PRACTICAL HANDBOOK OF MULTI-TIERED SYSTEMS OF SUPPORT

Also Available

Assessment for Intervention:
A Problem-Solving Approach, Second Edition
Edited by Rachel Brown-Chidsey
and Kristina J. Andren

Response to Intervention:
Principles and Strategies for Effective Practice,
Second Edition
Rachel Brown-Chidsey and Mark W. Steege

RTI in the Classroom:
Guidelines and Recipes for Success
Rachel Brown-Chidsey, Louise Bronaugh,
and Kelly McGraw

Practical Handbook of Multi-Tiered Systems of Support

BUILDING ACADEMIC AND BEHAVIORAL SUCCESS IN SCHOOLS

Rachel Brown-Chidsey
Rebekah Bickford

THE GUILFORD PRESS
New York London

A Division of Guilford Publications, Inc.
370 Seventh Avenue, Suite 1200, New York, NY 10001
www.guilford.com

Printed in the United States of America

This book is printed on acid-free paper.

Last digit is print number: 9 8 7 6

Library of Congress Cataloging-in-Publication Data

Names: Brown-Chidsey, Rachel, author.
Title: Practical handbook of multi-tiered systems of support : building academic and behavioral success in schools / Rachel Brown-Chidsey, Rebekah Bickford.
Description: New York : The Guilford Press, 2016. | Includes bibliographical references and index.
Identifiers: LCCN 2015036693| ISBN 9781462522484 (paperback) | ISBN 9781462522491 (hardcover)
Subjects: LCSH: Student assistance programs—Handbooks, manuals, etc. | Response to intervention (Learning disabled children)—Handbooks, manuals, etc. | School failure—Prevention—Handbooks, manuals, etc. | Problem children—Behavior modification—Handbooks, manuals, etc. | BISAC: PSYCHOLOGY / Psychotherapy / Child & Adolescent. | EDUCATION / Decision-Making & Problem Solving. | SOCIAL SCIENCE / Social Work. | EDUCATION / Educational Psychology. | EDUCATION / Teaching Methods & Materials / General.
Classification: LCC LB3430.5 .B76 2016 | DDC 371.7—dc23
LC record available at http://lccn.loc.gov/2015036693

In memory of Ken Merrell,
who taught us that implementing tiered supports
requires educators to think

And with love and thanks to David and Ellie
for all their patience over the years

—R. B.-C.

To Pat Red, who brought PBIS from Oregon to Maine
and inspired me with her passion and resolve

And with love to Mark, Sawyer, and Phoebe,
whose tolerance for a preoccupied wife and mother
has been greatly appreciated

—R. B.

About the Authors

Rachel Brown-Chidsey, PhD, NCSP, is Associate Professor of Educational and School Psychology at the University of Southern Maine. Prior to obtaining her doctorate, she taught middle and high school history and special education for 10 years. Her research areas include curriculum-based measurement, response to intervention (RTI), and scientifically based instruction methods. Dr. Brown-Chidsey is coeditor of *Assessment for Intervention: A Problem-Solving Approach, Second Edition*, and coauthor of *Response to Intervention: Principles and Strategies for Success, Second Edition*, and *RTI in the Classroom: Guidelines and Recipes for Success*. In addition, she has published articles about reading assessment and instruction as well as implementation of RTI. Dr. Brown is a nationally certified school psychologist and a licensed psychologist.

Rebekah Bickford, PsyD, NCSP, BCBA-D, is a psychologist at the Margaret Murphy Center for Children. She served on the faculty of the University of Southern Maine for 2 years after earning her doctorate there. Her research interests include consultation, the impact of teacher praise on student well-being, and the application of positive behavioral interventions and supports (PBIS) to specialized settings. Dr. Bickford is a founding member of the Maine PBIS Leadership and Policy Council, and has facilitated PBIS implementation in schools and districts around the state. She is a nationally certified school psychologist, a licensed psychologist, and a board-certified behavior analyst.

Acknowledgments

Special thanks to Kim Gibbons, Eileen Harris, Jennifer Knutson, Judy Loughlin, Dawn Miller, Mary Jean O'Reilly, Pat Red, Amber Roderick Landward, and others who provided important feedback on drafts of this work.

Contents

Purchasers can download and print select figures at *www.guilford.com/brown-chidsey3-forms* for personal use or use with individual students.

Introduction

OVERVIEW OF THIS BOOK

The goal of this book is to provide detailed guidance for educators who seek to establish multiple tiers of supports for students in their schools. The phrase *multi-tiered system of supports* (MTSS) refers to structures and procedures that schools offer to help each and every student be successful. Other phrases for an MTSS include *response to intervention* (RTI) and *positive behavioral interventions and supports* (PBIS). Both RTI and PBIS are types of tiered supports, but there are others as well. We have chosen to use the umbrella term *MTSS* to help readers learn about and use a comprehensive framework that can apply to all the students in a school. Note that we refer to such a *system* of supports in the singular, not plural. The reason for this is that the entire system needs to be integrated and universal, rather than separate mini-systems operating without connections to one another. In places, we refer to PBIS or RTI practices and research, but in all cases the larger framework of one, unified, MTSS is the goal.

The book is organized into six parts, each with several chapters designed to give practical and detailed guidance about how to set up and run an MTSS in your school. This book focuses on how to set up general schoolwide practices that are available to all students. The reason for the broader approach here is to offer educators the knowledge and skills to adopt as a mind-set and ethos rather than a set of isolated steps. Although details about specific procedures are provided, the first chapters in particular focus on prevention science and why all school personnel must learn and embrace a mind-set of prevention science as part of an MTSS in order for it to be successful over the long term. When first introduced, some educators thought that RTI and PBIS were passing fads that would eventually disappear. Instead, they now have lasted and been used in schools for almost 20 years (Walker et al., 1996). Those schools that have taken the time to set up the structures needed to support long-term implementation have observed improvements in student learning and staff engagement. We hope that this book will support educators in making schools successful for all students. Although the major goal of an MTSS is to provide supports when needed by any student, the book includes some information about how MTSS data can be used if a student is referred for special education.

PART I: PREVENTION SCIENCE IN SCHOOLS

Schools are complex social environments that face the challenge of providing effective instruction for students from diverse backgrounds. U.S. public schools have the responsibility to provide such instruction for any and all students who qualify for attendance. And, children ages 6 to 16 (and in some states 5 to 18) are required to attend school. Bringing about effective learning outcomes for all students on a daily basis is not easy, yet it is what educators do. The first section of the book (Chapters 2–5) explains the historical background and recent trends in U.S. public school policy that affect the daily work of teachers. Chapter 2 provides a history of the concept of prevention and how it has not historically been applied to public education. Following from an analogy made by Keith Stanovich (1986), Chapter 3 describes how important attention to details is in all aspects of an MTSS. Chapter 4 explains the many types of risk factors that public school students face and how such factors can influence school outcomes if not addressed. An important recent occurrence in public education is the development and adoption of the Common Core State Standards (CCSS). Chapter 5 explains the history of these Standards and how they are aligned with MTSS practices.

PART II: THE IMPORTANCE OF COLLABORATION AND TEAMS

The second section (Chapters 6–8) focuses on the importance of collaboration in making an MTSS work. Like any major systems-level project, an MTSS cannot happen if only one person directs it. It must be developed and implemented by teams of educators who work together with common goals. These chapters explain how to set up and maintain effective school teams to support an MTSS. Part II begins with Chapter 6, in which the important roles and functions of specific types of teams are described. Chapter 7 offers guidance on how to set up the specific types of teams needed to support an MTSS. Finally, Chapter 8 explores what is necessary for teams to be effective, including how to develop a team's identity and routines. This chapter is important for all readers, regardless of whether their school has many existing teams or is just getting started.

PART III: MAKING CHANGE HAPPEN

An MTSS is very much a *systems* approach to effective school outcomes. Such systems include the complementary and balanced integration of procedures that are activated when certain conditions are present. In order to understand and use an MTSS, it is important that educators know how complex social support systems operate and what it takes to bring about change within them. There is an emerging research base documenting what it takes for systems to function well and the chapters in this section (Chapters 9–13) draw from this research. First, in Chapter 9, there is an overview about the existing research on the science of change. Using findings from Fixsen, Naoom, Blase, Friedman, and Wallace (2005), this chapter gives an overview of the stages of change in organizations. Chapter 10 then describes the first three of these stages—exploration, adoption, and installation—as well as how such stages need to be addressed to set up an effective MTSS. Then, in Chapter 11, we detail the two levels of implementation and how careful planning is needed at both. Chapter 12 explains how innovation is an inevitable part of an ongoing MTSS, but needs to be anticipated so that it will be effective. Chapter 12 also describes what is necessary to sustain an MTSS as a permanent approach to student academic and behavioral success in schools. Finally, Chapter 13 discusses how carefully planned daily school schedules are an essential part of effective MTSS practice because they make it possible for interventions to be conducted regularly.

PART IV: EFFECTIVE INSTRUCTION WITHIN AN MTSS

As noted, this book focuses heavily on the "big picture" of system-level support for all students. Part IV (Chapters 14–18) examines essential research on effective instruction and how educators must use evidence-based instruction as the foundation for all parts of an MTSS. Chapter 14 reviews findings from a key meta-analysis, and other sources, about the most effective, research-based instructional practices for all grades and subjects. These practices are then juxtaposed in Chapter 15 with information about how to provide effective instructional sequences based on students' needs. Recognizing that U.S. schools are now more diverse than ever, and expected to become even more so, Chapter 16 reviews the research base on how to support students who are English language learners (ELLs). Although there are many types of diversity in U.S. classrooms, all students are expected to learn English as the language of instruction and this chapter explains how an MTSS is well suited to support ELL students. Chapter 17 provides a conceptual foundation and details about why having treatment integrity at all stages of an MTSS is essential and feasible. Finally, Chapter 18 explains why an MTSS will only succeed in supporting all students when at least 80% of each school's enrollment meets stated learning targets at Tier 1. With examples from a veteran MTSS leader, Chapter 18 details how the needs of each student can be addressed only when all students get effective instruction (Coyne, Kame'enui, & Simmons, 2004).

PART V: MTSS ORGANIZATIONAL STRUCTURE

In Part V (Chapters 19–22), the key organizational elements of an MTSS are explained. Some of the content of this section might be familiar to educators who have used certain components of an MTSS, but the descriptions in these chapters are designed to show how each step requires a comprehensive and well-designed infrastructure to be truly effective. There are four chapters in this section, starting with a discussion of universal screening. The conceptual foundations and practical requirements of universal screening are covered in Chapter 19. Using a cornerstone method pioneered by Stan Deno (1985, 2002) and colleagues, Chapter 20 explains why a detailed problem-solving process is a necessary component of an MTSS. Chapter 21 explains how progress monitoring is an essential pathway by which informative student data are collected in an MTSS. The last chapter in this section, 22, then gives detailed guidance on how to understand student progress data.

PART VI: CONNECTING MTSS WITH OTHER SUPPORTS

The final section of the book addresses the ways that an MTSS connects to other student supports already existing in schools. Chapter 23 explains how the final tier of an MTSS is a transition point where consideration of a student's long-term educational needs is the focus. Chapter 24 returns to the foundations of the book by discussing how prevention science can benefit all students and prevent the need for some special education placements. This chapter explains how an MTSS does not replace special education, but is an important complement to such services. Next (Chapter 25) there is a discussion of the continuum of services for students who have a disability, including both Section 504 of the Rehabilitation Act and the Individuals with Disabilities Improvement Act. Specifically, Chapter 25 identifies how students supported by an MTSS, but who do not make expected gains, might also benefit from other supports as well. This chapter concludes with information about how an MTSS complements, rather than competes with, special education as a system to help all students access effective education.

The book concludes with a case example that describes how all of the components can be combined to develop, implement, and evaluate an MTSS at the district level. Using examples from schools and districts in which we have worked, Chapter 26 seeks to explain the process of setting up an MTSS as it unfolds. This case example will not match the exact experience of all readers, but provides an idea of the level of detail required to make an MTSS successful.

SUMMARY

This book is designed to provide educators at all grade levels and career stages with an understanding of the infrastructure and system components needed to support effective learning outcomes for all students. Starting with a review of some historical foundations and emerging trends, the chapters offer information about the importance of developing strong teams of educators to implement and sustain an MTSS. The key details of an MTSS, including evidence-based instruction, screening, problem solving, progress monitoring, and decision making are explained through the lens of comprehensive system-level supports for all students.

PART I

Prevention Science in Schools

This section provides an introduction to the book through the framework of how prevention science can be used in schools to improve student academic and behavior outcomes. Prevention science is a distinct field of study that originated within the discipline of public health. It focuses on how specific planning steps and early intervention can identify students who are at risk of school difficulty. In recent years, researchers have identified key indicators of student risk, including poverty, frequent school changes, and early behavior and reading problems. Building on research about risk indicators, recent efforts have focused on using brief assessments of risk to learn which students need assistance right away. The chapters in this section provide a brief history of public education and the field of public health, and how integrating findings from both can benefit students. These chapters provide foundational concepts about the importance of prevention as a tool for educators as well as how certain details must be applied in relation to adopted standards, curriculum, and programs in schools in order for all students to succeed in school and life.

CHAPTER 2

Prevention as a Public Education Value

A multi-tiered system of supports (MTSS) is fundamentally a prevention system. While some professions have embraced prevention as a key conceptual framework, U.S. education has a history of being largely reaction oriented. For example, the 1965 Elementary and Secondary Education Act (ESEA) provided funding to schools with large numbers of students who were both impoverished and underperforming. The students, as a group, had to be both poor and underachieving for the school to get money to help them. Similarly, when the first federal special education law was passed in 1975, it established a procedure whereby students had to demonstrate problems before additional help would be provided. Both ESEA Title I funds and special education procedures involve having teachers, parents, and others *react* to student difficulty rather than anticipate and address it before a problem is observed. True, special education rules have from the beginning called for "child find" activities, yet the "found" children had to show evidence of a disabling condition to be eligible for needed services. Until MTSS became widely used, school personnel reacted to students' learning difficulties rather than prevent them.

Ironically, at the same period of time when schools developed and implemented programs like Title I and special education, the field of public health was implementing programs built on prevention science. MTSS is the application of prevention science in schools. The remainder of this chapter provides a brief history of public health as a field of study, levels of prevention, examples of school-based prevention, and general benefits to society that can occur when prevention measures are implemented.

HISTORY OF PUBLIC HEALTH

Public health became an identifiable area of study during the Scientific Revolution in Europe. This period of time, from approximately 1600 to 1800, saw the reintroduction of scientific ideas into European society. Practices such as recording and examining the number and types of deaths in different communities provided information about the variables that might be related to illness and death (Centers for Disease Control and Prevention, 2013b). Many of the major philosophers of the Scientific Revolution wrote about methods later used in public health practice, including sanitation and insurance. The Industrial Revolution (1750–1950) created the conditions that led to public interest and acceptance of widespread public health practices. Attention to the importance of clean water and basic sanitation resulted from the growth of urban centers with factories and large numbers of workers. At the same time, discovery of microorganisms and cell structures led to an understanding of how germs are spread. The culmination of the discovery of "germs" such as viruses and bacteria was the development of vaccines to prevent the outbreak of certain communicable diseases (Riedel, 2005). An indication of the importance of public health was the founding of the American Public Health Association in 1872 (American Public Health Association, 2015).

Over time, prevention efforts have been used to address a number of public health issues such as nutrition and smoking. Notably, the U.S. Centers for Disease Control, a government agency, changed its name to include "prevention" in 1992. In 1999 the Centers for Disease Control and Prevention published a list of the top 10 public health achievements of the 20th century (Centers for Disease Control and Prevention, 2013b). Many policies that are now considered commonplace, such as bans on smoking and seat belt laws, resulted from public health projects that used population data to identify trends and problems.

THREE LEVELS OF PREVENTION

The concept of prevention was further defined in a seminal book by Gerald Caplan (1964). Titled *Principles of Preventive Psychiatry*, Caplan suggested that there are three levels of prevention: primary, secondary, and tertiary. Primary prevention includes steps taken before any problem exists to prevent it entirely. An example is putting up safety gates at stairwells in a home so that a toddler will not fall down the stairs. Secondary prevention involves addressing the symptoms of a problem as soon as possible to reduce the effects of the problem. This could include taking a pain reliever at the first sign of a headache. Tertiary prevention includes providing long-term intervention for a problem to lessen its effects. Tertiary prevention is more intensive and includes steps such as taking insulin to treat diabetes. Caplan's main message was that we don't have to wait for a problem to be severe before taking action to reduce the effects. An MTSS is built upon Caplan's prevention model and provides a way to use prevention in schools. Caplan's three types of prevention are often known as a three-tiered model of support for all students.

EXAMPLES OF PREVENTION EFFORTS

There are numerous examples of how prevention can be used to improve outcomes across the lifespan. As noted, prevention was initially understood in the context of public health; thus, it has applications for making life better for everyone.

Vaccination

One of the first general applications of prevention in the general public was vaccination. Vaccination involves injecting a very small amount of a virus into the body so that antibodies can be developed. Once these antibodies are present, the body rejects later encounters with the same virus. Vaccination is possible because of research into the causes of diseases that were previously called "childhood" illnesses (e.g., chicken pox, measles, mumps). These illnesses used to be part of the experience of childhood and, before vaccinations, not all children survived these diseases and lived to become adults. Once the cause of certain childhood diseases was known, researchers worked to find a way to combat them. The first type of vaccine was for smallpox, and was developed by Edward Jenner in the 1700s as a result of his experiments with dairymaids who had developed cowpox (Riedel, 2005). Vaccination was probably known elsewhere before Jenner's experiments and descriptions, but it was his publication of findings with the Royal Society in England that made it an accepted practice in western Europe and beyond. Jenner's findings only showed that exposure to a low "dose" of a virus could prevent a full-blown case; there were many viruses that afflicted humans and many other researchers applied themselves to finding the right chemical formulas for vaccines that would prevent such diseases.

Despite advances, contagious diseases remained the leading cause of death in the United States in the first decades of the 20th century (Centers for Disease Control and Prevention, 2013a). A step toward ending the threat of such diseases came when public health nurses were placed in schools. New York City was the first school district to have nurses. The use of schools as centers for disease prevention was expanded after the development of the polio vaccine. Starting in the 1950s, vaccines were administered in schools to prevent as many children as possible from contracting deadly illnesses. Eventually, schools adopted requirements that all students be vaccinated prior to school entry for the most common childhood illnesses. This policy led to the effective elimination of many diseases such as polio, measles, mumps, and smallpox.

The preventative effects of vaccines are maximized when vaccines are administered during childhood. For this reason, medical professionals developed guidelines and policies recommending vaccines for children at specific ages. Vaccines remain an effective means of preventing childhood diseases even when some portion of the population remains unvaccinated. While the percentage of people who need to be vaccinated in order to protect the population varies by disease, if 80–90% of a community has been vaccinated against a given disease, the disease is unlikely to become an epidemic in that community (Centers for Disease Control and Prevention, 2013a). As a result of the clear benefits of universal vaccination of all children, preventative vaccinations were made mandatory; all 50 U.S. states have rules requiring that children be vaccinated before they can enroll in public schools and most private schools have similar requirements. There are some religious traditions that forbid vaccination (e.g., Christian Scientists, Jehovah's Witnesses) and the U.S. Constitution includes a provision protecting the free practice of religion. For this reason, an exemption from the school requirements is allowed for those children and parents whose religious beliefs disallow vaccination. Since vaccinations are an effective method of preventing childhood diseases even when 100% of a population is not vaccinated, exemptions for religious reasons do not threaten the general welfare of the public.

The requirement that all, or at least most, students in schools be vaccinated has resulted in many benefits for all. When enough people in a community have immunity to a deadly disease, it will not spread quickly. This means that there are not only fewer deaths but also fewer illness-related absences for students, teachers, and the workforce. Vaccination is a form of prevention because it leads to healthier children and adults as well as better school attendance and economic productivity.

Nutrition

Another area where prevention efforts have led to improved wellness and economic benefit is nutrition. Nutrition involves awareness and attention to the contents of what we eat, with the knowledge that certain foods have more benefits than others. Alongside the research into diseases and vaccines, public health researchers contributed to efforts to understand how eating patterns affect health and well-being. Prior to the 20th century, very little was known about the effects of food on general health. As advances in other aspects of wellness improved longevity, researchers turned their attention to the ingredients in food. It was long understood that when food was scarce, people perished. Less understood was how the specific ingredients in various foods influenced general wellness (Steckel & Rose, 2002). The systematic review and analysis of the components of food led to an understanding of how what we eat influences our well-being over time. The Food and Drug Administration (FDA) recognized the importance of nutrition in the 1990s by requiring "nutrition facts" on all food items sold in the United States (U.S. Food and Drug Administration, 2013). Based on research on the relationship between diet and health, the FDA acknowledged that the content of foods influences weight, health, and general wellness. The nutrition facts boxes on foods sold in the United States are designed to help consumers keep track of not only how many calories are consumed but also how many grams of fat, carbohydrates, and other nutrients. This information was developed because of convincing evidence that low-fat and low-calorie diets are associated with better health outcomes and longer lifespans. Additional efforts to improve nutrition at the universal level include posting nutrition facts in restaurants, using healthier foods in school lunches, and providing smaller portion sizes at meals.

Despite current prevention efforts, the United States and other nations are undergoing an epidemic of obesity. Current efforts focus on increasing all Americans' understanding of the importance of nutrition and its effects on general wellness. Public health officials seek to prevent conditions such as diabetes, heart disease, and certain types of cancer through campaigns that illuminate the fact that such diseases can be prevented if a healthy diet is followed. Diets that are low in fat and overall calories are associated with maintaining a healthy weight and general wellness. The ingredients in what we eat have a direct relationship to our immediate energy level and our long-term general well-being. Nutrition awareness is a form of prevention because good eating habits contribute to overall wellness, thereby preventing the development of disease.

Exercise

The most recent advance in research about well-being comes from the study of exercise. Starting in the 1970s, researchers identified a relationship between engaging in regular exercise and general wellness. In the preindustrial era, humans engaged in a great deal of physical activity each day just to survive (Steckel & Rose, 2002). With the rise of industrialization, humans have relied on the mass production of food to survive. No longer was hunting and gathering needed to survive. Unfortunately, this meant that many people became sedentary and did not get enough exercise. Humans still need a certain amount of daily exercise to be healthy. Research has shown that those who get out and walk, run, or engage in other physical activities are likely to be healthier over the lifespan than those who do not. For this reason, exercise is another example of prevention (Harvard School of Public Health, 2013).

Vaccinations, nutrition, and exercise are three examples of how data gathered as part of efforts to improve public health contribute to preventing problems at individual and community levels. All three of these examples have primary, secondary, and tertiary prevention components that can be applied depending on the status and needs of the individual or community. Doll, Pfohl, and Yoon (2010) have shown how prevention science can be used across a large number of challenges that children and youth face, ranging from social and emotional well-being to bullying to mental health and substance abuse. Until recently, prevention efforts were not widely used in schools. Instead, educators tended to assume that those students who could do well would do well, and when a student had difficulty, it was due to an inherent child deficit. Recently, the application of MTSS in schools has shown that many students' learning and behavior difficulties can be prevented through the application of multiple tiers of support.

SCHOOL-BASED PREVENTION

Prevention efforts in schools include all steps taken to have effective instruction ready and available for all students from the first day of each school year. Similar to Caplan's (1964) three levels, many schools have adopted three tiers of support for students. Figure 2.1 shows a model of Caplan's three stages of prevention that can be used in schools. Tier 1 is the universal level and includes any and all general education curricula and procedures. Sometimes this tier is referred to as the "core" or "universal" level because it is the foundation for all other supports. Tier 1 core/universal instruction is a form of primary prevention because it is provided universally for all students. The universality of Tier 1 instruction means that whatever materials and instructional procedures are selected to be used for core instruction need to be the best available. Tier 1 materials and procedures are the first and best opportunity to help all students access learning. When implemented correctly, at least 80% of students should be successful within the Tier 1 core programs. Tier 1 is a form of prevention because it optimizes the likelihood that a student will find school success.

While the Tier 1 core works for most students, it will not be sufficient by itself for all students. Some students will need additional support and instruction. This is when Caplan's (1964) secondary prevention becomes important. Secondary prevention includes steps taken at the first signs of a problem to reduce and eliminate the problem. In schools, secondary prevention is often known as Tier 2. Importantly, Tier 2 is always in addition to Tier 1 instruction. The reason for the additional support is that students who are struggling most often need more time to learn and master knowledge and skills. Tier 2 must be provided with enough frequency and at long enough durations to address the presenting problem. The content of Tier 2 instruction should come from the core materials and methods. This is important because if instructional materials and methods are different across tiers, students can become more confused. Tier 2 is generally provided to small groups of students who have similar needs at one time. Small-group instruction has been shown to be as effective as individualized instruction for most students (Vaughn et al., 2003). Tier 2 is a form of prevention because it

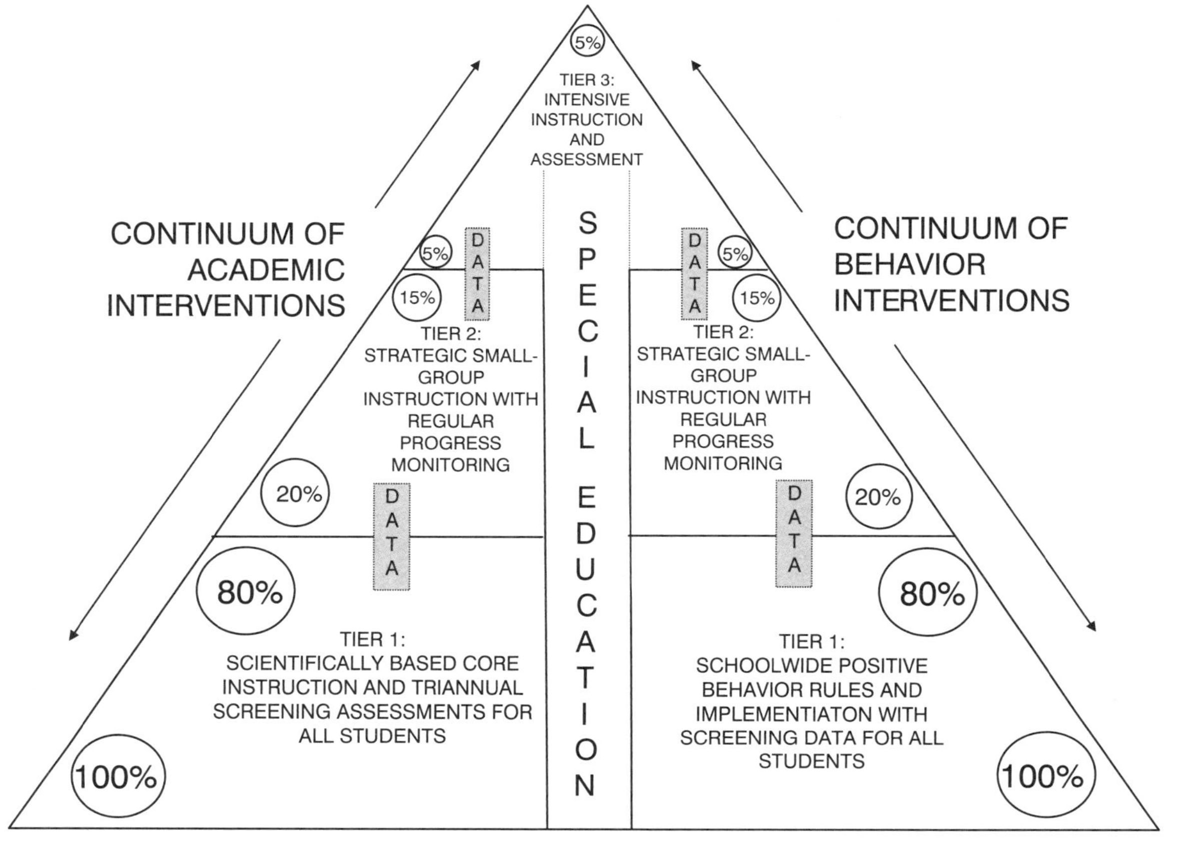

FIGURE 2.1. RTI model. From Brown-Chidsey and Steege (2010). Copyright by The Guilford Press. Reprinted by permission.

addresses a student's learning needs as soon as a problem is detected and creates a way for the student to get back on track to meet specific learning goals. In most cases, students will need Tier 2 for a short period of time and then will be able to transition back to Tier 1 alone. When implemented correctly, about 15% of the students in a school will need and benefit from Tier 2.

Caplan's (1964) tertiary prevention is the third and most intensive level of support. In schools this is known as Tier 3. This level includes efforts to limit and ameliorate the negative effects of a problem, even if the problem itself cannot be eliminated. Typically, if Tiers 1 and 2 are effective, no more than 5% of the students in a school require Tier 3 support. Tier 3 is usually individualized and includes more additional instruction. Usually Tier 3 includes more frequent and longer intervention, which is in addition to Tier 1 core and Tier 2 supplemental intervention. For example, a student with an academic deficit might participate in Tier 1 core instruction plus Tier 2 small-group instruction, plus an additional 45 minutes of daily one-on-one tutoring. Similarly, a student who is struggling with aggression would access the Tier 1 system for teaching and acknowledging expected behavior, as well as a Tier 2 intervention designed to provide frequent feedback, and a Tier 3 system such as a token economy designed to reinforce functional communication of feelings as an alternative to displays of aggression.

In other cases, Tier 3 might involve changing the core instruction in a particular content area. Often such replacement programs are very structured and include direct instruction methods. Such Tier 3 interventions are referred to as replacement core programs. Tier 3 interventions provide students with individualized opportunities to learn and practice specific skills. Providing Tier 3 instruction is a way to test the hypothesis that a student can succeed with more intensive supports. This is still prevention because it seeks to prevent the student from falling farther behind. Through the use of multi-tiered supports, schools can provide active and effective prevention for all students. These practices are associated with clear academic and behavioral benefits.

Academic Benefits

Students whose schools use prevention efforts to support all students are likely to experience numerous academic benefits. For example, where carefully designed and evidence-based core instruction is in place, students who begin the school year with school difficulties can catch up and be on grade level by the year's end (Moore & Whitfield, 2009). Some students will need Tier 2 supports and research shows that the additional instruction provided at Tier 2 can help such students "close the gap" and meet learning goals (Bryant, Bryant, Gersten, Scammacca, & Chavez, 2008; Koutsoftas, Harmon, & Gray, 2009). A small number of students will need intensive intervention or maybe special education, but with such supports these students can make gains, too (Denton, Fletcher, Anthony, & Frances, 2006). When school personnel provide research-based instruction as the core curricula and recognize that some students will need additional supports, they are engaging in prevention activities (Lembke, McMaster, & Stecker, 2010).

Behavioral Benefits

Recently, research has shown that there are many benefits gained from using an MTSS to support all students' behavioral learning as well. Based on research begun at the University of Oregon and continued elsewhere, a three-tiered model known as positive behavioral interventions and supports (PBIS) offers a very effective way to ensure that all students know what behaviors are expected in schools and how to exhibit those behaviors. Similar to the outcomes for academics, PBIS methods have been shown to reduce the number of students sent to the office for discipline problems as well as the overall number of problem behaviors in a school (Fairbanks, Sugai, Guardino, & Lathrop, 2007). The more that students are in the classroom and engaged in learning, the better their overall outcomes are likely to be.

The increasing diversity of U.S. schools makes teaching expected school behaviors essential. In the past, when most students in a school shared the same religious and moral values, it might not have been as important for teachers to be explicit about what behaviors were expected in each setting of the school. U.S. schools are becoming increasingly diverse and students in the same school do not necessarily have the same cultural, linguistic, and religious backgrounds. Given this reality, it is important that teachers are prepared to teach students the behaviors expected in school. For this reason, PBIS is a form of prevention because it ensures that all students have clarity on the expectations for their behaviors across multiple settings. When students know what is expected, they are more likely to meet those expectations and, therefore, this prevents students from engaging in behavior that will result in being sent to the principal.

Integrating Academics and Behavior

Using prevention across multiple tiers of support leads to benefits for both students and teachers. It is often not possible to separate academic and behavioral interventions. This is because the way that students behave in school can influence their academic performance and their academic skills can influence school behaviors. For this reason, researchers have developed tiered supports that integrate prevention for academics and behavior into one seamless system. The state of Florida has pioneered one of the first statewide integrated model of MTSS, which integrates prevention efforts for academics and behavior into one system (Florida Department of Education, 2014). Similarly, Michigan's Integrated Behavior and Learning Support Initiative (Michigan Department of Education, 2014) and the Kansas Multi-Tier System of Supports (Kansas State Department of Education, 2014) provide a unified model of MTSS. All three of these state initiatives provide support for students with academic deficits, support for students with behavioral deficits, and integrated support for students who have both academic and behavioral deficits.

Benefits to Society

Using prevention methods in schools also benefits the society as a whole. School completion (i.e., not dropping out) is related to a number of lifetime wellness indicators. Those who complete high school are more likely to obtain regular employment, have access to health care, and have higher levels of civic engagement (i.e., vote, serve on juries, run for office; Pacheco & Plutzer, 2008). By using prevention efforts in schools, we can improve the quality of life for everyone. Millions of dollars are spent on education each year; many of these dollars go toward remedial programs after students have fallen significantly behind. If we move a portion of the resource allocation so that prevention activities are foundational components of instruction, more students will succeed and the overall costs of education are likely to be lower.

Getting Started

Reflections on how one school district began using prevention practices are shared in Box 2.1. Dr. Mary Jean O'Reilly, a school psychologist in the Pittsfield, Massachusetts, public schools, describes how her district began the process of using prevention methods to support all students. As she notes, this process was made possible through two factors: districtwide leadership and gradual implementation over time.

SUMMARY

Prevention is a key concept in MTSS. By anticipating students' needs, educators can be ready to meet those needs from the first day of school. Prevention efforts have their roots in the field of public health, but have applications in many settings. Over time, public health researchers have shown that applying findings from research has led to many social benefits. The requirement for universal vaccination has greatly reduced the outbreak of deadly infectious diseases. Research in nutrition has shown that following a healthy diet prevents obesity and promotes wellness. Similarly, getting regular exercise ensures that the body is in shape and ready for daily activity. While the benefits of prevention have been clearly confirmed in medicine, application of prevention efforts in schools has lagged behind. MTSS and related efforts have created the opportunity to bring prevention methods into schools and use such efforts to improve outcomes for all students.

BOX 2.1. Reflections on Getting Started from Mary Jean O'Reilly, PhD, NCSP

The implementation of an MTSS is a natural progression in the development of our understanding of the most effective ways to address student needs. The implementation of the MTSS in our district is part of a continuum of change that started in the late 1990s when the special education director began sending staff to regional conferences on curriculum-based measurement practices led by national researchers such as Drs. Mark and Michelle Shinn and Dr. Roland Good. Our knowledge base and implementation efforts began to expand in 2001 when a small group of staff members were sent to their first PBIS training, led by Rob March of Successful Schools through the Urban Institute. After being inspired by this training, we began to implement PBIS in one middle and one elementary school. These trainings provided our first experience with using the perspective of a tiered model to look at the needs of our students. Over time our special education department was able to fund many more trainings for both special education and regular education staff involved in the implementation efforts.

The impetus to implement the PBIS framework came through our special education department. The catalysts included a relationship with a local university that had leading-edge training on multi-tiered systems in its school psychology department, which led to the placement in our district of doctoral interns with experience in the model, several of whom (including me) became full-time employees. The system was also fortunate to have a well-respected school and clinical psychologist who was a strong supporter of the use of direct instruction, response to intervention, and multi-tiered systems. The need for added levels of intervention was apparent due to our growing numbers of special education students who needed a wide range of supports, not just traditional pullout resource room services. As a small urban district, our special education leadership is always attentive to the data and aware of trends as they begin to appear. Creating an MTSS made sense on many levels.

Initial PBIS teams included regular education and special education teachers, administrators, school psychologists, and school adjustment counselors. Around the same time, we also began to use curriculum-based measurement, particularly for students in special education. Both of these initiatives were initially supported and implemented by special education leadership, and significant time, training, and resources were dedicated to implementation. Our special education director funded staff attendance at statewide and regional trainings, and also brought national trainers to our district in order to increase staff capacity to implement PBIS and curriculum-based measurement. Support from district administration was gained over time in order to implement these practices districtwide. Our district has been successful in its implementation of these practices, and we are regularly visited by other districts that are just beginning to implement tiered instructional and behavioral supports.

CHAPTER 3

The Importance of Details

In 1986, eminent reading researcher Keith Stanovich published an article in which he showed empirical data for something most teachers have known for years: those children who start school with limited prereading skills and whose reading skills remain below grade level are not likely ever to catch up and become strong readers (Stanovich, 1986). In fact, those who start with strong reading skills will remain strong readers, but those who start as weak readers will remain weak. Borrowing from the sociologist Merton (1968), who referenced a passage from the gospel of Matthew that described the phenomenon in which "the rich get richer and the poor get poorer," Stanovich referred to this compounding disadvantage in education as the Matthew effect. To say that Stanovich's initial conceptualization of this phenomenon was accurate is an understatement. Since 1986, evidence supporting the importance of strong reading skills has grown each year. Despite the emergence of the Internet and various forms of digital media, being able to read has remained a cornerstone skill that predicts high school completion, college success, and work outcomes (National Assessment of Adult Literacy, 2013).

In an effort to support the development of reading skills, many educators have embraced an approach to education that includes an MTSS. This approach was included in both the 2001 revision of the ESEA known as No Child Left Behind (NCLB) and the 2004 reauthorization of the Individuals with Disabilities Education Improvement Act (IDEA). In using MTSS methods, schools have the potential to intervene early with students so that "Matthew effects" can be prevented. A number of studies have shown that those students who are reading at grade level by the end of third grade are likely to be successful in the rest of school and graduate from high school (Snow, Burns, & Griffin, 1998). Efforts taken to improve the reading skills of students before third grade can reduce Matthew effects, but only if those efforts include attention to key details of instruction and assessment.

The importance of adhering to details when implementing an MTSS cannot be overestimated. An MTSS only works when all the necessary steps happen correctly and in the right order. Another verse from the Christian Bible captures the essence of this chapter's message. In the gospel of Luke, Jesus says to his followers: "Whoever is faithful in a very little is faithful also in much" (Luke 16:10, New Revised Standard Version). This idea is true of student support systems. In order for efforts like an MTSS to work, each and every detail of implementation must be carried out. When the "little" things are done correctly, students will benefit "in much." But when details are ignored, student support systems do not work and students who start behind will stay behind. This chapter explains the types of details that need to be addressed and how leaving out specific steps will undermine student success. By way of previewing essential details, Dr. Mary Jean O'Reilly offers advice for those starting the process of implementing an MTSS in Box 3.1.

BOX 3.1. Advice for Schools Thinking about Starting an MTSS from Mary Jean O'Reilly, PhD, NCSP

1. Plan carefully. Do an assessment of current strengths and weaknesses and decide on which areas to address first. Focus on either the most important change first or start with the simplest change likely to show the most improvement. Schedule time to review and retrain on a regular basis. Use the school or district calendar as an implementation tool. Write your goals into your school and district improvement plans, and make them measurable with a clear timeline. The PBIS framework provides an excellent implementation model for prevention practices. If you build it well, new initiatives that arise over time can be folded into existing structures.
2. Move at a reasonable pace. Be prepared to repeat key ideas, to provide regular training opportunities, and to pilot promising programs or practices. Peer coaching can be very helpful. Small successes that are replicable are often more convincing to staff than a mandate for change coming from the top. Focus as much on maintenance as on implementation. Have realistic expectations about the time it takes for institutions and people to implement lasting change.
3. Keep the practices in the forefront. Write them into the district and school improvement plans. Present them to parents and community groups for outside accountability. Plan to share your successes and challenges at regional and national conferences.
4. Collect useful data. Know what data should be generated by the changes you make and plan to collect it. Be open to new data sources that arise. Share that data with everyone involved, including teachers, paraprofessionals, and support staff. Make the change visible and the data accessible.
5. Strong administrative leadership is key. Without it you may make small changes, but a true prevention focus is really only sustainable if it becomes a part of the school culture and everyone "owns" it.

TRAINING

Appropriate training and preparation to implement tiered supports is essential. Ironically, educators have a history of not providing themselves with sufficient training when learning new practices (Hochberg & Desimone, 2010). There are recognized standards for effective preparation to implement an MTSS, but these standards are not always employed. The best training involves directly teaching the knowledge and skills, and then embedding practice in teachers' everyday work activities (Hawley & Valli, 1999). Because of constraints of time and money, this is not always done. Individuals currently training to become teachers may have more access to learning about an MTSS than in the past, but it's not clear that all schools of education are including such content (National Council for Teacher Quality, 2013). Experienced teachers in the field, often referred to as inservice teachers, are less likely to have access to high-quality training in MTSS practices (O'Connor & Freeman, 2012). Despite the fact that virtually all resources and guides for implementation indicate that intensive training is an essential prerequisite, many teachers have ended up being expected to implement tiered supports with little or no training in the specific steps. This is like asking students to take a multiplication test without first teaching them how to multiply.

O'Connor and Freeman (2012) outline important professional development (PD) and training considerations that schools and districts need to address before any tiered supports are offered to schools. These are (1) focused training in the specific assessment and data management methods to be used, (2) discussion and agreement about the school's culture and teacher beliefs, (3) targeted staff recruitment to hire individuals with necessary skills, (4) careful resource allocation, and (5) engaged leadership. Importantly, sufficient time must be allocated to addressing these five areas before the actual use of tiered supports should begin. Of the five areas identified by O'Connor and Freeman, the one that requires the most in-depth training is assessment and data management. Although teachers collect and use assessment data every day, many have not been formally trained to understand optimal test construction and interpretation. As noted above, the best training approach is one that provides initial direct instruction followed by embedded practice in teachers' everyday work. If teachers do not have adequate training to use and interpret the assessments matching each tier of support, the student data they collect will be meaningless and a waste of time.

ASSESSMENT INTEGRITY

A direct result of certain aspects of adequate training is the integrity of the assessment data. Data from student assessments will be only as helpful as the accuracy of the procedures used to collect the scores. Assessment integrity is an essential detail because if the data are inaccurate, decisions made from those data will be wrong. The effect of "bad" data is using instruction that is not matched to students' true learning needs. Thankfully, there are steps that can be taken to ensure assessment integrity. As noted above, proper training of those who will conduct assessments is essential. Educators should only administer, score, and interpret student assessments when they have been fully and properly trained to use the specific measure(s). Many assessment publishers offer trainings in their respective products and these are likely to be the best preparation because they are conducted by individuals who helped to create the assessments. Additionally, there are often training videos with accompanying practice items that can be used to learn and master specific assessments.

In addition to appropriate training to use assessments, both checklists and observations are important means of confirming assessment integrity. Checklists provide a tool that can be used for self-review or review by an observer. An assessment integrity checklist consists of a listing of the steps required to administer and score an assessment correctly. It gives a precise listing of each and every detail required for that assessment. Many test publishers have such checklists built into their training and review materials. For example, AIMSweb (NCS Pearson, 2014) and Dynamic Indicators of Basic Early Literacy Skills (DIBELS; Dynamic Measurement Group, 2013) both have checklists that educators can use to see if they have completed each step of the assessment procedure. A classroom teacher or specialist (e.g., school psychologist or special educator) can preview the checklist just before the assessment to be ready to administer it correctly and again right after giving an assessment to see if all of the steps were followed. It is also possible to record an assessment session and then use the checklist to confirm whether all of the steps were done correctly. Such stepwise review is recommended as part of the training procedures for learning specific assessments.

Checklist data should be reviewed as soon after administration of an assessment as possible so that the examiner can learn about and change errors in administration. The goal is to attain 100% accuracy as indicated by the checklist. Still, a certain amount of error in measurement is always present, thus, assessment integrity scores of 90% or higher are generally acceptable, depending on the type of error(s) made. When checklist data show that the assessment was administered with less than 90% accuracy, the obtained scores must be interpreted carefully and it may be better to throw them out and collect new data. Most of the assessments used in an MTSS have multiple alternate forms, so it is easy to gather new data about the same target skill(s). An examiner, whether classroom teacher, aide, speech and language pathologist, or other professional, is considered proficient with a specific assessment only after having data showing that he or she administers and scores the measure with 90% accuracy on three or more administrations.

Another way to check assessment integrity is to conduct observations of the assessments while they are being conducted with students. This is routinely done for research studies, but not necessarily at other times when assessments are used. The purpose in having assessments observed and evaluated in research studies is to ensure and document that the data are accurate. Having assessment data be accurate is important beyond research settings. Every time an educator collects data about a student and uses it to make an instructional decision, the accuracy of those data are crucial to effective instruction or intervention. For this reason, routine observation of assessments in schools is a recommended practice. Not every assessment needs to be observed; a sample of students participating in the same assessment can provide the needed information about assessment integrity.

A practical approach to getting such observation data is to assign one person to observe the others conducting assessments each time such data are collected. For example, if all of the classroom teachers in a building conduct triannual assessments using curriculum-based measures, a special education teacher, the school psychologist, or the principal could plan to observe each teacher once a year during these assessments. This would provide annual data on the assessment integrity of all teachers. Or, if the screening assessments are given at different times of the day across grade levels, one of the teachers could do the observations. The observations can utilize the assessment checklists described above and give more immediate and "real-time" evidence of how accurately a teacher is using a specific assessment. If the information collected about assessment integrity shows that one or more assessment users are less than 90% accurate, then retraining and additional checklists or observations should be completed. Remember, inaccurate data are useless and can even be harmful. Time spent ensuring that all personnel who conduct assessments are using them accurately will result in accurate data that provide useful information about student performance.

DATA VERIFICATION

Once data have been collected, it is important to conduct additional verification of accuracy. This does not have to be a time-consuming step, but it is an essential detail in making an MTSS effective. The first, best way to verify the accuracy of collected data is to conduct the "What?" test. This test is done by having the classroom teacher read down the list of his or her students' scores and if he or she says "What?" to any of the scores, that suggests that there might be an inaccuracy. The "What?" test involves the teacher comparing what he or she already knows about each student's skills with performance on the screening assessments. When a teacher says "What?" that usually means that the student's score on the list does not make sense in relation to the student's performance in class or on other assessments. Such a reaction must be interpreted as a red flag that the score(s) for that student are not correct.

Sometimes, even often, the reason for the teacher's "What?" response is that a score was entered incorrectly in the database. If a teacher sees that a student who is a very good reader has a low reading score or that a student who struggles with math has a high math score, the first thing to check is whether the score was entered correctly into the database. A surprisingly large number of "What?" responses are the result of data entry errors. The solution in such cases is to correct the student's score and then have the teacher use the data for adjusting instruction. But, if a check of the true scores reveals that the data report had the student's true score, then a different approach is needed. When a teacher says "What?" in response to a student's true score, there is definitely a difference between what the teacher expected and how the student performed on the given test. In such cases, it is best to retest the student using an equivalent form of the assessment.

Keep in mind that some amount of error is present in every assessment. It can occur for a number of reasons. For example, a student could have been having a very bad day because his or her family's pet dog recently died. Or, it could be that the air-conditioning system in the school was not working on the day when the assessment was given and the student's concentration was influenced because he or she was very hot. Or, it may be that the person giving the assessment made a mistake. There are many possible reasons that a student's score was inaccurate on a given day. The good news is that, by readministering the assessment, it is possible to see if the student's score changes. If the new score is more consistent with how the student has been doing in class, then the new score is considered accurate and the old score is thrown out. If the new score is similar to the first score, then it would be important to consider the accuracy of other data about the student's performance. If the student's new score is totally different from any other scores, then it may be necessary to conduct a more in-depth assessment in order to capture truly accurate information about the student's skills.

The main idea about verifying student data is that it is essential to check whether the scores we plan to use to make instructional decisions are accurate. Most of the time they are and we can move quickly on to planning instruction. But sometimes, data entry errors occur. When this is the case, the 60 seconds that it takes a teacher to complete the "What?" test is worth it because it means that no student will end up with the wrong instruction due to a data error. When the "What?" test reveals that the student's performance is inconsistent across settings and tasks, then the time spent on data verification is still useful because it means that additional information about that student is collected. It is very important that teachers take the time to verify student data so that accurate decisions about each student's instructional needs can be made. Failing to verify student data could result in making inappropriate decisions about a student's current learning needs.

TREATMENT INTEGRITY

After all students' data have been verified, the next step is to develop instructional plans that meet students' needs. Later chapters of this book provide details about how to do this, whereas this chapter is designed to remind readers that there are certain *details* that must be considered along the way. In addition to the importance of assessment integrity, the way that any instruction is delivered affects whether or not it will be effective. For example, a well-documented, evidence-based intervention could be ordered and delivered to a school, but if it is never unpacked or used by a teacher, it will not be effective. This is a simple example of a lack of treatment integrity. If a set of carefully designed, scientifically validated materials are never actually used, their integrity is totally compromised. Sadly, this has been known to happen in schools. For this reason, it is essential to check whether each and every "treatment" that is supposedly being used to help students is actually being implemented, and implemented correctly.

For the purposes of this chapter and book, "treatment" means both instruction and intervention. Essentially, a treatment is a set of procedures designed to help a person overcome a specific condition. The term *treatment* is widely used in medicine and psychology, but not as often in schools. Nonetheless, schools engage in treatments every day because they seek to change students' behaviors and outcomes. For a comparison, consider how a medical doctor often uses antibiotics to *treat* certain infections. When a patient presents with a serious infection that has not healed on its own, a physician can prescribe an antibiotic that will kill the organisms causing the infection. Most of the time, this works and the patient gets better. In such cases, the treatment of antibiotics is considered to be effective.

Teachers actually engage in many treatments with students. When a teacher observes that a student is doing something that is not effective for learning, the teacher is likely to intervene and use a treatment or intervention to change the student's behavior. The difference between a physician's treatment and that of a teacher is usually one of scale. Physicians usually work at the microscopic level by using medications that kill bacteria so that the child can be healthy and well. Teachers work at the macroscopic level. This means that the child's behavior can be observed easily by teachers and others instead of needing to look at the organisms under a microscope. For example, a teacher might work on having a student complete all work assigned. This can be observed by looking at what the teacher asked the student to do and comparing it with what the student actually did. In some cases, the student might not be accustomed to being asked to complete work. When this happens, the teacher is likely to break the assignment down into specific steps and explain to the student what needs to be done and why. This is a form of treatment because it is designed to change the student's reaction to the teacher's assignment. Just like we hope to see a change in reaction to an antibiotic for an infection, teachers hope to see students respond differently as a result of their instruction.

When a change in a student's reaction or behavior is desired or expected, the efforts put in place to make this change can be thought of as a treatment. But in order for treatments to be effective, they must be used as intended. For this reason, there has been a growing interest in examining the integrity of educational treatments. Sanetti and Kratochwill (2013) have written about the important components that must be in place in order to document treatment integrity. The key to evaluating treatment integrity is to use many of the steps outlined in this chapter. For a treatment to be effective it must be implemented as intended. Therefore, having a checklist of the required steps and using it to verify that the steps were actually used is important. While this sounds simple, it does not always happen in schools. This is why treatment integrity is highlighted as such a crucial step in this chapter and there is another chapter about it later in the book.

Checking on treatment integrity (i.e., observing to see that the required steps were actually put in place) is an important part of an MTSS because if effective treatments or interventions, or whatever they are called, are not actually used and used correctly, students will not see improvement. In order for an MTSS to work, it is essential that treatment integrity be checked along the way. Doing this is not as difficult as it may sound. The steps are the same as those required for checking assessment integrity. Essentially, it is a matter of having a checklist of the steps necessary to implement an intervention (remember, think of this as instruction) and to see if the teacher or interventionist is completing all of the steps. This can be done with a combination of checklists and observations, just as with assessment integrity. It is helpful to teachers to have the integrity checklist in advance because then they know what is expected. Also, as noted above, thorough training in the methods needed is important, too. Then, it is a matter of observing the teacher using the instruction or intervention with the student to see if all of the steps are completed. Similar to the standards for assessment integrity, if an intervention or treatment is used with 90% or more integrity, it is likely to be effective. In fact, 80% or more integrity is recognized as adequate for treatment integrity. When a teacher is below 80%, or when he or she wants to improve, steps to improve integrity are likely to enhance student outcomes.

MTSS READINESS CHECKLIST

Because of the importance of details in making an MTSS effective, in Figure 3.1 we provide a checklist that educators can use to consider readiness for implementing an MTSS. The checklist includes four essential areas in which the details of implementation should be planned out in advance: (1) training and staffing, (2) assessment integrity, (3) data verification, and (4) treatment integrity. We have intentionally explained the importance of these details now because without them, an MTSS will not succeed. As school teams work on developing MTSS plans, using this checklist will help them to include important details of implementing that might otherwise be overlooked.

SUMMARY

This chapter has provided information about the essential details that educators must attend to in order to implement an MTSS effectively. Four details are

1. **Training and Staffing**
   - ☐ Facilitate the community of educators in discussing the school's culture and teachers' beliefs, and coming to agreement about shared beliefs and values.
   - ☐ Provide existing staff with sufficient training, feedback, and ongoing support in the specific assessment and data management methods to be used.
   - ☐ Recruit and hire new staff with the necessary skills to implement an MTSS.
   - ☐ Carefully allocate resources to ensure adequate funding for the MTSS initiative.
   - ☐ Ensure that the education leaders are engaged and active participants in the development of the MTSS.

2. **Assessment Integrity**
   - ☐ Fully and properly train educators to use the specific measure(s) prior to administering, scoring, and interpreting student assessments.
   - ☐ Confirm the integrity of the assessment process with checklists and/or observations.

3. **Data Verification**
   - ☐ Verify the accuracy of collected data using the "What?" test.

4. **Treatment Integrity**
   - ☐ Based on the data collected, develop instructional plans that meet students' needs.
   - ☐ Provide any instruction, intervention, or treatment deemed necessary.
   - ☐ Ensure that instruction, intervention, and treatments are provided as intended (i.e., with integrity) using treatment integrity checklists.

FIGURE 3.1. MTSS Readiness Checklist.

particularly important in making tiered support effective for students: training, assessment integrity, data reliability, and treatment integrity. When these details are in place, an MTSS is likely to be very effective for students. Without these details, the data collected may be inaccurate, the decisions made about students' needs incorrect, and the efforts taken to help students useless. For these reasons, it is imperative that educators recognize the importance of details in the use of an MTSS, and that they take efforts to educate their colleagues about these details. Only when such details are understood and implemented correctly can educators be faithful to the promise of an MTSS.

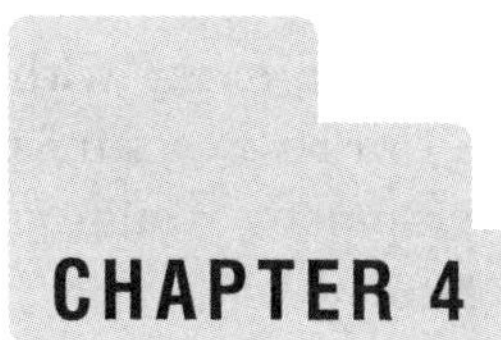

CHAPTER 4

Risk Factors and Student Success

Risk is abundant in childhood. Children are often born with risk factors and born into more. They face a multitude of environmental risk factors in the contexts of their families, in their relationships with peers, in their neighborhoods and communities, and finally from the structural inequality of the society at large. While children demonstrate notable resilience when faced with a small number of risk factors, the impact of risk becomes increasingly difficult to overcome as the number and intensity of risk factors increases (Burke, Hellman, Scott, Weems, & Carrion, 2011).

In fact, risk has the unique property of being both cumulative and multiplicative. The fact that risk is cumulative means that children do not leave their experiences of risk behind, even after a short-term negative experience has ended. For example, children who experience poverty at some point in their lives will be more vulnerable to other risk factors that they encounter at later points in their lives (McLoyd, 1990; Parker, Greer, & Zuckerman, 1988). Equally detrimental is the multiplicative, as opposed to additive, nature of risk. Risk is multiplicative in that each additional risk factor that a child experiences multiplies the overall impact of the risk. In other words, when it comes to risk in childhood, it can be exponentially worse to be exposed to three risk factors than two, and so forth.

There is no aspect of child well-being that is immune to risk. This is because bad things can happen at any time. As risk factors accumulate in children's lives, their cognitive, social, emotional, and physical development are increasingly compromised (Evans & Kim, 2013). Any of these aspects of development, and certainly the lot of them together, can impact a child's ability to develop the academic and social skills necessary for success in school (Rouse & Fantuzzo, 2009).

When risk factors are present, language and literacy development, along with numeracy and problem-solving skills, suffer. In fact, children in risky settings experience negative effects across all the domains of skill development, resulting in underdevelopment of the skills necessary for success in school.

THE MOST COMMON RISK FACTORS FACED BY SCHOOLCHILDREN

The nature of risk and its impact on children's development is complex, both in terms of the source of the risk and its effect on development and success at school. Children face risks from a host of social, psychological, and biological forces (Edwards, Mumford, & Serra-Roldan, 2007). Children are vulnerable from the moment of conception, with ample opportunity for harm prior to their first appearance in the world. A mother's quality of nutrition, level of stress, and use of drugs and alcohol are among the risks children face in utero. Children born prematurely—with low birth weight, or with a host of other complications—begin their lives exposed to risk. In addition, a child might begin life with a challenging temperament, an especially high activity level, or an especially low attention level, or be affected by other neurodevelopmental factors (Wasserman et al., 2003).

Similarly, children are exposed to risk throughout the contexts of their environments. Risk can result from parents' substance abuse, level of intelligence and education, level of functioning, approach to parenting, or antisocial behavior. Risk results when families face housing instability, with frequent family moves resulting in, among other things, the educational instability that results from changing schools frequently (Herbers et al., 2012). Other family risk factors include food insecurity (i.e., hunger and poor nutrition), unstable family structures, and violence in the home. Societal risk factors include peer and community influence, community violence, lack of community support, and racism (Condly, 2006). Despite the breadth of the risk factors listed here, this list is by no means comprehensive.

POVERTY AS A PRIMARY RISK FACTOR

At the heart of many of the individual and environmental childhood risk factors described above is poverty (Wagmiller & Adelman, 2009). Just as with risk to a child's development, there is no aspect of a person's life that is safe from the impact of poverty. Poverty contributes to poor maternal nutrition and low birth weight. Children born into poverty are far more likely to experience instabilities of home and family. They are also more likely to live in homes with substance abuse and physical abuse. When this happens, the disadvantages of parents become the disadvantages of their children. Indeed, poverty is intergenerational, compounding from one generation to the next.

In the 1960s during President Johnson's administration, the U.S. government initiated a "War on Poverty" by providing programs such as Head Start and food assistance. In the decades since the War on Poverty began, many attempts have been made to identify and address the factors that contribute to keeping people in poverty. Recent findings show that 21% of U.S. children live below the poverty level, representing an increase of 33% in the first decade of this century (Wight, Chau, & Aratani, 2011). When compared with other industrialized nations, the growing level of childhood poverty in the United States has placed the nation's child poverty rate second only to that of Mexico. There is a corresponding trend in the number of children living in single-parent homes, with 27% of U.S. children living in single-parent families in 2011 (Casey & Maldonado, 2012). The poverty rate for children living in single-parent households was 42.5% in 2012, which is more than five times the rate for children living with two parents who are married (Department of Commerce, Bureau of the Census, 2013). Due to the rise in single-parent families and the challenges that single parents face in supporting their children, more children live in poverty than any other age group in the United States.

While Caucasian children represent the largest number of U.S. children living in poverty, the poverty rate for African American children is triple that of Caucasian American children at 36% (Wight et al., 2011). That is followed closely by a 34% poverty rate for Native American children and a 33% poverty rate for Hispanic children. The rate of child poverty experienced by Asian Americans also exceeds that of Caucasian Americans at 15%. These statistics demonstrate the interplay between race and poverty in children's lives.

It is estimated that 35–46% of children born into poverty will remain impoverished as adults (Wagmiller & Adelman, 2009). Government programs have attempted to address the problem of intergenerational poverty through a variety of measures, including welfare programs, programs to move people from welfare to work, and early intervention initiatives (Hart & Risley, 1995; Phillips, Voran, Kisker, Howes, & Whitebrook, 1994). Despite these efforts, poverty remains a major problem in America, and intergenerational poverty persists.

Poverty plays a central role in many of the risk factors that children experience. In fact, poverty affects multiple and varied aspects of children's lives, and is associated with many of the circumstances known to undermine school success: maternal depression, poor nutrition, poor health, parental relationship instability, housing instability, food insecurity, discrimination, parental substance abuse, and parent conduct problems (Wadsworth et al., 2008). As a result of exposure to these risks, children from disadvantaged homes often start school lacking the academic, social, and behavioral skills necessary for learning (Ackerman, Brown, & Izard, 2004; Hernandez, 2012; Slopen, Fitzmaurice, Williams, & Gilman, 2010; Wagmiller & Adelman, 2009; Webster-Stratton, Reid, & Stoolmiller, 2008).

The multiple risk factors that low-income children experience can have a multitude of academic implications, such as impaired reading skills, a compromised vocabulary, delayed cognitive and language development, and increased risk for high school dropout (Hart & Risley, 1995; Hernandez, 2012; Neisser et al., 1996). In fact, the relationship between poverty and academic outcomes is so strong that the percentage of children in a school who live in poverty is the best predictor of a school's level of reading comprehension (Ransdell, 2012) and the reason that federal Title I funds are allocated to schools based on the percentage of students who qualify for free and reduced lunch.

The effects of poverty go beyond the academic factors commonly considered; equally problematic are the social, emotional, and behavioral challenges associated with exposure to poverty in childhood. Specifically, poverty has been shown to be associated both with increased levels of behaviors that interfere with learning as well as decreased levels of the foundational skills necessary for learning: social competence and emotional self-regulation (Ackerman et al., 2004; Kellam, Ling, Merisca, Brown, & Ialongo, 1998; Najman et al., 2010; Slopen et al., 2010; Wadsworth et al., 2008; Webster-Stratton et al., 2008).

Recent efforts have sought to clarify the relationship between poverty and behavior in childhood (Ackerman et al., 2004; Kellam et al., 1998; Najman et al., 2010; Slopen et al., 2010; Wadsworth et al., 2008). While it is clear that children who experience poverty are exposed to a number of risk factors that are believed to interfere with success at school, consensus regarding the specific factors responsible has not been reached. Answering this question is of paramount importance, as the behavioral profile that plagues many disadvantaged children interferes with academic and social success, and has implications over the lifespan.

SCHOOLS AS RISK FACTORS

One element in the behavioral profile that plagues impoverished students is aggression (Kellam et al., 1998). In fact, poverty has been found to be a significant predictor of aggression in kindergarten. Interestingly, though, other environmental factors are responsible for maintaining that aggression over time. Rather than poverty, the best predictor of continued aggression into middle school is the overall level of classroom aggression that a child experiences in the first-grade classroom. Specifically, a teacher's ability to manage aggression in the classroom during boys' first-grade year of school is the strongest predictor of how aggressive they will be in middle school. In fact, boys who were not aggressive in first grade but who spent the year in an aggressive classroom were significantly more likely to be aggressive in middle school (Kellam et al., 1998). Conversely, students who were aggressive entering first grade but who spent that school year in nonaggressive classrooms were not likely to be aggressive in middle school. Considering all family, school, neighborhood, and poverty variables, teachers are the determining factor in classroom aggression, with the level of aggression usually in proportion to the teacher's skills and training in classroom behavior management.

Persistent Poverty, Internalizing Behavior, and Externalizing Behavior

Students from impoverished backgrounds exhibit increased levels of both internalizing and externalizing behaviors (Slopen et al., 2010). Internalizing behavior refers to how a child experiences his or her problems personally through symptoms of anxiety or depression. Externalizing behavior refers to behaviors by which a child "acts out" or is disruptive in a classroom setting. Persistent poverty and the risks associated with persistent poverty have many effects on the behavior of elementary school children. Persistent poverty, defined as poverty evident at two or more times during childhood, has been found to be related to children's behavior, especially when it occurred recently (Ackerman et al., 2004). When one examines the factors of poverty that are at play in addition to income, the variables significantly related to externalizing behavior are maternal relationship instability, police contact, and harsh parenting. The mother's level of education provides an insignificant buffer against externalizing behavior. In contrast, a mother's history of mental illness is the only variable in addition to income that significantly increases a child's risk for internalizing behavior. Child cognitive ability, which is commonly considered to be an important aspect of resilience, provides an insignificant buffer against internalizing behavior. In other words, neither the level of a mother's education nor the child's IQ predict childhood behavior problems as much as a mother's mental health problems. While the parents' level of education can improve a child's outcomes, academic competence improves as family income increases, but worsens with relationship instability and harsh parenting within the family. That is, a family's income can improve student outcomes, but harsh parenting and limited emotional connections between the parent(s) and child can harm student outcomes.

The Role of Poverty-Related Stress

Attention has recently shifted to the role of poverty-induced stress as a mechanism by which poverty impacts children's behavior (Wadsworth et al., 2008). Poverty-related stress includes such experiences as economic strain, family conflict, family transitions, violence, and discrimination. Evidence suggests that poverty-related stress is more predictive of internalizing and externalizing syndromes than is socioeconomic status (SES). In fact, poverty-related stress has been implicated in certain mental disorders (i.e., those included in the *Diagnostic and Statistical Manual of Mental Disorders* [DSM]; American Psychiatric

Association, 2013) as oppositional defiant disorder, generalized anxiety disorder, obsessive–compulsive disorder, major depressive disorder, and persistent depressive disorder, as well as in some deviant behaviors. Race plays a role in children's experience of poverty-related stress, with Hispanic and Caucasian children more impacted by poverty-related stress than African American children. Interestingly, poverty-related stress impacts children of all ages equally, indicating that children find poverty stressful throughout childhood and adolescence.

The Timing and Duration of Poverty

Children's response to poverty is also related to the amount of time that they spend in poverty. Children who experience family poverty in early childhood, later childhood, and adolescence are more likely to engage in aggression and delinquency in adolescence and young adulthood than those who escape poverty at some point (Najman et al., 2010). Children who experience long durations of poverty are also more likely to use tobacco and alcohol as young adults. Compared with those who experience family poverty intermittently, children who experience poverty continually are the most likely to have negative behavioral outcomes.

Poverty, Food Insecurity, and Behavior

Food insecurity, or the experience of not having enough food due to limited resources, has been implicated in children's internalizing and externalizing behaviors (Slopen et al., 2010). Children living in low-income households and food-insecure households are significantly more likely to exhibit internalizing and externalizing behaviors than other children. Children from homes experiencing persistent food insecurity are significantly more likely to exhibit both externalizing and internalizing problem behaviors. In fact, findings suggest that the experience of food insecurity, above and beyond general poverty, increases a student's risk for displaying many types of problem behaviors at school. This is one of the reasons for school-based food programs, including free and reduced cost breakfast and lunch provided to students from low-income families.

The Relationship between Academics and Poverty

The academic impact of poverty was documented in a longitudinal study of nearly 4,000 children born between 1979 and 1989 that was conducted by the Annie E. Casey Foundation (Hernandez, 2012). The study found that, while the high school dropout rate was just 6% for students who had never experienced poverty, the rate jumped to 22% for children living in poverty and 32% for students who had spent at least half of their lives in poverty. The combined effects of poverty and compromised reading ability were found to be especially harmful. The dropout rate for children experiencing at least 1 year of poverty and reading below proficiency was 26%, and adding the risk factor of living in an impoverished neighborhood elevated that rate to 35%. Race was also found to exacerbate the effects of poverty and compromised reading ability, with dropout rates of 31% and 33%, respectively, for impoverished African American and Hispanic students who were not reading proficiently in third grade (Algozzine, Wang, & Violette, 2011).

EFFECTIVE INSTRUCTION FOR STUDENTS AT RISK

There is overwhelming evidence that poverty is associated with increased levels of externalizing and internalizing behaviors, and that such behaviors interfere with students' academic and social success (Ackerman et al., 2004; Kellam et al., 1998; Najman et al., 2010; Slopen et al., 2010; Wadsworth et al., 2008; Webster-Stratton et al., 2008). The multitude of risk factors to which children living in poverty are exposed contributes to the behaviors commonly seen in this population. The research reviewed demonstrates both the challenge and the importance of disaggregating poverty-related risk so that specific factors can be addressed (e.g., school-based meals and access to community food pantries). It is crucial that educators are aware of the factors that lead to interfering behavior, as well as approaches to ameliorating those risk factors.

Given that children spend a large portion of their days in schools, the problems faced by low-income children can and should be addressed with, and through, their teachers. With the necessary training and skills, teachers can promote prosocial behaviors, form closer and warmer relationships with their students, and prepare students for success. Many teachers faced with meeting the needs of at-risk students find that they have not been prepared to address the emotional and behavioral challenges that disadvantaged students often manifest (Aloe, Amo, & Shanahan, 2014; Phillips et al., 1994). Such teachers, especially those working in low-income school districts, benefit from the opportunity to learn effective classroom management practices that promote school adjustment and address learning and behavior problems. Effective classroom management training has the added benefit of reducing teacher burnout and increasing teachers' sense of self-efficacy with regard to managing their classrooms. In addition, teachers in schools with high-poverty populations benefit from support in conceptualizing their students as capable and employing effective positive and supportive approaches to teaching (Solomon, Battistich, & Hom, 1996). Finally, when taught to use supportive and effective strategies to manage classroom behavior, teachers become well positioned to alter students' trajectories (Kellam et al., 1998).

Unfortunately, some of the risk factors found to negatively impact students are not amenable to change within a school setting; such issues as persistent and recurrent poverty, and parent variables (e.g., relationship instability and police contact), cannot be readily ameliorated. But many of the other risk factors identified above can be addressed in educational settings. Schools can offer parenting classes and supports in order to provide parents with an alternative to harsh parenting, support parents' efforts to prevent their children from abusing substances, and reduce their children's externalizing behaviors (Mendez, Ogg, Loker, & Fefer, 2013; Webster-Stratton et al., 2008). Similarly, schools can offer training to students designed to prevent and ameliorate stress, poverty-related and otherwise (Seligman, Ernst, Gillham, Reivich, & Linkins, 2009; Seligman, Reivich, Jaycox, & Gillham, 1995). Likewise, schools can develop programs to address student hunger and support access to adult education programs to help parents further their education.

Given the enduring effects of poverty on students' school success, perhaps the variable that schools most need to address is the training provided to the teachers of disadvantaged students. Presently, low-income students are likely to encounter teachers who are inadequately trained for meeting their great and disparate needs (Kellam et al., 1998). That lack of training has been found to worsen the behavioral difficulties that such students are likely to have. Sadly, poorly trained teachers might also trigger problem behaviors in students who have not yet shown such tendencies. Kellam and colleagues (1998) speculated that students who were exposed to coercive and aggressive environments at home, then came to school and were exposed to hostile and aggressive teachers and classmates, could have come to believe that *aggressive* was the only way to be.

Because many teachers have not been prepared to address the emotional and behavioral problems associated with poverty, they too often respond with poor classroom management practices (Webster-Stratton et al., 2008). Such teachers, who are more likely to be found in low-income school districts, impede students' school adjustment and compound learning and behavior problems (Phillips et al., 1994). Compared with teachers in high-income schools, teachers in schools with high-poverty populations think of their students as less capable (even when objective measures show that they are not) and employ far less effective teaching approaches (Solomon et al., 1996). Rather than using positive and supportive approaches, such teachers tend to rely on harsh, punitive, and ineffective strategies to manage classroom behavior, further hampering students' school outcomes (Kellam et al., 1998). The good news is that the identification of these obstacles has led to the development of interventions designed to prepare teachers for addressing the needs and challenges of at-risk students (Webster-Stratton et al., 2008). Such interventions show significant promise in improving student outcomes.

SUMMARY

There are many and varied risk factors that contribute to the problems that impoverished students face in school. Experiencing poverty repeatedly and recently are significantly associated with students' interfering behavior. Students who experience both recurrent and recent poverty are likely to exhibit both externalizing and internalizing behaviors (Ackerman et al., 2004). They are also likely to be aggressive and delinquent, and to use alcohol and tobacco (Najman et al., 2010). Food insecurity also contributes to externalizing and internalizing behaviors (Slopen et al., 2010). Additionally, poverty-related stress contributes to the development of such behaviors, as confirmed by DSM diagnostic symptom categories (Wadsworth et al., 2008). Finally, poor classroom management by teachers can lead to aggressive behavior in low-income children (Kellam et al., 1998). Students living in poverty face many risk factors, both at home and at school, and those factors are interrelated in their lives. There are steps that teachers can take to offset the effects of poverty on school outcomes, but school teams must work together to make such efforts successful.

CHAPTER 5

What to Teach in the Era of the Common Core State Standards

Prior to the 2001 No Child Left Behind (NCLB) Act, curricula used in many classrooms were less standardized and teachers had more freedom to use a variety of teaching materials. Based on research indicating that the accurate use of specific materials and methods resulted in better outcomes for many students, NCLB introduced the idea of a "core" curriculum in each major content area. This requirement was included in the Reading First program, a component of NCLB (Gamse, Jacob, Horst, Boulay, & Unlu, 2008). Unfortunately, not all states and districts received Reading First grants, but those that did showed improved reading decoding outcomes (Institute of Education Sciences, 2013a). The goal of having a core program of instruction is to ensure that all students have access to effective instruction and many schools have continued to use core curricula in order to make the instruction provided to all students more consistent.

Although not the same thing as a core curriculum, in 2010, the Council of Chief State School Officers (CCSSO) began developing a set of common learning goals that all states could use; these are known as the Common Core State Standards (CCSS). The CCSSO is an affiliate of the National Governors Association, an organization that includes all 50 U.S. governors. The goal of the CCSS is to provide all U.S. schools with a uniform set of learning standards for what students should learn. As explained in Chapter 2, due to the history of U.S. schools such consistency has not been present in American classrooms before. The CCSS were designed to provide a level of instructional consistency in the United States like that observed in other industrialized nations. Nonetheless, the CCSS have been controversial and not all U.S. states have opted to use them. This chapter reviews the differences among standards, curricula, and programs, and how these align with MTSS.

STANDARDS, CURRICULA, AND PROGRAMS

Even though they all have a role in what gets taught in classrooms, learning standards, curricula, and programs are not the same thing. First, let's begin with some definitions.

- *Standards* are officially adopted learning goals for all students in a given school, district, or state. Sometimes they are called learning standards, and before the CCSS 49 out of 50 states had statewide learning standards. For those wondering, the holdout state was Nebraska. Standards are designed to indicate the observable and measurable knowledge and skills that students should have at the end of a period of instruction. Standards are designed to be curriculum-neutral, meaning that they state what students should learn, not what materials and methods teachers should use to teach. The CCSS have been criticized for dictating what and how teachers should teach, but technically they do not do this.
- *Curriculum* is an adopted set of courses or learning activities leading to a specific goal. When used in the plural the term is *curricula*. It is a Latin word and was traditionally applied to the combined set of learning activities used by a school or college leading to a specific degree. In modern usage, curricula are the specific teaching materials and methods that a school, district, or state has adopted to be used with all students. Curricula are different from standards in that they specify what the teachers teach, not what the students should learn. In the United States, it is usually schools and/or districts—both public and private—but not states that decide what curricula to use.
- *Program* refers to published materials developed for the purpose of teaching students specific knowledge and/or skills. Often, programs are adopted as part of a district's curriculum of study. Programs are usually designed to teach a specific content area or set of skills to students at specific levels. The presence and use of a certain program does not guarantee what students will learn. Instead, it includes the materials for instruction. Sometimes, programs also include directions that teachers are supposed to follow when using the materials.

It is important to understand the differences among the above terms. They have distinct meanings and uses in the planning and implementation of instruction. When considered and selected thoughtfully, standards, curricula, and programs can all have a role in an MTSS. But, MTSS leaders must take ownership of their role in selecting and using all three of these. Otherwise there is no integration and systematic review of the instruction that is taking place. Ideally, standards are selected first, followed by curricula, and then—last—programs.

In the years since NCLB and Reading First were implemented, many schools have adopted the practice of having core programs in one or more curriculum areas. Most often, such programs are used for reading instruction, but can be used in other areas as well. Selecting a core program before adopting standards and curricula is backward. When a program is selected first, the publisher and not the district leaders are taking charge of what students learn. Instead, core programs should be selected after careful consideration by a representative school or district committee that has reviewed and considered the research evidence for each program and how it meets the district's standards and curricula. Partly due to the CCSS, there has been much confusion about the roles of standards, curriculum, and programs in teaching practices.

CONFUSION ABOUT STANDARDS, CURRICULUM, AND PROGRAMS

The development of the CCSS has brought renewed attention to what is taught in U.S. classrooms (National Governors Association Center for Best Practices, Council of Chief State School Officers, 2010). The CCSS were developed because of frustration among governors and commissioners of education that comparisons of student outcomes among states failed to take into account that every state had different learning goals. Essentially, the students in all 50 U.S. states and six territories were expected to learn different things and, if compared on a common test, would show variable outcomes by design. The states' commissioners of education convened and realized that if they all agreed on a common set of learning standards for students in their states, comparisons among students in different states would be valid. Notably, most other industrialized nations (e.g., Great Britain and Finland) have such national standards. In developing the Standards, the National Governors Association sought a way for schools across the United States to have consistency in what all students would be expected to learn at each grade level. It is important to note that the Standards were neither developed by, nor will be implemented by, the U.S. federal government or the U.S. Department of Education. This is because under the U.S. Constitution providing education is a state's right and responsibility. As of 2015, 43 states and five territories, along with the District of Columbia and the Department of Defense Education programs, had adopted the Standards as the official learning goals for their states' students (Common Core State Standards Initiative, 2015).

In the time since the Standards were published and reviewed by states, there has been public discussion of whether the Standards are beneficial for students. Because of the proposed national scope of the Standards, some people may have mistakenly understood that they were developed by the U.S. Department of Education; as noted, the U.S. Constitution prevents this. Others have questioned whether it is best for all U.S. students to be held to the same learning standards (Bidwell, 2014). The rationale for questioning common standards appears to relate to an assumption that all students should achieve differently. Some teachers may worry that the CCSS will require them to change how and what they teach. Advocates for the CCSS have pointed out that when students move between states using the CCSS, the learning expectations will remain largely the same. It is possible that this might be a benefit because U.S. students have become increasingly mobile, which places them at greater risk for educational difficulties. In 2004, Education Week reported that U.S. census data indicate that about 15–20% of all students changed school systems during the previous school year (Education Week, 2004). Although there remain concerns about the CCSS, it is possible that having more consistent instructional goals across states could benefit some students.

While the CCSS have attracted a great deal of national and political attention, instructional practices in classrooms are what drive actual student learning. Such instruction should be based on the locally adopted curriculum; however, not all curricula provide a high degree of specificity to teachers about what to teach when, so that all students can achieve mastery. For this reason, core programs were developed with the goal of helping all teachers provide equitable instruction for all students. Once selected, there should be PD and training for teachers so they will know how to use the program correctly. Such training develops the practice of implementing the core program with integrity. Having core programs in key areas, such as reading and math, that are implemented in a consistent manner by well-trained teachers is a way to make sure that all students have access to equivalent instruction. This is in comparison to older practices where each teacher developed his or her own materials and methods and students in different classrooms might learn very different things.

CORE PROGRAMS AND MTSS

It is important to reiterate that core programs are not the same as the CCSS or an adopted curriculum. While there are efforts to align the CCSS with an MTSS, the use of core programs is a separate activity (National Center on Intensive Intervention, 2014). This section describes how core programs are integral to effective tiered supports. The basic purpose behind using core programs is that every teacher in a given school or district will use materials and methods that are the same for all students. In reality, the universality of instruction is for nearly all students because there will be a very small number (i.e., less than 1%) whose disabilities are such that they cannot functionally access the adopted core programs. For all other students, there should be equivalence in the manner and content of instruction by grade level. This is important for several reasons. First, as noted above, for students who move within the same district there should be minimal disruption to the student's learning. It may not always be so simple, but it will be better than if teachers in each school are using entirely different materials and methods.

A second important component of the use of core programming is that it can equalize learning experiences across teachers. When all teachers of each grade are using the same materials and methods, and pacing themselves to be near the same lessons during the year, it will not matter as much which teacher a student has. All of the students should have access to the stated core curriculum. This is very different from an era when parents of students in some schools would lobby the administration to get their child into a certain teacher's classroom. This practice reflects an understanding among parents that some teachers were better than others. While differences in teaching skill and experience will always exist, having a common core can limit the differences in student outcomes resulting from variation in teaching practices.

Finally, there are social justice implications to using core instructional materials. When a school or district adopts specific learning standards and accompanying materials and methods, it is committing itself to providing access to that learning to all students, regardless of race, gender, language, culture, and other variables. This is significant because there is a long history in the United States of disparities in educational outcomes related to the quality of instruction accessed by different students. If students in middle and upper socioeconomic status (SES) areas have access to different, and better, instruction than students in lower SES communities, equity in educational access is lacking. The 1954 seminal U.S. Supreme Court decision in the case of *Brown v. Board of Education of Topeka, Kansas* ruled that the segregated schools of the era failed to provide all students with equitable access to education. Using core programs is another step in the process of offering effective instruction to all students.

Any given "core" program may, or may not, be effective. This is why an MTSS includes the step of evaluating the evidence that a program will result in beneficial outcomes for students. Even before national technical assistance to implement tiered supports was available (e.g., the response to intervention [RTI] and positive behavioral interventions and supports [PBIS] centers), the U.S. Department of Education developed tools related to the quality of available teaching materials. NCLB included funding to create the What Works Clearinghouse (WWC; Institute of Education Sciences, 2013b). The WWC provides objective reviews of specific teaching materials and is designed to make sure all teachers have access to information about effective programs. Research teams at specific universities have also provided reviews of teaching materials and methods. A summary of university-based program reviews is found in Table 5.1. Both the WWC and university websites are helpful tools for teachers because they provide a way of comparing multiple reviews. The goal of all these web-based reviews is to provide teachers with information about which teaching materials have been

TABLE 5.1. University-Based Reviews of Teaching Materials

University	Program name	Website
Florida State University	Florida Center for Reading Research	*www.fcrr.org*
Johns Hopkins University	Best Evidence Encyclopedia	*www.bestevidence.org*
Vanderbilt University	IRIS Center	*http://iris.peabody.vanderbilt.edu*
University of Texas	Meadows Center for Preventing Educational Risk	*www.meadowscenter.org*
University of Virginia	Center for Advanced Study of Teaching and Learning	*http://curry.virginia.edu/research/centers/castl*

found to be the most effective with diverse learners. It is important to note that most materials published before 2012 were not designed to meet the learning expectations found in the CCSS. Publishers have revised materials in response to the Standards and school teams in states using the CCSS will want to examine the revised publications carefully, realizing that data about their efficacy will not be available for several years.

Before a school or district adopts a core program, it needs to review the evidence as to whether that program has been found to be effective in achieving the stated learning goals. There are two widely used terms that refer to whether a program has data to support its efficacy: (1) evidence-based instruction (EBI), and (2) scientifically based instruction. These terms are often used interchangeably, but they actually have different meanings. For the purposes of clarity in this book, we use the following definitions:

1. *Evidence-based instruction* includes those materials and methods that have been shown to be effective for a wide variety of learners in two or more experimental studies.
2. *Scientifically based instruction* includes materials and methods *based on* practices found to be effective in prior research, but which have themselves not been validated in two or more experimental studies.

Evidence-based practices (EBPs) have more research behind them than scientifically based practices. This is because all of the components of evidence-based programs have been fully tested in general education classrooms using methods that meet criteria for high-quality research. The entire program has been implemented and found to be effective, not just once, but at least twice, and sometimes more. Multiple examples of full and accurate implementation that yielded effective results for students provide the best indicator that if a school decides to adopt this program, its students will benefit as well.

Scientifically based practices are ones that are still in the experimental stage. These are instructional methods that have been developed based on available research, but which have not yet been shown to be effective in two or more experimental studies. This means that more research is needed to determine whether the program will work for diverse students across multiple settings. Often, scientifically based instruction goes on to become evidence-based instruction, but not always. Not all instructional innovations will work across diverse students. This is why evaluating instructional practices with a wide variety of students is so important. Health care has a long history of trying out new medications and devices. In fact, there are specific terms used in medicine to refer to the phases of research. Before a medication or device will be approved by the FDA, it must go through a phase known as investigational new drug or device. By applying a parallel standard by which instructional practices are studied scientifically, education will develop a body of knowledge concerning which materials and methods are truly evidence based.

The practice of selecting and using only evidence-based instructional materials and methods in classrooms is relatively new in U.S. education. As noted in Chapter 2, there is a history of individualism in U.S. education. As a result, some teachers may find it awkward that they will now be expected to teach from universal materials with more defined methods. The purpose in requiring that teachers learn and use uniform curricula and programs is to ensure that effective instruction that meets the stated learning goals is available to all students. Teachers will still have many opportunities to be creative in their instruction. While the use of core programs means that all of the teachers will use the same materials and stick to a schedule, each teacher can—and should—differentiate instruction for his or her individual students.

DIFFERENTIATION WITHIN CORE PROGRAM INSTRUCTION

An important component of effective use of any given core program is for the teacher to provide preteaching, enrichment, and reteaching of core lessons for selected students. Some students will "get" a lesson on the first exposure. Such students will need regular review of the learning, but probably do not need to have the lesson repeated or revised. These students may benefit from enrichment instruction that allows them to learn more beyond the basic ideas of the lesson. Other students will need to have the essential elements of the lesson broken down into distinct parts and repeated. Two main strategies for differentiating instruction are to preteach certain parts, and to reteach as needed. Preteaching refers to giving selected students an overview of words, ideas, or steps before doing the full lesson with the class. If some students in a class have difficulty with integrating new vocabulary with concepts, preteaching new words that will be in a lesson is a very effective method. This method can be used for all content areas and is particularly helpful for students who are English language learners (ELLs).

Some students will need more repetitions of the lesson, or its parts, to understand it fully. For these students, reteaching the lesson is important. Although all of the reasons that a student might need reteaching cannot be outlined here, there are students whose memory attributes are such that having two or three repetitions of new instruction is necessary to reach mastery. Reteaching can be done during core instruction as part of regular group rotations in the daily schedule. Chapter 13 provides details about how to construct schedules that incorporate regular reteaching for students who need it. Often, students will not need the entire lesson repeated, but only selected parts. In order for teachers to know what reteaching is needed, some type of regular classroom assessment is necessary. Many (if not all) core programs come with routine assessments designed to help teachers know each student's progress toward mastery. These assessments can identify which parts of lessons should be retaught. If a student requires the additional support of Tier 2 or Tier 3 instruction, regular progress monitoring will be needed (see Chapter 21).

ALTERNATE INSTRUCTION

Some students will require more intensive instruction than provided in the core program(s). It is important to note that only a very small number of students will ever need to have access to an alternate program, thus the work to schedule and implement such instruction is not likely to be overly demanding for school teams. Using alternative instruction for students who are struggling in school is a practice that comes from the field of special education. For many years before U.S. Special Education Law was passed in 1975, teachers working with students who had known or suspected disabilities would often use materials and methods different from those in the general education classroom or school. But, for those students who have not responded to Tier 2 intervention plus a first round of Tier 3 supports, an alternate core program could be an effective solution.

WHEN TO USE AN ALTERNATE CORE PROGRAM

Removing a student from the school or district-adopted core instruction is a decision not to be taken lightly. Indeed, the student's parents *must* be notified when such a decision is being considered. There is really only one circumstance within an MTSS when replacing the core program might be a logical step. When a student has not made effective progress in Tier 2 and Tier 3 supports that are built on top of the core program, then the school team could decide to try out a different program for that student. This is typically referred to as an alternate core program. If a team decides that trying a different core is justified, the step being taken is to test the hypothesis that a very different type of instruction will result in this student's success. Here we review the types of alternate core programs, how to select one, and how to conduct progress monitoring with the new program.

Types

Alternate core programs are characterized by including direct instruction of specific skills broken into distinct steps. These programs were initially developed for students with disabilities, but they can be used with any student who demonstrates a need for more intensive instruction. Examples of such programs for reading include any number of materials developed based on the Orton–Gillingham method of reading instruction, as well as materials that utilize explicit and scripted direct instruction. The reason that these are considered replacement core programs is that they diverge from the general MTSS requirement that additional instruction be provided *in addition to* the core instruction, they require a substantial amount of time to implement, and they are generally provided during the time when the student would otherwise be participating in the adopted core program. It is important for teachers and school teams to think about differences in the adopted and possible alternate core programs being considered for a student. For example, an important distinction about most reading instruction programs is that each one has a specific typeface (i.e., font) and keyword associated with each letter of the alphabet. Alternate core programs often have fonts and keywords that are different from those used in mainstream core programs. This is one of the reasons it is best for a student needing intensive intervention to use a full replacement core with a program that uses materials that will be very different from the general classroom core program rather than the core plus additional instruction.

One example of the differences in reading materials that could confuse a student is the program Reading Mastery. This program is a comprehensive reading instruction method that uses a distinct alphabet. The Reading Mastery alphabet has been carefully designed to make it easier for students to learn and recall each letter of the alphabet and the sound(s) it makes. Most students do not need the uniqueness of the Reading Mastery alphabet system, but a small number benefit from it. For those students, having them continue with the general core program while also using Reading Mastery's new alphabet can be very confusing. As a result, having these students switch to Reading Mastery as an alternate core program is the better option. In math, a program known as TouchMath uses a dot and counting system that is quite different from the standard way that numerals and their values are taught to students. TouchMath could be very confusing to a student if he or she stays in the general core math program and gets TouchMath lessons, too. Here, switching to TouchMath as the alternate core program would be an option.

Criteria for Selection

There are many possible alternate core programs available. This can make the process of selecting which one to use difficult. In order for any program to be used as an alternate core, it needs to cover the stated learning goals identified for the general core program. School teams considering the use of an alternate core program for a student have the responsibility to review and confirm that the alternate core will cover all of the learning standards adopted by the district for the student's grade. And, it is essential that the student's parents be notified and ideally included in discussions and decisions about any use of an alternate core program. Parent participation is important because changing a student's core instruction is equivalent to removing the student from the adopted general curriculum for all students and putting in place a different program of instruction. As noted in prior chapters, all U.S. students have a right to public education based on the constitutions of the 50 states. Amending the instruction that a student receives has implications for how a state is implementing its obligation to provide education for all students.

Progress Monitoring

As with any intervention, collecting progress data is a must. A student's progress in an alternate core program must be monitored weekly, just as with any Tier 3 intervention. Some alternate core programs have progress measures built in to them. When this is the case, these measures can be used for weekly progress monitoring. If a program does not have such measures, then general outcome measures (GOM) that match the target skills can be used (see Chapter 21). For example, when using a program like Corrective Reading, regular progress measures that document the student's progress toward mastery are included. Most replacement core programs have such progress measures because they are designed to show the student's relative mastery of the learning. Importantly, all students using an alternate core program must be included in the triannual universal screening assessments. This is because data are needed to show how they are doing in relation to other students and in meeting the stated learning standards for the grade level.

SUMMARY

In recent years, U.S. education has made a shift from having teacher-created instructional materials that vary across classrooms to widespread use of core instructional materials adopted by a district for each grade level. The National Governors Association (National Governors Association Center for Best Practices, Council of Chief State School Officers, 2010) developed and proposed the

CCSS as a national model for grade-level learning goals in reading and mathematics. These standards have been adopted by 43 U.S. states and four territories. Standards are learning goals and are different from curricula and programs. Curricula are the general teaching objectives for each grade level and programs are instructional materials for teaching the content. Core programs are important tools for implementing an MTSS because they provide a uniform foundation of instruction for all students. Most students will make effective progress with adopted core programs; however, some will need additional instruction. In a very small number of cases, students might benefit from an alternate core program that is more time intensive than the adopted core. Such alternate core programs are an option that can be tried as long as the replacement program covers the same learning goals as the core program, and parents are given the opportunity to participate in the decision.

PART II

The Importance of Collaboration and Teams

School teams are an essential part of an MTSS. Without them, the process of developing, implementing, and sustaining tiered supports cannot happen. For this reason, we have organized this section into three chapters about the essential role of teams (Chapter 6), the logistics of selecting team members and assigning roles (Chapter 7), and how teams can function most effectively (Chapter 8). The people who make an MTSS happen in schools must be ready to work as a true team and not as individuals or the dreaded "committee." Instead, the team members need to understand the importance of having a team develop and implement the MTSS as well as how to interact effectively with other team members and the larger school community in order to sustain programs over time. As we will share, the process of creating the team needs just as much effort and care as selecting instructional materials or monitoring student progress. Indeed, it is not possible for one individual to implement and sustain an MTSS and, unless effective teams are developed as part of the process, there is no point in trying. But, when effective teams are developed, they distribute the work appropriately and foster data-driven problem solving for all students.

CHAPTER 6

The Essential Role of Teams in Supporting All Students

In order for an MTSS to be effective, school personnel must work together as teams. This may seem obvious, but team-based approaches are relatively new in U.S. education. Prior to the 1990s, teachers tended to work independently. The importance of individualism in education was discussed in an 1891 article in the *Atlantic Monthly* (Shaler, 1891). Nathaniel Shaler explained that it was important that education include a focus on individualism so that students could learn to regulate their behaviors. Notably, Shaler also argued that teachers should use a military model of discipline in their teaching and that each teacher was in command of his or her classroom (Shaler, 1891). An iconic model of U.S. education is the one-room schoolhouse where one teacher had complete authority over his or her students. As schools became bigger, and more teachers were in each building, the tradition of the classroom teacher having complete authority did not go away. Indeed, teachers often closed their doors and interacted little with other teachers.

The tradition of isolation among teachers began to change in the 1990s. Although there are various possible reasons for this shift, one explanation is that efforts to improve student outcomes required more communication and collaboration among teachers. The focus on student outcomes culminated in major revisions in the U.S. Elementary and Secondary Education Act (ESEA), known as the No Child Left Behind Act (NCLB), in 2001. These revisions required schools to conduct assessments of students in grades 3–8 and show that students were making "adequate yearly progress" in order for the school to receive certain federal money. Many schools have shown improved student outcomes in recent years and many credit increased teacher collaboration as a component of this change.

One of the most widely adopted school collaboration models is known as the professional learning community (PLC; All Things PLC, 2013; Dufour, 2004). Collaboration and teaming are key elements of the PLC model.

Teamwork is essential for an effective MTSS. This is because of the "system" component of this work. An MTSS cannot be done by one person in isolation and it literally depends on having educators work together to support all students. Even in very small schools, collaboration between students and teachers is necessary to support success. There are several types of teams often used in an MTSS, including grade-level teams, problem-solving teams, universal teams, and intervention teams. In some schools, variations on these names have been used, such as student success team, student assistance team, or child study team. A summary of the common features and names of MTSS teams is shown in Table 6.1. The name of the team is not as important as the function it serves. The remainder of this chapter includes descriptions of teams according to their functions at each MTSS tier.

There are three main functions that MTSS school teams need to serve: (1) reviewing how groups of students are doing across the whole school; (2) reviewing individual student data; and (3) determining if more intensive support, or a referral for special education, is needed. For each of these types of teams, the members, types(s) of data considered, and type(s) of decisions made from the data are described. Box 6.1 includes reflections from veteran MTSS implementer

TABLE 6.1. Types of Teams

Tier	Key features	Examples
1	• Develops, oversees, and evaluates universal (schoolwide) procedures and data. • Includes members representing all stakeholder groups in the school. • Uses screening data to identify schoolwide instructional priorities for each academic year.	• Universal team • Building team • Administrative team (e.g., "A-team") • Problem-solving team[a]
2	• Reviews progress monitoring data for students participating in Tier 2 interventions. • All members understand how to make sense of single-case design (SCD) data graphs. • Members share from their collective expertise about interventions likely to be effective at Tier 2, especially standard protocol interventions.	• Grade-level team • Problem-solving team[a] • Student assistance team[a] • Student support team[a] • Child study team[a]
3	• Reviews progress data for students participating in Tier 3 interventions. • All members understand both SCD data graphs and the district and state rules about referral for special education services. • Activities include reviewing data for students participating in Tier 3 intensive interventions and deciding whether a student should be referred for special education.	• Problem-solving team[a] • Student assistance team[a] • Student support team[a] • Child study team[a] • Referral team • Building assistance team

[a]A team name that might be used at multiple tiers, depending on how many students are in the building and/or district.

BOX 6.1. Reflections on the Importance of Teams in Making an MTSS Effective from Mary Jean O'Reilly, PhD, NCSP

We began by implementing PBIS in two schools, and eventually rolled it out districtwide. As we continued to add to our prevention efforts, we used PBIS principles such as designating teams to address multi-tiered efforts and implement the framework within the culture of each building. Our prevention work broadened to include universal prevention curricula in each school, including Second Step and Steps to Respect social skills curricula, along with the Olweus Bullying Prevention curriculum, to address the requirement under state legislation that bullying prevention and intervention strategies be explicitly taught. As our mandate expanded, our district- and school-based teams morphed from PBIS-specific teams to school climate teams.

Our school climate teams address training and implementation in the areas of bullying prevention, positive behavioral supports, and social skill training on all tiers. Leadership of these teams generally includes the school adjustment counselor and/or the school psychologist, administrators, and both regular education and special education staff. The teams often also include paraprofessionals and other staff members.

Dr. Mary Jean O'Reilly, who has watched how school teams have both been essential and have evolved in her district. It is best if there are separate teams for each tier so that the team members can be very clear about the types of decisions needed. In larger schools, different teachers can serve on the teams and divide up the workload. In smaller schools, some teachers and specialists, and even the principal, might need to be on two or more teams. Still, in very small schools where the same teachers or specialists serve multiple roles it is best if separate meetings are held to meet the different functions. This will help team members avoid role confusion.

TIER 1: REVIEWING SCHOOLWIDE STUDENT PERFORMANCE

The most general function that a team can perform is to look at data from all of the students in a school and identify trends and instructional needs. Teams that consider schoolwide data are often referred to as universal, leadership, or problem-solving teams.

Membership

Schoolwide teams must have membership that represents all parts of the school community. If only certain groups are represented it will be difficult—if not impossible—for the team to work on behalf of the entire school. Team members should include classroom teachers, special educators, specialists (e.g., art and physical education teachers, speech pathologists, librarians), an administrator, and a parent. For secondary schools, having a student representative is advised as well. The number of team members to have really depends on the size of the school. In a small rural school, the "team" might be two to three people, but in a large urban setting, it could include eight to 10 people. Having too many members can interfere with team functioning (discussed below), so careful thought about the right number of team members for each school is important. Smaller teams are usually more effective than bigger ones. The members need to recognize that they represent their colleagues and work on their behalf.

Types of Data Considered

Schoolwide teams are in a position to review data that are collected from and about all students in the school, or from selected grades in certain cases. This is an important point because teams must have the right data in order to make good decisions. Examples of data that a schoolwide team might consider include triannual academic and social–emotional universal screening data, office discipline referral data, annual assessments for targeted grade levels, state-mandated assessments, and district-selected local assessments. By having data on all students, the team can reflect on how the school is doing in relation to student learning and behavior goals. Sometimes there may be scores missing for a few students in each grade, but that is not a problem assuming that most students completed the assessments. When large amounts of student data are pooled together, they are referred to as aggregated data and provide a valuable window into the functioning of the school.

Types of Decisions Made

The purpose in having aggregated data is to allow educators to review the general trends for all students. Importantly, these data are not designed to provide indicators of progress for individual students. Instead, the team looks at schoolwide data to see whether the efforts made by teachers and others to support all students are successful. For example, a team might look at the percentage of students in each grade level that met a specific learning goal. In an MTSS, we want at least 80% of students in each grade to meet such goals. If only 65% of third graders made the target last year, the team would be interested to know if more third graders made it this year. Similarly, the team can learn what percentage of students in the entire school met their respective learning and behavior targets. Schoolwide teams are responsible for looking at the "big picture" about how a school is doing and identifying what changes are needed.

TIER 2: REVIEWING INDIVIDUAL STUDENT PERFORMANCE

A different type of team is one that looks at data from individual students. Unlike schoolwide teams, student-focused teams are highly focused on incremental changes in individual student learning and behavior.

Membership

The membership of teams that support individual students is quite different from that of schoolwide teams. Instead of having members representing all school stakeholders, those who look at individual performance need to know the students personally and have the capacity to change instruction for students. For this reason, members are usually classroom teachers. Often such teams are known as grade-level teams (GLTs) and there are separate teams for each grade in the school. The GLT typically meets at regular intervals, from weekly to monthly, to examine individual student performance and develop instruction or intervention plans. In some schools, other staff join the GLT meetings either when requested by the team or on a rotating basis. For example, the instructional coach, special education teacher(s), school psychologist, or speech and language pathologist could rotate attendance at the GLT meetings for each grade level to answer questions specific to his or her expertise.

Types of Data Considered

As noted, individual student data teams review different data than schoolwide teams. There are two main types of data that such teams consider. First, a Tier 2 team is likely to look at the screening scores of the students in a specific class or grade level to see which students might need more help. Then, the team would pull additional information to learn if the screening scores are consistent with other information. If all of the data about the student indicate a need for help, the team would develop instructional ideas. After additional instruction (also called intervention) is put into place, the team would review the student's progress data to see if the change worked. The progress data would include student scores on brief measures completed weekly to monthly as a way to show if instructional change was effective. Examples of academic progress measures often used are AIMSweb (NCS Pearson, 2014), DIBELS (Dynamic Measurement Group, 2013), EasyCBM (Houghton Mifflin Harcourt, 2014), and FastBridge (FastBridge Learning, 2015).

Types of Decisions Made

There are two types of decisions that individual student data teams typically make: (1) identifying students who need extra help, and (2) whether an intervention is working. As noted above, the steps to identify the students who need help include looking at screening data as well as other sources of information about the students' progress. Importantly, decisions about providing student assistance should never be based on one type of data alone. If the team discovers that a student's data are inconsistent, it could recommend that additional assessments be conducted. Only when all of the data about a student show that there is a need for help should instructional change happen.

The other type of decision that individual student data teams make is whether an instructional change (i.e., intervention) is working. When considering this question, the team generally comes to one of three conclusions: (1) maintain the current instruction because it is effective, (2) intensify the current instruction because it is working but the student's progress is slower than needed, or (3) do something entirely different because the student is not making any progress. Later chapters provide details for how to interpret student data. An additional excellent resource is the Riley-Tillman and Burns (2009) book *Evaluating Educational Interventions*. Most of the time, the intervention is likely to be working and the team's review of the student's data leads to a decision to maintain the support as is. Sometimes, the data may show that the student is making improvement but very slowly. In such cases, the team could suggest that the intervention be "intensified." This means that it could be provided for more days per week, for longer time slots, or with fewer students in the group (Brown-Chidsey, Bronaugh, & McGraw, 2009). When the team sees data showing that a student is making no progress at all, it needs to recommend a new course of action. This could be trying a different intervention, or it could be recommending that a referral for special education be considered.

TIER 3: INTENSIVE SUPPORT TEAMS

While multi-tiered supports are generally very effective in helping students, not every student will "respond" to such intervention. If a student does not respond effectively to highly intensive intervention, then a team needs to consider the next steps. Some students will have learning profiles that indicate that a disability might be present. When a student does not show effective progress toward specific learning goals, despite multiple tiers of support, schools have a duty to consider whether the student has a disability and is eligible for special education. Such referral decisions are very different from the other types of decisions discussed above because all of the procedures related to special education are covered by both federal and state laws. Specifically, any time a student is referred for special education, there are due process considerations that must be included. Due process is short for the phrase *due process of law* and refers to the need for all required procedures related to special education to be carried out and documented. For this reason, the membership, data, and types of decisions of Tier 3 teams are typically handled according to district and/or state policies. Notably, there is a great deal of variation in state laws and guidance concerning whether or how a student who has received tiered supports (e.g., RTI) is formally referred for a special education evaluation (Hauerwas, Scott, & Brown, 2013). Readers are encouraged to review and learn their state and district policies concerning such referrals.

Membership

The composition of teams that make referrals for special education is typically governed by district or state rules. While federal special education law allows any interested person to make a referral, including parents, school districts and state departments of education often have guidance or laws concerning how school personnel should proceed. Such rules are typically most precise in relation to referrals for students who might have a specific learning disability (SLD). Since SLD is the single most common reason that students are referred for special education, understanding the rules about which personnel must be on the team is important. Some states require that all decisions about whether a student has an SLD be based on a process that includes multiple tiers of support and accompanying data (e.g., RTI data). Under the 2004 federal special education rules, all states must allow local districts the option of using such data (Hauerwas, Brown, & Scott, 2013). For this reason, it is often the case that a combination of the team members who served on the Tier 1 schoolwide team (e.g., universal team) and Tier 2 individual student data team (i.e., the GLT) will be members of the Tier 3 intensive support team.

Having both teachers who have worked directly with the student, as well as personnel who are familiar with the school's tiers of support on the team will make it possible to consider the individual student's progress in the context of the supports available at the school. In general, the intensive support team is likely to include the student's classroom teacher(s), a special educator, the specialist(s) who have worked with the student, and the building principal. Having a school psychologist on the team is also recommended because psychologists can review the data already collected and develop suggestions for the additional assessments to be conducted if a referral for special education is made. Notably, the parent is not typically part of the Tier 3 team but in some cases, the parent(s) may be invited so that other sources of information about the student's needs can be considered at the time of referral.

Types of Data Considered

The intensive support team has two main purposes: (1) develop and review intensive interventions, and (2) determine if a student should be formally referred for a special education evaluation. In order to do this, having the right data at hand is essential. First, all of the data collected and used by the other teams needs to be available. This means having all screening data, progress data, information about classroom performance, and state or district test data. Depending on the student's age and background, it might be helpful to have information from the student's cumulative folder about which schools have been attended, what attendance has been like, any discipline incidents, and other related information. Attendance data are particularly important because a student cannot benefit from instruction if he or she is not at school. When a student has a significant number of absences, the team needs to discuss the effects of such absences on the student's progress. If the team concludes that the student was not in attendance often enough to have sufficiently experienced instruction, the next intervention should focus on improving attendance.

Based on the data from Tiers 1 and 2, the intensive support team will consider whether another more intensive intervention should be tried. Such interventions are usually implemented in very small groups of no more than three students, or even individually. Once an intensive intervention is in place, the team will review the student's progress at regular intervals. Progress data for Tier 3 interventions should be collected at least weekly (see Chapter 21). If the student makes progress with this new intervention, the team's work is to figure out how to help the student catch up to classroom peers and return to less intensive intervention. But if the student's progress does not lead to meeting the stated learning goals for his or her grade, the team's other job is to consider a referral for special education.

Types of Decisions Made

Tier 3 intensive support teams have an important task: to decide if a referral is needed. When the team members agree that all of the student's data indicate the possibility of a disability, then a referral is the appropriate outcome. Typically, this means completing a paper or online form initiating the referral and activating due process rules. The actual evaluation cannot start until parent permission is obtained. In some cases, the Tier 3 team might conclude that there is a need for more data in order to make a decision. This could include additional progress data from the current intervention or other indicators of student performance. In that case, the team will need to meet again and review the additional data before making a decision. Because of the additional rules governing referrals to special education, it is best for the team to create written documentation of its meetings and any decisions that were made using a format such as the Team-Initiated Problem-Solving process (see Chapter 8). Such notes can be used if there is a question later in time about why a student was or was not referred.

CREATING "TEAMNESS"

So far, this chapter has described various types of school teams according to their functions. There is another major topic related to school teams: how teams are formed and learn to work together. When a group of people first come together, there is often no group identity. In order for school teams to be effective, each team needs to develop a purpose and identity. Tuckman (1965) and Tuckman and Jensen (1977) developed a well-known model for understanding how group members learn to work together. This model includes four main stages of group development: (1) forming, (2) storming, (3) norming, and (4) performing. Tuckman and Jensen (1977) also included a fifth stage, adjourning, which is not addressed here because MTSS teams are usually ongoing groups that do not adjourn. Forming is the stage when the group members first meet and get to know one another. Generally, members are cordial and curious about one another. Storming involves members advocating for their own personal goals and thoughts about the group's function(s). This is called storming because disagreement is likely and it could seem like a "storm" has developed among members. The next stage is when productive work usually begins. Called norming, this stage is when the group sets its operating rules so that it can get work done. The "norms" that the group develops also help it to create a group identity in relation to its purpose. Finally, the performing stage is when the group directly engages in productive work and addresses its task(s). This stage can last indefinitely, depending on the group's purpose and longevity.

Virtually all groups go through these four stages. Sometimes, the duration of the stages will vary. For example, if a group is formed but a set of specific rules for interaction are given to the group to use, the norming stage may be very short. Knowing that any given group will go through these stages is important because it can help school team members appreciate the time and effort needed to create and sustain effective teams. The first time that a new school team meets, it is not likely to be ready for the norming or performing stages. One way to help expedite the forming stage is to use a standard first meeting agenda; an example is shown in Chapter 7. This agenda can help the team navigate the forming and norming stages. Depending on the members, completing the norming and performing stages could take several more meetings. It can be helpful for all team members to learn and understand the stages of group formation and the time necessary for a group to develop its own identity. In addition, school leaders must recognize and give time to groups to work through these stages so that they can get to a functional performance level. If a group is expected to be fully cohesive and effective after one meeting, it is probable that the group will not be successful.

School-based teams are generally set up to meet and work together for at least an entire school year. Ideally, some team members will carry over from one year to the next so that there is continuity. Just like individuals grow and change, so do teams. The initial "norms" that a group develops may not work for the entire duration of the team. It is normal for a team to review and revise its operating rules as needed. In relation to an MTSS, school teams need adequate time to meet and conduct business. Setting up team norms that establish regular meeting times, members' duties, recording discussions, and the process for decisions will make the team more effective in the long term (Nellis, 2012). When there are multiple teams operating in a school, mechanisms for the teams to communicate with one another will be necessary. Planning for this communication as part of the overall preparation for an MTSS will enhance the likelihood that the efforts will succeed.

ONE TEAM OR TWO?

In developing MTSS teams and supports, schools will have to decide whether to have one team at each tier, or to have both an academic and behavior team at each level. There is no simple guidance about best practice. The decision about how many teams to have often hinges on the size of the school and number of staff. In large urban and suburban schools having separate academic and behavior teams is easily done because there are enough staff for each team. But, in small rural schools, having two teams could be impossible due to a limited number of staff. In addition to considering the school size and staff availability, it is important to consider how integrated tiered supports are and whether there is adequate understanding of both academic and behavioral needs to combine the teams. If one type of support (academic or behavior) was implemented several years before the other and is more fully developed, then it might be best to have separate teams for now. But once the two systems are operating fully, integrating the teams might make sense.

SUMMARY

Teams of educators who work together to support all students are essential components of an MTSS. School teams are known by many different names, but there are typically three main functions that such teams serve: reviewing schoolwide data and policies, supporting individual students, and referring students for special education evaluation. Each type of team has unique duties that contribute to having multiple levels of student support. In small schools, one group of people may be on all three types of teams; in large schools there are likely to be multiple separate teams with different members, though some overlap is common. It is important that both the school leaders and team members understand the functions of the various teams and how they work together to make an MTSS successful. Part of the process of using teams with an MTSS is recognizing that all groups go through predictable stages of development. School teams need time to develop their identities so that they can function well. Recognizing the unique roles of each type of team, as well as the importance of allowing time for group development, will foster the effective use of MTSS teams.

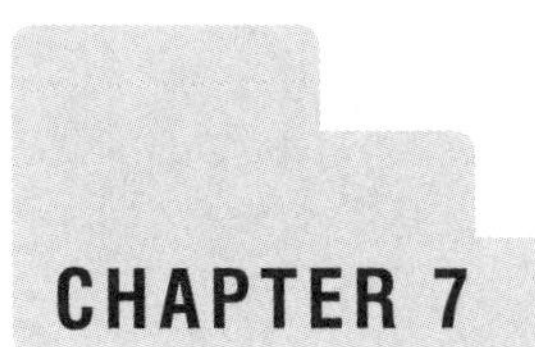

CHAPTER 7

The Logistics of Setting Up and Running Effective School Teams

A well-functioning problem-solving team provides the foundation for the successful implementation of an MTSS. Teams do the work to create systems that provide a structure for success. The key tasks in getting a problem-solving team off to a good start and keeping things going well are (1) developing a representative approach to teaming, (2) assigning roles and responsibilities to team members, (3) deciding how the team will make decisions, and (4) setting a meeting schedule for the year. The team's first meeting of each school year is an opportunity to establish or reaffirm these practices and begin the process of structuring for success (see Figure 7.1 for a recommended first-meeting agenda). In this chapter we describe the operational details of team activities. Throughout this chapter the term *team* is used generically for any and all school-based teams that support an MTSS. For a detailed description of different types of teams see Chapter 6.

DEVELOPING A REPRESENTATIVE MODEL

When a team forms in a school, the members of that team have been chosen to work together to bring about some change in the school. Team members are chosen for a variety of reasons and the selection of team members can impact a team's ability to bring about change. An educator might be selected for a team because he or she has a particular knowledge base or skill set that will be valuable to the team. Some team members might be chosen because they are well

1. Forming a Team
    a. Representatives
        i. What does it mean to represent a constituency of educators?
        ii. Whom are you representing?
    b. Roles and responsibilities
        ☐ *Team leader*: starts the meeting, reviews the purpose of the meeting, facilitates the meeting by keeping the team focused on each step; serves as the primary contact with the facilitator if there is no coach; sends a reminder before each meeting, including an agenda.

        ☐ *Minutes taker*: responsible for recording the team's decisions in the TIPS Meeting Minutes form.

        ☐ *Timekeeper*: responsible for making sure the meeting starts on time, monitoring the amount of time available, and keeping the team aware of time limits by giving "warnings" (e.g., "We have 10 minutes left").

        ☐ *Data specialist*: trained in accessing data from the School-Wide Information System (SWIS) or other school data systems.

        ☐ *Behavior specialist*: has been trained in and is competent with behavioral principles and assists in analyzing data.

        ☐ *Academic specialist*: has been trained in and is competent with academic interventions and assists in analyzing data.

        ☐ *Coach*: district-level (external) or school-based (internal) individual who has received or is receiving coaches' training; supports staff in implementing the action plan.

        ☐ *Archivist*: responsible for compiling all of the team's work into a handbook.

        ☐ *Facilitator*: facilitates the team through the process; becomes the school's main contact.

        ☐ *Administrator*: responsible for attending meetings and assisting the team with decisions that relate to school policies and procedures (principal or assistant principal).

2. Team Functioning
    a. Meeting minutes: How will we track our decisions and our progress?
    b. Voting: How will we make decisions?

3. Meeting Schedule for the Year

Agenda for the Next Meeting

1. Form an action plan for the year.
2. Develop a purpose statement for this initiative.

FIGURE 7.1. Recommended first-meeting agenda for a problem-solving team.

regarded or influential among their peers. Occasionally, a particular person might be placed on a team because he or she is resistant to change and is wielding negative leadership among peers as a result. Often, educators become team members because they are willing to be part of a new initiative and willing to work toward improving their school.

Regardless of how each individual comes to be on a team, once there, a new identity is formed. Each team member retains his or her individual identity, but the team also develops a distinct identity related to the work it does. The educators in any building who are not on a particular team are likely to be impacted by the work of the team and may have a vested interest in the team's work. Sometimes, this can result in resistance to change from nonteam members if they are concerned about being negatively impacted by new initiatives. In fact, the support of the entire community of educators is often critical for the success of any educational initiative and the way that a team operates within a school can determine whether that team's work will be accepted and implemented. With planning, school teams can include the entire school community in their work so that everyone is represented and all voices are heard and incorporated into the team's process. Developing the support and interest of all of the affected parties is critical to any school team's success.

In order to develop support and interest, which together are commonly referred to as *buy-in*, school teams should employ a representative model. Creating a representative model begins with assembling a team that represents the various constituencies in a school. Determining which members of a school community should be represented on a team depends on the nature of the work that the team will address. For some teams, such as a Tier 2 student assistance team, a representative team might include teachers from each of the grades along with academic and behavioral interventionists and a school psychologist. A schoolwide behavior support team, on the other hand, might include those educators as well as "specials" teachers (e.g., art, music, physical education, library), special educators, people who work as administrative assistants, teacher assistants, janitors, and cafeteria workers. This is because everyone who works in a school has knowledge of, or shares responsibility for, supporting prosocial behavior among students. Finally, many school teams benefit from the inclusion of an administrator (caveats to come).

It is especially important for school teams engaged in systems-level change to include representatives of all of the members of a school community in their efforts toward creating new systems that are sustainable, durable, and adapted to the values and culture of the school (Sugai et al., 2010). In order to function truly as a representative team, each team member should know whom he or she is responsible for representing, and every constituent should know who his or her representative is. As teams discuss problems, hypotheses, solutions, and action plans, educators who are not on the team can be kept informed of the team's discussions. Each member of the team can take those discussions back to his or her constituents. Not only can the representative keep nonteam members informed, he or she can give his or her represented educators a voice in the team's work by bringing their comments, concerns, and questions back to the team. This process has been likened to ocean waves, with information generated in team meetings going out to other educators, and then coming back to the team. While this process can feel time-consuming and cumbersome, it holds the most promise for creating durable change in a school.

Through this process, team members become representatives with the responsibility of communicating with constituents. The approach that representatives take to communicating with their constituencies can influence how well the information is received. Unfortunately, the most efficient forms of communication are often the least effective. While it is generally quick and easy to send an e-mail to a group of people with whom one wants to share information, e-mail often results in miscommunications and misunderstandings because it lacks the nonverbal elements of conversation. Misunderstandings can quickly ignite resistance and resentment in colleagues. While face-to-face conversation is more time-consuming, it is more likely to result in good outcomes. The change and consensus-building process is well served when team members acting as representatives attend constituent meetings, such as grade-level or other team meetings, and use those meetings as an opportunity to communicate the team's work to the broader school community.

ALLOCATING ROLES AND RESPONSIBILITIES OF TEAM MEMBERS

Another factor that is important to effective teaming is the designation of roles and responsibilities among the team members. As a result of wanting to use model practices, school teams often lean toward an egalitarian stance and are therefore reluctant to establish a hierarchy. The primary drawback of a nonhierarchical team is something that social psychologists call *diffusion of responsibility* (Whyte, 1991). Diffusion of responsibility occurs when people feel a sense of shared responsibility for something, such as the completion of a task, rather than a sense of personal responsibility. In other words, each team member thinks that another person on the team will likely do the work. When team members experience shared responsibility, tasks are less likely to be completed because each team member thinks that someone else will do what is necessary to complete the task. In order to avoid diffusion of responsibility, teams need to do two things: assign responsibility for tasks with their action plans (see Chapter 8) and assign roles to team members.

Assigned roles work to combat diffusion of responsibility by both designating who is responsible for various tasks during meetings, and also determining who is responsible for various tasks between meetings. Recommended roles within a team include (1) team leader, (2) minutes taker, (3) timekeeper, (4) data specialist, (5) behavior specialist, (6) academic specialist, (7) coach, (8) archivist, (9) facilitator, and (10) administrator. Not all roles must be filled for every team and sometimes one person might have more than one role. Teams must establish clear job descriptions for each of the roles on the team. Proposed descriptions of the recommended roles are below.

Team Leader

The most pivotal role on any team is that of the team leader. The team leader is responsible for managing team meetings. Management of team meetings includes sending the members of the team a reminder before each meeting, ideally including an agenda for the meeting so that members can begin thinking about the topics at hand. The leader is then responsible for starting the meeting on time and reviewing the purpose of the meeting with the team. A more challenging team leader responsibility is facilitating conversation, and sometimes disagreement, among team members. Leaders also facilitate the meeting by keeping the team focused on the current agenda and the problem-solving process. The team leader might also serve as the primary contact with an external facilitator and with a school administrator. It is paramount that teams choose a leader who has good leadership skills. For example, a leader who has the ability to guide members respectfully and assertively will be more effective than one who is passive or one who is combative. It has been said that good leaders get people to do what they want them to do without those people knowing that the leader wanted them to do something. Leaders who can get the work done without the need for coercion tend to foster a sprit of cooperation and goodwill among team members.

Minutes Taker

The minutes taker is responsible for recording the team's decisions in the TIPS Meeting Minutes form (see Chapter 8, Figure 8.3), which is ideally displayed from a computer during the meetings. Given the importance of the meeting minutes in guiding the problem-solving process and developing an action plan, the minutes taker is a more important position on a problem-solving team than it would be on a traditional team or committee. The best minutes takers are skilled with computers and technology so that they can do everything from running a projector to adding rows to a table on the Meeting Minutes form. The minutes taker is responsible for distributing the minutes to the other team members after each meeting. Ideally, the minutes should be finalized at the end of a meeting and the minutes taker should be able to e-mail them to the other team members before leaving the meeting. Sometimes the minutes taker might need to review the minutes after the meeting before sending them. The minutes taker should also place a copy of the minutes in whatever archival folder the team has decided to store them. Teams often store copies of the minutes on a computer server or cloud-based server that all of the educators in the building can access. Sometimes teams keep hard-copy paper minutes as well and the minutes taker will need to print and file the minutes after each meeting if this is the case.

Timekeeper

Effective teams manage and use their time together well. When members know that a meeting is going to begin on time, they are more likely to arrive on time. Ending meetings on time communicates respect for the team members' time and an understanding of the other responsibilities to which they need to attend. The timekeeper is responsible for making sure that meetings start on time, for monitoring the amount of time available for each agenda item, and for keeping the team aware of time limits by giving "warnings" (e.g., "We have 10 minutes left"). Timekeeping does not require any preparation or follow-up for meetings, but does require that all time deadlines be stated. For this reason, the timekeeper should be someone who is not afraid to interrupt others to state the time limits.

Data Specialist

In a data-based problem-solving team, it is important to have one or more team members who feel comfortable working with data. A team's data specialist is not necessarily responsible for managing any of the school's data systems; instead he or she is responsible for accessing those systems on behalf of the team so that key data are available during meetings. For example, data specialists typically run reports of relevant data to bring to (or project at) team meetings for the team to use in developing precise problem statements. He or she might also project images from a particular data system during team meetings so that the team can see the data while he or she is running data queries to answer the team's questions about a particular problem. Finally, the data specialist provides reports at all-school faculty meetings on the data trends that the team observes. The data specialist should be comfortable with technology and should receive training in how to access data from the school's data system(s).

Behavior Specialist

Many teams will benefit from the contribution of a member who has been trained in and is competent with behavioral principles, including applied behavior analysis (ABA). In addition to contributing knowledge of human behavior and of the school's intervention systems, the behavior specialist often assists the data analyst with analyzing data for and during team meetings. The person who serves the behavior specialist role on a team could be one of several specialists who work in schools, including special educators, school psychologists, and board-certified behavior analysts (BCBAs). U.S. states vary in their rules about the degree or credential needed to provide ABA services. In some states, a special educator might have extensive expertise in ABA, and in others a school psychologist could be the best person. The national and international credential for training in ABA is the BCBA. To earn the BCBA, individuals must complete and pass very specific graduate-level course work, supervised practice under specific conditions, and a national credentialing exam.

Academic Specialist

Similar to the behavior specialist, the academic specialist should be someone with specialized knowledge of academic instruction and intervention. The academic specialist should have knowledge of the academic interventions that are being provided to students in the school and should be able to assist with the analysis of academic data. Most often, the academic specialist will be a special educator, literacy coach, school psychologist, or speech and language pathologist. The majority of academic problems that students face are in the area of reading, but some students need help with writing, math, and other skills as well. There is no national credential for academic specialists, but often these team members have expertise in methods such as direct instruction (DI), curriculum-based measurement (CBM), and error analysis.

Coach

The education community has recently been home to a growing recognition of the benefit of having coaches in schools (Bradshaw, Pas, Goldweber, Rosenberg, & Leaf, 2012). As defined in research conducted by Jim Knight at the University of Kansas (Glasgow & Farrell, 2007; Knight, 2005; Jorissen, Salazar, Morrison, & Foster, 2008; Makibbin & Sprague, 1997; Marsh, Sloan McCombs, & Martorell, 2010), a coach is someone whose job description includes supporting the successful implementation of a school or district initiative. Coaches typically work at the district level or are based in an individual school. Coaches should receive very specific training, both in the initiative(s) that they are supporting and in the process of systems-level coaching. Within the context of a problem-solving team model, the coach supports staff in implementing the action plan that the team has developed and acts as a conduit between the staff and the team.

Archivist

One of the keys to sustainable systems-level change is the creation of processes and procedures that facilitate new ways of doing things. In order for those processes and procedures to have an enduring impact, they must be easily accessible year after year. Problem-solving teams can increase the probability that their work will be recorded for posterity by having a team archivist. The archivist is responsible for compiling all of the team's work into a handbook or other permanent product(s) that educators in the school can access. The team archivist is often a quiet, well-organized person who likes working behind the scenes to accomplish specific tasks. The archivist helps to maintain the team's collective "memory" by keeping copies of all important documents, especially the team's or school's handbook. Sometimes, the archivist also provides orientation and training for new team members.

Facilitator

Many systems-level initiatives benefit from the consultation of a facilitator who is not otherwise part of the school community. A facilitator is someone who works across different schools and districts to support initiatives; sometimes a facilitator might be known as a consultant. Facilitators have specialized training in the content of the initiative and in the process of supporting innovation in schools. The facilitator should be able to bring specific knowledge and skills to the team that in-school team members do not otherwise have. Importantly, facilitators should be objective about, and uninvolved with, the dynamics and personal and political factors affecting decision making within the school or district. Usually the facilitator guides the team through the innovation process, and becomes the school's main contact with state or national organizations that support the initiative.

Administrator

Teams responsible for creating change within a school must have the presence of at least one administrator at their meetings. The administrator, typically a principal or assistant principal, is responsible for attending meetings and assisting the team with decisions that relate to school policies and procedures. The administrator supports the team's work by making that work visible and endorsing any changes, both at the school and district levels. Such endorsement is important for creating long-lasting change. The one thing that an administrator should *not* do as a member of a problem-solving team is take on any role other than that of the administrator. It is especially problematic when administrators try to take responsibility for being the team leader because this undermines the team's goal of creating and leading change from the classroom level. Although having an administrator as a team member lends credibility to the work, it might be difficult because his or her time and attention are divided by many responsibilities. Overall, it is best to have one building administrator on the team who will make it a priority to attend all meetings.

TEAM DECISION MAKING AND AGREEMENT

There are several options for teams to choose from with regard to how they will make decisions. Teams might decide to adopt majority voting, in which the preference of the majority of members is adopted. At the other end of the spectrum, teams might adopt a consensus model by which they continue to discuss an issue until everyone comes to agreement about what the team should do. Both of these approaches have advantages and disadvantages. While the majority rule model might seem the most efficient way to make decisions, some important concerns could be ignored and members who hold those concerns could feel that their perspective is not valued. This can undermine group cohesion and make it difficult to make progress going forward. On the other hand, while a consensus allows for each member of the team to express concerns, full consensus can be difficulty to achieve. The model to use for final decision making is especially difficult for very small schools in rural settings. In such settings there might be only five faculty in the entire school. In such settings, consensus can be worth the effort because everyone must live with the decision.

A third option is what is sometimes referred to as the "thumbs-up" approach. In a thumbs-up decision-making process, each member displays his or her vote with his or her thumb: a thumb up indicates approval, a thumb down indicates disapproval, and a sideways thumb indicates that the member does not support the action, but that he or she will not prevent the motion from moving forward. In a thumbs-up approach, the team takes the time to ask anyone expressing disapproval to express his or her concerns. The team can explore possible solutions to the concerns raised and determine whether there are changes that could be made to the motion that would garner the support of the disapproving team member. This option ensures that every team member can be heard, but also ensures that the team can move forward with specific action steps.

CREATING A MEETING SCHEDULE FOR THE YEAR

It is always surprising how full educators' calendars become during the school year. Because teachers want to be able to manage their time while responding to students' needs, they often experience the temptation to schedule one or two meetings ahead rather than commit to a consistent meeting schedule. As a result of trying to meet students' and parents' needs, when a team of educators tries to schedule a meeting within the same month that the meeting is to occur, it can be very difficult to find a common time that is available. The best way to ensure that a team meets on a regular basis during a school year is to set a meeting schedule for the year at the first team meeting. It is a good idea to plan regular meeting times, such as every second and fourth Tuesday afternoon, so that the schedule is predictable and members can anticipate team meetings. Sometimes, the team might find that it is further along on its action plan than it anticipated, or that there is no urgent business to be conducted, for a previously scheduled meeting. If this happens, the team can opt to cancel that meeting and resume work at the next regularly scheduled meeting. See Chapter 13 for more information about schedules.

SUMMARY

Problem-solving teams can take steps to structure their work for successful implementation of an MTSS by putting certain systems in place. School teams are encouraged to adopt a representative model in which each team member is clearly responsible for representing a constituency within the school and every constituency in the school is represented. When the team develops procedures and materials (e.g., a handbook), each representative takes that information back to constituents for feedback. This process continues throughout system development, which allows for all of the educators in a building to have a voice in the system. In order to ensure effective systems operations, roles and responsibilities of team members should be established. Recommended roles within a team include team leader, minutes taker, timekeeper, data specialist, behavior specialist, academic specialist, coach, archivist, and facilitator. A building or district administrator should also be part of the team, but should not take on any of the other roles. Finally, teams are encouraged to create a meeting schedule at the first meeting of each school year in order to increase the likelihood that meetings will occur on a regular basis.

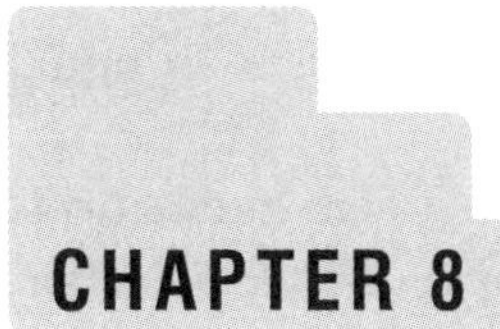

CHAPTER 8

Effective Team Processing

USING DATA AND A PROBLEM-SOLVING APPROACH

As described in Chapter 6, the shift to teaming in schools represents a move away from the largely solitary practice of teaching that came before. Teaming represents a different way of running schools and, as such, has generated both opportunities and challenges for educators. In keeping with the goal of the No Child Left Behind Act of 2001, the increased emphasis on teaming has had a number of positive effects on school functioning and school climate. Teachers and administrators have more opportunities to collaborate, resulting in the potential to learn from one another, support one another, and build stronger professional relationships. Correspondingly, students stand to benefit from the collective focus that school teams can bring to bear on issues that impact them. Efforts to standardize assessment, curriculum, and intervention, for example, could not be effectively accomplished without the collaboration of a team of educators.

Just as there are numerous benefits associated with teaming, educators face a number of barriers to effective teaming. Teachers might find that they need to learn to collaborate in new ways and this could be a change from past practices when teachers could be more independent. Generally expected to have all of the answers, teachers might struggle with the idea of working to arrive at an answer that is acceptable to all team members. Sometimes, the answer they know is "right" is not their own first choice. Collaboration, negotiation, and compromise can be especially challenging for teachers who care deeply about their practice and who recognize that the group decision will ultimately impact their classrooms and their students. Correspondingly, administrators might find themselves in need of a more egalitarian stance in their interactions with teachers than was needed in the past. Teaming assumes that, while each member brings a unique set of experiences and expertise, each member has an equal voice, regardless of hierarchy.

Team members might be challenged by shifting from social interactions about shared knowledge and experience, which were the staple of collegial interactions in educational settings prior to teaming, to interactions that are goal oriented. The fact is that, like the rest of humanity, educators are social beings who generally enjoy interacting with one another. While educators are a diverse lot with varied interests and hobbies, people working in the same school have a shared work experience and a shared student body. As such, in contrast to the goal-oriented nature of team interactions, conversations about students have historically served as opportunities to share and receive information, and perhaps engage in social interactions that serve to strengthen professional relationships.

The role of teams is to go beyond the exchange of information to the resolution of problems. This has been referred to as the move away from a *problem admiration* model and toward a *problem-solving* model (Shinn, 1989). Clearly, how well a group of people functions as a team depends on a certain set of collaboration and communication skills. Each member of a team brings a unique set of strengths and weaknesses with regard to that skill set. The primary means of creating a foundation for the development of group problem-solving skills is the establishment of a clear set of expectations and procedures for the group process.

A PROBLEM-SOLVING APPROACH TO TEAMING

The last decade has been witness to a push for the collection of data in schools, with very little guidance about *how* to use that data. Many of today's educators received little or no training in the collection and use of data in their teacher training programs. The motivation for collecting data is often lacking when educators cannot clearly see how that data will be used and how the data will benefit their students. Providing a clear model for the use of data, along with both training in the use of data and evidence that the use of data will impact student outcomes, can set the stage for effective data collection and the resulting ability to engage in data-based decision making. The Team-Initiated Problem-Solving (TIPS) process is an evidence-based approach to effective teaming for school teams charged with data-based decision making in the context of a problem-solving model (Newton, Horner, Todd, Algozzine, & Algozzine, 2012). TIPS is unique in that it embeds the use of data at each point in the model.

In addition, TIPS provides a universal method for teams to use data in a problem-solving context to improve student outcome. TIPS was originally developed to support teams in using office discipline referral (ODR) data obtained through the School-Wide Information System (SWIS) to guide the development of effective schoolwide behavior support systems (Newton, Todd, Algozzine, Horner, & Algozzine, 2009). The utility of the process for solving problems with data that TIPS provides has since been recognized as one that can just as readily be used with other sources of data available in schools, such as universal screening data derived from curriculum-based measures or attendance data available through various student information systems.

Bransford and Stein (1984) advocated for the use of a sequenced approach to problem solving for teams 30 years ago with their IDEAL model (in Deno, 2002; see also Chapter 20). IDEAL is an acronym for the process by which teams can "*I*dentify the problem, *D*efine the problem, *E*xplore alternative solutions to the problem, *A*pply a solution, and *L*ook at the effects of that application" (Deno, 2002, p. 38). As depicted in Figure 8.1, the IDEAL model is paralleled in the problem-solving model employed by TIPS, which comprises a five-step process that includes problem identification, hypothesis development, discussion of and selection of solutions, development and implementation of an action plan, and evaluation and revision of that action plan (Newton, Todd, et al., 2009). The TIPS model emphasizes the use of data in identifying and defining a problem, and the use of an action plan in solving that problem, making TIPS ideal for systems-level team efforts. Indeed, implementation of this problem-solving model provides school teams with an alternative to the *problem admiration* trap that is often the default approach of school teams (Algozzine et al., 2011).

Identifying Problems

The first step to solving a problem is accurately identifying that problem. This process is triggered when it has come to the attention of the team that a problem might exist. The first question for a team to answer when a concern has been raised is whether a problem truly exists (Deno, 2005). The process of answering this question is an assessment process, and the team must determine what, if any, data can be gathered to assist the team in determining the existence of a problem. For this purpose, a problem exists when there is a discrepancy between what is expected and what is happening. For some student problems, schools will have access to an existing source of data that can assist teams in problem

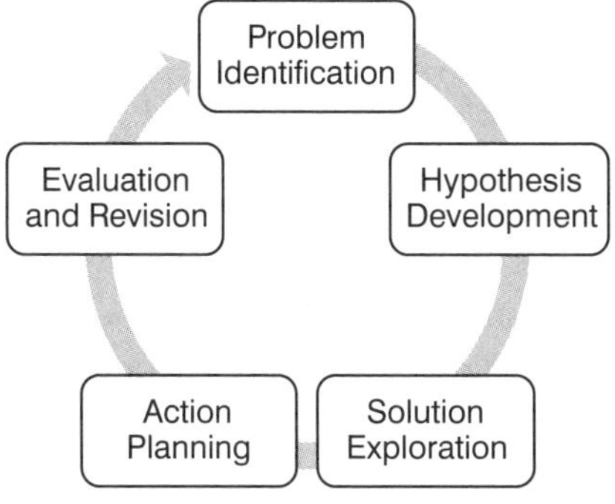

FIGURE 8.1. The TIPS problem-solving process.

identification. Examples of useful data for problem identification include universal screening data, attendance data, students' grades, and ODR data.

In the case of an individual student with a suspected academic problem, a team would look for a discrepancy between the level of performance expected for a student in his or her grade and the level of performance that he or she is exhibiting. With the evolution of curriculum-based measurement, we now have national norms to guide our assessment of this problem. Other potential problems might not be as easy to assess. For example, there is often a wide range in what educators within a building consider acceptable with regard to student behavior. When it comes to things like the voice level in the halls, physical contact on the playground, and the need to line up and quiet down before entering the building after recess, school communities must come to agreement on expected behavior before school teams can determine whether a problem exists. When a community of educators comes to agreement about the expectations for student behavior, the foundation is laid for problem-solving teams to identify and begin to solve problems.

With a clear understanding of what is expected, and access to useful and usable data, school problem-solving teams can begin to pinpoint the exact nature of a given problem. While an initial look at the relevant data might be enough to confirm that a problem exists, teams often need to run additional and more in-depth queries in order to gather enough information to form a clear definition of the problem. In TIPS, this is called forming a *precision problem statement* (Newton, Todd, et al., 2009). Teams need to know *who*, *when*, *where*, *what*, and *how many*—the dimensions commonly referred to as the "Big 5"—in order to develop precision problem statements (Educational and Community Supports, 2013). Access to data systems that are easy to manipulate makes this sort of data analysis possible and efficient for school teams. In fact, when school teams have access to effective and efficient data systems, the barriers to routine use of data to answer questions are eliminated and teams find that they do not need a mathematician or a spreadsheet wizard to answer the questions that they might have about the nature of a problem.

Example

It came to the attention of an elementary school's PBIS team that a high number of ODRs were happening at the end of the school's afternoon recess. At the team's biweekly meeting, the school's SWIS data account was open and projected for the whole team to see. The team selected the School Summary report and confirmed a spike in the number of ODRs issued between 12:15 and 12:30 each day. With a few more mouse clicks, the team learned the following information:

- *Who?* The team found that most of the ODRs issued between 12:15 and 12:30 were being issued to second- and third-grade students. Team members knew that 12:15–12:30 was the time during which recess ends for second- and third-grade students and those students were preparing to return to class.

- *When?* This was the piece of information that the team started with: 12:15–12:30.
- *Where?* The team confirmed that the majority of ODRs issued during the relevant time period were for behaviors occurring on the playground.
- *What?* The team found that, while there were some ODRs issued for disrespect and disruption, a large majority of the ODRs were written for physical aggression.
- *How many?* The team was surprised to see that there was an average of 15 ODRs per school day written to second and third graders on the playground between 12:15 and 12:30. The team also found that there were 30 students who had received ODRs during that time and in that location during the previous week.

The team then knew that 30 second and third graders were engaging in an average of 15 acts of physical aggression at the end of their afternoon recess. The team decided that it must then attempt to figure out why those students were engaging in that behavior.

Developing Hypotheses

Once a problem has been identified, school teams can begin to form hypotheses about why the problem is occurring. While the problem identification process prompts teams to gather information about who, when, where, what, and how many, hypothesis development is an attempt to figure out *why* something is occurring. In fact, hypothesis development often involves asking why about the answers to each of the Big 5 questions: why them, why then, why there, why that, and why that amount? It is important for teams to think through these questions and use them to guide the development of hypothesis statements (Newton, Horner, Algozzine, Todd, & Algozzine, 2009).

There are many factors that can contribute to the occurrence of a problem, and sometimes problems are a result of a combination of factors (Newton, Horner, et al., 2009; Shapiro & Lentz, 1985; Simonsen, Fairbanks, Briesch, Myers, & Sugai, 2008). The primary causes of problems in schools that teams must consider are:

- *Environmental factors.* Both academic and behavioral problems can occur when students are in an environment that is not conducive to success. Environmental factors can include such disparate elements as the condition of the building, classroom, or grounds; the extent to which the management of the classroom, the school, and the common spaces results in environments that are structured and predictable; and the degree to which the expectations for student performance are shared among faculty and staff and actively taught to and supported with students.

- *Curriculum and instruction.* Similarly, both academic and behavioral problems can occur when the curriculum and instruction in place are not effective, sufficiently rewarding, meaningful, and engaging.
- *Skill deficits.* Many problems are the result of the fact that students lack the skills necessary to meet the expectations that educators have for them. While we tend to focus on supporting students' development of academic knowledge, we often overlook the need to support their development of other skills necessary for success in school, such as self-regulation of emotions, self-management of behavior, and basic organizational skills.
- *Performance deficits.* For a variety of reasons, students often lack the motivation to use the skills that they have. While some students are intrinsically motivated to do what we would like them to do, others benefit from motivational support. All students benefit when the conditions of motivation and reinforcement in place are sufficient to encourage them to meet expectations.
- *Fluency deficits.* When students possess the skills necessary to be successful but fail to use those skills or to use them consistently, they are said to have a fluency deficit (Haring, Lovitt, Eaton, & Hansen, 1978). Fluency deficits tend to occur when students have not had enough practice with a new skill set for those new skills to have become their default response.

The team members in our example considered aspects of all of the common causes of problems in schools in an attempt to develop hypotheses regarding aggression on the playground. They began by discussing the activities that were usually taking place on the playground between 12:15 and 12:30. They knew from the school schedule that the time period in question was the end of afternoon recess for the second and third graders. A couple of team members had recess duty, and they knew from experience that the last 5 minutes of afternoon recess were spent getting the students to line up and quiet down in preparation for their return to class. One team member who was recently on the playground during this time noted that it was a chaotic time of day and that many students were uncooperative. Based on the additional information that they gathered, the team members developed the following hypotheses:

1. The second- and third-grade teaching team might have forgotten to teach the playground procedures to their students.
2. The recess monitors might not have been using effective methods of supporting students' prosocial behavior during this transition.
3. The second- and third-grade students were effectively forestalling their return to class by being disruptive, disrespectful, and aggressive because the recess monitors would not allow the students to return to class until they had quieted.

4. The second and third graders found it especially difficult to keep their hands to themselves and were simply engaging in physical contact with one another because they were in close proximity for an extended period of time while they waited to be dismissed from recess.

One team member agreed to check with the second- and third-grade teaching team to make sure that the playground procedures had been taught at the beginning of the school year. In response to this inquiry, the second- and third-grade teachers indicated that, not only had they taught the playground procedures to students in the fall, they had since retaught the procedures to their students several times in an attempt to reduce the number of behavioral problems arising during recess. This information allowed the team to eliminate Hypothesis 1. Two team members agreed to attend second- and third-grade recess for a few days to find out how well the recess monitors were supporting prosocial behavior during the end-of-recess transition. They found that, while there was room for improvement, the monitors were following the school policy of prompting, acknowledging, and rewarding students' adherence to the playground procedures and expectations. In fact, the monitors were found to be employing the same behavioral support methods that they used at the end of the other recess periods, during which high levels of aggression were not occurring. The team decided that Hypothesis 2 did not adequately account for the amount of aggression that was occurring between 12:15 and 12:30. With no easy way to eliminate the remaining hypotheses, the team decided to test Hypotheses 3 and 4 by discussing and selecting solutions, implementing those solutions, and monitoring their outcomes (Deno, 2002).

Discussing and Selecting Solutions

While many teams would prefer to start with a discussion and selection of solutions, the solutions derived when a team has taken the time to define the problem and develop hypotheses will be better solutions. The nature of any possible solutions will vary greatly depending on the nature of the problem. In general, solutions should consider whether the problem that is occurring is the result of something in the environment that could be changed (often referred to as an antecedent modification), or whether other variables are to blame. The same categories that are explored when developing hypotheses guide the selection of solutions:

- *Environmental factors.* Are there aspects of the environment that are undermining success?
- *Curriculum and instruction.* Are the curriculum and instruction in place effective? Are they sufficiently rewarding, meaningful, and engaging?
- *Skill deficits.* Are the expectations about what to do and when to do it

clear? Are the skills necessary to meet those expectations within the students' repertoire?

- *Performance deficits.* Are the conditions of motivation and reinforcement sufficient to encourage the students to meet expectations?
- *Fluency deficits.* Have the students had sufficient opportunity to practice the new skills with feedback and reinforcement?

After some discussion, the team realized that it might be able to address both Hypothesis 3, the *forestalling class hypothesis*, and Hypothesis 4, the *proximity hypothesis*, at the same time. A solution that would eliminate both the students' ability to prolong recess and their need to wait close to one another is an alternative to lining up known as *trickling*. With trickling, students are dismissed from one location to another in small groups rather than *en masse*. While trickling requires planning and supervision, it can reduce the likelihood of problem behavior that commonly occurs when students are required to line up and wait.

Developing and Implementing an Action Plan

Just as many teams would prefer to skip problem identification and hypothesis generation, many teams get stuck at discussion and selection of solutions. Now that your team has a solution that it would like to try, how will you carry it out? Effective teams take the solutions that they have developed and turn them into an action plan. While an action plan can take various forms, the critical elements are identifying what needs to be done, who is going to take responsibility for making sure that each step is completed, and when each step will be completed.

When determining what will be done, teams have the opportunity to think through the solution that they have in mind and consider all of the steps that will be necessary to implement that solution. For example, this school team identified that there was a problem with physical aggression among second and third graders on the playground between 12:15 and 12:30, and the team developed the hypothesis that this was occurring because students must line up after recess and wait until everyone is quiet before reentering the building. What steps must the team take in order to resolve this problem?

This team wanted to abolish lining up after recess and adopt a trickling procedure in which a smaller number of students reenter the building each minute. While this is a promising solution, there are likely several steps that will need to be taken in order to successfully implement this solution. For example, a new procedure for recess dismissal would need to be developed; the recess staff, teachers, and students would need to be taught the new policy and procedure; active supervision of students from the entry to their classrooms would need to be arranged; a system for encouraging and acknowledging student compliance would need to be put in place; and so forth. An action plan for this intervention is found in Figure 8.2.

Action step	Personnel involved	Time frame	Major activities	Outcome indicator	Status
Develop a trickling procedure.	Playground Subcommittee (Robin, Carla, and Stefanie)	Oct. 1–8	• Review the master schedule to determine time available for trickling. • Determine the number of students to be trickled. • Develop composition of small groups. • Determine the order by which groups will be dismissed.	Written procedure detailing the composition of small groups and schedule for their dismissal.	☐ In progress ☐ Done
Develop/ fortify an acknowledgment system.	Recognition Subcommittee (Ginny, Brianna, and Nancy)	Oct. 1–8	• Develop new secondary reinforcers (tickets) specifically for trickling. • Create a separate system for trickling ticket drawings. • Create a unique reward for trickling ticket drawings.	Trickling ticket acknowledgment system in place.	☐ In progress ☐ Done
Teach the new procedure to staff.	Teaching Subcommittee (Wanda, Laurie, and Linda)	Oct. 9–15	• Review the trickling procedure and trickling acknowledgment system with all faculty at faculty meeting. • Teach the procedure and acknowledgment system to playground staff on the playground. • Teach the procedure and acknowledgment system to and review active supervision with hall supervisors in the halls.	All relevant staff taught procedures.	☐ In progress ☐ Done
Prepare to teach the new procedure to students.	Teaching Subcommittee (Wanda, Laurie, and Linda)	Oct. 9–15	• Develop a lesson plan for students that details the expectations for student behavior and the procedure for trickling.	Lesson plan for students.	☐ In progress ☐ Done
Teach the new procedure to students.	Second- and third-grade teachers	Oct. 16–23	• Review the new procedure with students in the classroom. • Teach the procedure to students on the playground (including modeling, practicing, reinforcing, and reteaching as necessary).	All relevant students taught expectations and procedure.	☐ In progress ☐ Done
Implement a trickling procedure and acknowledgment system.	Playground staff, Recognition Subcommittee (Ginny, Brianna, and Nancy)	Oct. 23	• Remind students of new procedure. • Follow new procedure. • Provide a rich schedule of reinforcement during acquisition.	Trickling system implemented.	☐ In progress ☐ Done

FIGURE 8.2. An action plan to implement trickling.

Evaluating and Revising the Action Plan

By design, a well-designed action plan includes a plan to reflect on the problem-solving process. In a data-based decision-making context, teams have the luxury of reviewing the relevant data in order to determine if there has been improvement. Specifically, teams can visually analyze graphed data to look for improvements in the trend of the relevant data. In our example, the team checked the school's ODR data to determine whether there was a decline in ODRs among second and third graders between 12:15 and 12:30 after the trickling method was put in place. If the problem in question was found to be resolved, the team might feel comfortable assuming that the problem was accurately identified, the hypothesis confirmed, and the solution successfully identified.

If the data reveal that the initial problem has not been resolved, that can point to a problem at any step of the problem-solving process. At this point, the team would consider whether the problem was accurately identified, whether the hypothesis that was tested was valid, and whether the solution that was adopted was implemented with integrity. If the team is relatively confident that the problem was accurately defined and the hypotheses followed logically from the data, it might make the most sense to begin with a close look at implementation integrity. Specifically, the team could review each of the action steps in the implementation plan and evaluate the extent to which each step was carried out as intended.

The initial step of an implementation integrity check involves making sure that the action plan itself was carried out as agreed by the team. The easiest way to structure an implementation integrity check is to use the action plan that was originally developed for the problem as a checklist. The action plan provides the what, who, and when details necessary to assess implementation. The team can check whether each member of the team did what he or she agreed to do within the agreed-upon time frame. For example, did the ad hoc committee develop a new recess dismissal procedure by the end of the week? If so, was that procedure taught to the playground staff and the teachers by the following Monday? Did the teachers and playground staff work together to teach the new procedure to the students prior to implementation? Did the administrator arrange for active supervision in the halls from 12:15 to 12:30 in the time frame agreed?

In many situations, in order to answer implementation integrity questions, some members of the team will need to collect observation data. Specifically, two or three team members should observe the situation in question and collect observation data about what is happening. Those team members can use elements of the action plan, and any procedures developed as part of the action plan, as an observation checklist. In this example, key observation elements include:

- Did the playground staff begin following the new procedure?
- Are the playground staff following it as it was intended?

- Are staff present in the halls and actively supervising students' return to their classrooms?
- Are the active supervisors encouraging and acknowledging student compliance?

As the team members are observing the problem situation, they can also consider whether there are changes that could be made to improve the procedure that the team developed.

If the plan that was developed was being implemented with integrity, the team must then reconsider the first two steps in the problem-solving process. This process will generally look much as it did the first time that the team considered the problem and developed hypotheses. The team will again use the data to develop a precise problem statement, keeping in mind that they might have missed something the first time around. When possible, the team should reanalyze the data or consider other sources of data that might clarify the nature of the problem. Finally, the team should consider alternative hypotheses that might lead to different solutions. In the scenario that we have considered here, perhaps it is not lining up and waiting that is leading to problems, but some other factor(s), such as other students coming out to recess while the second and third graders are going in, lack of training for the students in the recess dismissal procedure, or poor staff practices during that transition.

IMPLEMENTING THE TIPS PROCESS

In order to effectively implement TIPS, school teams should seek training from a TIPS facilitator (Newton, Horner, Algozzine, Todd, & Algozzine, 2012). The developers of TIPS offer facilitator trainings at regional, national, and international PBIS conferences on a regular basis. The training teaches facilitators to support school teams in learning the TIPS process and procedures. TIPS training for school teams includes guiding teams through the process of assigning roles and responsibilities, using a meeting minutes template, and working through the problem-solving process using data at each point (Newton, Todd, et al., 2009). School team training involves both an initial training and ongoing support as teams implement TIPS. During the initial team training, the trainer introduces the logic, structure, and process of the TIPS data-based problem-solving process. The team is then guided through the structure and use of the TIPS Meeting Minutes template (Newton, Horner, et al., 2009; see Figure 8.3). The Meeting Minutes template is a form that is used to guide and structure the problem-solving process during team meetings. The form includes five major sections:

1. *Logistics*: a place to record the logistics and attendance of the present meeting, as well as the scheduling details for the next meeting,

School: ______

Meetings	Date	Time (begin and end)	Location	Facilitator	Minutes Taker	Data Analyst
Today's Meeting						
Next Meeting						

Team Members (Place "X" to left of name if present)					
☐	☐	☐	☐	☐	☐
☐	☐	☐	☐	☐	☐

Today's Agenda Items (Place "X" to left of item after completed)		**Agenda Items for Next Meeting**
1. ☐	5. ☐	1.
2. ☐	6. ☐	2.
3. ☐	7. ☐	3.
4. ☐	8. ☐	

Previously Defined Problems

Precise Problem Statement (What, When, Where, Who, Why)	Solution Actions (Prevent, Teach, Reward, Correct, Extinguish, Safety)	Who?	By When?	Goal and Timeline	Fidelity of Implementation	Effectiveness of Solution
					☐ Not started ☐ Partial imp. ☐ Imp. w/fidelity ☐ Stopped	☐ Worse ☐ No change ☐ Imp. but not to goal ☐ Imp. and goal met Current rate/level per school day = ______

Administrative/General Information and Issues

Information for Team, or Issue for Team to Address	Discussion/Decision/Task (if applicable)	Who?	By When?

New Problems

Precise Problem Statement (What, When, Where, Who, Why)	Solution Actions (Prevent, Teach, Reward, Correct, Extinguish, Safety)	Who?	By When?	Goal and Timeline	Fidelity of Implementation Measure (What/How/When/Who to Measure/Report)	Effectiveness of Solution (What/How/When to Assess/Report)
Current Level:					*Use Fidelity Check Board to collect fidelity ratings from staff, at least twice a month. ______ bring data for monthly review.*	*Collect ODR data, enter into SWIS, at least weekly. Review SW data at least monthly.*

FIGURE 8.3. TIPS Meeting Minutes template.

2. *Agenda*: a place to display the agenda for the current meeting, the agenda for the next meeting, and concerns to be discussed at another time.
3. *Administrative discussion*: a place to record the team's discussion of and plans to address administrative issues.
4. *Problem-solving plan*: a place to record the results of the team's problem-solving process, including the problem statement, solution, and action plan that the team developed during the meeting.
5. *Evaluation*: a place for the team to self-assess the team's functioning.

The template is designed to be projected during meetings. Just as the template provides structure to team meetings, the visual display of the template during meetings cues the team to follow that structure. With the meeting minutes prominently displayed, all team members can refer to the agenda throughout the meeting. This allows team members to gauge how much time to allot to each topic and where they are in the agenda. Publicly displayed meeting minutes also allow the members of the team to collaborate and accurately record the team's discussions and plans. A benefit is that the team minutes taker does not have to revise the minutes after the meeting, send them out for feedback, revise them, and have them approved at the following meeting. Rather, he or she can incorporate input throughout the meeting, end the meeting with the final version completed, and e-mail them to the other team members or post them in a shared folder before leaving the meeting. This efficiency ensures that each team member has an accurate and immediate record of the action plan, the steps for which each member took responsibility, and the time frame for completion. Finally, having a displayed Meeting Minutes form facilitates integration of team members who arrive late. Rather than stopping the meeting to bring a late arriver up to speed, the late member can read the agenda, action plan, and decisions made so far in order to orient to the meeting.

SUMMARY

The TIPS process is an evidence-based approach to teaming that is designed to improve the effectiveness and efficiency of teaming in schools (Newton, Horner, Todd, et al., 2012). TIPS employs a problem-solving model approach to teaming, which comprises identifying problems, developing hypotheses, discussing and selecting solutions, developing and implementing an action plan, and evaluating and revising that action plan. TIPS is unique in that it embeds the use of data at each point in the model. TIPS provides a viable alternative to the "problem admiration" trap that is often the default approach of school teams. By learning the TIPS process and following the TIPS structure, school teams can transition to resolving problems for their students.

PART III

Making Change Happen

This section of the book provides information about how to create effective change in schools. Building on seminal work by Fixsen et al. (2005), these five chapters walk through the six stages of change identified by Fixsen and colleagues: (1) exploration, (2) adoption, (3) installation, (4) implementation, (5) innovation, and (6) sustainability. Chapter 9 gives an overview of the Fixsen et al. model as well as why attending to the process of change is as important as the actual changes themselves. In Chapter 10, the exploration, adoption, and installation stages are described in relation to developing an effective MTSS. This chapter emphasizes the importance of having teams be highly selective about what changes should be considered. Due to the many details and critical importance of the implementation stage, it is discussed in a chapter by itself (Chapter 11). This chapter explains how no detail is too small during implementation and how teams need to plan each step carefully and review outcomes often. Chapter 12 is about innovation and sustainability and reminds readers that some suggested school innovations will not be worth considering and that the teams hold the responsibility of maintaining effective practices over time. Finally, the section ends with a chapter on schedules (Chapter 13). Information on daily school schedules is included here because teams will need to review and adjust the school schedule in order to be certain that there is time each day for tiered supports.

CHAPTER 9

The Science of Change

As anyone who has tried to implement change in an organization knows, it is not easy and takes time. There is a big difference between having a great idea and getting others to go along with it. This chapter introduces the idea of implementation science and is followed by several other chapters that focus on the individual steps needed to actually implement an MTSS. Alongside careful team development, the science of change is an important precursor to building an effective MTSS. The importance of the science of change in the process of implementation has become far better recognized in recent years. Many types of organizations, including businesses and schools, have recognized that for any change to be effective and lasting, there must be a plan for its implementation. In other words, one cannot make a policy change today and expect it to be in force tomorrow. Instead, careful planning for the change is needed.

IMPLEMENTATION SCIENCE

Thanks to the growing awareness that implementation of change does not happen automatically, there is an emerging body of research concerning implementation science. This research was spearheaded by Fixsen et al. (2005). As a science, this research provides information about the systematic use of specific procedures across settings and time. Forman and colleagues (Forman et al., 2013) provide an excellent overview of implementation science as it relates to schools. As Forman et al. note, there are two main ways that implementation science has been conceptualized. The first way utilizes the concepts of "elements" that must be present for implementation to be effective. Both Rogers (2003; in Forman et al., 2013) and Fixsen et al. (2005) suggest that implementation depends on the correct elements being available. This is analogous to a chemical compound that depends on having certain elements present (e.g., H_2O). Fixsen et al. suggest that the necessary elements are (1) source, (2) destination, (3) communication link, (4) feedback, and (5) influence.

In addition to elements, proponents of implementation science suggest that there must also be stages. This adds a time element to making change happen. Both Fixsen et al. (2005) and Durlak and DuPre (2008; in Forman et al., 2013) have suggested that the stages of implementation must be considered. Having enough time to implement a given change is very important. All the best elements could be present, but without sufficient time, the change cannot happen. Together, the combination of implementation elements and stages provides concrete details for how change can be implemented effectively. More recently, Fixsen, Blase, Duda, Naoom, and Van Dyke (2010; in Forman et al., 2013) have suggested that there are very specific procedures that must be followed for implementation of any change to be effective. In particular, they suggest that there must be (1) an organization that promotes the initiative, (2) an operational definition of the intervention, (3) preparation for competent use, (4) organizational supports, and (5) facilitative leadership. The number of variables that implementation researchers have identified as important to effective implementation reveals how complex it is.

Because of this complexity, implementation models are often referred to as "frameworks." A framework provides the structure for a more fully developed entity, but not the complete product. Frameworks serve to support implementation by providing general principles that have been found to be important in other settings. Forman et al. (2013) identify four factors that are important in school settings: (1) barriers to implementation, (2) intervention integrity, (3) diverse client populations, and (4) implementation in diverse settings. The main barrier that Forman and colleagues suggest is present in schools is the lack of EBIs. Schools do not have a good track record of implementing EBIs, despite many calls to do so. Indeed, compared with use in other fields like health care, education's use of EBIs is dismally low.

A related concern is the level of implementation integrity. This has been recognized as a concern with school-based use of EBIs. Educators have a tradition of modifying practices as they see fit (see Chapter 2 regarding this history). As a result, teachers may not be using interventions as they were used in the research that found them to be effective. There are two sides to this issue, as some teacher modifications have worked. When educators modify interventions, however, they are essentially conducting an experiment with students who have not agreed to be part of a research study. In addition, when the modifications are not documented, it is not possible to know what was done, nor what accounted for the resulting outcomes. Forman et al. (2013) suggest that there needs to be far more definition of intervention components so that consumers are clear about what constitutes a specific intervention practice. Such documentation will make it possible to examine accurate implementation integrity. Finally, Forman and colleagues (2013) note that at the same time schools are trying to understand and use EBIs and implement them effectively, schools are becoming far more diverse in many ways. The linguistic, racial, ethnic, cultural, religious, and other backgrounds that students bring to schools are more varied than ever, and expected to become even more so. This is important to recognize because most of the available research on both EBIs and implementation has been done in settings with primarily Caucasian students who speak English. It's simply unknown how educational innovations will play out in more diverse classrooms.

This point is affirmed by Scott, Boynton Hauerwas, and Brown (2014), who found that U.S. states' implementation of RTI policies among students who represent culturally and linguistically diverse (CLD) backgrounds was minimal. Scott et al. found that, although many states cited the benefits of RTI/MTSS for students from diverse backgrounds, very few had concrete policies and practices incorporating variables such as language, race, and culture into their RTI regulations and guidance documents. A few studies have found that MTSS practices can be effective for students from diverse backgrounds (i.e., Orosco & Klingner, 2010; Vaughn, Mathes, Linan-Thomson, & Francis, 2005), but there is a need for far more research on the implementation variables to ensure that all students have access to effective instruction.

IMPLEMENTATION SCIENCE AND MTSS

The remaining chapters in this section go into detail about how to use implementation frameworks to support an MTSS. First, however, it is important to recognize that an MTSS is not a list of simple steps checked off on a form and then forgotten. Instead, an MTSS includes interwoven networks of services that students access as needed so that they can be successful in school. At the very least, an MTSS functions in three dimensions: students, teachers, and time. This would not be too difficult if there were only one student at a time who needed help. But there will always be multiple students who need different kinds of help from teachers with different backgrounds over various lengths of time. As a result, the planning and details to implement an MTSS are numerous. The good news is that, with planning and regular systems review over time, an MTSS can be implemented effectively. Chard (2013) identified key areas of focus that schools should address when planning and implementing tiered supports. Specifically, it is important for schools to (1) ensure a strong Tier 1, (2) align Tier 2 with Tier 1, (3) focus on high-quality professional development (PD), and (4) build visionary leadership. Chard also pointed out that attention to the details of implementation was crucial in schools where tiered supports like RTI have been successful. Box 9.1 provides thoughts from Dr. Mary Jean O'Reilly about her district's process to plan and sustain an MTSS.

BOX 9.1. Comments on the Importance of Planning for Change from Mary Jean O'Reilly, PhD, NCSP

PBIS has been a primary core prevention practice in our district. We have focused on using the development, teaching, and acknowledgment of schoolwide expectations to increase positive relationships between students and staff; reduce discipline referrals; address any existing disproportionality in discipline or suspensions; and create positive, prosocial school climates. Our special education leadership initially sent a small group, including myself, to a meeting for urban districts in our state in 2001, so that we could learn about PBIS and the three-tier model and begin to pilot it in one elementary and one middle school. We spent the next year planning for implementation and rolled it out in the spring of 2002. Within a few years, training and coaching had been provided to staff across the district, and we continue to maintain and evolve our schoolwide plans to this day.

In the last few years our state began focusing on bullying prevention, eventually passing legislation requiring all districts to have bullying prevention plans. Our district bullying prevention plan was used as a model by the state. We chose to adopt the Olweus program, and invested in sending several school adjustment counselors to be certified trainers. We have also implemented the use of the Second Step and Steps to Respect social skills curricula in our schools. Over the last few years, we have worked on aligning both PBIS and Olweus, and on transitioning prior PBIS teams into school climate teams that address both bullying prevention and PBIS.

A recent body of literature that complements implementation science is work by Danielson and colleagues about supporting and assessing effective teaching practices (Danielson Group, 2013). Danielson has created an evaluation framework that includes four domains and 22 specific components of teaching. The domains are (1) planning and preparation, (2) classroom environment, (3) instruction, and (4) professional responsibilities. The framework is aligned to the Common Core State Standards (CCSS) with the goal of helping teachers be prepared to provide instruction matching what students are expected to learn. The framework is available for individual teacher use for free from the Danielson Group website.

An important feature of the Danielson framework (Danielson Group, 2013) is that it is accompanied by a specific teaching evaluation tool. For each component within the domains, a teacher can be rated as meeting the criteria for one of four levels: 1 (*unsatisfactory*), 2 (*basic*), 3 (*proficient*), or 4 (*distinguished*). There are descriptions of teacher performance for each component at each level so that teachers and evaluators can identify how each level compares with the others. In addition to the descriptions of performance at each level, the tool provides critical attributes and possible examples that would document a teacher's attainment of a specific level. The evaluation tool is designed so that a teacher's progress toward distinguished performance can be monitored over time. In this regard, it offers a means by which teachers can be evaluated using formative measures just like students. Such a tool can be an important resource for an MTSS because teachers will not necessarily already have all of the teaching skills needed to ensure effective instruction in every classroom or at every tier.

As noted by Fixsen et al. (2010) and Chard (2013), effective implementation in schools requires making sure that teachers have the skills to carry out each step required of them. To do this well, school personnel, especially school leaders, must anticipate that some or all teachers will need initial and ongoing PD in order to implement tiered supports. But, in order to know if the PD is effective, there must be some method for evaluating teacher practices. Danielson's work provides one such teacher evaluation tool that can be used to complement implementation science in schools (Danielson Group, 2013). It is worth noting that the Danielson tool is deigned for evaluating general teaching practices, but is not something that can verify treatment integrity. This is because generally good teaching is not the same thing as implementing a given program as intended. For this reason, implementing an MTSS requires understanding and using treatment integrity checks as well (see Chapter 17). Importantly, before using any teacher evaluation tool, the teacher(s) must have a chance to learn about the expected practices, have access to additional training opportunities, and be able to discuss evaluation outcomes with the observer. This is the same set of practices we would use when evaluating student work.

IMPLEMENTATION OF AN MTSS

As the following chapters describe, implementing an MTSS effectively requires attention to many variables at one time. This challenge is one of the reasons that collaborative teams are essential for an MTSS. As will become apparent in reading these chapters, no one can or should implement such efforts alone. As a general overview of the implementation variables that must be considered when planning an MTSS, a very simple beginning is to think in terms of people, place, and time. The people include students, teachers, parents, specialists, administrators, and others who will have key roles to play. For the sake of simplicity, they will be referred to here as *stakeholders*. A number of places come into consideration when planning an MTSS. Certainly, the entire school building, including classrooms, hallways, playgrounds, lunchrooms, libraries, and gyms can play a role. But in addition, there are interactions between and among the places, such as home–school dynamics, and how similar or different each classroom's rules are. For our purposes, the places will be referred to as the *environment*. Time plays an important role in tiered supports. Not only can students not make big gains immediately, educators need time to develop new systems and practices, learn new skills, and undergo any paradigm shifts that may be necessary (although paradigm shifts often occur after new systems and practices are put into place).

For this reason, it is essential to think about how time must be considered and valued in an MTSS implementation.

Stakeholders

Everyone who has something to gain or some level of involvement in an MTSS is a stakeholder. The central stakeholders are the students who benefit from instructional supports. But they are not the only stakeholders, because many other people are part of an MTSS, too. Attention to the specific needs of different types of stakeholders is a very important part of implementation. As the importance of using implementation science has become more widely known, researchers have looked at the effects of using multi-tiered supports on various stakeholders. Most of the research thus far has examined the effects on students and teachers, but in different ways. The research on students has been primarily in relation to their learning outcomes. Among teachers, there have been some studies that have examined actual implementation of tiered supports. Sanger, Friedli, Brunken, Snow, and Ritzman (2012) found that general education teachers, special educators, and speech clinicians saw benefits from RTI, but that more attention to implementation details was needed. In a study of teachers' perceptions of RTI implementation in Michigan and Texas, Wilcox, Murakami-Ramalho, and Urick (2013) found that teachers were more confident of their increased skills with assessment than with their instructional methods. The participants noted that they wished for more support for themselves in developing better teaching skills. This finding from 2013 resonates with guidance from Danielson, Doolittle, and Bradley (2007) that urged schools to invest in PD of instructional skills as a key implementation step.

Hoover (2011) noted that while many of the components in tiered supports can be broken into steps, there is still a need for more attention to exactly when and how to adjust instruction for students. Teachers may need more support during initial implementation so they can learn how to make instructional changes. Many researchers have pointed out that unless interventions are implemented with integrity, they are not likely to be effective. As noted, Forman et al. (2013) found that accuracy of implementation is an area in which teachers tend to lag behind other professionals. Seeking to understand why accurate implementation of school interventions remains a concern, Sanetti and Reed (2012) surveyed school intervention researchers. The findings showed that many of these researchers had little training themselves in treatment integrity, and that when it was not required for publication of a research article, it was not considered important. This finding is salient to implementation because if intervention researchers don't know or use integrity procedures, how can schools expect this of teachers? Keller-Margulis (2012) has recommended steps for ensuring that interventions are implemented correctly and this is information that needs to be considered as part of overall implementation planning (see Chapter 14).

Environment

The second key area that schools need to address when planning for implementation is the environment. This is intentionally a broad term that covers all the places and settings where students can learn. Importantly, not only do individual settings need to be considered, but it is also important to consider how different settings interact with each other. A key example is the home–school connection. Home and school are both specific settings where students spend some part of each day. What happens at home can influence how school goes and vice versa. For this reason, it is important that educators think about the interactions among various environments and how they affect student learning. A very powerful and important body of research about the effects of environmental variables on students is found in the literature on PBIS. Using a well-defined model, PBIS provides a way for educators to shape how every school environment is set up so that students can be successful in all of them (Sugai & Horner, 2010). This means planning out the expectations and procedures for classrooms, hallways, gyms, lunchrooms, playgrounds, and buses. There are even ways to extend supports to the home.

Thinking about environment when planning and implementing an MTSS may seem obvious, but it is essential that the planning consider not just how the environments are currently configured, but also how they could be *re*configured to help students. For example, are the seating arrangements in classrooms ideal for the students, or are they set up to benefit the teachers? Are rules about the playground ever explicitly taught to students, or are students just expected to know them? How does such an expectation work? One of the key aspects of environments to think about is transition. How well are the many school environments set up to make transitions from one activity or location to another easier for students? Considering all environmental variables is an important step toward effective implementation.

Time

Many teachers say that time is the most precious resource in schools. Without enough time, neither teaching nor learning is possible. There are two main ways that time needs to be considered for effective implementation. First, there needs to be enough time set aside for the planning and preparation stages. As noted, it is not possible to make an MTSS happen overnight. In addition, educators must attend to time in the daily, monthly, and school-year schedules. Specifically, a review of how time is used each day during the school year is necessary. Students who are struggling in any area of school are likely to need additional time in order to catch up. If there is not enough time set aside in the schedule, students will never be able to catch up. Educators have a duty to plan ahead for the time needed to provide interventions when students need them.

The MTSS planning process requires time set aside for planning and review. It is generally recommended that a school will require at least 1 academic year for planning to implement an MTSS. The planning year needs to have a plan unto itself as well. There needs to be time set aside for a representative team to map out the activities that will be used to create the longer-term MTSS implementation plan. In some cases, the planning time may need to be extended or adjusted in some way. If there is major staff turnover or a leadership change, more time may be needed to work on planning. If there is an unexpected event in the community such as a natural disaster, this will affect planning time. Rinaldi, Averill, and Stuart (2010) studied teachers' reactions to RTI implementation and found that planning and implementation time was very important. The teachers in the study noted that it took 3 years for them to have a full understanding of what they were doing and how it benefited students. Time invested in good planning will pay off later during actual implementation.

Part of the planning phase includes reviewing existing schedules to consider how time is currently used and how it might be used differently. In particular, there must be time in each school day for interventions to be provided. The best way to make sure that interventions will be provided is to set aside time for them. If enough time is not set aside in the schedule, it creates a major barrier to effective implementation (Brown-Chidsey et al., 2009). In addition, effective implementation requires that educators review their time use annually and determine if additional schedule changes should be tried (see Chapter 13).

SUMMARY

Research on how well a major change is sustained has led to the field of implementation science. By studying the details of implementation, schools can identify which factors must be considered in their own planning. Effective implementation requires both the right elements and enough time to build capacity among staff, students, and community members. Schools will benefit from thinking about how the proposed change will affect stakeholders, environments, and time demands. In addition, there needs to be a commitment of resources for PD and teacher evaluation so that educators will be expert with the selected practices. Only when interventions are implemented with integrity will they work. Planning for implementation, as well as reviewing progress along the way, will lead to the most effective MTSS.

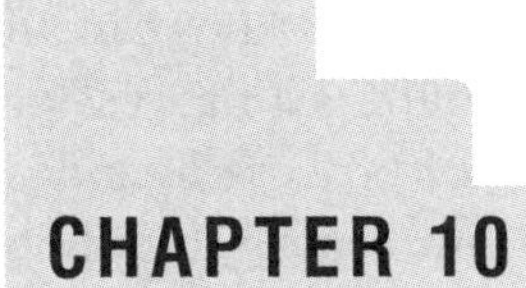

CHAPTER 10

Exploration, Adoption, and Installation

Exploration, adoption, and installation are the first stages of the Fixsen et al. (2005) implementation framework. This chapter describes the typical ways that new ideas (e.g., innovations) are considered by educators and how certain ones end up getting adopted. Although the research base on how educators select programs and materials is not large, prototypes of decisions made at the school and district levels are discussed. By the end of the chapter, readers should understand both how the history of an idea and how it is spread through a school can make a big difference in whether it ultimately gets "adopted." Importantly, this chapter examines how many education leaders think that exploration, adoption, and installation are the endpoint of making change happen in schools. In reality, these are the very beginning points for true change to take place.

Researchers have examined the processes by which innovations are adopted and implemented in educational settings for more than four decades (Rogers & Mortimore, 1969). This area of inquiry stems from a recognition that there are two separate and distinct components to improving schools: the intervention itself and the effective implementation of that intervention (Fixsen et al., 2005). In order to create optimal learning environments for students, we need to attend to both halves of the innovation equation: we must choose effective interventions and we must implement them with integrity. Attainment of the desired outcome depends on both selecting the right intervention and implementing it well, while failure to attain the desired outcome can result from the selection of a poor intervention, poor implementation, or both.

The process by which schools and districts explore and adopt new innovations can vary greatly. While some employ a very deliberate and thoughtful process, many innovations are adopted with little contemplation and research.

The people involved, the nature of the innovation, and external mandates can all play a role in determining whether adoption of a new innovation is a process or an event, and whether it is ultimately successful. A thoughtful process includes establishing the need for change, generating excitement for innovation, building buy-in by demonstrating how educators will benefit by supporting innovation, and working toward consensus for adoption of the innovation. Research suggests that it is worthwhile for educators to take the time to explore innovations, plan for implementation, and prepare school communities for change.

HOW WE HAVE TRADITIONALLY SELECTED NEW IDEAS: THE NEXT GREAT THING IN EDUCATION

We have a long history in education of being seekers: we recognize the need for improvement in our schools and we look for solutions to the problems that impede our ability to achieve desired outcomes. Educators become aware of educational interventions in a variety of ways. You might hear about something that is being done in a neighboring district, in another state, or in another part of the world that sounds like it is making a difference for students. You might read about a new approach to reading intervention or improving school climate in a professional journal and recognize that it is targeting a challenge that your school faces. Alternatively, educators might become aware of innovations as a result of a district, state, or federal mandate.

Those who have been involved with education for 5 or 10 years or more have likely seen more education "innovations" pass through the halls than they care to remember. While some innovations might have resulted in meaningful change, many were probably just ideas that seemed like they would benefit students, but which had not been subjected to scientific research to assess their effectiveness. Great ideas come and go and we move from one initiative to the next at what would be considered breakneck speed from a systems change perspective. While this almost constant change is generally well intentioned, the result for many can be innovation fatigue. Teachers who have been through this process a time or two might come to ask themselves: Why should I study this new system, attend trainings, and struggle to implement this new approach when I don't know if it will work and I don't know if my leaders will continue to support it next year? The history of rapid change in the practices that are used in schools is among the barriers to truly effective and lasting change.

BARRIERS TO AND FACILITATORS OF CHANGE

One of the important contributions that Fixsen and colleagues (2005) have made to the knowledge base about effective change in schools is that there are always barriers and facilitators to change. But the good news is that, by recognizing these factors, organizations can put in place steps to reduce the barriers and strengthen the facilitators (Klingner, Ahwee, Pilonieta, & Menendez, 2003). Fixsen et al. (2005) note that an important step in addressing barriers is to identify those barriers as well as the person(s) who have the authority to remove them. Just listing the barriers will not make them go away. Instead, it is important to recognize why they exist and to know who can remove them. In the case of an MTSS, the process of removing barriers might involve learning which staff do not support such a model and then setting up individualized meetings between the principal and other MTSS leadership with those who do not support the initiative. These meetings will provide reticent staff with the opportunity to explain their concerns as well as hear about the strengths of using tiered supports.

It is important to recognize that some barriers must be removed, but some might not need to be eliminated in order for an MTSS to move forward. For example, having both the legal authority and financial capacity to implement an MTSS is essential. If the school district administration, either the superintendent or board, has decided not to support or approve an MTSS, then it is not feasible to keep trying to make it happen (yet). Similarly, if there are not enough dollars allocated for the model of an MTSS that is desired, then implementation as desired is not possible. In these cases, efforts to obtain administrative support and funding are the best next steps. Trying to move forward on other steps of an MTSS without administrative support and funding is not recommended. But other types of barriers may not be insurmountable impediments to implementation.

If there are one or two teachers who are against an MTSS in a building, the feasibility of implementation depends on the size of the staff. In a school with 25–30 teachers and other staff, one or two naysayers are not likely to prevent the rest of the staff from moving forward. This is because the majority of the staff support an MTSS and will make it happen. Even if two out of 25 staff members oppose an MTSS, the remaining 23 are more than enough to make it happen. However, if the school has five teachers (and this happens in very small rural schools), then moving forward might not be possible. It is generally accepted that 80% of the faculty must support an innovation in order for it to move forward (Sugai & Horner, 2005). In every group or organization, there can be some people who oppose any and all innovations. It's not always clear why they are in opposition, but often these are people who disagree just to be disagreeable. Thankfully for the rest of the group, having a small number of naysayers does not mean that every change will be stopped. Indeed, the principles of democracy are such that a very small number could not prevent change for the majority. So, determining how to address the barriers to an MTSS will be a process that must be worked out at the building and district levels. When the barriers can be overcome, or at least tolerated, then the next step is to examine the facilitators.

The term *facilitators* refers to those environmental variables that enhance the likelihood that something will happen. Fixsen et al. (2005) suggest that examining the facilitators of change is essential for long-term innovation to happen. Facilitators can include having a principal and superintendent who embrace an MTSS as well as a budget that will allow purchasing evidence-based curriculum materials. In terms of the change process, those advocating for an MTSS need to sit down and consider the facilitators that exist in their situation. By knowing the people and circumstances that are likely to support an MTSS, a team is in a better position to develop a coherent implementation plan. Based on their review of successful change, Fixsen et al. (2005) developed the term *implementation drivers*. Also known as core implementation components, the "drivers" are steps that the organization takes so that any given innovation is effective. There are six main drivers/components and these are listed in Table 10.1. Note that the six components are not necessarily in the order used, and that "compensatory" supports for existing staff are always provided as explained below.

Staff Selection

Deciding who will be part of an innovation or change is important. The top tier of leadership staff need to understand the innovation thoroughly. That being said, most school-based innovations depend on existing staff. This means that the innovation leaders need to get to know the existing staff and develop relationships that will help create a community of professionals. While this might seem like a simple step, it is very important because it is through a sense of community and common purpose that an MTSS happens. When school leaders truly get to know, appreciate, and cultivate the interests, needs, and diversity of their staff, a true learning community is formed.

TABLE 10.1. Fixsen et al.'s (2005) Change Implementation (Driver) Components

Component	Example
Staff selection	Personnel who have the requisite training and expertise in the desired change are hired.
Training	When needed, additional training of staff is provided. This can include both new and existing staff members.
Ongoing consultation and coaching	Once the change is put into place, the key staff are provided with ongoing support in the form of consultation and coaching to ensure the delivery of the change with fidelity.
Staff and program evaluation	After one cycle of implementation, the key staff and the program itself are systematically and objectively evaluated.
Facilitative adminstrative support	In response to the evaluation data, supports are provided to the key staff so that needed improvements or enhancements are delivered.
Systems interventions	The adminstrative leaders engage in ongoing efforts to secure the resources necessary to support the innovation.

Training

Once a community with common goals is present, it is much easier to evaluate what additional learning is needed to support the school's objectives. Identifying training needs is not a once-and-done step, but is a continuous process. The training provided should always reflect the school's and district's stated student instructional goals. Thus, if a teacher asks for training in a program or method not endorsed and used by the school, it should not be supported. Instead, regular training in all of the programs and methods that the school uses to support an MTSS should be provided. Such training includes initial preparation as well as annual or more frequent refreshers so that all adopted programs are implemented with integrity. Some educators might object to the idea of "training" because it seems like any individual creativity is impossible. Consider the preparation and training that other professionals experience in order to do their jobs well. Physicians, accountants, lawyers, and others all engage in regular (e.g., at least yearly) updates in order to know the latest and most effective methods of treatment and service. If teachers are going to be regarded as professionals, and provide effective instruction, ongoing training is essential.

Ongoing Consultation and Coaching

Once an innovation is put into place, it needs to be supported in order to be effective. In order to make any innovation, including an MTSS, effective for students, school staff need consultation and coaching. There are a number of ways to provide such supports for staff. When staff are uncertain about whether they are implementing a step correctly, they need to be able to access consultation with an expert. Such expertise does not have to be an added expense, but can include access to specialists who already work in the district. For example, literacy and math specialists, school psychologists, speech and langauge pathologists, and others with advanced training can provide the consultation that teachers need. Such consultation does not always need to be in person, but can include e-mail and telephone communications. When staff know that they can access such supports quickly and without penalty, they are more likely to take advantage of available expertise.

Staff and Program Evaluation

After an innovation or program has been in place for a reasonable period of time, it is important to evaluate whether it has met its goals. There are two types of evaluation that can show the effectiveness of an innovation. *Staff* evaluation includes individualized appraisal of the staff responsible for implementing the program. Such evaluations are important because they indicate whether the staff members are meeting the overall goals of the program and their specific jobs. Many (if not all) schools have staff evaluations built into employment contracts. The contractual evaluation systems have a legal status in determining if a staff person will maintain employment. Such evaluations are important if a staff person is seriously negligent in basic job responsibilities, but may not give feedback about how the staff person could improve acceptable job performance. For this reason, school leaders need to consider both formal and informal feedback as important tools in enhancing staff performance. In addition to the required annual performance review, staff will benefit from more frequent feedback about how they are doing. Such reviews can include informal suggestions, and especially praise, for how a staff person supports students on a daily basis.

Facilitative Adminstrative Support

In order for an MTSS to be effective, individual staff members must do their jobs each day. But it is also essential that school leaders do their part as well. When a staff person, whether a teacher or paraprofessional, shows a need for support, it is very important that the school leaders identify the specific need and provide support. This can include additional training as well as more frequent coaching or consultation. While the day-to-day operations and success of an MTSS depend on well-trained and engaged staff, having school leaders who understand and advocate for student supports is essential as well. Examples of administrative support include celebrating MTSS activities at monthly staff meetings, highlighting building accomplishments at district meetings, and including MTSS priorities in budgets and advocacy at school board deliberations.

Systems Interventions

A sixth, but not necessarily final, component in effective systems change is the use of systems interventions to support the daily work of teachers. Systems interventions include steps taken by administrators and others to sustain the hard work done by teachers. Such interventions include developing budgets that have professional development (PD) funds and instructional coaches, as well as other supports, that teachers need so that they can help all students get the support they need. In addition, systems interventions involve explaining to school board/committee members why an MTSS is important and that using multi-tiered supports prevents some students from developing conditions that would require more expensive special education services. Basically, systems intervention means that the school and district have an ethos (i.e., mind-set) that *all children can learn* and that every effort will be made to help all students access effective instruction.

A BETTER ALTERNATIVE FOR SELECTING INNOVATIONS

In order for an intervention to be worthy of adoption, it needs to be more than something that is being done in a neighboring district, school, or classroom, and it needs to be more than just someone's good idea. If we are to ask educators, schools, and districts to invest time, money, and effort in a new way of doing things, we must ensure that the innovation is evidence based, it meets the needs of the students, and it is culturally relevant to the schools. This requires that educators invest the time it takes to examine the evidence in support of a program or intervention, evaluate its ability to address the goals that educators have for their students, and assess its applicability to the culture and values of the school. One helpful resource for examining how instructional materials are selected is the hexagon tool by Blase, Kiser, and Van Dyke (2013). Based on work by the National Implementation Research Network (NIRN), the hexagon format helps school teams consider possible interventions in relation to:

1. Needs
2. Fit
3. Resource availability
4. Evidence
5. Readiness for replication
6. Capacity to implement

Each part of the hexagon reminds team members that for any intervention to be effective in the long run, the context in which it will be used must be carefully considered.

In the current climate of evidence-based practice (EBP), virtually every program or product being advertised for schools claims that it is evidence based. They are easy words to say, after all, and there are no EBP police in education. Educators' understanding of what constitutes EBP varies greatly and there has been little consensus on the matter in the research community (Nelson & Epstein, 2002). Some of those advocating various innovations claim that theirs is an EBP because it is grounded in several popular books that were published by well-respected authors. Others claim that the practice they are promoting is EBP because it has been effective in settings outside of education, such as juvenile justice facilities. Perhaps the most egregious offenders cite their own books or non-peer-reviewed articles as supporting evidence. Such testimonials are not true evidence, yet may lead some educators to think otherwise.

How can educators know if an intervention is an EBP? In order to answer this question, educators need to know if a practice has been subjected to scientific research and, if so, what the outcomes of the research were. The NCLB Act of 2001 established a definition of ***scientifically based research*** that includes "the application of rigorous, systematic, and objective procedures to obtain reliable and valid knowledge relevant to education activities and programs." The act goes on to say that research

- employs systematic, empirical methods . . .
- involves rigorous data analyses that are adequate to test the stated hypotheses . . .
- relies on measurements or observational methods that provide reliable and valid data . . .
- is evaluated using experimental or quasi experimental designs . . .
- is presented in sufficient detail and clarity to allow for replication, and . . .
- has been accepted by a peer-reviewed journal or approved by a panel of independent experts through a comparably rigorous, objective, and scientific review. (§9191[37])

If an intervention has not been subjected to scientifically based research and shown good outcomes, it is not an EBP. Without examining the research, it is sometimes difficult to tell the effective interventions from the ineffective ones. For this reason, educators need to be able to gather information to determine whether an innovation meets the criteria set forth by NCLB. Doing so is worth the effort, as it provides a means of comparison between intervention options. By considering the existing evidence base for an intervention, educators can prevent investment of time, money, and effort in something that is not likely to have the desired outcome, and redirect those resources to an intervention that is.

An MTSS is an evidence-based framework in which many EBPs play a part in supporting and responding to students' needs. Having an MTSS for reading will only improve students' reading abilities if the practices employed at each tier are evidence based. The assessment tools that are employed for screening (benchmarking), the core reading curriculum, and the interventions for struggling readers, nonreaders, and students with reading disabilities must all have evidence that demonstrates their effectiveness. Similarly, a system for supporting students' behavior at multiple tiers must comprise evidence-based assessment, instruction, and intervention practices across those tiers.

CONTEMPLATING CHANGE

Thanks to NCLB and other efforts (e.g., What Works Clearinghouse), there is greater national focus on the importance of using only EBPs in schools. But, of course, just thinking about change does not make it happen. Instead, there needs to be a planned and focused process for implementing the right change(s). As will be explained, the major work in bringing about change is to facilitate conditions whereby all, or at least 80%, of the school staff endorse and will implement the change. But well before getting to such acceptance there needs to be a process for proposed changes to be suggested. While having such a process might seem obvious, many schools and districts do not have a formal system for new ideas to be initiated. This is in contrast to most businesses, and even to the democratic system of government, which have well-established proposal systems. For example, does your school and/or principal have an "idea" box or other mechanism for innovations to be considered? Are such suggestions welcomed at any time, or are there change "windows" when new ideas are considered?

There is virtually no research about how changes are initiated in schools, but schools seem to embrace change with great enthusiasm. There is a solid body of research on change in individuals, and this research informs the conceptualization that Fixsen et al. (2005) have developed regarding organizational change. Prochaska and DiClemente (1992) developed a model of change at the individual level that is worth reviewing before we move on to organizational change. This model includes five stages and is summarized in Table 10.2 along with examples of each stage related to weight and dieting. The first stage is called precontemplation and is really a state of nonawareness of the need for change. At this point, there is no plan or interest in change. For example, an individual might be content with his or her weight, even though he or she is overweight. The second stage brings the need for change into awareness and is called contemplation because it occurs when the individual starts thinking about change. This could happen when someone visits the doctor and learns that he or she is overweight.

At the third stage, preparation, steps to make change possible begin to happen. This can be a short or long process, but it is an important process because it brings the materials or other required elements into the environment where change can occur. This could include getting rid of unhealthy foods and purchasing only healthy ones. The fourth stage, action, is probably the most difficult and

TABLE 10.2. Prochaska and DiClemente's (1992) Transactional Change Stages

Stage	Activities	Example
Precontemplation	There is no awareness of a need for change by the individual.	"I am happy with my current weight and level of wellness."
Contemplation	There is an emerging awarenss of the need for change.	"I visit the doctor for my annual physical and learn that I am overweight and at risk for diabetes."
Preparation	Steps are taken in the direction of change.	"I clean out my cupboards and remove unhealthy foods; I visit the grocery store and purchase only healthy foods."
Action	The individual engages in regular use of behaviors that are different from the past.	"I eat a healthy diet of 1,500 calories per day and walk 30 minutes per day."
Maintenance	The individual engages in behaviors likely to keep the changes constant over time.	"I purchase a scale and weigh myself weekly while continuing to eat a healty diet and get exercise."

the longest. This is when the actual dieting and/or exercise for weight loss would occur. This stage lasts as long as necessary for the desired change to take place. The last stage, maintenance, involves the end of active change but includes steps to keep the recent change(s) in place. For example, it could include purchasing a scale and weighing oneself regularly to keep track of weight over time. If needed, the maintenance stage can involve a return to the action stage to reinstall desired change. Prochaska and DiClemente (1992), as well as others, have shown that using the fives stages of the change process can make change more likely to happen and last longer. Examples from their research include not only weight loss but also smoking cessation, as well as overcoming addiction to other harmful substances.

A possible key to the success observed in use of the Prochaska and DiClemente (1992) change model is that it recognizes change as a process and not an event. This is in contrast to the way change often happens in schools. Many classroom teachers have had the too-frequent experience of starting a new school year with a different "program" or curriculum. Sometimes, the teachers might have known that the change was coming, but not always. And, despite research showing that providing PD training for new materials increases their accurate and effective use, there is often no such training given for teachers before they are expected to use a new program. The way that new programs and materials are often introduced in schools (i.e., with little warning or preparation) might suggest to educators that change is an event instead of a process. Although the research on effective school change needs to be enhanced, available findings suggest that only when change is viewed as a process, and appropriate planning and resources are allocated to support the change, will effective and lasting change be possible in schools.

One of the steps that has been documented to support effective school change is the creation of a team that will oversee the change process. All models of school change recommend such teams and research supports their use. Prior to giving serious consideration to a new program, curriculum, or any other way of doing business, a school needs to create a process by which change is considered. Such a process can be overseen by a team representing all school community members, but needs to be set up according to the principles outlined in Chapters 6 and 7. The team can then utilize available research on change to develop plans and procedures for exploration, adoption, and installation of the MTSS steps.

ADOPTION

Adoption refers to the formal decision by a school board or committee to use a specific program or set of practices with their students. Adoption is important because it is a matter of policy and applies to all students. Ideally, school boards or committees adopt an instructional program only after very careful review and because they believe it to be in the best interest of all the students in their jurisdiction. Once a program has been formally adopted (usually a matter requiring a formal vote by the school board or committee), the resources needed to implement it effectively must be approved and the formal training needed to make it happen must be implemented in a timely fashion.

INSTALLATION

Adoption of an innovation is the beginning of implementation, not the end. Although much work might have been required to reach an adoption decision, there is still much work to be done. What we have learned from implementation research is that starting with an effective intervention is not enough to ensure success. One might say that an EBI is necessary but not sufficient to produce a meaningful change for students. Once we have identified an intervention that has been shown to be effective when subjected to scientifically based research, there are still important steps necessary to get that intervention from research to practice. In short, we must have a plan for implementing our intervention that is as strong as our intervention. While adoption of a program is an important step, installation of the program is far more important if it is to be lasting and effective.

For any change in policy to become a practice in a school, a large amount of background work must happen. Specific steps such as creating short- and long-term action plans, ordering materials, providing training, and creating a schedule must occur. After adoption, schools must pay attention to the "behind-the-scenes" preparation needed for the innovation to be effective over time. In order for this to happen, it is important that schools employ the "work smarter, not harder" principle, and audit existing practices so they can eliminate those that are not integral or demonstrating efficacy. Installation refers to the first actual steps required to make change happen. Installation is a process used in other fields as well. Museums must install exhibits before they can open to the public and the installation work takes careful planning and resources. Examples of installation of an MTSS include selection of evidence-based instructional materials as well as thorough training of all staff who will use them. Just purchasing the materials will not make change happen, but it is an important first step.

As with all other steps in effective change, it is important that there be a plan for installation and that it not come as a surprise to anyone. One of the simplest but most important steps that school teams can take in preparing for installation is communicating often about the plans. Such communication needs to start several months before the installation begins, and be frequent as well as consistent. Advertisers understand well the power of such communication and they often create a key message for the "rollout." School teams can do the same thing, and having everyone use the same message will promote both consistency and general readiness. In addition to having a key message, educators will want to know why the change is happening. Teams should offer information sessions for their colleagues to explain the history and rationale for the change as well as all the steps involved. Teachers deserve to be well prepared for any instructional changes and they are more likely to "buy in" to change if they know that they will have time to prepare and be fully supported in using any new methods.

RECOMMENDATIONS

Based on the research conducted by Fixsen et al. (2005) and others, we recommend the following six key steps for initiating the change process to support an MTSS:

1. Establish a team.
2. Establish the need for change.
3. Ensure that your *next great thing* is truly an EBI.
4. Generate excitement for change.
5. Build buy-in and consensus.
6. Create a thoughtful plan.

The remaining chapters in this section describe the next steps in effective change, including implementation and sustaining change over time.

SUMMARY

While the research on the science of change is still new and limited, available findings document that there are specific steps that a school can take to make innovation successful. These steps include recognizing that change is a process and not an event, appointing a team to oversee changes, selecting and using only truly EBPs, and providing support for each and every step of the change process. In the past, schools have tended to view change as an event, and this has contributed to distrust and frustration among teachers who have been left feeling both unprepared and not valued for their expertise. An MTSS is a very different way of thinking about instruction and learning, and the changes necessary to make it successful must be considered carefully. By using guidance from research on the change process in general, schools seeking to make an MTSS effective, durable, and sustainable over the long term will be in a strong position to facilitate lasting change.

CHAPTER 11

Implementation

With a firm foundation of understanding the change process, and a team committed to utilizing only evidence-based practices (EBPs), the next stage in making an MTSS happen is implementation. Given all the work needed to consider, adopt, and install MTSS practices, one might think that similar effort toward implementation is a given. As this chapter shows, actual daily use of the adopted practices requires careful planning and support, too. As noted by Fixsen et al. (2005, p. 16) as soon as a new idea is rolled out, the "compelling forces of fear of change, inertia, and investment in the status quo" emerge and block the way. There are steps that educators can take to make implementation much more successful and these are described below. A key point highlighted in this chapter is that school personnel often rush to put new practices in place, but do not consider or invest in the training, consultation, and procedures needed to be sure that the teachers fully understand the nature of the innovation and why it is needed. The focus of this chapter is on identifying what preparatory work must be done for initial and long-term implementation so that the environment will welcome rather than reject the change.

INITIAL IMPLEMENTATION

One of the keys to successful implementation is momentum. As described in the previous chapter, careful planning long before the change is actually implemented is necessary for it to succeed. The activities surrounding such planning create an energy and expectation for the way that things will be once the change is in place. In order to get staff to buy in to the change, we usually spend time convincing them that the changes will result in something better than what they are experiencing now. In the case of an MTSS, the planning stages often include explaining to teachers how traditional school practices, such as students having to "wait to fail" before they can get help, are inefficient and ineffective. In contrast, an MTSS offers methods that provide students with additional instruction as soon as they need it. With that promise made, it is very important that those in charge of an MTSS implementation do whatever they can to make it succeed.

There are several key steps that planning and implementation teams can take to make sure that the first days, weeks, and months of an MTSS are successful. These steps include (1) creating and distributing a long-term implementation schedule; (2) implementing with one grade, subject area, or tier at a time; (3) holding frequent check-in meetings with teachers; and (4) acknowledging successes and failures right away. By following these steps, the initial implementation of an MTSS is more likely to succeed.

Implementation Schedule

One way to make initial implementation successful is to let all stakeholders know what the schedule will be. Such a schedule can be developed during the planning process and should be distributed to anyone who wants it. The schedule should indicate which students, teachers, grades, and other personnel will implement the change first, who will follow, and so forth. Having a schedule and sticking to it will create a sense of trust that the change will happen in a predictable and orderly manner. It is important to minimize changes to the schedule. If numerous changes are made to the projected schedule, it might be hard for staff to trust that it has any meaning. Sometimes the planning team might recognize a needed change in the early days of implementation, but unless it is truly a mission-critical one, it is best to wait and make that change in the next phase so that it can be built into the schedule and communicated with all staff.

One Grade, Subject, or Tier at a Time

The starting point for an MTSS generally varies depending on whether the focus is on academics or behavior. Initiatives to implement an MTSS for behavior begin with building a universal, or Tier 1, system of support for all students. This is the best approach to take for behavior in part because schools typically do not have a universal curriculum available to all students to support prosocial behavior. Some academic implementations of an MTSS have started with one grade level or subject area at a time and this is an effective practice. Still, some schools will opt to implement the system with all grades at the same time and this is okay too. Most implementations of an MTSS for behavior begin with building a Tier 1 system. Having too much change at one time can be overwhelming for anyone. By carefully selecting one grade level, one content area (e.g., reading), or one tier (i.e., a schoolwide system of behavioral support) as the starting point, it leaves other routines unchanged and helps students, teachers, and other staff not be overwhelmed. Many implementations of an MTSS have started with reading, but this is not required. Certainly reading is important, but so are all the other things taught in schools.

The planning team implementing an MTSS for academics should consider which content area or which grade level is most in need of change during the planning process. By reviewing any existing data and considering the school's highest need, the team can identify the best starting point. In some cases, it might make sense to start with both one grade level and one content area such that only first-grade reading instruction is modified to use MTSS methods. Such a limited change could make sense if the building has a large number of teachers per grade level. An MTSS for behavior, or PBIS, requires schoolwide engagement and depends on having participation by the entire school. The planning team must think about all of the effects on school routines and how much is involved in the change as it decides where to begin.

Check-In Meetings

A step that planning and support teams can take that will foster trust and support from staff is to hold frequent check-in meetings during the initial implementation. Such meetings do not have to be long, but are an important type of communication between those planning the change and those who are on the ground implementing it. Such check-ins can happen as part of existing meetings. For example, one or more planning team members can attend each weekly grade-level team meeting to ask how the implementation is going and to answer questions. Similarly, time can be set aside at the monthly faculty meetings to address implementation issues. Setting aside time for questions and feedback is important because it demonstrates that teacher and staff input matters and that not everything will go perfectly right away. Planning team members need to record and discuss the feedback, and when there are urgent problems or requests affecting the entire process, develop a way to address the problem right away. Eventually, the need for the meetings will be smaller and they can be faded over time.

Acknowledging Success and Failure

A final way that implementation can be enhanced is for school leaders to communicate the successes and failures of the implementation on a regular basis. This is important because it provides public recognition for events that staff are experiencing. In times of change, it is very important to recognize and celebrate successes along the way. Such celebrations affirm that the energy and work needed to make the change happen were worth it. But it is just as important to recognize and address problems. If only successes are made public, it can send a message that the leadership is ignoring the problems. By acknowledging things that need to be fixed, and how that will be done, staff are more likely to trust that the process is worth it and that glitches will be addressed.

An overall theme in making initial implementation succeed is good communication. In times of change, we all have more questions and may feel more anxiety. Providing clear schedules, expectations, opportunities for feedback, and open lines of communication fosters trust and collaboration. There is no guarantee that every step of implementation will go smoothly, but frequent and open communication is something that can happen no matter what. Fixsen et al. (2005) note that much of the work of initial implementation is to get the organization past the initial awkward stage where everyone is uncomfortable. The amount of time it will take for initial implementation to occur will vary, but implementation is generally understood to be in place when most or all of the staff recognize the change as the adopted practice of the school.

LONG-TERM IMPLEMENTATION

There is a distinction between initial and long-term implementation in that initial implementation gets the change started, but there is more work to be done to make the change permanent. Long-term implementation is realized only once the new practices become the accepted norms of the school. Notably, many innovations in education never reach this stage because necessary procedural guidance and infrastructure were not put in place ahead of time. The importance of fully defining what full operation will mean and then breaking it into manageable parts is essential for educational innovation to succeed. Consider how many times schools have tried to implement something new and it seemed to work for a while, but then there were problems and the change was abandoned. Planning for long-term implementation is designed to prevent abandonment of effective changes that will succeed with the right support.

The distinction between initial and long-term implementation is something like experiencing initial success on a diet and then realizing that it will require ongoing discipline to stick to the diet to keep the weight off. The excitement associated with initial implementation eventually fades, but the daily steps necessary to maintain success are still needed. In order for schools to achieve long-term MTSS success, attention to this stage is needed. In fact, it is sometimes the case that after the initial implementation, the steps needed to keep it going will actually seem harder than at the beginning. This is because the process of implementing the change may shed light on previously overlooked student needs. For example, after putting into place a schoolwide PBIS system, the initial data on office discipline referrals (ODR) might show that there are many more playground fights than anyone actually realized. Learning about this higher incidence could be difficult and frustrating to teachers who are already working hard every day. It is at just this moment in implementation when attention to the long-term needs is most important.

Joyce and Showers (2002) found that in order for long-term implementation to succeed there must be ongoing support for those responsible for daily implementation. Fixsen et al. (2005) noted that one of the most essential features of effective long-term implementation is the presence of a feedback loop between the implementers (i.e., teachers) and developers/planners. To support an effective feedback loop, both coaching and evaluation are needed. Together, coaching and evaluation provide important communication about implementation, but also create a shift in the types of communication about daily practices that occur.

Communication Changes

Recall that an important component of initial implementation is frequent and open communication between the planners and staff. At the initial stage, the planners often have a large amount of detail to communicate, and the staff may have important, but brief, feedback. This communication pattern shifts as initial implementation becomes long term. After a sustained period of implementation, a body of data will accumulate and that information can be used to inform program improvements and next steps. How data about implementation are collected and shared will have a substantial impact on long-term effectiveness. For this reason, it is important that there be careful consideration of how information is collected and shared. In order to set up and support effective communication loops, Fixsen et al. (2005) recommend the use of both coaching and evaluation. In Chapter 10 we shared the basic framework for effective implementation that Fixsen and colleagues (2005) developed. This model includes six main components, of which coaching and evaluation are included. Importantly, these steps follow a specific order so that there can be enough time for initial implementation as well as effective communication and feedback loops.

Coaching Comes before Evaluation

Although the Fixsen et al. (2005) model allows for multiple points of entry, there is a specific direction to the process. In relation to implementing an MTSS, the selection of specific methods and staff training would always come before consultation and coaching. Similarly, consultation and coaching will always come before staff evaluation. This directionality is very important because it sets up an environment in which both students and teachers can succeed. Planning team members need to keep the order of operations for long-term implementation in mind as they set up supports.

Consultation and Coaching

Both consultation and coaching are very important supports for successful long-term implementation. There is a longer research base for consultation, but recent findings suggest that coaching is important as well. While consultation and coaching share the goal of supporting teachers' effective implementation of new practices, these two methods are distinct from each other. Consultation is typically conducted outside of the classroom and is initiated by the teacher, who seeks out the consultant to ask for advice and support about a specific situation or student. In comparison, coaching usually happens in the classroom and is initiated by the coach, who has been assigned to support the teacher in specific ways (Denton & Hasbrouck, 2009). It is important to note that assignment of a coach to a teacher does not, in any way, reflect on that teacher's core teaching skills. Instead, the coaching model is designed to provide universal support to all teachers rather than depend on the teachers to ask for help.

Despite the long history of consultation in schools, it has not often been specifically mentioned as part of an MTSS (Erchul, 2011). This oversight might be the result of the implicit role of consultation in tiered supports. By definition, implementing supports that are available for all students depends on effective communication among staff members, but the dynamic may not always fit the traditional description of consultation. Regardless of this, consultation does play an important role in long-term implementation. Consultation provides school teams, classroom teachers, and others who might be serving as interventionists (e.g., paraprofessionals) with access to ideas from people with specific expertise. In schools, those who provide consultation often include school psychologists, speech–language therapists, occupational therapists, physical therapists, literacy and math coaches, and special educators. Schools implementing an MTSS also benefit from consultation provided by people with expertise in systems-level change, behavior, reading, and other specific areas.

One does not need to have a certain credential to provide consultation, but rather must have expertise that is viewed as helpful to other educators. There is an extensive research literature on consultation in schools (Erchul, 2011), however, for the purposes of an MTSS implementation, the main point is that it is important that it be made available. Even in small schools, the MTSS planning team needs to set up procedures so that everyone involved in the long-term implementation can access consultation when needed. Often, the planning team members might serve as the initial consultants and then, over time, staff members come to recognize and seek out others who have the best expertise for their questions. Having access to consultation is important because it means that staff can get help at the moment in time when they perceive it is needed, rather than on a schedule set by others.

Coaching is a much newer approach to supporting teachers. Although classroom coaching has been around for several decades, it was given a major boost from inclusion in the Reading First program sponsored by the U.S. Department of Education (Denton & Hasbrouck, 2009). While there is much less research about coaching, the available findings have largely been sponsored by Jim Knight and colleagues at the University of Kansas (University of Kansas Center for Research on Learning, 2013). Although there are many approaches to coaching, a defining feature is that the coach observes the teacher in the classroom at various times. The observations are followed by feedback sessions in which both the coach and teacher share impressions and ideas for improvement. At the time of this writing, there are no large-scale empirical studies of the effects of coaching on student outcomes, but findings from initial research are promising. A team of researchers at Johns Hopkins University is studying the effects of coaches on the implementation of PBIS in a model they are calling PBIS Plus (Bradshaw et al., 2012). This study's preliminary findings in 42 elementary schools indicate that coaches can have a significant impact on both the effectiveness of participating teachers and the academic and behavioral outcomes of their students. Teemant (2014) found that coaching of 36 urban elementary teachers was linked with improved student outcomes. In another study, Garcia, Jones, Holland, and Mundy (2013) found similarly positive results for middle school students whose teachers were coached. More research on the best coaching practices is needed; nonetheless, initial findings suggest that students benefit when coaches help teachers improve their practices.

In terms of an MTSS implementation, coaching is poised to play an important role in helping teachers and interventionists get feedback on their actual use of specific teaching practices. In this regard, it provides another important communicative function in the overall implementation of an MTSS. Planning teams need to pay close attention to how coaches are selected and trained and the evaluation procedures that will be used to monitor coach effectiveness. It may be that teachers will vary in their preference for coaching or consultation, and some amount of choice by teachers could be allowed. By offering consultation, which is teacher directed, and coaching, which is observer directed, schools provide important ways that educators can improve and sustain their daily practices related to a successful MTSS.

Staff Evaluation

The other critical feedback loop that helps to make long-term implementation successful is staff evaluation. This evaluation is distinct from contractually required evaluation procedures and, instead, refers to each staff person's application of procedures specific to a given change (i.e., an MTSS). Such evaluation is very important because it offers a different type of feedback concerning implementation. While consultation and coaching provide formative information and ideas that teachers can decide whether to use, evaluation offers a snapshot of each staff person's actual implementation in real time. The level of formality associated with staff evaluations related to an MTSS implementation can vary; however, if the goal is to use data about staff practices as a component of overall program evaluation, a high level of consistency and standardization in staff evaluation is needed. Specifically, if a larger goal is to learn the overall level of treatment integrity among the instructional practices being used, then formal and standardized observations that measure treatment integrity will be needed. More information about treatment integrity is provided in Chapter 17.

In addition to observing each staff person's basic implementation, staff evaluations can include other components. For example, there is abundant evidence that teachers can improve many student outcomes through the use of praise (see Bickford, 2012, for a complete review). If changing the schoolwide number of praise statements is a goal of the MTSS effort, then capturing data about teacher praise would be necessary. Alternatively, a school might have a goal of increasing the total number of minutes for daily math instruction and therefore would count the total minutes of math per day for each teacher. The decision about which staff behaviors to measure needs to be based on the school's and/or district's specific MTSS plan and goals. In order to put staff evaluation into effect, plans must be made well in advance and all staff included in communication about the evaluation process. Some staff may be anxious about being evaluated and, therefore, it is very important that steps be taken to prepare staff for the process and to help them appreciate their importance in the overall success of the MTSS.

SUMMARY

The success of an MTSS implementation depends on careful attention to many details. The work done in the exploration, adoption, and installation stages is certainly important, but must be followed by supports for both initial and long-term implementation. With supports such as advertised schedules, careful selection of which grade(s), subject(s), or tier to implement first, regular check-in meetings, and acknowledgment of both successes and failures, a school is poised to make the first days, weeks, and months of an MTSS successful. But in order for initial success to last there must be attention to additional details for long-term implementation. In particular, having a more detailed feedback loop about classroom practices can guide long-term efforts. By using collaboration and coaching, as well as staff evaluation, school teams can support teachers as they refine their implementation skills. In addition, important information about how an MTSS implementation is happening will be gained. These data will serve an additional purpose as we explore innovation and sustainability in Chapter 12.

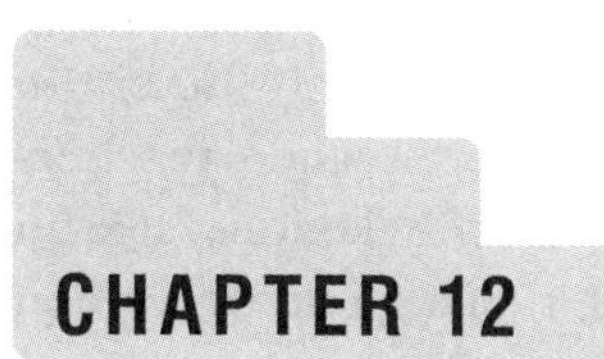

CHAPTER 12

Innovation and Sustainability

Often, educational innovation breeds other changes. Teachers are familiar with the many frequent changes in educational policies and practices and some refer to them as a "pendulum" that swings too often back and forth, not staying in one place long enough to have lasting effects. By using research about change, schools can select the most worthwhile innovations and then implement them effectively so that they will last. Once an MTSS is effectively implemented, there will be useful modifications and enhancements that can be made. It is important, though, to have a system for knowing which modifications are worth putting into place. Schools have a history of changing programs too quickly; rarely has enough time passed to see if one good idea worked before another replaced it. The importance of giving an innovation enough time to be effective, as well as using outcome indicators to document effects, is explained. By using a planful change approach, schools will be able to sustain an MTSS for many years. But, like all other aspects of change, attention to the steps necessary to sustain the MTSS is needed as well.

INTEGRATING INNOVATION INTO AN MTSS

A reality of life, as true in schools as anywhere else, is that change is inevitable. Once the MTSS is up and running well, educators have the opportunity to refine and improve the system. Over time, many of the mechanisms that support the MTSS can be enhanced. There are two types of change that can occur once an MTSS is initiated. One type of *enhancement* is when a particular innovation is improved by subsequent revisions. A second type of change is when the entire system of supports leads to an *evolution* in practices, such as when teachers come to think of data as mission critical to planning their daily lessons. Fixsen et al. (2005) identify innovation as a distinct phase of their change model. When innovations are brought into an existing system, they will affect the daily flow of operations, thus they need to be planned for as carefully as other stages. For example, the DIBELS (Dynamic Measurement Group, 2013) were recently revised with important and useful changes. While the "old" DIBELS were certainly good, the new seventh edition has components not available in the old version such as DIBELS for math (Dynamic Measurement Group, 2014). Although all of these changes are potentially useful, it is important that educators think about how and when to incorporate a change, rather than rush in too quickly and end up with other problems. We recommend that school teams ask the following questions (all of which should be asked as part of initial exploration) before putting MTSS innovations in place (see Blase et al., 2013).

1. "Is there an evidence base for the innovation? If so, are the data strong enough to support wide-scale use?"
2. "What training is needed for the innovation to be used effectively?"
3. "What schedule would make sense for integrating the innovation?"
4. "How should we communicate about the innovation?"
5. "How will we know if the innovation is truly 'better' than what we did before?"

Each of these questions needs to be carefully reviewed by the planning team before any innovation is put into place. The colleague(s) who support the innovation might be eager to get started right away (e.g., after hearing about it at a conference), but it is far better for everyone to proceed slowly so that only effective and value-added innovations are put into place.

"What Is the Evidence Base?"

The first question that the team needs to ask is whether there is research that documents outcomes of the proposed innovation. This step is no different from what the team would have done when reviewing programs and materials at the start of the MTSS planning. Asking about the research for a specific innovation is important because the change might still be in an exploratory phase, such as a pilot test. Good research follows a specific order and progression. It starts with initial pilot studies and then proceeds to field trials and finally multiple replications. When an innovation to an existing product or method is developed, it must be researched through this process just like the original version. Sometimes, educators might hear about an innovation at a conference where the researchers present early findings from a pilot test. Such findings might be encouraging, but it would be premature for a school to begin using the innovation based on pilot test data alone. Instead, it is best to wait for confirmatory findings and then consider whether the innovation is worth trying. This means that the team needs to look for and review additional data about the intervention. In addition to public websites like WWC, educators can find research on recent innovations in journal articles.

"What Training Is Needed?"

Once an innovation has been confirmed to have adequate research evidence, then the team needs to plan for the training necessary to implement and use it. The seventh edition of DIBELS provides a good example of how this can be done. When the seventh edition (also known as DIBELS Next; Dynamic Measurement Group, 2014) was published, training opportunities for educators to learn how to use this edition were also made available. Such trainings were offered in multiple formats so that both online webinars and site-specific trainings were available. The benefit of online training is that it is often less expensive and not as logistically challenging. But, when a large number of people all need the same training, it can be just as effective to have a trainer come to the school. The planning team needs to decide how staff will demonstrate their training level and readiness to use the innovation. Often, this is included in formal training procedures, but not always. For any innovation to be effective over the long term, all staff need to use it as intended and with consistency so—just like with initial preparation—training is essential in order for an innovation to succeed.

"What Schedule Should Be Used?"

After mapping out the training plans, another important consideration is the schedule for both the training and implementation. This is very important because using two different versions of a program at the same time can be confusing and lead to uninterpretable data. Usually, it is best to bring in the innovation at the start of a school year or teaching cycle. For example, if a team decided to adopt DIBELS Next for its universal benchmark screening measure, it would be best to begin its use in the fall of the next school year (Dynamic Measurement Group, 2014). This would give time for all necessary adaptations to be arranged. While both forms of the DIBELS have many similar features, it's not a good idea to screen students with two different versions in the same year because the data are not equivalent. The schedule for introducing a new instructional program should follow the same principle. It would be confusing and cumbersome for both students and teachers to switch core materials in the middle of a school year. An exception can be made for interventions used with a small number of students. Once staff are properly trained, it is possible to use a new intervention with a subset of the student population during a school year. As noted in

Chapters 22 and 23, it is important that any intervention changes be recorded on graphs and in other records so that those who review the data know what happened and when changes were made.

"How Should We Communicate?"

The next step after deciding on the schedule for introducing an innovation is to communicate about it with the entire school. As emphasized in earlier chapters, communicating on a regular basis with all school personnel is an important aspect of implementing lasting change. Fixsen and colleagues (2005) point out that ongoing communication with all stakeholders is essential for effective change of any kind. The MTSS team needs to plan ahead for how it will share the innovation plans and schedule with all members of the school community. Communication examples include announcements at staff meetings, written information in newsletters, and more detailed meetings with small groups of staff as needed. If the innovation will affect one group of teachers more than the others (e.g., second-grade teachers), then a meeting with those teachers to go over the changes in detail makes sense. Keep in mind that for communication to be effective it needs to be heard, not just said. This means that the planning team will need to disseminate information about the planned changes as many times as necessary for staff to understand what is happening; in addition, the planning team will need to check for understanding.

"How Will We Evaluate?"

The final step in planning for innovation is to map out how the changes will be evaluated. Like all parts of an MTSS, it is important to know if the selected practices are working as intended. The evaluation procedures for innovation can be the same as those for existing practices, but it is important to plan for gathering such data. The general outcomes from student and teacher performance will serve as sources of data, but additional ones may be desired as well. For example, it might be helpful to ask all those using the new innovation to complete a brief survey after a certain number of weeks into the change. This can capture information about how well the innovation is working from the perspective of those who use it most often. There can be minor differences in materials or data entry that affect teachers' daily practices. If these are problematic, the planning team can investigate whether an adjustment is possible. It can also be useful to collect data about an innovation after it has been in place for one full cycle. For example, after changing to a different method for universal screening and using it for an entire school year, having staff give feedback can help planning team members be prepared for later innovations.

Given that innovation is inevitable, it is important for MTSS teams to be prepared to integrate new practices into existing ones. But such integration needs to be done with thought and planning to be sure it will have the intended impact. Teams are advised to consider the evidence base, training needs, schedule, communication plan, and evaluation steps when thinking about any changes to existing MTSS procedures. There will likely be more suggestions for change than truly need to be integrated, and with such planning, effective innovation can enhance tiered supports.

SUSTAINING EFFECTIVE CHANGE

In order for the hard work invested in implementing an MTSS to last, there must be attention to sustainability. There are specific steps that schools can take to foster sustainability, including developing expertise within schools, documenting the systems-level work that has been done, planning for ongoing PD, and creating an annual schedule for the components of the MTSS. In order for systems change to be sustainable, the policies and procedures that have been developed must be documented. The last section of this chapter provides direction for teams in how to document their work and maintain the fruits of their labor. We recommend that each school develop faculty and staff handbook(s) for MTSS. Handbooks provide durability and sustainability through changes in administration at the district and school levels, as well as through team and staff changes. Schools can use their handbooks for employee training and as a reference for implementation. Finally, handbooks can and should be updated on an ongoing basis throughout the development of a multi-tiered system.

HANDBOOK DEVELOPMENT

Due to differences in the scope of MTSS practices for academics and behavior, we suggest creating two separate handbooks, or having one handbook with two distinct sections for academics and behavior. Creating handbooks that document all parts of the school's MTSS might seem like a daunting task. In order to make the work feasible, it is important to divide up the tasks and set a reasonable timeline.

Academic MTSS Handbook

The exact contents of the academic handbook will vary from school to school, but some suggested chapters are listed in Table 12.1. First, the team needs to decide what chapters to include. Once this is decided, then primary authors for each chapter can be assigned. In some cases, a team member might write more than one chapter. In order to keep the "publication" of the handbook on schedule, it is important to have firm deadlines for each draft. It is best to ask team members to determine the deadlines that they think are reasonable and then

TABLE 12.1. Suggested Academic MTSS Handbook Chapters

Topic	What is covered
Introduction and history	Includes a brief history of how MTSS came to the school and what specific model, methods, and programs are currently in place (e.g., PBIS).
Tier 1 materials and programs	Provides a concise summary of all the Tier 1 core instructional materials that have been approved by the school board or committee for use in all classrooms.
Universal screening	In table and narrative form, this chapter gives an easy-to-understand overview and schedule of the screening (or other) assessments used with all students.
Tier 2 interventions	In order to help teachers know what interventions might be tried in a given learning area, this chapter lists and describes what the district has approved and purchased.
Progress monitoring	Provides a table and description of progress measures for all learning areas for which intervention might be provided. These measures would be used at Tiers 2 and 3.
Tier 3 interventions	Although perhaps similar to the chapter on Tier 2, this one explains what variations of Tier 2 interventions, or other different Tier 3 interventions, have been approved for use.
Comprehensive evaluations	Gives guidance on how to use MTSS data and what is required in full and individual evaluations conducted for special education referral.
Appendices	Other reference materials such as district or state policies as well as any forms that should be used as part of an MTSS.

have one person serve to remind them of the deadlines and collect the drafts. Exactly who serves in the leadership capacity for such work is totally up to the team members and does not have to be the team leader or principal. An additional resource that can be used to assist with the handbook development process is an article by George Batsche on the RTI Network website (Batsche, 2013). This article provides additional information about materials to consider including in the academic handbook.

Behavior MTSS Handbook

The PBIS, or MTSS for behavior, handbook is typically created differently. This is because schools will already have some form of existing academic instruction and curricula, but may or may not have existing behavior instruction and support systems already in place. Using the teaming processes described in Part II, the universal (Tier 1) behavior team develops each component of the system and handbook. You will recall that this process includes team proposals that are adapted to account for the feedback of the community of educators. Given the nature of this process and the number of elements that must be created, development of the system takes place over a period of time. As each element is developed, the team archivist adds it to the handbook. As such, the handbook is a living document that can be amended and expanded over time.

The final behavior MTSS handbook should include everything from the school's expectations for behavior to its ODR form and corresponding procedures. Examples of the school's acknowledgment system and the guidelines and procedures associated with it should also be documented in the handbook. In addition, the archivist should include the lesson plans that have been developed for teaching the schoolwide expectations and the agreed-upon schedule for teaching those lessons each year. Other items that should be documented in the PBIS handbook include matrices for the schoolwide expectations across settings and events, the operational definitions of minor and major behaviors, and any products or procedures associated with the secondary and tertiary systems of support. A list of suggested chapters for a behavior MTSS handbook can be found in Table 12.2.

TABLE 12.2. Suggested Behavior MTSS Handbook Chapters

Topic	What is covered
Purpose	Provide a statement describing why the school has adopted MTSS for behavior.
Schoolwide expectations and plans for teaching the expectations to students.	That chapter includes documentation of the agreed-upon schoolwide expectations for student behavior, matrices and lesson plans for teaching the expectations to students, and a schedule for teaching the lesson plans.
Acknowledgment system	This chapter should include all elements of the system for acknowledging expected student behavior. Include examples of tickets or tokens that are part of the system, the procedures for staff to follow in providing acknowledgment, and the procedures for managing the acknowledgment system.
System for responding to challenging behavior	The entire system for responding to challenging behavior should be documented, including the lists of minor and major behaviors, the operational definitions of those behaviors, a flowchart depicting how staff should respond to challenging behavior, and the school's ODR form.
Advanced tiers	Include the school's process and form(s) for providing assistance for struggling students. In addition, the interventions provided at Tiers 2 and 3 should be documented.
Data management	This chapter provides guidance on how behavior data will be collected, managed, analyzed, and reported to staff. Importantly, this chapter should document the process for using the data to make decisions regarding the schoolwide system as well as with regard to individual students.
Appendices	Other reference materials such as district or state policies as well as any forms that should be used as part of the MTSS.

Student and Parent Handbooks

In addition to having handbooks for all staff that explain the MTSS practices for academics and behavior, most schools have some form of student and/or parent handbook. The student/parent handbooks provide an opportunity to inform parents about the school's efforts to support all students, as well as to generate parent and student buy-in for the school's systems. While more concise, the student and parent handbooks should be consistent with the staff handbooks. The student and parent handbook(s) will not need the level of detail about assessment and instruction procedures that the staff handbook has, but information about annual screening schedules, behavior expectations, whom to contact with questions, and how MTSS procedures and data are used should be put into the student and/or parent handbooks. It will be easier to write the staff handbook(s) first, and then copy and paste relevant details into the student/parent handbook(s). This way the information will be consistent.

The key to deciding how to organize the handbook(s) is to consider the "work flow" of the school's MTSS process. The suggested chapter topics for the handbooks in Tables 12.1 and 12.2 are only suggestions. The topics for the academic handbook are based on a chronological flow of information as it would apply to a teacher seeking more intensive supports for a student. In contrast, the topics for the behavior handbook are organized in the order in which a behavior MTSS system is typically developed. It is certainly possible to organize the chapters in a variety of other ways. For example, a school might prefer that the academic handbook be organized such that assessments are in one chapter and all interventions are in another. This is why the handbooks are typically written during the process of implementation. For both handbooks, only once the processes have been validated should procedures be given the authority of a handbook. It is best to work on drafting the handbooks while each stage of the change model is being implemented, but it is important that the handbooks be marked as drafts until formally adopted. Each school or district will vary in who must have a say in adoption of the handbooks. In some districts, there are very formal procedures for such materials. It is important that the writing team find out what review and approval steps will be necessary. Below are considerations about how to discuss key MTSS components that should be covered in the handbooks.

Core Instruction

The starting point for an MTSS is core instruction. This includes any and all instructional materials, procedures, and programs that have been officially adopted or developed for use by the school district. With the implementation of the Common Core State Standards (CCSS (see Chapter 5), the word *core* is often misunderstood to mean only materials aligned with the CCSS. Readers should note that in this book the term *core*, as it applies in an MTSS, refers to all instructional materials and methods that are universally available to all students. They are referred to as core instruction because they form the core of the learning students will experience. They also form the base of the MTSS triangle, thus serving as the core of the process. In all U.S. school districts, there are rules and procedures for how instructional materials and methods are adopted for use. Typically, it is the school board or committee that has the legal authority to make the decision about what will be used for instruction, but it usually acts on guidance from the district's leadership staff. Technically, only those materials and methods formally approved by the school board or committee can be used in the classrooms.

One of the reasons that the CCSS were developed, and so many states adopted them, is that there was (and perhaps still is) a large amount of variety in what was actually being taught in classrooms. As detailed in Chapter 5, for many years the learning available to students in U.S. public schools was based on what the teacher decided to teach that day. This lack of consistency is not effective when students change teachers each year, so having a more consistent approach to the scope and sequence of the learning goals is a better method. Many schools have been in the process of selecting and adopting new instructional materials to serve as their core programs, including development of behavior expectations. In cases where the school is using the CCSS, the term *core* will have a dual meaning such that the materials serve as the foundation for learning as well as align with the CCSS. Some teachers may not understand why their old familiar instructional materials need to be changed. Including information in the handbooks about why and how the core instructional materials were selected can answer questions of veteran teachers as well as provide a history and context for new teachers. Given that most schools hire some new teachers each year, having an annually updated description of what is being taught in the general education classroom can provide a tool for helping new instructors understand why the school uses the materials and methods that it does.

As noted in Chapter 5, the CCSS exist for core academic skills only and not for behaviors. As every teacher knows, student behavior is very important to overall learning outcomes. PBIS was developed to address the problems resulting when students don't know, or are not motivated to engage in, the behaviors that are appropriate in different settings of the school. Although there are numerous academic programs that schools can select for teaching literacy and math skills, the resources necessary for teaching expected behaviors do not come in the form of a packaged curriculum. For this reason, schools will need to develop the content and process for teaching appropriate behaviors across school settings. There are several excellent resources to support schools and districts in this work, including Colvin (2007) and the National PBIS Technical Assistance Center website (*www.pbis.org*; U.S. Department of Education Office of Special Education Programs, 2015).

Assessments

A variety of assessments are important to a successful MTSS and explaining how each type is used will help staff recognize the unique role each one plays. It is possible to have just one chapter in the handbook(s) on all assessments, or they can be broken into subtypes such as screening and progress monitoring are in Table 12.1. It may make sense to organize the information on assessments in relation to who collects the data and how it is organized and distributed. In some schools (usually small ones), the classroom teachers conduct both screening and progress monitoring assessments. In other schools, the assessments are conducted by special teams. How the information is shared with teachers is an important part of the way it needs to be described in the handbooks. If the teachers never conduct the assessments, it might be important to provide a high level of detail and even pictures of assessment items so they can understand what the students are asked to do.

The most important information to include in the assessment chapter(s) is how the data are used. Assessment scores by themselves are meaningless. Teachers and other staff members need to have a reference tool that tells exactly how all types of data are used. The easiest way to convey this information in the handbooks is to use examples taken from the school's existing data. Certainly, all identifying information about individual students needs to be removed, but once de-identified, local examples will convey the way that the data are used for decision making. Ideally, multiple examples are included so that the most common scenarios are available for teachers and others to review. For example, descriptions and graphs for students who are doing well, as well as ones for students who are struggling, will help teachers understand the school's data better.

Interventions

One of the first things educators often ask about in relation to setting up an MTSS is "What are the interventions?" In reality there is no single list of interventions that can be provided to and adopted by every school. The choice of which interventions to use must be based on which core instruction is being used. There needs to be complementarity across the tiers. Each school needs to conduct an inventory of what interventions it already has in place, whether they are working, and then decide what else to add. Importantly, this provides an opportunity to evaluate the effectiveness of existing interventions and consider the elimination of any that have not proven effective (a concept commonly referred to in PBIS as "working smarter, not harder"; U.S. Department of Education Office of Special Education Programs, 2015). This is the work of the planning team that will eventually result in a well-functioning MTSS process and the handbooks to guide it. But through that process there will be identified programs and materials that are being used at Tiers 2 and/or 3. In one or more handbook chapters, there need to be listings and descriptions of the interventions available for struggling students.

By the time the handbooks are written, team members will be able to explain how each one was selected.

Having a place where available interventions are listed and described will be useful for both veteran and new educators in the school. Veteran teachers may not know all of the available options, and new teachers will want to know what is available for them to use. In all cases, the intervention descriptions should be accompanied by information about how to get trained to use the intervention. In fact, a team might decide to have entire chapters on training! Educators need to understand that they cannot use an intervention until they have been trained properly. Some interventions will require very brief training and others will take more time. The training requirements for interventions should be made available to all educators so they can decide what additional skills they want to learn.

Some interventions will be overseen or organized by someone other than a student's teacher. For example, check-in/check-out (CICO) is a Tier 2 intervention provided to students who need additional feedback and support for meeting expectations for behavior that is organized at the building level. For interventions such as CICO, that are managed outside of the classroom, it is important for teams to create and document a process through which a teacher can request that a student gain access to an intervention and for the teacher to be kept abreast of the student's progress.

A final detail about the intervention chapters pertains to the level of review and oversight needed to approve the interventions listed. This topic should be discussed along the way as the team reviews and selects interventions, but it is also necessary to be sure that any additional approvals are obtained prior to publishing the list of interventions. A principal or superintendent who should have been consulted about such approval does not want to read that a program he or she has never heard about is being used. This is important not only because of the official approval process but also because once the list of interventions is published, teachers (and sometimes parents) will want to know how to access them. By listing interventions as selected and approved for use at each tier, the school or district is making a commitment to have those interventions available for all students who need them. Certainly no student will need to use all of the interventions, but there needs to be a plan for how they will be accessed and to ensure that such access is equitable. Handbook writing teams are encouraged to include language in the handbooks that reserves the right of the school or district to make changes to available interventions at specified intervals.

In some cases a school might have adopted a specific MTSS model and have developed an identity associated with that model. For example, a school might have undergone extensive training to use PBIS and refer to itself as a PBIS school. When such is the case, it is both acceptable and a good idea to include this in the handbooks and related materials. There are now, and likely to be in the future, specific applications of MTSS like PBIS and when a school has invested time and resources into learning and using a specific model, it is helpful to make that clear and also explain the specific vocabulary that goes with that model. Having such information in the handbooks helps staff to understand and value their training as well offer a consistent message and image about the school.

Alternatively, a school might have used a variety of different support procedures and models over the years but is no longer committed to just one of these. When this is the case, the handbooks provide an excellent opportunity to explain that history as well as the adopted methods that will be used moving forward. This is one of the reasons why it is good to have an introduction and history section in the handbooks. It can tell the story of what came before so that it is public information, and then guide users to the procedures that are now in place. Given that schools have a history of bouncing back and forth from one new thing to another, sharing the history and then "pinning the pendulum to the wall" with the remaining chapters of the handbooks can prevent future confusion (Tilly, 2009).

Schedules

A final important topic, but one that may not exist entirely in the handbooks, is the school's annual calendar for MTSS activities. All of the careful planning that the school will have done to set up its MTSS will have an associated calendar of what happens and when. If the handbooks will be updated annually, then the actual real calendar can be included in them. This allows all staff to be able to refer to one common document and know when screenings are scheduled to occur, what time of day seventh graders have skills block, and so on. In some cases, the handbooks might not be updated every year and then the calendar of events for each specific school year will need to be set up elsewhere. Regardless of where it is located, schools need to have a common calendar that includes all MTSS-related events. These include each of the three triannual academic benchmark screening dates, deadlines for when data will be returned to teachers, meeting dates for the grade-level and problem-solving teams, and other details related to the MTSS.

Most schools already have annual calendars established and the easiest way to get the MTSS-specific details added is to talk with the person who manages that calendar. Depending on the size of the district there may be guidelines about how items get added, but it is very important to MTSS success that certain activities be on the school calendar. With nearly universal access to the Internet in all U.S. schools, an excellent tool to use for making the annual calendar easy to manage is to set up a perpetual calendar. There are many free and low-cost computer softwares for setting up a calendar for a specific purpose or group. Google has a free calendar tool that allows users to add entries to multiple calendars or even subscribe to multiple calendars. These tools allow the creation of "perpetual" calendars that hold details about events that need to recur every year so that a planning team can just update the details from year to year. If the bus behavior assembly is held on the first Friday of every school year, then a recurring entry in the online calendar can remind the staff who run it the exact date it will be held this year, next year, and thereafter. Such annually occurring events should also be recorded as a perpetual calendar in the handbook (e.g., lunchroom expectations and procedures are taught the first day of each school year, playground expectations and procedures are taught the second day of each school year, etc.). Getting MTSS activities onto the school's calendar is an important step in the long-term sustainability of the MTSS. When such events become as regular and expected as July 4th and Thanksgiving, they are truly part of the school's culture and values.

HANDBOOK PUBLICATION AND DISTRIBUTION

Once the handbooks are done, they will need to be "published" in some way. These days, that usually means putting them onto a website. The benefit of web-based publishing is that the cost is low. The downside is that it may be invisible because the target audience does not know where it is or how to find it. It is up to school teams if they want to print copies of the handbooks. This is certainly an option if helpful. Most of the time, the final version will not be printed, but will be posted on the school's or district's website. There are some decisions about exactly where the handbooks are posted that are important to their use and value.

Public or Private?

All websites have the option to be either public or private. Public sites can be viewed by anyone in the world who knows the address. Private websites require a username and password. The team will need to decide whether the handbooks should be posted on the public or private side of the website. Posting the handbooks publicly means that all possible stakeholders and consumers can access them. Generally, such a posting means that the school wants to be known and held accountable for the practices in the documents. A private posting will be available only to those given access. This can offer the benefit of limiting access to those who are using the handbooks or need access to the forms they contain. The downside of private posting is that some stakeholders, such as parents and community members, will not know the MTSS process being used. We recommend posting the handbooks on the school's or district's *public* website and making it clear that the procedures were carefully developed with the goal of supporting every student. Making the handbooks public documents affirms that the school is serious about using tiered supports to help all students.

Another decision that the writing team will have to make is whether to post the handbooks as one complete document, or to break them into sections. The easiest solution is to do both, but the Internet manager or instructional technology (IT) department may have specific guidelines that direct what format will be allowed. The most easily downloadable type of file to post is a PDF. This stands for *portable document format* and is readable by virtually every computer in the world. Either the entire handbooks or each chapter can be posted in PDF format. The other major way to post content on the Internet is to use the webpage programming language called HTML. This means that the contents of the handbooks would be converted to actual webpages and posted. There are pros and cons to each format and teams should consult with IT staff about what is possible locally. Teams are encouraged to keep in mind how often they anticipate revising the handbooks when they select the format(s) for publication.

Finally, once the handbooks are posted on a website, the location(s) will need to be advertised and distributed so they can be accessed and used. It will be important to share the link(s) to the handbooks annually so that all staff can access and use them. If the handbooks are public, it is a good idea to share the link(s) with other stakeholders such as parents and district leaders so they can learn more about MTSS and how it helps students. The handbooks can be a very helpful and important staff training and development tool. The more prominently they are highlighted on the school's or district's website, the more they will be understood to serve as key resources and tools for student improvement. When possible, teams are encouraged to have the link(s) to the handbooks placed in multiple places on a website so that they are easy to find and use.

SUMMARY

Once an MTSS is up and running in a school, there is still more work to be done to make it truly lasting. In the process, there will be innovations that can make the tiered supports better and more effective for students. The same careful planning used for exploration, adoption, installation, and implementation needs to be applied to consideration of innovations and for sustainability over time. While some innovations will be worthwhile, others will not. School teams need to consider the evidence base, training, communication needs, and evaluation plans before adding any innovation into existing MTSS procedures. Similarly, teams must think about how to sustain MTSS over the long term. One of the best tools for making the MTSS "permanent" is to create one or more handbooks that will be used with current and future staff. Importantly, there should be separate handbooks or sections relating to academic and behavioral supports. These handbooks put all of the policies and procedures in one place and provide information for new staff to understand how all the parts of the system fit together. Once completed, the handbooks can be published in paper or on the website, and can serve to educate the public about how the school uses tiered supports for the benefit of all students.

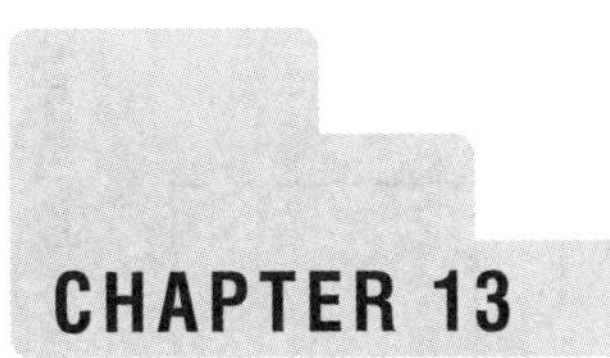

Schedules

In order for an MTSS to work, each school must review its daily schedule. Most of the time, it will be necessary for the schedule to be revised so that there is time in each day for tiered supports. Unless there is adequate time in the daily schedule for instruction and intervention, students cannot make progress. Revising the schedule is often one of the most difficult parts of setting up an MTSS. It is difficult because it requires change, coordination with others, and compromise. This chapter explains what amount of time is needed for supports at each tier, how to initiate and try out schedule options, and steps for evaluating schedule effects.

HOW MUCH TIME IS NEEDED?

Tier 1

Tier 1 is the most important part of an MTSS and it requires the most time. Although time allotments for all subject areas have not been developed, there is guidance on the amount of time required to teach reading and math. As part of its Reading First grant programming, the Florida Center for Reading Research (2013) reviewed available research on Tier 1 core reading instruction. This review resulted in the recommendation that all classroom teachers in grades K–5 spend 90 continuous minutes each day teaching reading. Figure 13.1 shows a sample elementary grade reading block schedule. As shown, not all of the instruction is whole class. The 90 minutes need to be organized into chunks of time for specific activities. In the case of reading instruction there are five main skills that the teacher needs to cover every day: phonemic awareness, phonics, fluency, vocabulary, and comprehension. How much of each of these skills will be included in each day's lesson depends on the age and instructional needs of the students.

<table>
<tr><th>Instruction</th><th>Range of Time</th><th colspan="6">Class Configuration</th><th>Examples of Teacher-Led Activities</th></tr>
<tr><td></td><td rowspan="2">25–45 minutes</td><td colspan="6" rowspan="2">Whole Group</td><td>Work with Core Comprehensive Reading Program (CCRP)</td></tr>
<tr><td rowspan="7">Initial 90+ minutes daily</td><td>Phonemic Awareness:
• Segmenting sounds
• Blending sounds
Phonics and Fluency:
• Sound–letter relationships
• Blending and decodables
• Dictation and spelling
Vocabulary and Comprehension:
• Robust Vocabulary Instruction
• Prereading strategies
• During-reading strategies
• Postreading strategies</td></tr>
<tr><td rowspan="5">TOTAL TIME: 45–65 minutes</td><td colspan="6">Small Groups (Group 1–5)</td><td>Group 1: segment sounds with Elkonin boxes</td></tr>
<tr><td>15–20 minutes</td><td>M</td><td>T</td><td>W</td><td>Th</td><td>F</td><td>Group 2: word building with letters and pocket charts</td></tr>
<tr><td>Session 1</td><td>1</td><td>4</td><td>2</td><td>5</td><td>3</td><td>Group 3: review complex blending strategies</td></tr>
<tr><td>Session 2</td><td>2</td><td>5</td><td>3</td><td>1</td><td>4</td><td>Group 4: reread the decodable book</td></tr>
<tr><td>Session 3</td><td>3</td><td>1</td><td>4</td><td>2</td><td>5</td><td>Group 5: choral reading of a new poem</td></tr>
<tr><td rowspan="2">Immediate Intensive Intervention</td><td rowspan="2">20 minutes</td><td></td><td>M</td><td>T</td><td>W</td><td>Th</td><td>F</td><td>Work with Supplementary Reading Programs (SRPs)</td></tr>
<tr><td>3x per week</td><td>1</td><td></td><td>1</td><td></td><td>1</td><td>Group 1 also needs iii, which requires work on the following skills in addition to work with Elkonin boxes:
• Phonemic segmentation with mirrors
• Common syllable patterns with spelling
• Reading a decodable book at instructional level</td></tr>
</table>

FIGURE 13.1. Sample elementary grade reading block schedule. Copyright by the Florida Center for Reading Research. Reprinted by permission.

In Figure 13.1 there are 25–60 minutes allocated for whole-class instruction. For a kindergarten class, the amount of whole-class instruction is most likely near 25 minutes, but for fourth and fifth graders, it's closer to 60 minutes. This reflects the students' developmental readiness and needs. In addition to whole-class instruction, the teacher needs to organize the time so that he or she can meet with each of the smaller reading groups in the class. These groups are based on the students' current reading level and learning needs. As the schedule shows, the teacher meets with three of the five groups each day. Having daily small-group time allows the teacher to work with students on skills that each one needs to improve. While the teacher works with a small group, the rest of the class will be doing either independent work or peer tutoring such as found in the program Peer Assisted Learning Strategies (PALS; Vanderbilt Kennedy Center, 2014).

There is much less research on how much time is needed for math, but the National Council of Teachers of Mathematics (2013) has recommended that elementary grade students should have at least 60 minutes of math instruction each day and that secondary students need about 70 minutes each day. Schools have begun to implement this recommendation by reviewing their schedules and creating time in the schedule. Research has shown that when schools allocate more time to math instruction, students' math scores improve (National Council of Teachers of Mathematics, 2013). Similar to reading, not all math instruction should be whole class, but should include small-group and individualized methods as well. In recent years there has been an increased awareness of the importance of math skills; in addition, related skills such as science, technology, and engineering have been recognized as important for students' future employability. Together, these skills are often referred to as STEM: science, technology, engineering, and math. STEM skills have been recognized as very important for success in the job market (Rothwell, 2014). If schools are going to support the development of STEM skills, they will need to be vigilant in developing daily schedules that will include enough instructional time in math and related areas.

Tier 2

By definition, Tier 2 instruction—also called intervention—is provided *in addition* to Tier 1 core instruction. This means that students have access to more instructional minutes so that they can strengthen skills. The good news is that adding instructional time at Tier 2 is a very effective way to support most students who are struggling. But it also means the time must be found in the schedule for Tier 2 sessions. Tier 2 time blocks for a given grade or class cannot overlap with Tier 1 instruction.

Most Tier 2 instruction is provided in units of 20–30 minutes, 3–5 days per week. The variations in time relate to the age of the students and amount of help needed. Younger students (e.g., K–1) cannot pay attention as long, so often will have 20-minute sessions. Older students should have 30 minutes per day at least four or five times per week. But it is important for teachers to realize that those students who are very close to meeting a learning goal may need support only a few days per week, while others might need daily sessions. The best way to make sure that all students who need help can access it is to include intervention blocks in the master schedule (Brown-Chidsey et al., 2009). Such blocks of time are sometimes called "skills" or enrichment blocks, and they offer a way to provide all students, regardless of ability, with support or enrichment. By having a skills block in the school schedule at a time when all students are available, the time can be used in flexible and responsive ways. Those students who need additional instruction to meet grade-level goals will have daily access to it. Those students who are doing fine, and even those who are ahead, can use the time to learn and explore advanced topics of interest to them. In this way all students benefit from having a skills block in the schedule.

As students transition from needing more to less help, the daily skills activities can be adjusted. If a student starts out needing support 5 days a week but then makes gains so that less support is needed, the skills block time can be varied across the week. For example, on Mondays, Wednesdays, and Fridays, the student might attend Tier 2 reading or social skills lessons, and on Tuesdays and Thursdays he or she can attend an enrichment activity. Often, there will be another student who needs support only 2 days a week and this student can share the intervention time with the first student. In this way, more students can access the help they need. If a student who was doing fine struggles with a new learning unit, he or she can be moved into a Tier 2 group for a short time to strengthen skills and then move back to enrichment once the skills are secure.

Tier 3

When an MTSS is implemented effectively, only a very small number of students will need Tier 3 support. Outcomes from schools where tiered supports have been in place for many years show that as few as 5% of all students are likely to need the kind of intensive support typical of Tier 3; this means about one student in each classroom of 25 students. Students who need Tier 3 have already been provided with many other supports, but they still need help. For this reason, Tier 3 time allocations and activities tend to be more individualized and unique. The other reality present at Tier 3 is that there are only so many minutes in each school day. This means that Tier 3 supports must be in addition to the Tier 1 core instruction as well as to what has been provided at Tier 2. In rare cases, Tier 3 support in an academic area might include a "replacement core" program. Replacing the Tier 1 core academic instruction program should be done only after data show that the student has not responded to Tier 1 + Tier 2 + Tier 3 implemented with integrity and with stable data points showing nonresponse. Tier 3 support for a behavioral concern could range from an individual behavior support plan, which typically would not require a modification to a student's schedule, to an individualized therapeutic or skill-building intervention, which would.

CHANGING A STUDENT'S SCHEDULE AT TIER 3

When adding time to the other instruction already in place, the biggest challenge is finding time in the student's schedule. Usually students are already booked for the entire school day. This means that the team must make a decision about whether to replace some current instruction with additional intervention. With regard to academic areas, there are two main scenarios that usually happen at this stage: (1) the student is making some progress, but not enough to catch up; or (2) the student has not made any progress at all.

Some Progress

When a student has made some progress with Tier 1 + Tier 2, but is not improving fast enough to catch up by the end of the year, it makes sense to see if adding additional instructional minutes to the existing Tier 2 intervention is the best answer. To do this, the student might have to give up another class for a period of time. Such a decision must always include the student and his or her parents. The amount of time needed will not always be known at the start of Tier 3, but it is practical to look for another 20–30 minutes such as is provided during Tier 2.

A strategic way to identify whether a current class or subject could be replaced with Tier 3 instruction is to find out if there are any nonessential classes that the student does not like. Often this means reviewing the student's schedule of special classes or electives. When a student has a nonpreferred class and it's possible for the Tier 3 instruction to be provided then, that is a good option to try. Keep in mind the function of doing so is to test the hypothesis that additional time with the same instruction will make it possible for the student to catch up to specific learning goals. The switch is temporary and designed only for catch up and not a permanent solution. The daily session length as well as the number of weeks during which the additional instruction will be provided must be decided in advance. In addition, it is essential that the interventionist collect weekly student progress data so that the effects of the additional instruction can be reviewed. In many cases, a brief student schedule change to allow participation in Tier 3 instruction will help that student to catch up. Once the student reaches mastery, the additional instruction can be faded and then ended.

Replacing Core Instruction

If a student's Tier 1 + Tier 2 progress data shows no improvement, despite instruction delivered with integrity, a more drastic change of instruction might be needed. In such cases, using more intensive instruction is recommended, or the team might consider using a replacement core program. A replacement core refers to an entirely different set of materials and instructional practices. For example, if a school's elementary level core reading program is Reading Street (Pearson Education, 2013), a replacement core would be another program altogether. So, if a third grader has significant reading delays, a replacement core might be the Sonday System 1 (Winsor Learning, 2013) or the Wilson Reading program (Wilson Language Training, 2010). The benefit of using a replacement core is that it can be implemented during the time blocks already present in the schedule. Usually, such a replacement core requires a significant time commitment (e.g., 120 minutes each day), so it is provided in place of Tier 1 and Tier 2. This approach means that the student does not give up any classes but has new instruction in place of core and Tier 2 instruction. In other cases, the replacement core might require additional time and the team must determine if such a time commitment is appropriate.

When using a replacement core program, the team is testing the hypothesis that the instruction that was already tried was not well matched to the student's needs and that another type of instruction will work better. Again, it is essential that the team collect weekly student progress data so that the effects of the replacement program can be known. Ideally, the student will show necessary gains with the new program. If this happens, then the team can conclude that the replacement core program, which typically requires 90–120 minutes each day, is what the student needs to meet the learning goals. If the student does not meet the goals with the replacement core program, then the team is advised to make a referral for a special education evaluation. This is because the student is struggling despite high-quality instruction implemented with integrity. When a student is not making effective progress despite coming to school regularly and getting good instruction, it's possible that the student has a disability that is affecting school outcomes. Some people might say it's not a question of whether the student has a disability, but what disability the student has. When a student has not responded to instruction over three tiers of support, these data alone suggest that there is some other reason for the student's difficulty, thus a comprehensive evaluation is justified. At this point more changes in the student's schedule are not logical because they are not likely to improve outcomes.

SCHEDULE PLANNING

Reviewing Current Time Use

In order to begin the process of developing an effective schedule that supports tiered interventions, school teams must first start by reviewing what they currently have in place. The number of people involved in this planning can vary, depending on the size of the school. For very small schools, having all teachers and related staff be part of the conversation makes sense. For medium and large schools, it is a good idea to have a smaller working group review the current schedule and come up with suggestions for change. When a smaller working group develops ideas for a revised schedule, it's best to get input from all teaching staff. One method is to use a brief anonymous survey that asks teachers for specific information about their schedule preferences. For example, a survey could have three questions such as (1) What is your least favorite aspect of the current schedule?; (2) What is your favorite aspect of the current schedule?; and (3) If you could change one thing about the current schedule, what would it be? Keeping the survey short increases the likelihood that more teachers will complete it.

Developing Options

When considering how to revise the school schedule it is important to keep the long-term goal in mind. Generally this means creating a schedule that includes the time needed for Tier 1 core instruction plus Tier 2 interventions every day. As noted above, Tier 3 interventions do not have to be included in the master schedule because they apply to a small percentage of students and are generally individualized. At the elementary school level, there should be 90 minutes per day for reading instruction and 60 minutes per day of math instruction. If the reading block also includes spelling and writing, it should be 120 minutes total. Additional course time blocks will be based on the number of other core courses (e.g., science and social studies) and special courses such as art, music, physical education, and world languages.

At the secondary level, the number of minutes per class is usually determined by the number of classes that students attend each day. Some secondary schools have fixed schedules with the same courses in the same order each day. Others have all classes every day, but the order of classes rotates. Still other secondary schools have "block" scheduling with longer class periods, but every class does not meet every day. Regardless of the type of schedule, the priority needs to be on making it possible for students who need additional assistance to access it every day. This is more difficult with block schedules because of the course rotation. One approach to ensuring that secondary students have access to tiered supports every day is to have a fixed "skills" block in the daily schedule. This time block is usually much shorter (e.g., 30–40 minutes) than long blocks, but it is enough time for struggling secondary students to get needed help.

Often, there is not a perfect schedule that works well for everyone, so it's helpful to develop several options that capture benefits and drawbacks to be discussed. Using feedback from a brief survey as well as the important goal of daily access to tiered supports, the schedule team can create one to three options. Having too many choices will make it difficult to narrow down a final selection. Yet, having some choices allows the staff to see the pros and cons of different schedules. Eventually, a decision about which schedule to use must be made.

This choice can be based on a vote by all staff, a vote by teaching staff, consensus of a committee, or a leader's individual decision. It's best to let all staff know how the decision will be made. Usually the final decision will not be popular with everyone, but the process should be objective and transparent. The benefit of having a vote to decide the schedule is that no single person can be blamed for the final choice. But, in some cases, there may be reasons outside the teachers' control that a specific schedule must be used and then the principal's choice must stand. Keep in mind that schedules can and should be changed at reasonable (e.g., yearly) intervals.

GRADE-LEVEL TIME BLOCKS

A scheduling feature that can be very helpful to the implementation of an MTSS is having some time each day when all the students in each grade are available at the same time. This can be helpful at all grade levels because it makes it possible to group students according to their current instructional need. In many secondary schools, flexible grouping for instruction is already in place. At the elementary level, such grade-level scheduling may not be as common because classroom teachers often have been able to control their schedules. Elementary school personnel in charge of scheduling are encouraged to consider making it possible for all students in each grade to have core instruction at the same time. For example, this would mean that all third graders would have math and reading at the same time each day.

The benefit of grade-level scheduling is that the students can then meet in groups according to their current skill level. In a third-grade class there might be some students still working to master addition and others already working on division. If the students can be grouped for math instruction according to what they need to work on now, both the teachers and students will find the lessons easier. A key distinction about such grouping is that it should not be a form of "tracking." Tracking was a widely used system for grouping students, mostly in high schools, that meant that students tended to be in leveled classes with the same students year after year. Tracking was found to be a form of segregation by the courts and significant efforts were made to end tracking (Welner & Oakes, 1996). As a result, the backgrounds and experiences of students in classes were more varied. The challenge for teachers when students are grouped heterogeneously is that it's much more difficult to teach well because the students have so many different instructional needs.

A solution to this dilemma is to use flexible instructional groups. In a seminal article about grouping, Esposito (1973) found that grouping itself was not helpful to students. Instead, it was when the teacher modified the *instruction* to meet the needs of group members that students benefited. This finding is exactly why using short-term flexible instructional groups is recommended as part of tiered supports (Castle, Deniz, & Tortora, 2005). In contrast to tracking, where students never had the chance to get extra support or "catch up" to higher-achieving peers, flexible instructional groups include specific steps for reviewing student data and regrouping students based on their changing learning needs. Flexible groups are typically built on students' initial screening and classroom data and then the groups are changed after every 6–9 weeks of instruction.

Flexible groups can be created in classrooms, but sometimes there are not enough students with the same learning needs to create groups that are about the same size. The solution to this problem is having all the students in the same grade have core instruction at the same time. If all the students in the same grade have core instruction at the same time, then students can be grouped across classrooms according to their needs. This method can be used for any area of the curriculum, but is most common in math and reading. The model is sometimes known as "walk to read" because the model was developed for an approach in which students walk to another classroom for certain parts of reading instruction. Importantly, no student should be in the same instructional group all year. In order to be sure that the instruction is matched to students' needs, teachers must meet and review student data on a regular basis. These data reviews then guide regrouping of students at frequent intervals.

PERSONNEL

Another component of planning effective schedules is to consider the personnel who will be available during each time block. The best model is when the most qualified staff work with the most struggling students. But it's not reasonable to expect teachers to be available to work with students every minute of the school day. Teacher and staff contracts include precise language about how many things can be included in each employee's workday. Nonetheless, it is important to think about which personnel will be available for supports during scheduled times. Classroom teachers usually have the most specific schedules. Their contracts typically specify how many minutes or subjects will be taught each day; what duties will be covered; and how many breaks must be provided, including lunch. Classroom teachers typically participate primarily or exclusively in Tier 1 core instruction only because it is their main job. But classroom teachers can differentiate instruction according to student needs during small-group times. This leaves the question of who will provide Tier 2 and Tier 3 supports.

Tier 2 Personnel

There are two main ways to think about Tier 2 personnel. The first is to use the model suggested above in which the most expert staff work with the most struggling students. The second is to use nonclassroom staff, such as paraprofessionals and specialists. It is better to assign the most expert staff to the most struggling students because those students both need and benefit from that expertise the most. School schedules sometimes present significant barriers to implementation of the preferred model. When this is the case, a specialist or paraprofessional could work with the struggling students. The types of staff who might be assigned to Tier 2 groups are special education teachers, specialists such as speech–language pathologists and other therapists, general paraprofessionals (i.e., those not assigned to students with disabilities), and trained volunteers. In addition, schools that receive Title I money can use Title I teachers for tiered supports as long as the requirements of the Title I grant are met. A provision in IDEA 2004 allowing special education money to support prevention of disabilities means that special education teachers can spend up to 15% of their time teaching tiered supports to general education students. Specialists also can provide such instruction, but they are more likely to support Tier 3 interventions since the cost for their time is higher than that of other staff.

An excellent and low-cost option for staff to run Tier 2 groups is trained volunteers. Such volunteers can include parents, grandparents, and high school or college students who can use the teaching time toward their required community service hours. Importantly, the volunteers must be trained well in order to ensure that their time with students will be effective. To be successful, it is best if there is a volunteer coordinator who recruits, trains, and schedules those who come in to work with students each day. While there are costs for having a volunteer coordinator, they are very small in relation to the benefits to the students. These costs are usually much less than those needed to pay additional teachers or paraprofessionals, making this an option worth considering. Although well-trained general paraprofessionals and volunteers can be a viable option for small-group instruction, a drawback is that the classroom teachers may not get to interact with struggling students as much. This can lead to teachers having less "ownership" of the students' progress over time. Teams need to think carefully about the benefits and drawbacks of each staffing option and work to address any limitations during training and implementation.

Tier 3 Personnel

When a student needs Tier 3 supports, he or she has likely been struggling for a long time. For this reason, it is common to see more advanced professionals working with such students. For example, it may be that special education teachers work with students at Tier 3 and not Tier 2 because of their training to support struggling students; as at Tier 2, special educators are allowed to do this for up to 15% of their time. As noted, a specialist could work with students at this level as a step in the process of determining why the student is struggling. When a specialist works with a student for the purpose of identifying the source of an academic difficulty, this is known as diagnostic teaching. The information from such teaching should be included in any evaluation reports about the student, including a comprehensive evaluation. Specialists with behavioral expertise, such as behavior analysts, should be employed at Tier 3 for students who are struggling with behavior. Students who need Tier 3 support for behavior typically require function-based behavior support that a specialist with behavioral expertise can provide. Volunteers can be used for some Tier 3 supports, but this is less common because of the higher level of need that such students have. Some schools might decide to use paraprofessionals and volunteers at Tier 2 and have Title I and/or special education staff work with students requiring Tier 3 supports. There are many options for how tiered supports are staffed, but it's essential that planning teams think about how the necessary time set aside for different types of instruction and intervention will fit with the personnel available at those times.

FIELD TESTING A SCHEDULE

Once the school has decided on a schedule, it is a good idea to try it out and see how it works. The "field test" is typically 1 week and gives staff the opportunity to see if the schedule works as well in real time as it appeared on paper. This is important because it provides time to see if there are any unexpected problems. For example, if the schedule results in a "traffic jam" in the lunchroom that causes lunch to run overtime, a change in some part of the schedule could be needed. Field testing can also be a way to compare two different schedules to see which is preferred. And, it can be used to give staff who are wary of a certain schedule a low-risk way to experience the schedule. If a schedule will be tested before being adopted, it is important to have a specific plan to collect data on how it worked. In addition, it is essential that there be a formal process for making the decision whether to adopt the schedule or not. If staff are told that a schedule will be tried out and then voted on, the promised vote must be held.

EVALUATING SCHEDULES

After a new schedule has been adopted, it is important to review how it is working over time. Just as data about the schedule should be collected along the way to developing a new one, each year staff should be asked to provide feedback on the schedule and whether changes are needed. There is no rule about how often the schedule should be updated, but it is a good idea to review it systematically each school year. Collecting feedback each spring allows time to review the schedule and make plans for the following year. Sometimes, small changes in external factors might affect how well the school schedule is working. For example, in parts of the country that experience snowy winters, the time that it takes for elementary students to get snowsuits and boots on and off for recesses can impact adherence to the schedule. Or an equipment change in the cafeteria could result in a different flow of students during lunch, which could influence whether students return to class on time. All of these are factors that could influence how well the school schedule is working.

SUMMARY

In order for an MTSS to work well, there must be careful attention to the school schedule. There must be time allocated for each tier of support. An effective MTSS includes ensuring that students have access to *additional* instruction when needed. Not only must there be sufficient time for Tier 1 core instruction, but there must be time in the daily schedule for 20–30 minutes of Tier 2 instruction as well. Tier 3 support is more individualized and is typically provided in addition to Tiers 1 and 2 (e.g., in place of an elective course) or as a replacement core program. In addition to creating a schedule that has time blocks for tiered supports, school teams need to consider which personnel will be available in each time block to work with students. Once a new schedule has been put into place, it needs to be evaluated to be sure that it is working as needed for students and teachers.

PART IV

Effective Instruction within an MTSS

Effective instruction is the foundation of all student success. This section describes the features of effective instruction and how teachers can customize their teaching for individual students. Chapter 14 provides a summary of important research about effective instruction. Beginning with a review of important work by John Hattie and colleagues (2009), this chapter describes the research that has identified the most effective classroom teaching practices. One of the challenges that teachers face is how to match specific teaching practices to individual student needs. Chapter 15 describes the instructional hierarchy developed by Haring et al. (1978), and provides examples of how teachers can use the stages of the hierarchy to design individualized instruction for each tier. While all students benefit from tiered supports, the growing number of English learners in U.S. classrooms requires educators to learn more about the unique needs of these students (Chapter 16). The best instruction in the world will be ineffective if not delivered accurately, and Chapter 17 describes both the importance of and methods for evaluating treatment integrity. Finally, Chapter 18 integrates the information in this section into an explanation of why educators must start by focusing on making Tier 1 instruction as effective as possible. This chapter makes the case for making 80% student success at Tier 1 a primary MTSS goal because, otherwise, the supports at Tiers 2 and 3 will not be sustainable.

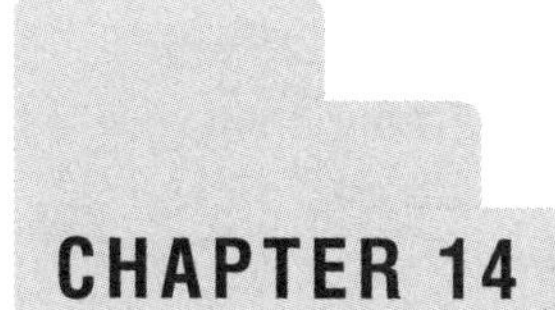

CHAPTER 14

What Is Effective Instruction?

Although politicians like to lament the poor state of instruction in U.S. classrooms, there is a strong body of research documenting effective instructional methods. Despite this strong research base, educators have a tendency to use a variety of methods, rather than stick with what has been shown to work. This chapter reviews the research base on effective instruction and identifies key teaching methods that must be present in all tiers of support. Importantly, instructional practices that are effective for academic skills are equally effective for social skills.

VISIBLE LEARNING

One of the best summaries of what is known about effective instruction was compiled by John Hattie (2009, 2011; Hattie & Yates, 2013). Hattie's initial work (2009) is a synthesis of over 800 meta-analyses of research studies about instructional practices. This review of effective practices is important because he and his team organized the results in relation to one key statistic: effect size (*d*). Effect size is a statistic that tells how much bigger the gains of one group were over another. Effect size is given in relation to the standard deviation (*SD*) of what was studied. This means that the effect size tells how much more variation one group had over another after normal variation (e.g., *SD*) is considered. In addition, Hattie categorized the general types of methods studied in relation to whether each method was specific to the (1) student, (2) home, (3) school, (4) teacher, (5) curricula, or (6) teaching. Of the top 10 methods, six were related to the teacher or teaching practices, two to the student, and two to the school. This chapter

TABLE 14.1. Top 10 Teacher- or Teaching-Related Instructional Methods Identified by Hattie (2009)

Method	Effect size (*d*)
1. Providing formative evaluation	0.90
2. Microteaching	0.88
3. Comprehensive interventions for students who are learning disabled	0.77
4. Teacher clarity	0.75
5. Reciprocal teaching	0.74
6. Feedback	0.73
7. Teacher–student relationships	0.72
8. Spaced versus massed practice	0.71
9. Metacognitive strategies	0.69
10. Self-verbalization/self-questioning	0.64

focuses on classroom-specific practices, so it will review Hattie's top 10 methods related to teachers and teaching (see Table 14.1).

An important distinction that Hattie (2009) makes is that when it comes to evaluating change in education, there needs to be an effect size of at least 0.4 for the difference to be meaningful. This is because in education some differences in outcomes can be expected regardless of instructional conditions. These typical changes are the result of student maturation over time (developmental effects) and the presence of a caring adult in the classroom (teacher effects). The combination of naturally occurring developmental and teacher influences creates an effect size of $d = 0.4$, on average. Since some changes (hopefully improvements) in student outcomes can be expected no matter what the instruction, Hattie set the criterion for meaningful student improvement to include effect sizes of 0.4 or greater. All of the methods listed in Table 14.1 meet this criterion. Also notable is that all of these methods are recommended MTSS practices.

Providing Formative Evaluation

Formative evaluation is a core MTSS practice that has abundant research support (Stecker, Fuchs, & Fuchs, 2008). Formative evaluation includes regular and frequent assessments of student progress. Hattie's (2009) review showed that formative evaluation had an effect size of 0.90, almost a full *SD*. One of the best types of assessment to use in formative evaluation is curriculum-based measurement (CBM; Shinn, 1989, 1998; Reschly, Busch, Betts, Deno, & Long, 2009). CBM is excellent for formative evaluation because the measures are brief (i.e., 1–4 minutes) and can work with any curriculum. Formative evaluation is important because it shows the student and the teacher exactly how the student is responding to instruction in real time. Usually, such assessments are used weekly to monthly to keep track of student progress during interventions. The measures can be scored immediately and this gives the student and teacher feedback about whether the intervention is working. Formative evaluation is an effective teaching practice because it provides a feedback loop about student progress.

Microteaching

This term refers to the practice of having a mentor observe short lessons and give feedback to the teacher. It is referred to as microteaching because the feedback is based on a small part of a larger lesson and not the entire lesson. This practice yielded an effect size of 0.88 in Hattie's (2009) research. The purpose of focusing the observation and feedback on a portion of the lesson is so the observer can give detailed feedback about everything observed. Microteaching is typically used with student teachers, but can be used with veteran teachers as well. The benefits from microteaching result from giving immediate feedback to the teacher so that he or she can change practices right away. Research on student performance as a result of observations of teaching does support the benefits of teachers being observed and getting immediate feedback. Taylor and Tyler (2012) found that Cincinnati students did better on districtwide assessments during the years following structured observations and feedback to their teachers.

Feedback

Feedback to students is a component of the formative evaluation methods described above, however, specific studies of teacher feedback to students show how important it is. Hattie's (2009) analysis showed that feedback produced an effect size of 0.73. Not all feedback is equal and other researchers have shown that feedback that is immediate and specific to the situation is the most effective (Konold, Miller, & Konold, 2004). When feedback is received right away, it is more likely to make sense to the learner because the context is more immediate. In addition, when the feedback addresses the exact steps or behaviors the student needs to correct, the student is better able to make the adjustment. Another aspect of feedback that is important is whether it is positive or negative. Research has shown that learners do best when there is a positive to negative ratio of 5 to 1. This means that for every negative, or corrective, feedback statement a teacher gives to a student, there need to be at least five positive (i.e., praise) statements (Bickford, 2012).

Teacher–Student Relationships

Researchers are sometime accused of explicating the obvious and in the case of research on teacher–student relationships, this may be the case. Studies show that the quality of the relationship that a teacher has with his or her students influences student outcomes; Hattie (2009) showed an effect size of 0.72 for teacher–student relationships. Specifically, the more that the teacher has person-centered connections with students, gets to know them as individuals, and works to develop an ongoing relationship with them, the better the student is likely to do in school. Positive relationships do not remove the need for good curricula and direct instruction, but they do help students stay engaged in the classroom and stay in school. It is important to note that the teacher–student relationship must be professional and respectful too. Overly permissive teachers are not any more effective than strict disciplinarians. Instead, it is teachers who get to know their students as people and who have clear, effective, and supportive (i.e., the classroom management system is structured so as to promote student success) classroom discipline who are the ones most likely to have positive relationships with their students.

Teacher Clarity

Hattie (2009) included one meta-analysis of teacher clarity. This refers to how well the teacher conveys to students exactly what is expected and how to do the assigned task. Notably, teacher clarity had an effect size of 0.75. This is important because for students to do well in school they need to know what is expected. It appears that when teachers are clear about expectations, students do better. Additional research on the importance of clarity is found in the PBIS literature. An important component of PBIS is having teachers work together to define the expectations of students in every setting in the school. When expectations for behavior are made clear to students across the school, important effects are seen. Not only do the number of behavior problems drop, but student learning outcomes improve (Sugai & Horner, 2010). Teachers making their expectations clear to students is an important component of effective instruction.

Reciprocal Teaching

Reciprocal teaching (RT) is a specific type of peer tutoring. It was developed by Palinscar and Brown in the 1980s and has very solid research findings (Hacker & Tenent, 2002). RT involves teaching the students a very specific way to work with each other in teams and Hattie (2009) found an effect size of 0.74. First the teacher must be sure that the students understand how to use the RT steps and then the students teach and coach each other using the methods. RT is specifically designed to help students understand and recall what they read, but can be used with readings in any content area. The way that RT helps students is by having all students engaged in discussing an assigned reading in small groups. By having all students participate at the same time, student engagement is increased. Student engagement is widely connected to improved student outcomes (Reyes, Brackett, Rivers, White, & Salovey, 2012). RT and similar peer-tutoring methods (e.g., PALS) are effective because they keep students engaged in the classroom and connected to the instruction.

Spaced versus Massed Practice

The type of learning activities that students complete in the classroom can have a significant effect on outcomes as well. Spaced practice refers to having students learn, then review, knowledge and skills in a planned sequence so that prior learning is reviewed at regular intervals. Massed practice refers to "cramming" types of activities that involve spending a large amount of time on one topic but then never returning to that topic again. Research has shown that spaced practice is best because it allows the learner to develop a deeper understanding of the material or skills. Hattie's (2009) research showed that it had an effect size of 0.71. Using spaced practice as a core teaching method benefits students because it means that prior learning is continuously reviewed and mastered (Toppino & Cohen, 2010). It is important that teachers know the difference between spaced and massed practice and can use each as appropriate.

Metacognitive Strategies

Metacognitive strategies are "tricks" or steps that learners use to make sense of information. Metacognition refers to the capacity to plan one's thinking. For example, before starting to work on a research paper about Napoleon, a student might recall to mind what he or she knows already and what search terms woube best to use to locate resources about Napoleon. Or, a student might create a mnemonic to help recall specific science terms. These are types of metacognition because they require thinking about thinking. Research shows that when teachers teach metacognitive strategies, students do better, with an effect size of 0.69. Such strategies can be taught in different ways. A teacher can model strategies by using a "think-aloud" approach. This means the teacher would say out loud what he or she is thinking when he or she engages in certain learning or study behaviors. Or, a teacher can also explicitly teach certain strategies or well-known "tricks" such as the acronym for mathematical operations PEMDAS: please excuse my dear aunt Sally. Teaching students not only the learning content, but also how to recall and study it, is an effective way to boost student learning outcomes.

Self-Verbalization/Self-Questioning

Another learning strategy that teachers can teach their students is self-verbalization. Self-verbalization is the practice of repeating ideas or steps to oneself while learning and using the information. Self-questioning is similar and involves asking oneself questions while learning. Although these had the lowest of the top 10 effect sizes (0.64), they are still effective methods that teachers need to prepare students to use. Both are types of self-regulation and have been shown to enhance learning by increasing engagement and rehearsal. Both of these strategies can be taught via teacher modeling as well as direct instruction. Students whose teachers show and use these strategies are likely to have better learning outcomes. As with the other methods in this list, it is important that teachers know how such methods work and be able to teach them to students. The presence of this and other learning strategy methods on Hattie's (2009) list shows the importance of teaching not only content but also teaching the process of learning as part of everyday instruction.

Comprehensive Interventions for Students Who Are Learning Disabled

For students who continue to struggle despite well-planned instruction, research supports using very specific and comprehensive interventions. Most of the research on these interventions has been conducted with students identified as having a learning disability (LD) and Hattie's (2009) work showed an effect size of 0.77. The findings from the research support the practice of using very intense and systematic instruction to help students with an LD achieve success. More recently, research has suggested that not only students with an LD benefit from such comprehensive interventions and that a reconceptualization of LD is needed (Fletcher & Vaughn, 2009). Regardless of whether students are labeled learning disabled, there are teaching practices that appear to benefit not only those with an LD profile, but also many other students. Notably, since the adoption of MTSS policies in U.S. federal and state laws, the number of students identified with a specific learning disability (SLD) has declined (Samuels, 2010). This decline may not be the result of MTSS practices, but does suggest that it is possible to support students with general education interventions.

All of the methods in Hattie's (2009) "top 10" teacher and teaching methods can be grouped into two main categories about their effects on learning: engagement or feedback loop. Table 14.2 lists the methods according to these categories. Both engagement and a feedback loop are essential for any learning

TABLE 14.2. Hattie's (2009) Top 10 Teacher- or Teaching-Related Practices Categorized in Relation to Student Engagement or Feedback Loop

Student engagement	Feedback loop
Comprehensive interventions for students who are learning disabled	Providing formative assessment
Teacher clarity	Microteaching
Reciprocal teaching	Feedback
Teacher–student relationships	Cognitive strategies
Spaced versus massed practice	
Self-verbalization/self-questioning	

to happen. A learner must be physically present and mentally engaged in order for the initial acquisition of learning. In addition, there must be feedback to the learner about whether his or her understanding or skills are correct in order for the student to achieve true mastery. Hattie's synthesis identified the most effective teaching practices across a wide range of studies. Many of the practices that Hattie identified are ones that are part of a specific type of instruction called direct instruction.

DIRECT INSTRUCTION

Other research provides additional information about specific instructional methods that have been shown to be effective regardless of learner age and the content of the learning. One of the specific types of instruction with a strong research base is called direct instruction (DI). There are really two types of DI: "big" DI and "little" di. Big DI refers to scripted instructional materials developed and published for sale. Little di refers to the methods embedded in the scripted lessons. Little di methods can be used with any instructional materials and include four main teaching practices: (1) teacher modeling, (2) errorless teaching, (3) immediate feedback, and (4) regular practice and review.

Modeling

Modeling refers to having the teacher literally show the students what to do. It is a way of showing students what to do before expecting them to do it themselves (Methe & Hintze, 2003). It is best if the teacher has a specific practice model or procedure in mind that includes all of the steps that students will be expected to follow. Modeling is most effective for skills-based instruction, but can be used for teaching knowledge as well. For example, in teaching handwriting, the teacher can use a chalkboard or projector to demonstrate to students how to form the letter *a*. In this example it is important that the teacher model the actual writing in front of the students and not just put up a preprinted letter *a*. Whenever the process for completing a task is important to doing it correctly, the teacher needs to model the entire process. By having the teacher model the steps, students learn both the process and the completed correct answer. For knowledge-based instruction, modeling is done by having the teacher give examples of the correct answer. For example, the teacher can model how to categorize animals by specific attributes (e.g., mammals, reptiles).

Errorless Teaching and Learning

After the teacher has modeled the knowledge or skill, having the students practice it in a way so that they cannot make a mistake is very effective. This method is known as errorless teaching because the way the information is presented reduces the chance of student error to virtually zero (Mueller, Palkovic, & Maynard, 2007). Errorless teaching involves having the teacher model the target knowledge or skill and then having the students repeat it back verbatim. This method was developed initially for use with students who have developmental disabilities, but it has been found to be effective with all learners. For example, if a teacher wants students to learn the meaning of the word *ornithologist*, an errorless teaching lesson would be as follows:

TEACHER: An ornithologist is a person who studies birds. What is an ornithologist?

STUDENTS: An ornithologist is a person who studies birds.

The benefit of errorless teaching is that students get the answer right from the very first attempt. This means that the information is never encoded incorrectly, and it takes less time than either having the students guess, or allowing the students to learn it wrong and then having to reteach the information correctly. When students practice something incorrectly, as is the case with an incorrect guess, it often takes many repetitions of answering correctly to replace that initial incorrect encoding.

Immediate Feedback

As noted in the section above, feedback is one of the most important aspects of learning. An example of the importance of feedback is found every time a learner asks him- or herself or the teacher "How did I do?" on an assessment. Learners want to know the outcomes of their efforts. Feedback is more effective when given more often than just after a test (Kulik & Kulik, 1988). There are two main types of feedback that teachers can give: corrective feedback and praise. Corrective feedback includes telling a student the right answer when a mistake is made. Praise includes telling the student that his or her efforts are good or the answers are correct. Both types of feedback are very important. Praise serves as a reinforcer to the learner and helps to maintain momentum. Corrective feedback tells the learner if his or her attempts are correct and informs the learner about what to do differently the next time. Importantly, if there is only one type of feedback, learning may be affected. When the student hears only praise, he or she will not know of his or her errors and will carry them forward into new learning situations. This means the student will most likely make errors again in the future. Alternatively, if the student only hears corrections, he or she may give up on the learning because it could seem like he or she is not doing well. A small number of errors may not derail the student, but when the student is making many errors and the teacher gives feedback only on the mistakes, the student's effort toward learning could seem useless.

Researchers have examined how many and which types of feedback students need to receive in order to learn best. Across disciplines, research is consistent in showing that a 5:1 ratio of positive to negative feedback is best (Walker, Ramsey, & Gresham, 2003–2004). When students hear five positives for every correction, they are likely to stay engaged in learning because most of the time they are hearing praise. But, importantly, they are not hearing only praise. While being told one is doing something right creates a nice feeling, it is not effective instruction when provided in isolation. As noted above, when only praise is given, students learn a false sense of accuracy. The result of only praising when there are actually errors is that students don't actually develop true mastery. This means they might end up embarrassed later when saying the wrong thing. In addition, it means that the student has to unlearn the wrong answer and learn the correct one. In the end that takes at least twice as much time as learning it correctly at the beginning. Providing immediate corrections to students lets them correct errors right away before errors become solidified.

Regular Practice and Review

The final method that is widely used as part of little *di* is regular practice and review. This refers to having students complete daily practice of what was just learned, as well as reviewing past learning. This is the independent stage of learning where students try out the knowledge and skills from the lessons. There should be a practice component to every lesson. In order for students to stay fresh with prior learning, the practice sessions should include some review work as well. If today's lesson was about multiplication facts but students had previously learned addition and subtraction, then the practice work should include a few of all the problem types learned so far. This will keep the prior learning fresh while adding new learning. Importantly, practice work should include only items that have been taught. This is because asking students to do work they have not been taught sets them up for failure.

One type of practice and review is homework. It is important to note that homework should not be the only time that students practice. Instead, there should be some practice time at school during class so that students can get teacher assistance as they try out the assigned work. Homework can be an effective way to give students more practice opportunities, but it needs to be assigned carefully (Cooper, 1989; Cooper, Robinson, & Patall, 2006). Research suggests that homework is not very effective until students are in about fourth grade. This is probably because before then their brains are not developed enough to carry over the events and learning from the school day to the home. As they approach age 10, students are better able to reflect on what they learned in school and practice it at home. Homework should only include items that have been taught and that the student knows how to do independently. This is because homework should be a time for independent practice. As noted above, asking students to do things they have not been taught is unfair and will usually lead to animosity between the students and teacher (Cooper, Lindsay, Nye, & Greathouse, 1998). Finally, homework needs to be collected and reviewed daily so that students get immediate feedback on how they did.

SUMMARY

The research on effective instruction shows that there are specific instructional practices that have been shown to work with most learners across settings. As school teams work on setting up an MTSS, it is important that they review and consider which types of instruction will be used at each tier. Notably, the instructional practices ideal for use at Tier 1 are the same that should be used in Tiers 2 and 3. Likewise, the methods used to teach academic skills should also be used to teach behavioral skills. Simply put, effective instruction is effective instruction. Some students will master the learning with Tier 1 instruction only. Others will need the additional instruction provided in Tiers 2 and 3. Two main characteristics of effective instructional practices are that they engage learners and include a feedback loop. Hattie's (2009) work showed that, despite the availability of many different teaching practices, not all work equally. The most effective teacher and teaching practices offer a place for teams to start identifying the instruction needed by their students. Additional research has supported practices known as DI, especially modeling, errorless learning, feedback, regular practice, and review. The combined use of learner engagement, a feedback loop, and DI will likely result in better outcomes for all students.

CHAPTER 15

The Instructional Hierarchy

Chapter 14 provided an overview of effective instructional practices. This chapter explains how various instructional practices can be put together to meet students' learning needs. While there is ample research on which instructional practices work, there is much less about how to design instruction in relation to student needs. Nonetheless, one specific model stands out as the best starting point for planning instruction. Known as the instructional hierarchy (IH), it is a way of understanding the "order of operations" that teachers should follow when teaching specific content. The IH model was first published in 1978 by Haring et al. in a book titled *The Fourth R: Research in the Classroom.* It was published well before the current era when education has a heavy focus on research and data. Haring et al. suggested that practices used in classrooms should have been validated through research prior to their use. While this may seem like a reasonable expectation now, in 1978, when the book was published, it was a novel concept. At the time, there were many "fads" in education and very little oversight to determine if practices actually worked.

For many teachers it is hard to think back to a time when they did not know how to read, write, or do math. Likewise, most future educators were quick to learn the social skills necessary to be successful at school. Most teachers were good students and learned academic and behavioral skills easily; their own success in school led many teachers into the profession. While some students will acquire new learning easily, not all will. At least 20% of the students in every school can be expected to struggle when new learning is introduced. Depending on the backgrounds of the learners, another 20% may struggle as well, meaning that as many as 40% of the students in any classroom will find new learning difficult. Coyne et al. (2004) have suggested that all educators have a responsibility to teach each and every student. All students have a right to effective instruction, but some students will "catch on" and understand instruction more quickly than others. For this reason, teachers must pay attention to the needs of each student in the classroom.

The first chapter of Haring et al.'s (1978) book includes a description of a proposed IH. This hierarchy is based on research that shows how students progress through predictable stages of learning. Think back to learning to drive a car. Most people did not become expert drivers right away. Instead they had to learn each step, practice each step, and practice again until it became automatic. As Haring et al. suggest, learning anything requires the same stepwise progression. If teachers are knowledgeable about the steps students go through when learning, they can modify instruction within each step, as needed, to help each student reach mastery.

The steps—or stages—of the Haring et al. (1978) IH are shown in Table 15.1. The four stages proposed by Haring et al. are acquisition, fluency, generalization, and adaptation. The importance of the IH is that it shows how learning follows a predictable sequence. Any learning will start with clumsy attempts to mimic the teacher, and then progress to more fluent approximations. If the student sticks with it, he or she can develop mastery and may progress to generalization and adaptation. The easiest way to envision the IH is in relation to music and sports. Learning to play a musical instrument usually includes a difficult early stage when just knowing where to put one's fingers and hands is hard. Similarly, learning a new sport requires having to learn the basic technique of how to hold a golf club or how to throw a ball.

TABLE 15.1. Haring et al.'s (1978) Stages of Learning

Stage	Description	Activities typical at this stage
Acquisition	Initial learning begins; the student learns the most basic steps of the overall skill.	The student learns the vocabulary and behaviors necessary for the skill. For example, in learning to play the guitar, the student would learn and use the names of guitar parts and mimic the teacher's hand positions.
Fluency	The student practices the skill and works toward independent use of the skill.	The student would have learned certain notes and practice playing them over and over. For example, the student might have learned the notes C and E and used them in a simple song, practiced daily.
Generalization	The student is able to use the skill with materials different from those used in practice.	The student is able to use the learned skills to play songs that the teacher did not teach. For example, the student might go to a music store and get the music to play a new song on guitar.
Adaptation	The student changes some feature of the skill to make it work in a new situation.	The student could create a new piece of music to be played on the guitar, using the skills learned.

Once a basic skill is learned, then it can be perfected only through practice. Malcolm Gladwell (2011) provided a description of the benefits of practice in his book *Outliers*. Those who become truly great at a skill get there by practicing, and practicing, and practicing. Gladwell uses examples from sports (hockey and basketball) and computing (Bill Gates and Steve Jobs) to point out that the people who become really good at any given thing spend many more hours practicing it than other people. Both Bill Gates and Steve Jobs spent countless hours playing with computers before they came up with their successful ideas. Michael Jordan spent day after day on the basketball court practicing his throws before he played in high school, college, or for the Chicago Bulls. These examples remind us that in order to be really good at something, practice matters. The same is true for academic and social skills. The way to get good at reading, math, or interacting with friends is to do those things over and over again. This chapter provides descriptions of each stage of the IH and then translates them into the instructional practices needed to support students at each stage.

STAGES OF THE IH MODEL

Acquisition

Acquisition of learning is the stage at which students are totally new to the concept or skill. In acquiring the information or behaviors, the students are "trying on" new things for the first time. Lesson components at the acquisition stage include teacher modeling and student attempts to mimic the steps. Depending on the complexity of the skill, the teacher may need to provide many models and repeat them. The goal of instruction at the acquisition stage is for students to learn what the target skill or knowledge is. Neither fluency nor mastery should be expected at this stage because the learners are still novices. The duration of the acquisition stage depends on the content and the students' learning histories. Some students will be ready to move on to the next stage before others. For this reason, teachers need to expect to do some reteaching during the acquisition stage.

Differentiation of instruction is one way that teachers can support students who don't readily "get" initial instruction at the acquisition stage. Sometimes, this will include reteaching in the manner that was first used. Other times, it may be that the student needs the information presented in another way. This is why teachers need to get to know their students and have data showing how students are doing on a regular basis. Ideally, when a student struggles at the acquisition stage, the teacher is able to use his or her knowledge of the student as well as his or her knowledge of the content to adjust instruction to match the student's need. When several students in a classroom are struggling at the acquisition stage, the teacher may want to reteach the lesson to all of those students while the rest of the class does independent practice. When more than 30% of students in a class do not "catch on" to instruction at the acquisition stage, that is a clue that the teacher needs to reteach the lesson to the entire class. In such a scenario, it is likely that there are other students who, unbeknown to the teacher, did not learn as intended. Yes, there will be some students who did get it the first time, but hearing it again will not be harmful.

Fluency

Once at least 80% of the students in a class have shown basic acquisition, it is time to move on to fluency instruction. This is the stage when the focus of the instruction is on having students practice the skill or knowledge. Fluency is a measure of a student's rate of task completion. Fluency is important because it shows how automatically a student can complete a task. In the case of reading, the more automatically that one reads words, the more brain power is available for overall comprehension. It is essential to understand that, in the case of reading, fluency does *not* connote speed reading. The actual reading speed of fluent readers will vary in relation to the text being read. But it will always be fluent if the reader is 95% accurate and understands what is read. For example, reading a novel by a favorite author will usually lead to faster reading than reading a textbook about a topic new to the reader. But, in both cases, the reader can be fluent if he or she reads carefully. Reading something too fast does not lead to effective reading. Instead, effective reading comes from reading at the appropriate rate.

Like acquisition, the best way to build fluency is with practice. However, the practice needs to be with materials at the student's current skill level. If the material is too hard, the student is likely to give up. If it is too easy, the student could be bored, lose interest, or think the work is silly. A helpful way to think about how to match students to their instructional level is to think of the "Goldilocks" rule: the material needs to be "just right" for the student's current instructional need. Just like Goldilocks was able to eat the porridge that was just the right temperature, students need materials that are just right for their current learning needs. It is essential that the materials that students use for practice are at just the right instructional level (Burns, 2007; Burns, VanDerHeyden, & Jiban, 2006; Parker, McMaster, & Burns, 2011).

For an MTSS to be effective, teachers must understand and use instructional levels when planning instruction and intervention. This means that the teacher needs to know what the student can currently do, and what the student needs to learn. Instructional levels are not established identically across all content areas. While it is essential that students understand at least 95% of reading content, Burns and colleagues (2006) have shown that instructional levels for math and writing need to be constructed differently. In the case of math, the number of digits correct in 1 minute is a helpful metric for instructional level. On the other hand, an instructional level for writing should be locally derived, as more research is needed to learn global writing instruction levels. In the meantime, teachers should know and use local instructional standards, including the CCSS, to work toward having all students meet the expectations.

Generalization

Once students have developed fluency, the goal is to help them generalize what they have learned to other settings. Generalization is important because it is what allows students to use school-based learning in settings outside of school (Stokes & Baer, 1977). Being able to behave, read, write, or do math in school is not very helpful if the student cannot do these things in other settings across the lifespan. For example, if a student can go to a restaurant, use appropriate social skills, read the menu, and mentally calculate whether an entrée is affordable, the student has applied what he or she has learned in school to a nonschool setting and generalization has occurred. Teachers can facilitate generalization by setting up classroom situations in which the students apply what they are learning in novel situations.

Unfortunately, generalization is notoriously difficult to achieve without explicit planning and teaching for generalization. A difficult aspect of this stage of the hierarchy is that in order to know if it is working, the student must be engaged with material that has not been seen before. The good news is that the more teachers prepare students for generalization, the more effective it will be (Alessi, 1987). Therefore, teachers need to include "tests" of student learning in daily activities as a way of monitoring whether generalization has happened. This can be done by including learning opportunities in daily classroom activities so that students can apply their skills in new situations. For example, a teacher could see if a student has generalized math skills by having the student count and enter the daily attendance. Similarly, students could be given menus from local restaurants to practice ordering their preferred items. Students generally like the chance to apply their skills in "real-world" situations, including those contrived in school.

Adaptation

The final stage of the hierarchy is adaptation. Not all learners reach this stage, but teachers should expect students to be able to adapt their learning to other circumstances. In essence, adaptation is when the student takes what has been learned and generalized (i.e., used) and changes it to meet a new need. For example, if a student has learned to read in English and then goes on to learn to read in another language, that is a form of adaptation. But adaptation can take many forms and be more creative. A student might have learned that there are theorems or "rules" in math and go on to develop his or her own theorem about a specific mathematics phenomenon. Or, a music student might go on to write his or her own pieces of music. This goes beyond generalization because it is not just performing an untaught piece of music but creating music itself. Adaptation is important in the IH because it is where innovation happens. Without adaptation, there would be no progress. Adaptation gives us a pathway to improve on what has come before. But in order for students to adapt, they must first acquire, become fluent, and generalize learning.

Differentiation

Differentiation of instruction refers to how a teacher adjusts how he or she works with each student based on the student's specific learning needs. The term captures the importance of making instruction relevant to individual students by making it *different* for each student's needs. In this regard, differentiation is a way of thinking about how to meet the needs of each student in each classroom (Huebner, 2010). Differentiation is the practice of adjusting instruction based on the unique needs of individual students, or small groups of students. In practice, this means that the teacher would use formative assessment data to identify which students need additional help. Then, he or she would adjust instruction according to the students' learning needs. Often, such differentiated instruction can be done with small groups of students who have similar learning needs. As shown by Vaughn et al. (2003), instruction differentiated for small groups of students is just as effective as instruction differentiated for individual students in most cases. Importantly, differentiation can be used at each stage of the IH.

Usually, differentiation includes having the teacher review what was taught at a given learning stage and having the student practice more. Most often, it is additional practice that will help the student make gains. Sometimes the student does not understand the basic concept being taught (e.g., adding involves putting things together). When this happens, the teacher needs to consider whether the student is ready for the current instruction, or needs to have additional instruction at a prior level to be ready for the current content. Pushing a student through instruction for which he or she is not ready will not be effective. The student will probably not be able to take advantage of the instruction. As noted above, the Goldilocks rule can be helpful when considering differentiation; what instruction will be "just right" for each student? Any steps taken to individualize instruction for one or more students are considered differentiation.

STANDARD PROTOCOLS AND PROBLEM SOLVING

Being able to teach according to the four stages of the Haring et al. (1978) model is an important skill for all classroom teachers. By knowing that learners progress through four learning stages, teachers will be able to identify each student's current learning need and provide instruction matched to that need. A helpful way to understand the types of instruction that students need was developed by Fuchs, Mock, Morgan, and Young (2003). In this article the authors suggested that there are two main ways to plan for students' instructional needs: standard protocols and problem solving.

Standard Protocols

Standard protocols are teaching methods that are used with all students, regardless of background. In order to become a standard protocol, a teaching method must have been shown to be effective across many research studies and with students from diverse backgrounds. Standard protocols follow the IH by helping students to acquire, become fluent, generalize, and adapt learning so that they master the knowledge and skills in a given area. Standard protocols are important because they utilize effective methods such as direct instruction to foster learning mastery for all students. Such methods are helpful to both students and teachers because they use "standard" methods for all students and yet achieve strong outcomes for most students. An example of a standard protocol is the use of an evidence-based core math program in the general education classroom. Such a program is designed to meet the needs of a majority of students by incorporating the four stages of learning. The value of standard protocols for teachers is that they reduce planning time for everyday lessons.

Problem Solving

For students who do not make effective progress with a standard protocol approach, a more intensive level of instruction is needed. Fuchs et al. (2003) suggest that such students need a problem-solving approach to instruction. This refers to the IDEAL model suggested by Deno (2013) and others. Problem-solving instruction includes two stages: identifying what instruction the student needs and providing it. Because of the more individualized nature of this instruction, problem-solving instruction is more time-consuming and intensive. Still, such instruction can be used at both the Tier 2 and 3 levels, depending on the student's needs. At Tier 2, the instruction would be provided for a small group of students who have similar learning needs. It would be called problem solving because it would be based on difficulties that the student experiences in the Tier 1, whole-class, environment. Students who do not make effective gains with Tier 2 will need Tier 3 supports. Here the instruction is likely to be individualized based on the student's response to Tier 2 intervention. At Tier 3, problem-solving instruction is much more intensive because it seeks to identify and use exactly the type of student–teacher interactions the student needs.

Triage

Another important principle that should be part of determining what type of instruction a student needs is triage. *Triage* is a French term, often used in medical settings, that reflects a series of steps used to determine the level of care that a patient needs. Most often it is used in emergency rooms, at crash sites, or in other critical care settings. It overlaps with the three-tier model in that patients are sorted into three levels of need. Tier 1 patients need no or little care, Tier 2 need some care, and Tier 3 need immediate and intensive care. This same idea should be applied in school settings to determine the instruction that a student gets. Students who are on grade level and meeting expected learning standards meet a triage level 1 (i.e., Tier 1). Students who are a little behind and could catch up with daily extra instruction meet a triage level 2 (i.e., Tier 2). This means that they are likely to make the needed gains in the current school year with Tier 2 supports. But students who are so far behind the learning standards that they will need intensive instruction to catch up are at triage level 3 (i.e., Tier 3). This means that they need intensive additional instruction right away.

It is very important that MTSS teams understand and use the principles of triage in their work. If a student has significant skill gaps on the first day of school and is 2 or more years behind, the student should receive Tier 3 intervention right away. Requiring that the student participate in Tier 2 supports does not make sense because that will only extend the amount of time that the student remains behind. By definition, Tier 2 supports will not be intensive enough to help a student make 2 or more years of growth in 1 year. Instead, the student needs immediate intensive instruction with weekly progress monitoring. Many such students will make needed gains when provided with Tier 3 supports. Delaying intensive intervention for such students will only perpetuate the "Matthew effect" whereby they fall farther behind their classmates.

By combining the principles of standard protocols, problem solving, and triage, an MTSS will be most effective. Standard protocols should always be used at Tier 1 and most of the time at Tier 2. This is because such instruction involves groups of students with similar learning needs; using one instructional program with all of the students is likely to be both effective and efficient. Instruction based on problem solving is most often used at Tier 3 and in special education. This is because students needing more intensive instruction have not responded to the standard protocol and individualized methods are needed. In order to decide which type of instruction students need, teams should utilize a triage method so that students are matched to the instruction that meets their current level of need. Students who are significantly behind should not have to wait to receive the instruction that they need now. Another tool that teachers can use to determine a student's instructional need is to consider skills and performance deficits.

SKILLS AND PERFORMANCE DEFICITS

In addition to helping teachers identify and use standard protocol and problem-solving methods, the IH offers a way to help educators understand whether a student's difficulties are the result of skills deficits or performance issues. In pioneering work, Amanda VanDerHeyden and Joseph Witt demonstrated that students usually have difficulty in school for two main reasons: a lack of skills or a lack of interest (VanDerHeyden & Witt, 2008; see also Chapter 7). Also, known as the "can't do, won't do" assessment, this approach evaluates whether a student is not completing work because he or she does not know how (i.e., can't do it) or because he or she does not want to do it (i.e., won't do it). The "can't" situation means that the student has a skills deficit and does not know how to complete the assigned task. The "won't" situation means that the student knows how to complete the task but does not want to do so.

VanDerHeyden and Witt (2008) provided directions for how to conduct an assessment to learn whether a student's difficulties are because he or she "can't" or "won't" complete assignments. The main components of such an assessment include having the student complete assigned tasks under two conditions. First, the student is asked to complete the activities under typical classroom conditions; this is the "can't" condition because it tests whether the student does any work at all. Next, similar tasks are assigned, but this time the student can earn prizes for completing the tasks; this is the "won't" condition because it tests whether the student will do the work if there is an incentive. The "can't" condition shows if the student has the basic skills needed to complete assigned work. The reason that the "won't" condition is helpful is that it mimics a situation in which a student clearly knows he or she can do something but is not motivated to do it. If a student is able to complete the assigned tasks initially, then the student's skills for the area of concern are understood to be intact. But if the student is successful with the assigned activities only under the "won't" condition, then the assessment suggests that the student has the necessary skills but will complete the tasks only when motivated to do so.

Students who don't (yet) have the skills will need direct and systematic instruction in the specific skills that are lacking. Students who have the skills but perform them only when reinforced, will benefit from an incremental reinforcement program. Such students need instruction that helps them to use the skills across all conditions where they are needed. Interventions for students with performance deficits include using reinforcement strategically and less often over time so that the student uses the requisite skills based on task demands and naturally occurring reinforcers and not only in relation to personal interest. Importantly, using reinforcement to help students complete work must be done correctly so that the student does not develop either dependence or saturation. The key to effective use of reinforcement as part of such instruction is to fade it over time so that the student eventually completes work independently.

SUMMARY

The IH is a four-phase progression of learning stages. In most cases, learners progress through each stage to become more proficient in many areas. It is important that teachers are knowledgeable about the hierarchy because it has implications for differentiating instruction. If instruction is too hard or too easy, in other words if it is not at the right instructional level for that student, it will not be effective. Teachers must understand how to match a student's current stage of the hierarchy to instruction. In order for teachers to know students' needs, they need to use and interpret formative assessments of learning. These assessments will show whether a student needs differentiated instruction; this includes reteaching and providing additional opportunities to practice so that students can become proficient. Students might demonstrate either skills or performance deficits. A skills deficit refers to a student not possessing the skill required for a certain assignment. A performance deficit refers to a situation in which a student has the skills necessary to complete an assignment, but fails to do so. Performance deficits suggest that a student is not sufficiently motivated to complete the task. In such cases, the student is likely to need external motivation in the form of temporary reinforcement until the completion of the task becomes inherently motivating. Use of Haring et al.'s (1978) IH, in combination with can't do/won't do assessment, helps teachers know whether students have skills or performance deficits and how to address individual learning needs.

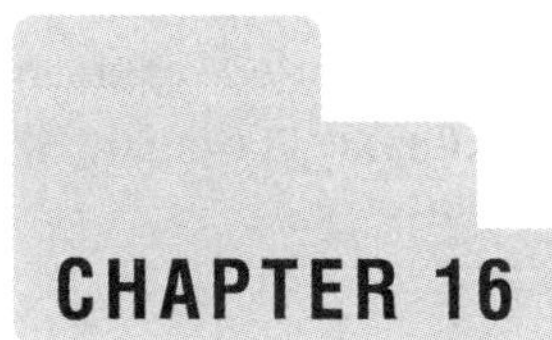

CHAPTER 16

Effective Instruction for Students Who Are ELLs

English language learners (ELLs) are the fastest growing group of students in U.S. schools (National Center for Education Statistics, 2013b). Already in California, students whose first language is Spanish outnumber those whose first language is English. Although the number of Spanish-speaking students continues to increase, English remains the dominant language in terms of economics and business (Castro, 2013). For example, Castro reported that 83% of websites worldwide are in English, assuring its role in world affairs. Learning English remains an important step for those who wish to be successful in U.S. and international business and politics (Genesee, Lindholm-Leary, Saunders, & Christian, 2005). In U.S. schools, the dominant language of instruction is English. The U.S. Department of Education requires schools to keep track of data on English learners and provides supports for these students under Title III of the Elementary and Secondary Education Act (Federal Register, 2008; U.S. Department of Education, National Center for Education Statistics, 2010).

Despite efforts to help students learn English, there is a legacy of too many students who are ELLs ending up in special education (Gravois & Rosenfield, 2006; Klingner et al., 2005; Samson & Lesaux, 2009; Shifrer, Muller, & Callahan, 2011; National Center for Education Statistics, 2013b). The main reason that ELLs end up in special education instead of getting more English instruction is that it is sometimes difficult to distinguish between a learning disability (LD) and language learning difficulty (Barrera, 2006; Barrera & Liu, 2010; Collier, 2011; Figueroa & Newsome, 2006; Lesaux, Lipka, & Siegel, 2006; Wagner, Francis, & Morris, 2005; Wilkinson, Ortiz, Robertson, & Kushner, 2006). Identifying an LD requires having a student complete tasks using language. If a student's language skills are not strong, then the accuracy of LD identification might be compromised. For this reason, researchers have long recommended caution when conducting evaluations of ELLs for special education (Ortiz, Flanagan, & Dynda, 2008).

FEATURES OF LANGUAGE DEVELOPMENT

In order to understand the needs of students who are ELLs, teachers must understand certain aspects of general language development. Ideally, all teachers would have taken a course in language development, but this may be impractical. Instead, the work of Cummins (1981) is very helpful in making sense of how school-age children develop their language skills. Cummins suggested that there are two main stages to second language development: BICS and CALP. BICS stands for *basic interpersonal communication skills*. These skills are the ones most essential to daily survival. For example, knowing how to locate a bathroom in another language is an example of BICS. BICS are the skills that ELLs need in order to get through each day in a second language. By contrast, CALP are *cognitive academic language proficiency* skills. CALP refer to advanced language skills needed for students to participate in instruction using a second language. CALP include being able to read advanced texts and write fluently in another language. BICS and CALP are not the definitive description of language development, but they are helpful tools for classroom teachers because they shed light on how ELLs often use language in classrooms.

For example, BICS are often observed in students soon after they join a new classroom. They might be seen asking classmates questions about typical daily activities or what is for lunch. Such questions have to do with getting through each day. As those readers who have traveled internationally will understand, ELLs are typically quick to learn and use a few key words and phrases that facilitate classroom survival. Knowing how to find food and a bathroom are very important survival skills. It is estimated that ELLs will develop BICS in 1–2 years. They are the first new language skills to emerge because they are survival related. By contrast, the language skills necessary to be a successful student in a new language take a much longer time to develop. Importantly, CALP skills are built on top of BICS, so the latter supports the former. But the time and effort needed to be a strong student in a new language is very different from finding the bathroom and a restaurant.

BICS

By definition, BICS are very basic skills related to getting through each day in a new language environment. It is not a surprise that ELLs learn these first, as BICS help the student to feel comfortable with the new environment and be able to get basic needs met. Classroom teachers often observe that ELLs are using BICS on the playground, in the lunchroom, or in side conversations with classmates. A teacher might think that when a student can speak with English-speaking classmates, "hang out," and be popular on the playground, that the student has mastered English. Unfortunately, this conclusion is premature. While the student may have learned how to use BICS to make social connections and survive each day at school, that is not the same as mastering academic English. BICS require an informal and functional version of English that lets others know one's intentions and plans. This is very different from CALP, which involves mastering formal English. Formal English has many rules that go beyond the skills necessary for BICS. Instead, CALP serves to provide a thorough foundation in the rules of English. Consider how students raised in English-speaking countries like Canada, the United Kingdom, and the United States take many years to master the formal rules of English. While children usually start speaking at age 2, using language correctly takes many years of practice and learning. Indeed, most of the elementary school years (grades K–5) focus on learning and using the rules of one's language. For this reason, it is imperative that teachers understand the academic aspects of language use.

CALP

CALP is the mastery of a language to such an extent that one can learn in that language. Typically, this happens by default in one's first language. When a student is learning another language, it takes time to reach the point of being able to think and function in that language. That is why CALP takes much longer to master than BICS. Every language has many rules that are important to making meaning of words. ELLs need time and support to reach CALP. Cummins (1981) suggested that CALP requires 5–7 years to develop. This is due to the more complex language rules and demands of academic language. In order to assist ELLs, it is imperative that teachers understand the difference between BICS and CALP and have skills to teach ELLs in general education classrooms.

The reason that CALP takes so much longer is that it requires mastering the rules of a language well beyond the limited functional use of certain words. There may be an excess of grammar rules in any language, but to become an expert and strong student in that language, knowing these rules is required. CALP activities include many of the tasks that students in U.S. elementary schools experience when learning formal English. Learning things like how English verbs are conjugated and the spelling of irregular verbs and nouns are tasks that must be mastered and that English-native students take years to learn. The challenge for ELLs is that they often enter the education system later than their English-native classmates. If a non-English-speaking student moves to the United States in first grade, he or she is already 6 years behind her classmates in learning oral

English. Imagine what it's like for an ELL to enter a U.S. school in eighth grade. This is why additional supports are provided for ELLs of any grade. It's not easy to learn both the language and the content at the same time. Although recent analysis has provided more details about the needs of ELLs (Dixon, Zhao, & Shin, 2012), it is clear that such students require additional supports to be successful in school.

EFFECTIVE INSTRUCTION FOR ELLs

The good news is that an MTSS appears to be an effective way to support ELLs. Although Scott et al. (2014) found that states do not presently have many tiered programs developed for ELLs, other research shows that tiered supports are actually very effective for such students. A small number of studies have shown that when tiered supports are put in place for all students, ELLs benefit the same or more than other students (Cirino et al., 2009; Gilbertson, Maxfield, & Hughes, 2007; Kung, 2009; Leafstedt, Richards, & Gerber, 2004; Orosco & Klingner, 2010; Vaughn et al., 2006). Two factors likely account for the effectiveness of tiered supports among ELLs. First, ELLs typically benefit from additional instruction time so that they can master both English and the content material. An MTSS is set up so that additional instruction is available to students every day (Linan-Thompson, Cirino, & Vaughn, 2007). Second, students who are learning another language, English or otherwise, benefit from direct and systematic instruction of that language (Ortiz et al., 2008). An effective MTSS includes using EBPs at each tier. Direct and systematic instruction has been shown to be an EBP for teaching English and other languages. Thus, tiered supports are poised to offer benefits for ELLs.

Despite the promise of benefits for students learning English, an MTSS developed and practiced among native English speakers may not fully address all the needs of ELLs. Scott et al. (2014) found that most states have little or no specific procedures or guidance for how to apply tiered supports for culturally and linguistically diverse (CLD) students. Importantly, language is just one part of the diversity that students might bring to school. Culturally responsive instruction involves the teacher understanding the students' cultural values and teaching in ways that take those values into account (Cartledge & Kourea, 2008; Ortiz & Artiles, 2010; Utley, Obiakor, & Jeffrey, 2011). Although tiered systems have been found to be effective for students learning English, there is virtually no research on the effects of an MTSS in relation to culture and ethnicity (Blanchett, Klingner, & Harry, 2009; Haager, 2007; Klingner & Edwards, 2006; Ortiz & Artiles, 2010).

Implementing tiered supports that are culturally and linguistically sensitive requires more than assuming that the general MTSS procedures will work the same for all students. It is important that school teams consider and plan for how tiered supports can be appropriate for all students in the school (Ortiz, Wilkinson, Robertson-Courtney, & Kushner, 2006; Rinaldi & Samson, 2008). Specific details that teams must think about include considering what types of overall language instruction are needed, in addition to Tier 1 and 2 supports. While EBPs have been shown to work for ELLs, they may not be sufficient without other supports. For example, should explicit instruction in oral language also be provided (Pollard-Durodola, Mathes, Vaughn, Cardenas-Hagan, & Linan-Thompson, 2006)? The general working dynamics of the tiered supports need to be discussed as well. How and when are parents included in the process? What kinds of outreach for parents in certain cultural groups might be needed? Essentially, there needs to be planning for every step along the way to provide supports for all students.

A few guiding principles have been developed that can be used by teams as they plan for an MTSS that will work for all students. First, it is best to examine and teach language skills before considering or assuming that a disability is present (Ortiz et al., 2008). States' policies concerning how to evaluate ELLs for an LD vary a great deal (Scott et al., 2014), but there is agreement that language must be considered first. This is because some form of language is necessary to evaluate other cognitive and academic skills. Educators will need to know the relative strengths of the students' overall language development before judgments about the presence of a disability can be made. In some cases, especially when a student has very recently moved to a U.S. school, it can be best to start by monitoring the student's progress in learning English. Such progress data are generally more reliable than one-point-in-time assessments and such data indicate the general strength of the student's learning capacity.

Second, when a student has been provided with evidence-based English instruction but is not making effective progress, a full psychoeducational evaluation might be needed. In such cases, it is important that the team consider who is best qualified to conduct the evaluation (Barrera, 2006; Figueroa & Newsome, 2006; Ortiz et al., 2008). Ideally, a psychologist who is fluent in both English and the student's first language will be available. Sadly, there are not enough bilingual school psychologists to meet the needs of all bilingual students. When no bilingual psychologist is available, a translator might be an option (Wagner et al., 2005). Translators can provide a bridge between the student and assessment materials, however, translated items do not always mean exactly the same thing in another language. For this reason, school psychologists and other examiners must be very careful about who conducts the translation and whether the translation conveys the intended meaning.

In addition, care should be taken when selecting translators. Sometimes, it might be tempting to use a family member as the translator. This is not recommended because the family member will find it difficult to be totally objective. Instead, a school-recognized translator who has been formally trained in school-based translation requirements is the best choice. When a formally trained translator is not available, the team will need to decide how best to proceed with the evaluation. It may be best to delay the process until a trained translator is found. However, such a delay might cause more harm to the student than moving forward with a less-skilled translator; in such cases the evaluator will need to verify the meanings of words to ensure assessment integrity. Ideally, all translated material should be converted back into English using "backward translation." This means checking the meaning of the translation when put back into English; this step allows for confirming that the meaning was not lost in translation.

SUMMARY

Students who are ELLs can benefit greatly from an MTSS, but additional considerations are needed to ensure that the practices take into account their learning needs. Some research shows that tiered supports can be effective for ELLs, but few states have policies requiring additional steps to include ELLs in planning an MTSS. Although initial research suggests the benefits of direct and systematic instruction offered with additional intervention sessions, very little research has examined how well an MTSS supports students with other types of diversity, including cultural diversity. As schools move forward in developing MTSS practices, attention to how the plans fit with the values and norms of CLD students and their families is needed.

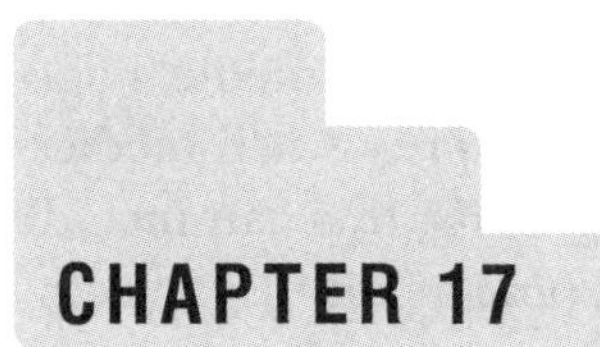

CHAPTER 17

Treatment Integrity

The benefits of effective instruction are easy to identify in student outcomes, however, such benefits are not possible if instruction is not implemented correctly. This chapter describes the concept of treatment integrity and how effective materials are useless if they are not used correctly. We have selected the term *treatment integrity* instead of *treatment fidelity* because the word *integrity* means both "the quality of being honest and fair" and "the state of being complete or whole." By contrast, the word *fidelity* comes from the Latin root *fides* and means faithful. Although being faithful in using interventions might be a good thing, it connotes beliefs rather than actions. While the concept of intervention rests on the belief that educators can and should alter students' trajectories, intervention is ultimately about taking action. Recent research on treatment integrity has shown that teachers can evaluate integrity without interrupting instruction by collecting teaching accuracy data as a routine part of instruction (Sanetti & Kratochwill, 2013). Despite such evidence, the extent to which teachers actually collect such data remains unclear (Sanetti, Gritter, & Dobey, 2012; Sanetti & Reed, 2012). Yet, treatment integrity is of singular importance to an MTSS because the data documenting student performance are only as useful as the integrity of the instruction provided (Fryling, Wallace, & Yassine, 2012). As schools work to set up an MTSS, they must pay attention not only to ensuring treatment integrity, but also to documenting it so that the reliability of gathered data can be known. Ideas for how to establish a school culture that values treatment integrity are provided.

BASICS OF TREATMENT INTEGRITY

Treatment integrity is a concept and practice that evolved from work in clinical and medical settings. In such settings, physicians and psychologists frequently face the challenge of having patients complete treatment steps. For medical doctors, this can include having patients who do not take their prescribed medications. For psychologists and other mental health professionals, this can include patients who do not complete essential steps such as keeping a daily log of activities. In such cases, the intended treatment, as planned by the clinician, was never implemented. When this happens, it is impossible to know if the treatment (would have) actually worked. Educators face the same difficulties, but with different vocabulary terms. We have students who need to complete lessons and assignments. When the lesson or assignment is done differently than intended, then there is no lesson/assignment integrity. Most teachers have faced the frustration of having students who do not follow-through on some action steps that likely would have helped them improve. This is a lack of treatment integrity in action.

It is pretty easy to understand the effects of treatment integrity when explained in relation to one student at a time. The most extreme form of student-specific lack of treatment integrity is when a student does not come to school on a regular basis. Such truancy most likely has a direct effect on that student's learning outcomes because he or she is not there to benefit from instruction. But there are implications from treatment integrity at the whole-class and small-group levels as well. Consider the example of a middle school that has adopted a specific science curriculum and materials. If there are three seventh-grade science teachers at the school, in order for students to have equal access to that adopted curriculum, all three of the teachers need to implement and use it in similar ways. What would be the outcome if one of the science teachers decided he or she did not like the unit on magnetism and left it out when he or she taught? What if he or she left out other topics, too? What would happen when the students took the spring state-mandated assessment? If there are questions on that assessment about magnetism and other omitted topics, the students in the class that never had that instruction would be disadvantaged. When there is an official, approved curriculum or program that all teachers of a level or subject are expected to teach, and some of them don't teach it, there is a lack of "treatment" integrity because some students will be denied access to the learning intended.

One of the reasons that states adopted a unified set of learning standards in the 2000s, which have recently been replaced by the Common Core State Standards (CCSS) in most states, is that having consistent and unified teaching goals makes it much easier to know what all students are expected to learn. In this regard, the lessons that provide instruction in the standards are a type of treatment for students. By requiring that all children attend school at certain ages, and by having state-adopted learning standards, our society expects that children will acquire the knowledge and skills necessary to become effective and engaged citizens. But the combination of these sets of laws means that there must be careful coordination of instruction so that all students have equal opportunities to benefit from instruction and meet the standards.

TREATMENT INTEGRITY AND MTSS

An MTSS puts a huge emphasis on having and using student data to evaluate whether instruction is working. But the data from each tier are only as good as the instruction provided. Technically, the outcome data reflect whatever instruction happened along the way. If all the teachers were using the methods and materials adopted by the district for their grade and subject area, the system should work well. But what if some teachers teach other things or in other ways? There is an ongoing discussion among teachers about whether having mandated core curricula eliminates all creativity from their work (Webster-Stratton, Reinke, Herman, & Newcomer, 2011). This debate cannot be answered here, but is important to acknowledge because achieving treatment integrity requires sufficient adherence to a planned lesson that all students can access, while simultaneously differentiating instruction enough so that each student's needs are met. This is very hard to do and it is what makes teaching a tough profession. Coyne et al. (2004) addressed this issue when they discussed the challenge of reconciling the needs of *all* students with those of *each* student. Teaching in ways that all students in a classroom benefit, while also paying attention to the needs of individual students, is not easy, but it is what teachers must do to maximize their impact on students.

Each classroom teacher is charged with the task of providing instruction for all of the students in his or her classroom(s). Many teachers have suggested that this means they end up "teaching to the middle," meaning they provide instruction for those students who are average but not for those who are above or below. It is logical that teachers would end up teaching to the average and "middle" students because they make up the majority in each class and usually are ready for the learning standards at each grade. But what does this mean for students who are well ahead of or far behind their classroom peers? For these students, there is an issue of *teaching integrity* because the instruction most likely provided to them does not match their needs. Although core curricula and standard protocols can be a part of supporting the needs of all students, there will always be a need to differentiate such teaching so that students across the range of abilities have access to effective instruction.

USING SCIENCE TO SUPPORT TEACHING INTEGRITY

The term *teaching integrity* is really the same as treatment integrity, but focuses on how it is possible to provide instruction that will work for all students. The good news is that an MTSS is a way to achieve effective teaching integrity. As described in earlier chapters, there is a body of research that defines both effective instruction (Chapter 14) and how to organize instruction to support all students (Chapter 15). These methods are the result of many decades of scientific research about effective instruction. An MTSS is an enhancement of this research because it utilizes the core methods, but also provides supports based on each student's level of need. Instead of offering only one instructional program with the assumption that it will work for all students, an MTSS recognizes that students' needs differ and provides multiple levels of support for that range of needs. But, to be effective, the supports need to be provided with integrity and according to the evidence base by which they were developed.

An effective MTSS is the combination of effective instruction with differential response to student needs over time. The methods incorporated into an MTSS should have been tested in research studies in order to offer the best instruction available. Thus, they provide a way to bring science to teaching. However, they will work as intended only if used as intended. This is why teaching integrity is so important. When teachers adapt steps of a research- or evidence-based teaching method, they violate the rules attached to evidence for that method. As discussed in Chapter 12, innovations are an important part of science, but they must be evaluated using the same scientific process used to validate the overall method they seek to improve. The rest of this chapter describes steps to affirm teaching integrity so that the data collected as part of the MTSS will be useful.

TEACHING INTEGRITY AT EACH TIER

Each tier of an MTSS requires somewhat different steps to make teaching integrity happen. Across all tiers, there are two components to integrity that are important: training and observation. These are first explained and then examples from each tier are provided.

Training for Integrity

Throughout this book, the importance of training staff to use each and every method that is part of an MTSS has been emphasized. Such training is a cornerstone of teaching integrity because it provides educators with a common understanding of what a specific lesson or procedure looks like when done correctly. When staff are provided with high-quality training, as well as ongoing consultation and coaching to improve their skills, they will have a valid model for what they are expected to do. Such training must be based on implementation of evidence-based instructional methods and programs. Educators will observe the effects of their training and the science behind it in their students' success.

Recent research suggests that one of the elements of the teaching profession that most frustrates teachers is the lack of quality PD and training (Hill, 2009). Teachers themselves are aware of ineffective training practices and are eager for opportunities to learn methods that really work. Offering high-quality training and development for educators is the first and best way to foster teaching integrity. Any time we expect a teacher to do something new and different, we need to provide appropriate training and development. By providing teachers with training from the start, we help them know what excellent teaching looks like and give them the means to evaluate their own practices. Such training also helps teachers to recognize that becoming an expert will require time and practice. But, by having a model for what effective instruction looks like, teachers are able to compare their own practices on a regular basis.

Observations of Integrity

In addition to providing teachers with effective training, conducting observations of teaching is an important part of supporting teaching integrity. Sanetti and Kratochwill (2005) suggested that a starting point for observations is for teachers to conduct self-evaluations of how well they implemented a lesson as planned. More recent guidance suggests methods for how teachers can develop teaching integrity measures (Sanetti & Kratochwill, 2013). More and more published programs include integrity observation checklists as part of the materials available for educators who utilize the programs. Observing whether a planned lesson is implemented as intended is the best possible way to determine whether teaching integrity is achieved. There are many factors that could affect a lesson's integrity. For example, an unplanned fire drill (or actual fire) would immediately preclude a teacher's plans to deliver a specific lesson. In such cases, doing the lesson over again on another day will be necessary. Regardless of the reason that a lesson is interrupted, it is a good way of understanding teaching integrity.

Teaching integrity involves the teacher completing each and every step in a planned lesson as intended. No one is perfect, so achieving 100% integrity is not the goal. Instead, having an integrity rate of at least 80% is desired, although rarely met (Schulte, Easton, & Parker, 2009). Any lesson can have a teaching integrity observation form created for it (Sanetti & Kratochwill, 2013). This means that any lesson can be observed to evaluate teaching integrity. As outlined by Sanetti & Kratochwill (2013), the steps include defining the (1) intervention components, (2) implementation steps, (3) details of the intervention plan, and (4) the assessment method to be used. Using these steps, a teacher or interventionist can develop an observation checklist that can be used to determine if all of the planned steps were used in a given lesson. Observation of lessons is important because it provides evidence about whether the steps that should be included in a lesson were actually implemented. This is essential for evidence-based instruction because it is the only way to document whether true teaching integrity was achieved.

Tier 1

Determining teaching integrity at Tier 1 involves observing one or more classroom teachers while they provide daily instruction. This might seem routine, but is necessary to document that Tier 1 core instruction was provided. The first step is to decide who will conduct the observation. It will be less stressful for the teacher if the observer is someone known to the teacher and not an administrator. The best way to document teaching integrity is by having a trained observer conduct at least three observations of a teacher providing instruction in the same content area. Having three observations provides a way to avoid error in measurement. While this is the goal, sometimes only one observation will be possible. If one observation verifies integrity, then others are not required, but if there is a question about teaching integrity, additional observations should be conducted.

The classroom teacher can provide the details of the planned lesson in advance for the observer. Many Tier 1 core instructional programs now have observation checklists that can be used for such teaching integrity evaluations. The easiest and best way to conduct the observation is to compare the actual lesson with what was planned. Sometimes an observer will meet with the teacher ahead of the observation, but this depends on time availability. More important is a meeting after the observation to go over what was observed and steps for improvement, if needed. Calculating basic teaching integrity involves dividing the number of implemented lesson components by the number planned. This will give a number and percentage, but it is more important that the observer discuss the lesson with and provide feedback to the teacher. During this discussion, ideas for improvement can be discussed, as needed.

Tiers 2 and 3

For interventions provided at Tiers 2 and 3, the process of conducting observations is analogous to those used at Tier 1. Nevertheless, the process can feel different since there are fewer students involved and the stakes are higher given the level of risk that the students receiving intervention face. First, the person to conduct the observation needs to be identified. Next, the specific lesson to be observed needs to be determined. The teacher or interventionist then provides the observer with an observation checklist listing the planned parts of the lesson. As with Tier 1, many interventions have integrity checklists and these can be used for observations. The goal for interventionists is for the intervention to be implemented with a high level of accuracy. As noted by Schulte et al. (2009), 80% is a goal; while that level of integrity is rarely achieved outside of research, it is a worthwhile target. The actual teaching integrity percentage should be reported to the school team responsible for interpreting student progress data. This will help the team decide whether the intervention was conducted with enough integrity to have resulted in valid data, or whether more interventions with greater integrity are needed. Teaching integrity data is also necessary for an advanced tier team to determine whether or not a student should be referred for a special education evaluation. Specifically, if the student has had access to evidence-based intervention delivered with integrity and has still failed to make progress, the team has cause for concern about the student. On the other hand, if the team finds that a student has failed to make progress, but that the intervention was not delivered with integrity, the team has cause for concern about the intervention and, rather than rushing to a referral, must take immediate action to ensure that the student be provided with an effective intervention. As noted, there is no universal rule for an acceptable level of treatment integrity, but an intervention with 10% integrity should be viewed differently from one with 90% integrity.

SUMMARY

Treatment integrity, or teaching integrity when applied in schools, is very important to the MTSS process. When instruction or intervention is done according to the rules of a scientifically based study, the outcomes are more likely to be better and more likely to boost the student's progress. For this reason, school teams are encouraged to think about treatment and teaching integrity as they develop MTSS policies and procedures. MTSS blends scientifically based instruction with a tiered system of supports that uses a student's response to instruction to indicate whether more help is needed. When schools use teaching integrity measures as a tool to verify that evidence-based methods were used correctly, they will have data indicating whether student progress was based on practices that are truly evidence based.

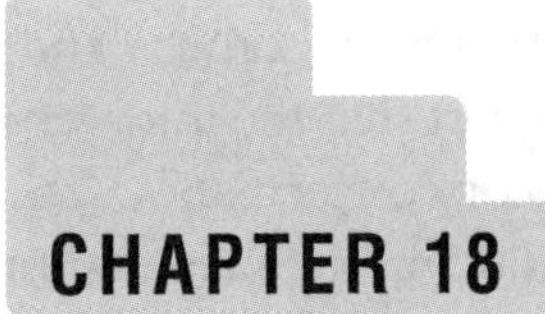

CHAPTER 18

Critical Mass

WHY 80% STUDENT SUCCESS MATTERS

The term *critical mass* comes from physics and means the "minimum amount of a given fissionable material necessary to achieve a self-sustaining nuclear chain reaction under specified conditions." Despite its beginnings in physics, this phrase has become common in everyday use and generally means "a size, number, or amount large enough to produce a particular result." Both meanings of the term require a minimum amount for something to happen, but do not specify a maximum. Critical mass conveys the idea of a threshold that must be met before other things can happen. In an MTSS, a key critical mass is having at least 80% of students meet the grade-level learning targets through Tier 1 support alone. This chapter explains why the 80% "critical mass" of students is essential for an MTSS to be successful.

THE PREVENTION TRIANGLE

Those who have learned about and used various types of an MTSS in recent years are likely to be familiar with the "triangle" (see Figure 2.1 in Chapter 2). It is a graphic that shows how tiered supports offer a framework for helping all students access all parts of the curriculum. Note that there are percentages in small circles next to the edges of each part of the triangle in the figure. At the base of the triangle 100% of students enter the support system. All students in a school, regardless of ability or other supports, are considered to be part of the tiered system. Tier 1 is the general education curriculum for academics and behavior and is what every student should experience every day. In other words, Tier 1 is provided to 100% of the students. The public health prevention model presented in Chapter 2 suggests that, if Tier 1 is effective, about 80% of the students in each school will be successful with Tier 1 supports alone. The current chapter addresses why it is essential that at least 80% of students meet the learning goals at Tier 1.

As noted by Mahdavi and Beebe-Frakenberger (2009), schools often start the process of using an MTSS with less than 80% of students experiencing success at Tier 1. However, schools that start out with less than 80% of students meeting the learning standards at Tier 1, with time and careful attention to student needs, can ultimately meet this goal. The MTSS team members need to keep in mind that planning for and supporting all students is more like a marathon than a sprint. In order to have an MTSS system work, each tier fulfills certain types of student needs. The essence of Tier 1 instruction is the core curriculum. It is the first and best opportunity to help all students be successful in schools. Therefore, educators need to understand the importance of having a core curriculum that meets the needs of most students. There are three main reasons that the 80% goal is so important to an MTSS: (1) resources, (2) statistics, and (3) student success. Each of these reasons are explored in this chapter.

RESOURCES

As the earlier chapters in this book have explained, setting up a system in which students can move easily across the tiers as needed is not easy and requires a great deal of time and resources. Typically, it takes a school 3–5 years to get such a system running well. One of the most important steps in having the supports work well is making sure that all resources are being used both effectively and efficiently. For example, if too many students are not meeting the Tier 1 learning goals and staff try to support them at the next level, the Tier 2 capacity will be overwhelmed as educators try to support more than a fifth of the student body with small group instruction. The same thing will happen if there are too many students requiring Tier 3. The reality is that most schools have limited resources and therefore cannot afford to have ineffective instruction at Tier 1. For this reason, it is essential that teams understand and act on the importance of the 80% rule. For tiered supports to be sustainable, each part of the system must function as planned. This means that at least 80% of students must meet the Tier 1 core learning goals. If there are too many students needing additional supports in Tiers 2 and 3, the system will not work because there will not be enough people, places, and minutes in the day to support more than 20% of the students at that level of intensity.

THE STATISTICS BEHIND 80%

The 80% criterion comes from the public health model (see Chapter 2) and Caplan's work in 1964. This model suggests that, if universal interventions are effective, it is reasonable to expect at least 80% of people exposed to those interventions to demonstrate the intended outcome. Interestingly, the "80% rule" holds true across domains. Whether you are engaged in an antismoking campaign, implementing an evidence-based reading curriculum, or providing schoolwide positive behavior supports, if you are doing it well you can expect 80% of recipients to respond to your intervention. Correspondingly, if your intervention is having the desired effect on less than 80% of your intended audience, a change in the intervention is warranted.

Psychologists pioneered the use of statistics as a method for studying and understanding a wide array of phenomena. Statistics is the study of how probability can be used to test the accuracy of data. Specifically, statistical tests are designed to compare a given number with what would have been expected based on probability. Probability refers to the random occurrence of events over time. For example, the probability that a person will be struck by lightning in a given year is 1:280,000 (National Lightning Safety Institute, 2013). This number is based on using available data to compute a probable statistic. Probability is based on both available data and randomness. Probability refers to the chance of an event occurring based on prior data about the occurrence of such events. But in reality, not all events happen at random. For this reason, probability is not the same as actual occurrence. The actual occurrence of events such as lightning strikes and volcanoes is different from their probable occurrence. The reason for the difference is that random "error" comes into play. In other words, other events occur that influence the actual occurrence of things like lightning and volcanoes.

However, comparing the actual occurrence to the statistical probability does give a way to make sense of natural phenomena. And, statistical comparisons are generally correct. Therefore, statistics are based on taking a "sample" of data from the known actual occurrences, and calculating an estimate of probable future occurrences. Given the accuracy of this method, most major sports organizations, as well as "fantasy" sports groups, use such data to estimate how a given player should do in a season (Major-League Obie Role-Based System, 2013). Over time, and based on the general accuracy of statistics predicted from actual data, the field of statistics has adopted this method as a useful way to know if an obtained result is accurate and useful. For example, it is often the case that statisticians can predict who will win the World Series each year. The predicted winner may not be the actual winner every year, but such predictions are accurate enough to make them valuable. Another example is how prior success picking the winner of the Kentucky Derby is likely to suggest future success at this task (Mayam, 2013).

Knowing the typical or expected performance of any "event" can be a helpful tool in planning. For example, coordinators of a road race might want to know the expected number of participants so they can plan for how much water to have ready. Similarly, emergency room staff might want to know, on average, how many units of each type of blood are used each week of the year so they can alert the blood bank when supplies are low. There are expected variations in the demand for blood but these can be predicted using statistics. These types of data are sometimes referred to as "population-based" metrics because they are based on what can be expected in relation to what is known about the population at large. Doll et al. (2010) discuss important population-based statistics related to children and youth. As Doll et al. explain, there are two main benefits of learning about typical events in the population at large: (1) it provides an idea of expected outcomes, and (2) it serves as a basis of comparison for cases that are very atypical.

Over time, statistics have become so normal in daily life, few may question them. For example, weather prediction, the stock market, and sports are all heavy users of statistical methods. Ironically, statistics have not been as widely used in schools. Until recently, few educators thought about what typical school performance was. Often, teachers might be hesitant to define average school performance, but they tended to rely on a mind-set that they "knew it when they saw it." Waiting to see which students struggle and then providing supports is not as effective as a prevention-based system. For this reason, there is a growing interest among educators to utilize research about prevention to improve student outcomes.

As mounting research shows, having systems in place to identify and support students who are struggling from the first days of school is more effective. How each student does in the early years of school has a direct effect on that student's long-term success. In addition, how all students do influences society as a whole, at least in industrialized societies. This is because mass production of goods, and other features of industrialization, rely on an educated workforce. If there are not enough educated workers, businesses cannot produce the goods and services that run the economy. So that means there needs to be "a critical" mass of educated workers for modern society to function.

STUDENT SUCCESS

The reason that having 80% or more of students meet learning standards is so important is that it shows that teachers are actually teaching what is expected. The St. Croix River Education District (SCRED) in Minnesota has for many years published its learning outcomes and attainments. This is because the leadership in SCRED believes that the public should know how its students are doing (St.

Croix River Education District, 2013). If 80% or more of students are meeting the school's learning expectations, then the district considers itself to be meeting expected progress. This metric takes into account that up to 20% of students might not meet the expectations and will need more help. The good news is that teachers are in the business of providing such extra help, and the tiered supports available for the 20% of students who need them can help those students reach the learning goals.

If 80% or more of a school's students are meeting the learning goals, teachers can feel confident that the core curriculum and instructional strategies are effective for most students. But at the same time, it means that some students are not finding success. Setting the goal for Tier 1 MTSS success at 80% acknowledges that some students will need extra help despite an effective universal system. Here is a little secret about typical MTSS data: most of the time—based on statistical probabilities—85% of students will be successful with Tier 1 instruction alone. That is a good thing. That leaves about 15% of students who need extra help. Sometimes more students will need extra help, so setting the criterion at 80% leaves "wiggle room" for a school that might have a few more struggling students.

Being able to expect that 80% or more of students will succeed with Tier 1 is helpful to teachers because it makes the work of providing extra supports to the 20% of students who need them feasible. For example, if the average class of students includes 25–30 students, then five to six students in each class are likely to need additional support. The good news is that five to six students is a manageable number. These are the students who did not meet the learning standards with Tier 1 instruction alone and need some additional instruction. The best way to help these students is to offer additional instruction for those five to six students. But it's possible that one or two of the students needing extra help have very significant school problems. These students might need Tier 3 right away and that's okay (see "Triage" in Chapter 15).

Tier 2 instruction for academic deficits should be provided 3–5 days each week for about 30 minutes each day. The extra time spent on this instruction will make it possible for most struggling students to master the learning and meet the grade-level goals. In order to know if the students are making the desired improvements, regular progress assessments should be used. These assessments usually take 1–4 minutes and show whether the student is making progress toward the specified grade-level standard. Most of the students will have made the needed gains and will be ready to reduce the amount of Tier 2 instruction needed (Vaughn et al., 2009). As noted, one or two students in each classroom will need the intensive intervention available at Tier 3. Tier 2 intervention for behavioral deficits is often provided in the form of check-in/check-out, which occurs throughout the school day. Data are generated at each check-out and an overall percentage is calculated at the end of each school day. That percentage is compared to a goal that was set for each student based on baseline data, providing an effective means of progress monitoring the impact of the intervention. Like Tier 2 interventions for academic deficits, some Tier 2 interventions for behavior, such as social skills instruction, will occur in concentrated times throughout the school week.

As shown in Figure 2.1 (Chapter 2), only a very small number of students require Tier 3 support. If Tiers 1 and 2 are effective, no more than 5% of the students in a school should require this level of intensive intervention. As shown in the figure, the category for Tier 3 services is not exclusively general education. Instead, Tier 3 could include a combination of students in general and special education. The reason for such combining is that the nature of the intensive instruction that students need at Tier 3 is not necessarily going to be different from what could be provided as part of special education. There is no cache of unique special education interventions that are used only once a student qualifies for such services. Therefore, students who did not respond to Tier 1 + Tier 2 might benefit from instruction already being provided for students with individualized education programs (IEPs). IDEA 2004 allowed schools to use up to 15% of their federal special education money to support students at risk for developing a disability. This provision is explicitly preventive in nature.

The process for deciding whether a student needs Tier 3 intervention involves using a problem-solving process (see Chapter 15). In some cases, students who need Tier 3 instruction can join an existing intervention group such as those provided in special education. In other cases, the team might need to select a specific and different intervention to use. In the case of interfering behavior, a Tier 3 intervention will typically include a function-based behavior support plan. Typically, Tier 3 instruction is individualized because the student needs something different from what has been provided at Tier 2. The goal at Tier 3 is to test the hypothesis that a certain type of much more intensive intervention will result in student success. Providing Tier 3 intervention may or may not be linked with evaluating whether a student is eligible for special education. Since student progress data are collected at all tiers, the data from Tier 3 might be very helpful to an evaluation team, but the presence of such data does not mean that a student qualifies for special education. Importantly, these data cannot be the only data used to evaluate a student's needs. IDEA 2004 requires that a comprehensive evaluation be conducted every time a student is referred to special education.

Ideally, when a student is being evaluated to determine eligibility for special education, data from all tiers will be reviewed and used in the evaluation report, alongside other sources of information (see Chapter 25). Some students receiving Tier 3 support will qualify and then receive special education services. This may or may not mean that the type of instruction actually changes. As noted above, good instruction does not "belong" to general or special education and students might be part of small groups of students with similar learning needs. However, if a student is not referred or does not qualify for special education but still needs intensive intervention, Tier 3 could be the best solution.

The good news is that getting at least 80% of students meeting the goals is quite possible. One example of a district that decided to meet, and exceed, the 80% goal is the Kennewick School District in southeast Washington state (Fielding, Kerr, & Rosier, 1998). Kennewick is not an affluent town. At the time it began the work of boosting reading skills, the residents included current and former employees of the decommissioned Hanford Nuclear Reservation and migrant farmworkers. Led by a group of teachers, administrators, and school board members, Kennewick set the goal of having not only 80% but 90% of its third graders meet end-of-year reading goals. To make this happen, the entire daily schedule and structure of the elementary schools was changed. It was not an easy process, and one of the most important steps in Kennewick's success was changing how reading was taught from the first day students arrived at school. The primary focus was on using every minute of the school day as carefully as possible to maximize student reading skills.

This transformation began at the general classroom level. The schedule and resources for reading instruction were changed and built on a foundation of research-based instructional methods. At least 90 minutes of every school day were devoted to Tier 1 reading instruction. Teachers gathered and used student data in planful ways. There was no "downtime" in these classrooms; every minute was used to improve reading skills. As a result of these efforts, 90% or more of the students in Kennewick have met the third-grade reading goal for many years. The important lesson from Kennewick in relation to tiered supports is that the teachers do not assume that someone else will help their struggling students. Instead, every teacher takes responsibility for ensuring that all students learn to read. This is an example of excellent resource allocation because Tier 1 is being used to its best potential: having students meet learning goals in the classroom.

LONG-TERM IMPLICATIONS OF THE 80% RULE

As noted in earlier chapters, the importance of having enough educated citizens began to dawn on U.S. policymakers in the 1980s. Under the Reagan administration, a seminal report known as *A Nation at Risk* suggested that U.S. schools were ineffective and not on a par with schools in other industrialized nations (U.S. National Commission on Excellence in Education, 1983). Soon thereafter, three decades of educational reform began. The focus of the reforms was making U.S. schools more effective in reaching and teaching all students.

One of the current metrics used to gauge U.S. progress in educational improvement is the Trends in International Math and Science Study (TIMSS; U.S. Department of Education, National Center for Education Statistics, 2015). TIMSS offers a unique way to compare the performance of students across countries because it measures only math and science skills, which are less influenced by the presence of different languages than reading-related skills. TIMSS is conducted every 4 years in as many countries as possible. It was administered in 1995, 1999, 2003, 2007, 2011, and 2015 (U.S. Department of Education, National Center for Education Statistics, 2015). In 2011, the most recent year for which data were available, the scores showed that U.S. fourth graders scored ninth and sixth in math and science, respectively, out of 57 participating countries. Although the United States did not come in first in either math or science, the 2011 rankings do show improvement over time. Table 18.1 provides a summary of U.S. student scores from 1995 through 2011. Although the United States did not rank in the first place, U.S. students did place near the top 10 in many years.

The TIMSS scores suggest that U.S. students have scored among the top 10 nations in both math and science over time. While some politicians may think that U.S. performance in math and science is not adequate, the more important issue is whether there is a critical mass of students who have the skills needed to support the U.S. economy. To assist with understanding U.S. students' competitiveness globally, it is helpful to review high school dropout data. A review of data about how many students have dropped out of high school in recent years shows that the percentage of dropouts has actually declined since 1990 (National Center for Education Statistics, 2013a). In that year, about 12% of U.S. students dropped out of high school and did not get a diploma. By 2010, the rate was 7%. On the surface, this seems like an impressive gain, but it is important to review the data by ethnic group. A closer review of the data shows that students who are black, Hispanic, American Indian, or Alaska Native are almost twice as likely to drop out of school than other students. Such data suggest that current practices in U.S. education appear to work well for English-speaking white students, but not necessarily as well for students of color.

The lack of improvement in graduation outcomes for students of color in the United States is part of the reason that NCLB required that schools tease apart their data and report outcomes by ethnic group. In essence, these data show that the U.S. public education system works well for middle- to high-income students from Caucasian backgrounds, but is failing students from American Indian/Alaska native, black, Hispanic, and low-income families. This is despite research evidence that EBPs can work for *all* students. The reality of such data requires

TABLE 18.1. U.S. TIMSS Rankings over Time

	Math		Science	
Year	4th	8th	4th	8th
1995	12	3	18	12
1999	19		18	
2003	12	6	15	9
2007	11	9	8	11
2011	11	9	7	10

that educators think about their daily practices and whether they are truly teaching in a way that makes an effective education available to *all* students.

Although students from many different states have participated in the TIMSS, there is another assessment that has been used to compare student performance among U.S. states. Known as the National Assessment of Educational Progress (NAEP), it is given every 2 years to selected students in grades 4 and 8 across the United States. The report from the 2009–2010 school year is the most recent on the U.S. Department of Education website and shows the percentage of students meeting state learning goals broken down by sex (gender), grade (4 or 8), content (math or reading/language arts), and ethnicity (American Indian, black, Hispanic, white). NAEP data are consistent with other indicators of student outcomes reported in this chapter. Specifically, students from minority backgrounds do not do as well in the U.S. education system. This is why educators are encouraged to consider whether at least 80% or more of their students in each demographic area are meeting the learning targets.

Tier 1 is the first and best place where students encounter new learning. When taught well from the start, students are able to add new learning to prior learning every day. Each student's potential is optimized when every day of instruction adds to what came before. This means that there is little downtime each day. Because of the importance of Tier 1 instruction, teams must focus their initial efforts on ensuring that the general education instruction and classroom management in each classroom is as effective and efficient as possible. Resources invested in preparing classroom teachers to teach excellent lessons and build positive relationships with each student every day will yield huge benefits as students can appreciate the cumulative effects of learning over time. For all of these reasons, one of the initial steps in setting up tiered supports is to learn what percentage of students at each grade level are meeting the learning goals. Often, schools start with reading but this can and should be done for math, writing, and behavior as well.

In cases where 80% or more of students are meeting the learning goals in all areas, the next steps will include setting up Tier 2 and 3 supports for those students who need extra help. But when less than 80% of students are meeting the goals, the team must focus its energy on getting to the 80% goal in all areas. Box 18.1 shares guidance from Dr. Kim Gibbons of the St. Croix River Education District (SCRED) about how her district went through the process of getting to the "critical mass" of 80% student success at Tier 1.

GETTING TO 80%

There are five key steps that teams can take to get at least 80% of their students achieving the learning goals: (1) evaluate student data carefully and note patterns; (2) invest in the most effective materials; (3) examine the current teaching

BOX 18.1. Guidance from Kim Gibbons, PhD, NCSP, about how her district, the St. Croix River Educational District (SCRED), Reached the 80% Tier 1 Goal

The St. Croix River Educational District (SCRED) was a pilot site for CBM in the early 1980s for the University of Minnesota Institute for Research on Learning Disabilities. As a result, these measures were widely used within the context of a problem-solving model. Beginning in about 1995, we began formally implementing what is now known as RTI/MTSS. We began by screening all students three times per year, setting target scores, and progress monitoring at-risk students. When our state began publishing the results of Basic Skills Tests, our district realized that we had a core problem with reading instruction. This problem was validated through our CBM screening measures as well.

Our initial data indicated only 20% of students were proficient across SCRED. Initially, we didn't set a goal to get to 80%. We realized it would be a long process, and thus, we set realistic but ambitious goals for improvement. We focused on improving core reading instruction through:

- Guiding schools through a process for selecting research-based curriculum.
- Aligning district reading programs with the National Reading Panel standards (no state or national standards existed). When we found gaps (e.g., phonemic awareness instruction), we developed materials for teachers to use to add to their core curriculum.
- Deploying high-quality PD in the area of beginning reading instruction followed up with coaching to grade-level teachers.
- Establishing grade-level teams where teachers would regularly examine screening and progress monitoring data and discuss how to improve instruction.

We have focused on the three big areas of MTSS through:

- Measurement:
  - Purchasing universal screening and progress monitoring system for all schools.
  - Providing training to teachers on how to collect and use data to improve instruction.
  - Sharing data regularly (e.g., three times per year) with grade-level teams, principals, superintendents, and curriculum directors.
  - Assisting schools in collecting diagnostic data on some students to inform intervention selection.
  - Developing a data warehouse to store all data and create user-friendly data reports for teachers and administrators.
  - Creating criterion-referenced target scores for CBMs, Individual Growth and Development Indicators (IGDI), and Measures of Academic Progress (MAP), and using data analysis to predict performance on statewide tests.

(continued)

- Curriculum/instruction and tiered services
  - Providing assistance to districts on curriculum alignment to standards.
  - Providing staff development (regularly) on research-based instructional strategies.
  - Educating staff on "tiers of service" and establishing options for helping kids other than special education. We provided lots of assistance on scheduling and research-based interventions.
- Schoolwide organization and problem solving
  - Worked with districts to establish grade-level teams. Established a grade-level team facilitator project to train facilitators at each grade level to facilitate meetings using a variety of data reports.
  - Established problem-solving teams. We have provided 5 days of problem-solving model training per year since 2000.
  - Provided coaching to grade-level teams and problem-solving team facilitators.
  - Established a district MTSS team.

schedule; (4) invest in teacher professional development (PD), including coaching; and (5) conduct observations. It is essential that efforts to move student outcomes to 80% or higher utilize the team organization and planning described in earlier chapters. The work needed to support student improvement across an entire school or district is complex. Developing team norms and using a meeting protocol such as Team-Initiated Problem Solving (TIPS) will make the process much easier for everyone. It may not be necessary to apply all of these steps in all cases, but considering each of these is necessary before making changes.

Evaluating Student Data

The first step is to look at the available student data. In order to do this, universal data are needed. This means that there must be a score for each student on a common assessment at each grade level, as well as schoolwide data about social climate and behavior. Having universal data is essential because the goal is to examine patterns in all students' performance to determine how well the Tier 1 system is working. The data should be reviewed according to several grouping variables. First, how far away from 80% success is the student body overall? This is the first and most important question that we ask of our universal data, as the answer to this question tells us whether or not our Tier 1 systems are effective. If possible, compare students in relation to race and ethnicity, free- and reduced-lunch status, special education and other supports, and attendance patterns. If the data show that the scores of students with poor attendance are bringing down the school percentage, then the focus of "intervention" needs to be on boosting attendance for those students, and so forth. Second, what is the percentage of learning goal attainment for each grade? Comparisons by grade may reveal important differences in teaching practices that need to be addressed. If 80% or more of the students in first grade are meeting the learning goals, but then the percentage falls to 64% at the end of second grade, it may be that changes in second-grade instruction are most urgent. With regard to race and ethnicity, it is especially important to ensure that minority students are not disproportionately represented in the school's discipline system (Skiba et al., 2011).

Within the grade levels, comparisons by teacher can be made, too. This is often the most difficult kind of comparison because it will feel very personal to each teacher. It is a worthwhile endeavor, though, since research consistently shows that teaching practices are one of the most powerful predictors of student outcomes (Hattie, 2009). When comparing student outcomes between classrooms, it is best to have the principal meet with each teacher individually to go over the data before having a team discussion of outcomes. In some cases, a teacher might readily agree that his or her practices need to change. In other cases, he or she may need help accepting this reality. Finally, a review of student-specific scores can be conducted, but this should be limited because the focus at this stage is on how to ensure that a critical mass of all students—80% or more—meet the learning targets. The review of student-specific data comes during progress monitoring.

Instructional Materials

In some cases, it may be necessary to invest in new materials. While it is true that *materials don't teach, teachers do*, teachers need certain materials to make effective instruction happen. Time and planning spent on careful selection of instructional materials can pay off with better student outcomes. Some districts have a schedule for reviewing and updating all curriculum materials. Others may conduct reviews as needed. It is best to have a formal system for reviewing materials and selecting new ones. By having a formal review process, all stakeholders can have a role in knowing how materials are selected. In recent years, there has been more focus on ensuring that materials are either evidence based or research based. You will recall from Chapter 5 that evidence based means that a specific product was shown to be effective in two or more experimental research studies, while research based means that the product is based on established research about effective instruction, but may not have a separate evidence base for itself yet.

It is important that those who serve on a materials and selection committees understand the basic principles of education research and how to know whether a product has either an evidence base or a research base. In the United States, there are no rules barring educational publishers from claiming research evidence, whether it exists or not. For this reason, review committee members must be cautious and wary of publisher claims. An investment in new teaching materials is a considerable cost for any district and publishers have the goal of getting the contract. By having a committee conduct the review, the decision will not rest on one person, but will be made by a group that has hopefully considered all of the options and evidence. When new materials are adopted, it is essential that there be PD to support the teachers in using the materials. This is another significant cost, but even the best evidence-based materials will not work if used in the wrong way. If a district is not willing to invest in the PD needed to use a new program correctly, it may be better off not purchasing it at all.

In addition to ensuring that all teaching materials are evidence based, it is important to review how the materials link with the state's learning standards. As outlined in Chapter 5, most U.S. states have adopted the Common Core State Standards (CCSS). As a result, most publishers of instructional materials have sought to align their products with these standards. Nonetheless, there is no current system to validate whether a publisher's claim that a product covers the standards for a grade level is true. The selection committee must review and confirm that materials indeed include the learning activities and materials necessary for students to master each standard.

Examining the Current Teaching Schedule

Once patterns in student outcomes by group and grade level are identified, and instructional materials selected, the next step that a team can take is to look at the daily schedule and see how instructional time is being used. Often, teachers will report that they know they should be doing additional activities as part of the core instruction, but that there is not enough time for them. A system-level change that could be helpful to students and teachers alike is to adjust the daily schedule so that there is enough time for instruction in each area (see Chapter 13; and Brown-Chidsey, Bronaugh, and McGraw, et al., 2009). Gumm and Turner at the Florida Center for Reading Research (2013) have suggested that there should be 90 minutes devoted to elementary reading instruction every day. There are no such formal guidelines for math, science, or social studies, but it is clear that there must be a sufficient amount of time set aside for instruction and that those instructional minutes need to be used well. It may be that some changes in the daily schedule can make it possible for more time to be spent on instruction in one or more areas.

Professional Development

The process of examining student outcomes may lead to a recognition that the teachers in a grade, building, or district need assistance refining their practices. When the process of reviewing student data, selecting new materials, and examining the schedule suggests that teachers would benefit from learning and using different practices, it is appropriate to invest in significant PD. Importantly, this effort needs to be considered a true investment that will lead to improved student learning outcomes. Sadly, some of the programs offered to teachers in the name of PD do not achieve any meaningful change. This is because they are often too brief or not connected to specific school goals and practices. In considering a true investment in PD, a team must think through the specific goals of the activities and how teacher and student progress will be measured. Readers are encouraged to use the guide to selecting PD developed by Lewis, Barrett, Sugai, and Horner (2010).

Also important is a recognition that effective PD needs to happen in consistent increments over time. This is in contrast to the "once-and-done" PD events that teachers sometimes experience for an afternoon once a year (Ferguson, 2006). Effective PD needs to be planned in advance, happen at regular and consistent intervals (i.e., at least monthly), and be connected to what the teachers are doing in the classroom. Effective PD is not cheap and the district must be ready to support effective PD in order to yield better student outcomes. PD can focus exclusively on teaching practices, or it can be bundled with a specific product or program. The nature of the data and observed practices should guide what type of PD is selected. An important aspect of effective PD is the presence of a coaching component. Recent research suggests that when PD includes having an expert teacher serve as a coach for other teachers, the actual implementation of specific practices is more frequent and accurate (Cantrell & Hughes, 2008; Driscoll, 2008; McCollum, Hemmeter, & Hsieh, 2013; Onchwari & Keengwe, 2008; Patti, Holzer, Stern, & Brackett, 2012). Such coaches observe teachers delivering lessons as well as provide immediate feedback on lesson delivery.

Conducting Observations

Once data about student performance and instructional time are known, it can be helpful to have teachers watch each other teaching. In the past, teacher observations were considered the duty of the principal and something to be feared. Over time, research has shown that teachers can benefit from more frequent observations by a variety of colleagues. One model used to review and improve instruction is known as the "walk-through." The walk-through is a method for having the principal, instructional coach, or another colleague come and observe instruction on a regular basis (David, 2007). Walk-throughs are typically very brief and initially help teachers become comfortable having other adults in the classroom. Over time, observers can provide feedback to teachers about what was observed. Some principals make it a point to walk through every classroom every day.

A newer observation model is known as an instructional tour. This approach includes having teachers invite colleagues to visit their classrooms to demonstrate specific teaching practices. This model is more teacher driven, but can be facilitated by a principal. For example, there can be an expectation that every teacher in a building will "host" a tour each year. These tours offer teachers the opportunity to learn what colleagues are doing and discuss best practices. The tour model may require more resources than walk-throughs because teachers need substitutes in order to leave their classrooms and observe others. However, if the principal, other leaders, and/or guest speakers are used, teachers can take instructional tours without the additional cost of substitutes.

Getting feedback from observation is a very effective way to improve teaching (see Hattie, 2009). And unless classroom observations are conducted, there is no way to be certain whether teachers are consistent in their application of teaching practices. The data collected from observations can be used to refine practices and improve student learning outcomes. For example, inconsistencies in student performance noted when comparing outcomes across grade levels may make sense in relation to the types of teaching practices observed. If the teachers within a grade level are using very different methods across their classrooms, it may be worth focusing on having instruction be more consistent within the grade level.

All of the above methods for getting at least 80% of students meeting the learning goals are strategies that can and must be done at Tier 1. As noted earlier, all the best Tier 2 and 3 efforts will fail if there are too many students who need them. The first and best place to help all students succeed is the Tier 1 general education classroom. When a team observes that less than 80% of students are meeting the goals, then its primary MTSS efforts must be on improving Tier 1 core instruction. Having effective core instruction is the only way that tiered supports can be effective and sustainable over the long term. Nonetheless, even when less than 80% of students in a school are demonstrating success, those students who are very significantly behind (i.e., more than 2 years) will need immediate help. For this reason, a school cannot justify delaying intensive supports for students based on the need to improve Tier 1 instruction. Instead, there must be a plan that includes improving Tier 1 instruction while providing Tier 2 and 3 supports for those students who need them (see "Triage" in Chapter 15). As will be addressed in Chapter 25, the U.S. Department of Education has issued administrative guidance that schools cannot use an MTSS as an excuse to delay needed instruction for students.

SUMMARY

An effective MTSS is built on guidelines and research in the fields of prevention and public health. These guidelines show that only when a "critical mass" of a population meets a standard or goal will the entire population be safeguarded.

This principle holds true in education as well. Only when there are enough educated citizens can business, government, and society work. This is one of the premises behind universal public education, but it has not been uniformly applied in all schools. When schools recognize and use the 80–15–5 rule for student success, tiered supports will be very effective. But if schools attempt to help struggling students without first having at least 80% of all pupils meeting the learning goals, they are not likely to succeed because it will be like trying to bail out the *Titanic* with a thimble.

PART V

MTSS Organizational Structure

A strong MTSS requires an organizational structure that is carefully planned. This section includes information about all of the necessary steps and structures in an MTSS. Identification of students who need tiered support begins with screening data (Chapter 19). By collecting universal screening data about both students and the school environment, as well as other sources of information, teachers can organize tiered supports for selected students. The process of determining what type of intervention a student needs is based on a problem-solving process (Chapter 20). The details of how to organize supports are explained in relation to both uniform small-group interventions and an individualized problem-solving process. In order to know whether an intervention is working, there must be progress monitoring data. Chapter 21 explains how to select progress measures for academics and behavior. Finally, Chapter 22 describes how to interpret and understand progress data collected as part of an intervention.

CHAPTER 19

Universal Screening

Screening all students is an essential feature of an MTSS. The status of students' academic skills, as well as their behavior and social and emotional well-being, can be assessed through universal screening programs. Such screening helps teachers know which students might need more help. While screening is not diagnostic, it provides brief information about every student's current learning needs. Screening data will not necessarily tell us who is going to graduate at the top of his or her class, but it will provide a starting point for identifying the students who could use extra help to meet learning goals. This chapter provides information about the purpose of universal screening, how to set up screening procedures, how to understand the obtained data, and next steps for implementing universal screening programs.

SCREENING FOR PREVENTION

Like the three-tiered model itself, the basic idea for screening comes from public health and prevention methods. As the field of public health developed (see Chapter 2), it became clear that certain reliable indicators were very strong predictors of health outcomes. For example, weight and body mass index (BMI) are very stable indicators of risk for Type 2 diabetes (American Diabetes Association, 2013). For this reason, people are routinely weighed and measured at checkups. Unlike the other types of diabetes, Type 2 diabetes is preventable through diet and exercise. Physicians use the information gained by screening each patient's weight and BMI to guide their lifestyle recommendations for each individual. In other words, the data gained are used to determine which patients need additional instruction or motivation with regard to daily habits.

There are other types of screening indicators that can help promote wellness. Another commonly assessed wellness indicator is cholesterol. There are two types of cholesterol: HDL, which is the "good" type of cholesterol, and LDL, which is the "bad" type (WebMD, 2013). Physicians routinely screen their patients' cholesterol levels because they know that keeping cholesterol at healthy levels promotes wellness by keeping the heart healthy. For these reasons, physicians recommend having cholesterol checked at least every 5 years in adulthood (WebMD, 2013).

Nonmedical screening methods exist as well. For example, having a network of close friends—from church or elsewhere—is an indicator of strong social support, which is itself another wellness indicator (Robinson & Jon, 2004). In the last 20 years, education researchers have realized that prevention research applies equally well in education. Specifically, when teachers know which students need more help, and they provide such help, later problems can be prevented. This is the rationale behind using universal screening procedures in schools (Cook, Volpe, & Livanis, 2010). When teachers know which students need more help at the start of each school year, they can provide the help needed right away or arrange for other supports. This is in comparison to traditional school assessments that tend to happen once at the end of the school year. If a student does poorly on the end-of-year test, there is no more time in that year to do anything to help.

Educators can use universal screening to monitor students' response to instruction as well as their behavior and emotional well-being (Kalberg, Lane, & Menzies, 2010). Specifically, regularly scheduled, brief measures that span the skills that schools seek to improve can provide a window into how well students are responding to Tier 1 instruction and which students will benefit from additional support. By briefly "taking the pulse" of each student's ability to read and do math, as well as his or her social and emotional behavior, educators can create a profile of each student across domains that provides the information needed to best support each student.

SCREENING PROCEDURES

The steps needed to screen all students are not difficult to follow, but attention to details is important (see Chapter 3). There are five key components that need to be addressed in order for screening to be effective: (1) planning, (2) selecting materials, (3) setting up schedules, (4) identifying and preparing personnel, and (5) providing training.

Planning

The first step in screening is to make plans for when, where, and how the screening(s) will happen. The schoolwide (universal) Tier 1 team should be in charge of such plans. The planning includes deciding what assessments will be used, when, and by whom. There are a number of universal screening measures available for purchase and for free that schools can use.

The Common Core State Standards (CCSS) have created a helpful environment for selecting screening assessments for academic concerns (Common Core State Standards Initiative, 2013). As detailed in Chapter 5, the CCSS are learning standards that have been adopted by the majority of U.S. states and territories. These standards were developed by the National Governors Association Center for Best Practices and the Council of Chief State School Officers (2010; i.e., the commissioners of education in U.S. states). The goal in creating national standards for U.S. schools was to have a common set of learning outcomes for all students. For many years, other industrialized nations (e.g., France, China) have had learning outcomes and standards for all public school students. By comparison, U.S. students have been held to the standards of the states in which they go to school. This means that there have been 50 plus sets of standards (i.e., including U.S. territories). This is a problem in that many U.S. students move at least once during their K–12 education. When the learning standards change with each move, the student has to "start over" in meeting those standards. Having a comprehensive set of learning standards for all grades helps ensure that students will access essential knowledge and skills regardless of family mobility.

At the planning phase of universal screening, the team needs to identify which skills will be measured at each grade level. By reviewing the CCSS or state standards, the team can specify which key skills are most essential and should be included in screening. At the younger grades, basic reading and math, as well as school discipline referrals, are frequently selected because they are predictive of later achievement (Pas, Bradshaw, & Mitchell, 2011). In upper-elementary and middle school, the number of office discipline referrals (ODRs) a student has remains an area of interest, while academic attention shifts to reading comprehension and applied math problems. At the high school level it is generally not necessary to screen all students three times each year. This is because students who meet academic and behavior learning targets at the start of ninth grade typically will be successful in the rest of high school. In addition, there are numerous other assessments given in high school that can indicate that a student is having difficulty, and ODRs remain an important indicator of behavioral need. While universal screening typically does not take place in high schools, we strongly recommend that high schools have a clear process by which educators can request assistance for students who are struggling socially, behaviorally, or academically. The process for planning to use universal screening assessments typically takes about one school year. This is because many details must be considered in the process. The planning team needs to consider and make decisions about the materials, schedule, training, and personnel before the entire plan can be rolled out in the school or district.

Selecting Materials

Even though not all states have adopted the CCSS, there are a number of screening assessments matched to the CCSS; this means that there are universal assessments for the expected outcomes in most states. The available screening assessments are general enough to work for almost any state or territory's learning standards. It is important that schools do not add on too many additional tests when screening students. Teams should start by reviewing all current grade-level common assessments to see if there is already a screening measure being used. If not, the team should think about whether at least one current test could be removed if an additional screening assessment is added.

The National Center for Response to Intervention (NCRTI; 2012) created a matrix of academic screening tools that school personnel can use to select appropriate measures; this tools chart has been updated by the National Center on Intensive Intervention (2014). Similarly, the National Technical Assistance Center on Positive Behavioral Interventions and Supports has many resources about how to conduct behavior screenings (U.S. Department of Education, Office of Special Education Programs, 2015). Aside from social and emotional screeners, screening materials need to match what is being taught to students. Importantly, most published universal screening assessments are "curriculum-neutral" measures that can be used with any program. The school team should take time to explore the options before adopting universal screening materials. There are considerations of cost, alignment with instruction, assessment methods, and training requirements. No single screening measure is truly "better" than others. All of the options have strengths and weaknesses and school teams must consider the goodness of fit with their students' needs. Some screening measures are completed on a computer or "tablet" like an iPad. Others are paper-and-pencil tests, and some of these have an optical scanning system for computer scoring. The planning team needs to think about where and when students or teachers will complete the screenings. If a computer-based measure is used, computer access is essential. If paper measures and scoring are used, teachers will need time to score and enter data. Every option has benefits and drawbacks that the team must discuss.

Setting Up Schedules

In addition to selecting the measures to use, the team must set up academic and behavior screening schedules. This is often the most difficult step because every school day is so busy. Creating a screening schedule that will reserve time for screenings throughout the year is best. Then, teachers and other staff will know when to expect the screening activities. Both academic and behavior screening are recommended three times a year in the fall, winter, and spring (Brown-Chidsey et al., 2009; Kalberg et al., 2010; Shinn, 1989). In addition, schoolwide data on ODRs can be used as an ongoing indicator of students' behavior difficulties. Screening academic skills several times a year is important because these skills should change in predictable ways over each school year. By screening students' academic skills three times a year, teachers can learn which students need help and provide that help while there is still time in the school year. Similarly, frequent screening for behavioral concerns allows schools to quickly provide support to students who are struggling in social and emotional areas.

With the development of norm-referenced academic screening materials, having identified screening "windows" of time helps schools to compare their students' scores with the norms. There are two major screening schedules used in the United States and these are based on when the school year starts. Some schools start in early to mid-August (typically in the South and West), and others after Labor Day in September (typically in the Northeast and Midwest). Table 19.1 shows the screening "windows" for schools based on start dates (Dynamic Measurement Group, 2011). Each window is about 1 month long, although some months will not have as many school days as others. In the fall, screening starts about 2 weeks after the first day of school. The reason for this is so students and teachers can become familiar with each other. Often, elementary schools begin screening the oldest students first, and work "backward" to the youngest. This practice gives the youngest students more time to become familiar with school routines before the screening happens.

It is best to put the screening dates on the school's or district's annual calendar so everyone will know when screening will happen. Most schools can conduct screening in 1 week, with some extra time needed for any students who were absent when their class was screened. Some schools set aside a single day on which to complete all academic and behavior screenings (Kalberg et al., 2010). The actual time needed will depend on who does the screening (see below) and what measures are used. Some types of behavior screeners can be completed by teachers during a faculty meeting (Kalberg et al., 2010). For example, the Student

TABLE 19.1. Screening "Windows" Based on School Start Dates

Fall		Winter		Spring	
August	September	August	September	August	September
August 15–September 15	September 15–October 15	December 1–December 31	January 1–January 31	April 1–April 30	May 1–May 31

Risk Screening Scale (SRSS; Drummond, 1994; Michigan's Integrated Behavior and Learning Support Initiative, 2015) and other teacher rating forms can be done at a faculty meeting. Using a small portion of a faculty meeting to complete behavior screeners provides teachers with the time to complete the process, as well as with an opportunity to ask questions that might arise during the process. Other types of behavior screening tools are conducted "automatically" through collection of existing data. For example, ODR data is collected each time a student is sent to the office for a behavior incident. When using ODR data for screening, the steps involve entering it into a data system and then making it available for the universal team to review.

Individual academic screening measures take anywhere from 1 to 45 minutes to complete. Some can be completed by students in groups, but others require individual administration. The planning team needs to think about how many total minutes will be needed to screen all students, and then add some time for unexpected events like fire alarms, assemblies, announcements, and so on. The first time a school does a screening it will take more time than subsequently. Similarly, the fall screening often takes longer than the winter and spring ones. After going through the screening cycle during one full school year, the process will seem much easier the next year.

IDENTIFYING AND PREPARING PERSONNEL

Rating scale forms of behavior screeners must be completed by classroom teachers and ODR data are collected with each incident. As a result, the personnel involved in behavior screenings includes all classroom teachers and the principal(s). Academic screening involves having students complete specific academic tasks, and a number of different people can conduct academic screenings. Classroom teachers, specialists, administrators, paraprofessionals, other staff, and volunteers are all possible screeners. The most important thing in deciding who will do screening is training (see below). As long as the screeners are well trained and have been observed in order to document screening accuracy, there is no "rule" about who conducts academic screening.

There are practical considerations about deciding which personnel should participate in academic screening. The more people who serve as screeners, the more training that is needed. There are three main options for which personnel to involve in screening: (1) a small screening "team" of districtwide experts, (2) all classroom teachers, or (3) all staff who can read and attend the training. The more people who conduct screening, the more variability in scores, though this has not been found to be a problem (Brown-Chidsey & Gritter, 2012). The main difference in outcomes related to which personnel conduct academic screening is the amount of time that screening takes; the more people who screen, the less time it takes. Teams need to think about the best way to get screening done in a timely fashion.

The Screening Team

The most time-consuming but reliable approach is to train a small number of personnel who will be known as the academic screening team. This team usually includes assessment specialists such as school psychologists, special educators, speech–language pathologists, occupational therapists, and physical therapists. The benefit of using a small screening team is higher reliability. If the members of the screening team are well trained using the methods outlined above, the overall reliability of the obtained data should be very high. The drawback of using a screening team is that it will take more time because there will be fewer people working with students. This means that the screening schedule will need to take into account when the team will be able to work with students in each classroom. In addition, the team will have to decide where screening will occur. Often, screening teams work in offices and small "pullout" classrooms that are quiet. In some buildings, it may be possible to conduct screenings in hallways or common spaces such as the library or cafeteria. When a small screening team is used, fewer spaces will be needed.

Classroom Teachers

Another option is to have every classroom teacher conduct his or her own academic screenings. To make this happen, all classroom teachers will need to be trained. Scheduling is much easier when classroom teachers conduct screenings because they can schedule the sessions based on the classroom schedule but within the screening "windows." In the long run, having classroom teachers do the academic screening is the best option because it is still efficient and the teachers get to see firsthand how every student is doing in relation to the learning goals. Such information can be very helpful to teachers as they plan support and interventions for individual students.

In order for classroom teachers to conduct academic screenings, some additional staff support might be necessary, depending on the age of the students. Older students (e.g., grades 3–8) can complete screening assessments that are given in a whole-class format. This means that the teacher can conduct the screenings for older students with the entire class at one time. Essentially, such screening assessments are no different from other assessments (i.e., tests) that the teacher might use. Younger students will require individualized screenings and this requires careful planning so that the teacher can work with students one-on-one while the rest of the class does an assigned activity. One approach to making it possible for the students to complete the individualized sessions is to hire "roaming" subs who work with the whole class while the teacher conducts the individual academic assessments.

Staff and Volunteers

The last major option for academic screening is to use an "all-hands-on-deck" approach. This means that all staff who are available participate in the screening. In addition, parent volunteers might participate. This is the most time-efficient option because having more screeners means that it takes less time to get the screening done. The people who participate include all certified staff plus paraprofessionals, secretaries, cafeteria workers, custodians, bus drivers, and volunteers (e.g., parents and grandparents). When this option is used, it is possible to conduct a screening in 1 day! But it is essential that all those who work as academic screeners participate in training to be sure that they know what to do and will be able to do it right. The benefit of having all staff and volunteers be part of training is that the entire community will know about and be part of the academic screening experience. This increases the likelihood that people who are not in the schools every day will understand that triannual universal screening is important. The downside to including all staff and volunteers is that there may be more variability in the procedures and the accuracy of the data might be slightly less than when teachers or a team conducts the assessments.

PROVIDING TRAINING

In order for the data from screening to be useful, the screening measures must be completed correctly. This is no different from other screening tests. If a lab technician applies the wrong analysis to a blood sample, the doctor and patient will have no idea what the results mean. Similarly, school screening measures are standardized and require using the right methods in order for the data to be useful. This means that the measure is administered in the same way with every student. It is important that screening measures be standardized because otherwise it would be impossible to compare the results from one student with those from another student. To ensure that screening measures are used correctly, training is essential. Most publishers of screening assessments have training available for users. In some cases there are online webinars, or DVDs, that users can watch while practicing with the measure. Other measures have trainers who will come to a school or offer trainings in major cities. It is essential that any personnel who conduct universal screenings participate in training and show mastery of the assessment procedures so that the data will be interpretable and helpful for teachers.

It is a good idea to have at least one person in each building become the "expert" on the screening measures. This person can then train others as needed.

Regardless of the training method, it is important for those who will administer the screenings to practice ahead of time to be certain of accuracy. All screening assessments should be used with at least 95% accuracy. A good way to confirm readiness for using the measures is to have a trained examiner observe each screening team member and "score along" on another copy of the measure. Then the two scores can be compared. This process is known as ***interobserver agreement*** (IOA) and there should be 90% or higher IOA between any two people using the same measure. Well-known screening measures like AIMSweb (NCS Pearson, 2014) and DIBELS (Dynamic Measurement Group, 2014) have IOA forms in their administration manuals. These can be used during initial training as well as for "booster" training sessions to help those with prior training to be ready for the next screening.

UNDERSTANDING SCREENING DATA

After universal screening data are collected, it is imperative that key school leaders sit down and review them to understand their importance. The first step is to put them into a format that is computer ready. Many of the screening programs are set up so that they can be reviewed in a computer-generated table or graph. The main thing that educators will want to know from the screening data is what percentage of students met the learning goals. As noted in Chapter 18, an MTSS calls for having at least 80% of students in each school meet the stated academic and behavior goals. When 80% or more of students meet the goals, the school staff can focus on finding interventions for students who are still struggling. When less than 80% of students meet the goals, educators need to pay attention and work on changing the core instruction so that the 80% criterion can be met. Focusing on core instruction means that all teachers in each school need to be observed to confirm that they are using the core curricula with integrity. In addition, the school team needs to consider and choose appropriate Tier 2 interventions for students who are struggling and Tier 3 interventions for students who are significantly behind. Such interventions can include both group and individual interventions.

SCREENING EXAMPLES

Figure 19.1 provides an example of a district-level screening report for all first graders on selected DIBELS Next measures. This report was printed using sample data from the *DIBELS.net* data system. For each of the selected measures used over the school year, there is a pie chart showing the percentage of students meeting recommended benchmark scores for Tiers 1, 2, and 3. This type of report provides a clear idea of how well first-grade reading instruction is working throughout the district. Figure 19.2 shows a classroom report of screening scores from the CBM system formerly known as the Formative Assessment System for Teachers and renamed FastBridge (FAST; FASTBridge Learning, 2015). These are sample data and all student names are fictitious. The first column after the students' names includes each student's raw score on the CBM reading measure. The percentages shown in small boxes immediately after most scores are each student's oral reading accuracy. There are one or two exclamation marks after some students' accuracy percentages. These marks provide quick visual indicators of each student's level of risk. Students without an exclamation mark are at low risk and do not need intervention. Students with one exclamation mark have reading scores that put them at some risk. Students with two exclamation marks

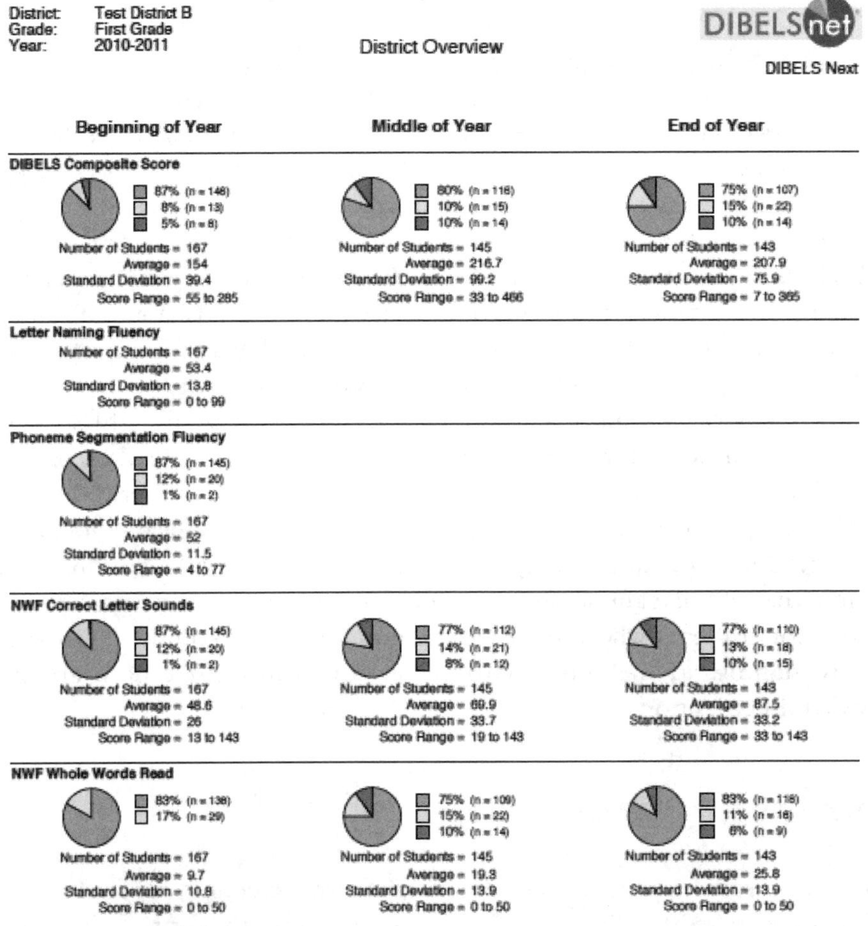

FIGURE 19.1. Sample *DIBELS.net* district-level report for grade 1. Copyright by DIBELS. DIBELS, DIBELS Next, and DIBELSnet are registered trademarks of Dynamic Measurement Group. Reprinted by permission.

fast CBMReading

Group Name: 02-CBMRe-2014 | CBMR English Screening Report

Teacher: Nicole DiCarlo | Grade: 02 | School: FAST Academy Elementary | District: FAST Academy District | School year: 2014-15

Class -							
Student name	Words Read Correct (WRC)			Percentile rank in grade ()			
	Fall	Winter	Spring	Class	School	District	National*
Bacon Sarah	80.0 [91%]			56	56	54	58
Bunch John	117.0			64	64	65	88
Childs Katherine	66.0			46	46	41	43
Covington Angel	63.0 [89%] !			44	44	40	39
Crowley Dylan	72.0 [91%]			48	48	47	50
Goss Rachel	2.0 [20%] ! !			1	1	1	1
Helms Aidan	77.0 [94%]			54	54	51	55
Kendall Joshua	74.0 [94%]			52	52	50	52
Lucero Gavin	28.0 ! !			28	28	24	11
Mayfield Ethan	82.0 [88%]			58	58	55	59
Meeks Devin							
Newell Lauren	216.0			92	92	91	90
Oconnell Peyton	13.0 ! !			8	8	7	1
Plummer Sara	15.0 [79%] ! !			16	16	14	2
Proctor Bradley	61.0 [90%] !			42	42	38	37
Rangel Benjamin	14.0 [88%] ! !			14	14	11	1
Rosado Gerard	147.0 [90%]			68	68	72	99
Schaefer Calib	26.0 [81%] ! !			26	26	22	9
Sinclair Susan	37.0 [90%] !			32	32	28	18
Spivey Luca							
Stinson Marti	37.0 [86%] !			32	32	28	18
Whaley Casey	13.0 [81%] ! !			8	8	7	1
Yoder Sophie							
Zuniga Brandon							

FIGURE 19.2. Sample FAST (now known as FAST Bridge) CBM reading class-level report. Copyright by the University of Minnesota. Reprinted by permission.

are at high risk and most likely need immediate intensive intervention. While a low score on this screening assessment could mean that a student needs help, the data must be compared with other sources of information.

The School-Wide Information System (SWIS; Educational and Community Supports, 2015) provides a mechanism for schools to screen and monitor student behavior. A sample schoolwide report is presented in Figure 19.3. Data for this report are aggregated to demonstrate the key variables of student behavior in a school. For example, educators using SWIS in their schools can monitor the average number of ODRs that have occurred per day across the months of the school year. Likewise, educators can see what times of day and which days of the week ODRs are the most likely to occur, and where on campus problem behaviors are being documented. The SWIS School-Wide Report also allows educators

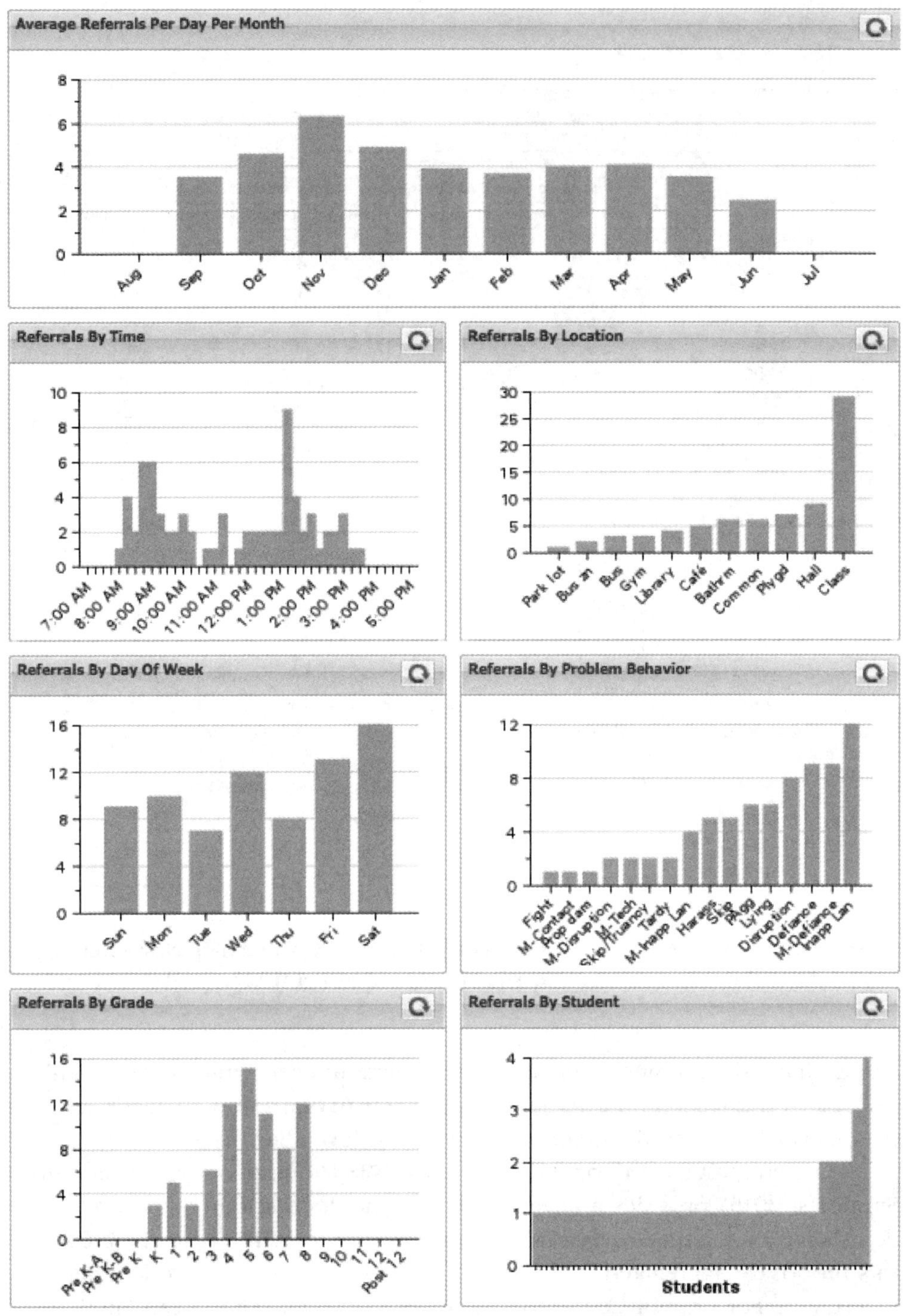

FIGURE 19.3. Sample SWIS School-Wide Report. Copyright by the University of Oregon. Reprinted by permission.

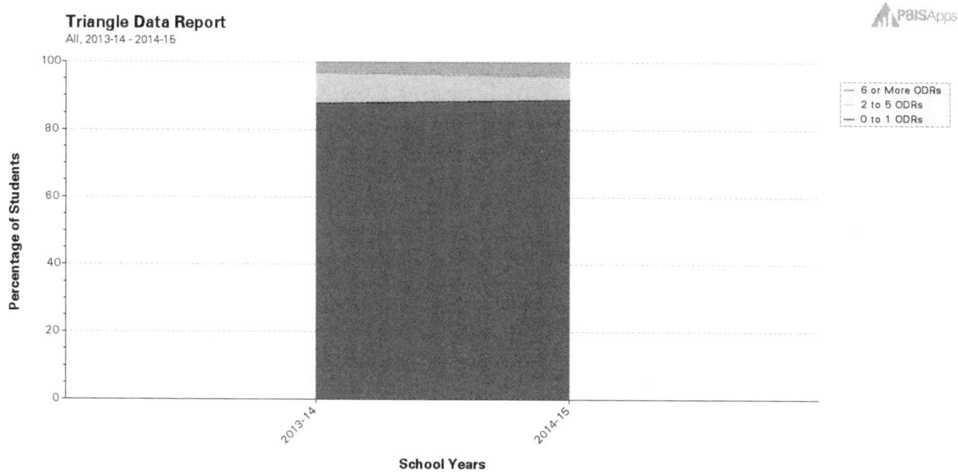

FIGURE 19.4. Sample SWIS School-Wide Report. Copyright by the University of Oregon. Reprinted by permission.

to compare ODRs by grade level. The SWIS Triangle Data Report shown in Figure 19.4 provides a graphic representation of how many students are being supported at each tier.

SWIS also provides a graph depicting referrals by student, which demonstrates the number of students engaged in problem behavior and their number of ODRs. The Student Referral Report graph presented in Figure 19.5 provides a more in-depth depiction of the behavior of individual students. Students who have received three or more ODRs are represented by their student identification number. This report can be used to screen students in a number of ways. For

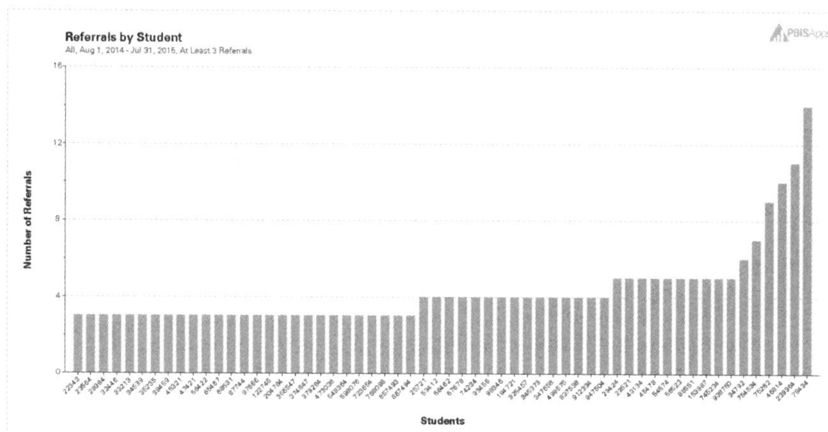

FIGURE 19.5. Sample SWIS Student Referral Report. Copyright by the University of Oregon. Reprinted by permission.

example, educators can use the Student Referral Report in October to identify the students at greatest risk of engaging in problem behavior throughout the year. Specifically, if they are not identified and provided with an effective intervention, students with two ODRs in October are very likely to demonstrate a pattern of interfering behavior as evidenced by six or more ODRs by the end of the school year (McIntosh, Frank, & Spaulding, 2010). In addition, school teams can monitor this report on a regular basis to ensure that students who have received one or more ODRs are being monitored and that the students who have received the most ODRs are being provided with Tier 2 or 3 behavior supports.

The six universal screening reports included here show the range of different types of information that educators can obtain from academic and behavior screening data. The first two reports show the effectiveness of Tier 1 academic instruction at the school and district level. The district-level DIBELS report (Figure 19.1) indicates that the first-grade reading instruction was very close to the 80% goal in most areas tested. Similar reports by school can be generated to learn if there are differences in the number of students meeting learning benchmarks across all the schools in a district. The classroom-level FAST CBM report (Figure 19.2) does not include the percentage meeting the benchmark goal, but this can be easily calculated from the data given. The large number of exclamation marks quickly shows that less than 80% of students in this class met the goal. As noted in the next chapter (Chapter 20), screening scores must be used alongside other indicators of student performance to identify the best interventions. The FAST classroom-level report also includes information about how the students' scores compare with four types of normative groups: class, school, district, and national. These comparisons are important because they show how well each student is doing compared with other students locally and nationally. Comparing student screening data with national norms is very important because it shows whether the students are developing the target skills in ways similar to their age- and grade-level peers in the United States.

The SWIS School-Wide Report (Figure 19.3) demonstrates how well a school's Tier 1 behavior support system is functioning across key dimensions. In contrast, the SWIS Student Referral Report (Figure 19.5) depicts how well individual students are responding to the Tier 1 system and allows schools to identify those students who need additional support with their behavior. The school whose Triangle Data Report is depicted in Figure 19.4 knows precisely what percentages of students in their school require support at each tier and how well they are doing at improving their system so that more students are supported at Tier 1. You can see that this school made a slight gain in the percentage of students who are responding to Tier 1 (the dark gray zone on the bottom of the graph) from the first year to the second, but there was also a slight increase in the percentage of students requiring Tier 3 support (the light gray zone at the top of the graph).

While the ODR data available in SWIS provide an important source of information, there are two limitations to using ODRs as the only behavior screener.

First, ODRs are likely to capture the most noticeable behaviors, but they can be less sensitive to more subtle or low-level behaviors. Secondly, it is important to keep in mind that ODRs only capture students' externalizing behaviors. It is equally important to identify and provide intervention to students who have significant internalizing behaviors (Cook et al., 2011). Specifically, students' ability to access and benefit from instruction can be hampered when they are withdrawn, anxious, or depressed. As such, teams are encouraged to use multiple sources of data to identify students whose behavior is likely interfering with academic success (Lane, Menzies, Oakes, & Kalberg, 2012).

Schools can overcome both of the limitations of relying exclusively on ODR data by employing universal screeners that rely on teachers' ratings of their students' internalizing and externalizing behaviors. While there are a number of options, the Student Risk Screening Scale for Internalizing and Externalizing Behaviors (SRSS-IE; Lane, Oakes, Carter, Lambert, & Jenkins, 2013) is a free and easy screener that schools can employ to capture the spectrum of interfering behavior. As represented in Figure 19.6, a shared spreadsheet can be created with a tab for each teacher. A few minutes of a staff meeting can be devoted to each teacher logging in and rating his or her students across 12 behaviors, resulting in a total score that can be considered in the context of other data to determine the need for intervention.

NEXT STEPS FOR IMPLEMENTING UNIVERSAL SCREENING PROGRAMS

Using universal screening involves selecting and administering assessments that indicate whether students are meeting the established learning standards. When a student is not at the standard, some form of additional instruction is needed. If less than 80% of students in a classroom, grade, or school attain the benchmark target on screening measures, a significant part of the work that the school team needs to do is to review and revise Tier 1 core instruction so that more students meet the goal. It is important to note that efforts to improve Tier 1 core instruction cannot replace tiered supports for students who are already significantly behind. As described in earlier chapters, teachers must "triage" students based on multiple data sources and provide increasingly intensive supports as needed. The good news is that many students will find success as a result of Tier 2 interventions. These interventions include group-based instruction that reviews the essential learning for behavior, math, reading, and writing. In most cases, students will be successful in response to Tier 2 direct instruction. Such lessons include four to six students and cover the steps needed to complete important school tasks. Tier 2 support for behavior can also include a schoolwide intervention such as CICO, which has been shown to be effective for as much as 67% of students who are struggling to meet behavioral expectations (Filter et al., 2007).

Student Risk Screening Scale for Internalizing and Externalizing Behaviors (SRSS-IE)													
	Directions: Please rate each student on each behavior using the following scale: 0=Never, 1=Rarely, 2=Occasionally, 3=Frequently												
Student Name	Steal	Lie, Cheat, Sneak	Behavior Problems	Peer Rejection	Low Academic Achievement	Negative Attitude	Aggressive Behavior	Emotionally Flat	Shy	Withdrawn	Sad; Anxious	Lonely	SRSS-IE TOTAL
Black, John	0	0	2	0	2	0	0	3	3	3	3	3	19
Childs, Sue	0	0	0	0	0	0	0	1	1	2	0	0	4
Conley, Rebecca	0	0	0	3	0	0	0	0	0	0	0	0	3
Deveraux, Angela	0	0	0	0	3	0	0	0	0	0	1	1	5
Everett, Bill	0	0	0	0	2	0	0	0	0	0	0	0	2
Floyd, Henry	1	1	2	0	0	3	0	0	0	0	0	0	7
Greene, Amanda	0	0	0	0	0	0	0	0	0	2	0	2	4
Hill, Garth	0	0	0	1	1	3	0	0	0	0	0	0	5
Johnson, Susanna	0	0	0	0	0	0	0	0	0	0	3	0	3
Lewis, Cindy	0	0	0	0	0	0	0	0	0	0	0	3	3
Marsh, William	0	2	3	1	1	3	0	0	0	0	0	2	12
Neal, Robert	0	0	0	2	0	0	0	0	0	0	0	0	2
Roberts, Allyson	0	1	0	0	0	0	0	0	0	1	1	3	6
Sutherland, Steve	3	3	3	3	3	2	2	0	0	0	0	0	19
Thompson, Parker	0	2	2	0	2	2	0	0	0	0	0	0	8
West, Tabitha	0	0	0	0	0	0	0	2	3	1	1	3	10

FIGURE 19.6. Sample Student Risk Screening Scale (SRSS) class screening.

If a student is not successful with Tier 2 support, then Tier 3 individualized support can be used to see what type of instruction the student needs to be successful.

SUMMARY

Universal screening is a method established by the field of public health to identify people at risk of developing problems and those who have developed problems that need to be addressed. In education, academic universal screening includes having all students complete assessment measures that show whether each student is meeting the stated learning objectives, while screening measures for behavior are completed by teachers about all students. In recent years, U.S. efforts have focused on using national assessments to identify students who need additional support so that they can meet the learning goals. Using universal screening measures helps teachers identify which students need extra help. When extra help is provided to students before they fall seriously behind, they are often able to catch up and meet grade-level learning goals. For this reason, schools are encouraged to embrace universal screening as an effective tool for promoting effective outcomes for all students.

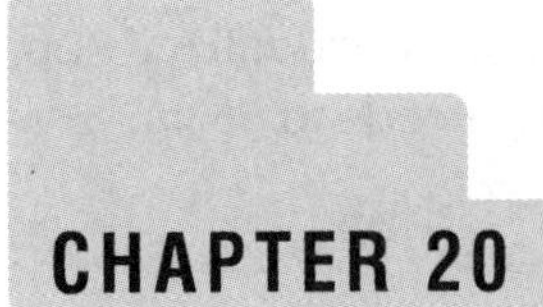

CHAPTER 20

Problem Solving

Problem solving is a central component of an MTSS. This chapter describes how problem-solving steps can be used to assist students with school difficulties. As mentioned in Chapter 8, work by Bransford and Stein (1984) and later Deno (1985) led to the development of the IDEAL problem-solving model for schools. The IDEAL method includes five steps that can be used at all stages of an MTSS to support student learning. This method focuses on understanding that students experience problems and difficulties, but that they themselves are not problems. An important aspect of the IDEAL method for school problem solving is that it offers a variety of options that provide additional instruction for students who need it.

BACKGROUND

When the first U.S. special education law (Education of All Handicapped Children Act [EHCA]; Public Law 94-142) was passed in 1975, the goal was to make sure that all students could access an effective education. Prior to this law, children with disabilities were often denied access to education even though it was provided for other children. Without this federal legislation, each state provided varying degrees of education for children with disabilities, but there was no consistency. Leading up to 1975, legal cases brought by advocates for children with disabilities created precedents for all children to have access to a free public education; EHCA created a new system to ensure that all children, regardless of ability, could access this right. Much of the advocacy for passage of EHCA was by advocates for children with severe and profound disabilities such as orthopedic impairments or Down syndrome. As a result of this advocacy, early understanding of the law included a belief among teachers and parents that those served by the law would include only children with a medical diagnosis of a specific, and generally severe, condition.

Starting in the late 1970s and well into the 1990s the U.S. Department of Education, as well as the state departments of education, worked to ensure that all teachers, school administrators, and other school personnel understood the special rights and legal protections afforded students with disabilities under EHCA and its successor laws (i.e., Individuals with Disabilities Education Act, or IDEA). Many states passed laws requiring that all teachers and most other professional school staff take a college-level course or other form of professional development to be knowledgeable about the federal and state special education laws. As a result of such requirements, many classroom teachers and administrators came to think of students with disabilities as very different and separate from other students. After the passage of EHCA and through the 1980s, the term *mainstream* was used to refer to students in "regular" or "general" classrooms, while students with disabilities were largely taught in separate, stand-alone classrooms (see Chapter 25 for details).

Perhaps due to this separateness and isolation, some educators came to think that all of the school difficulties of children with disabilities were due to the inherent nature of the disability itself and not related to the classroom environment or teaching methods. This is an important point because if there is an assumption that a student's difficulties are all within the child, then there is little need or motivation to consider whether different teaching practices could help the student. But the assumption that all of a student's school problems were caused by severe disabilities—and labeled with a medical diagnosis—did not match the demographic data about students served in special education as it was implemented in the 1980s and 1990s. While many of those who advocated for special education laws expected that the majority of students who would be served under these laws would be children with severe disabilities, by the time that the law was revised and first updated in 1986 there were data showing that the majority of students served under EHCA were primarily students with so-called mild disabilities such as specific learning disability (SLD).

In the school year 1980–1981, the second year of EHCA implementation, students with SLD made up 3.6% of all students in U.S. public schools and those with SLD were the largest subgroup of all students with disabilities served under the law (National Center for Education Statistics, 2013c). By 1991, when the EHCA law was revised for a second time, and when the title was changed to IDEA, students with SLD made up 5% of all U.S. public school students, and their numbers were more than double any other special education category. These data surprised many advocates for children with disabilities. A more detailed history of efforts to improve special education is found in Chapter 25. Important to understanding the history of problem solving is that these numbers worried education policymakers because if they kept growing, the resources needed to support special education would not be available at the federal or state levels. Thankfully, there were educators and researchers who realized that another approach to supporting students with school difficulties might be needed to address the problems of students with "mild" disabilities.

Concurrent with the passage of Public Law 94-142, the U.S. Congress funded research centers at several major universities with the goal of developing research-based methods for identifying and supporting students with disabilities. One of the centers funded was at the University of Minnesota. The grant support at this center was used by researchers Stan Deno and Phyllis Mirken (Shinn, 1989) to develop assessment and intervention materials for students with disabilities, including SLD. In 1985, Stan Deno summarized the research in a seminal article titled "Curriculum-Based Measurement: The Emerging Alternative." In this article, Deno described how research on tools to identify and progress monitor students with SLD had contributed to a new understanding of the types of difficulties that students sometimes face in schools. Importantly for MTSS, Deno's work described how using a problem-solving approach for understanding students' learning difficulties could offer faster and much more effective solutions for students and teachers.

Since 1985, Deno has updated the problem-solving model and described how it continues to offer the best way to support students who exhibit school difficulties. Initially, this model was conceptualized as a tool for supporting students with academic difficulties, but its applications have been expanded to include students with behavior and conduct problems such as attention-deficit/hyperactivity disorder (ADHD), oppositional defiant disorder (ODD), and others. Deno credits two noneducation authors for the nucleus of the acronym for this problem-solving method. In 1984, John Bransford and Barry Stein published a book titled *The IDEAL Problem Solver: A Guide for Improving Thinking, Learning, and Creativity*. This book described the basic five steps in a general problem-solving model like what Deno and colleagues (Deno, 1985) had been developing in their research. A key feature of both the Bransford and Stein (1984) and Deno (1985) definitions of a "problem" was that it was separate and distinct from the person(s) who was experiencing it (Shinn, 1989). This is important for education because instead of defining a student as being the problem, the IDEAL model defines a problem as the difference between what is expected and what is occurring. This means that the problem is not inherent to a single person, but that a problem exists and needs to be addressed.

Consider how radically different it is to think of a problem as separate from an individual. If a teacher thinks that a student's difficulties are because of a genetic disorder that cannot be changed in any way, will that teacher think that changing his or her instruction could be worthwhile? But what if the teacher thinks that changes in classroom instruction and routines could improve outcomes for the student? Most teachers go into education because they want to help children. If doing something different in the classroom might help an individual student, would a teacher be willing to try it? We like to think that the answer is "yes." An MTSS is based on having teachers adjust instruction based on student need, and research suggests this is the better approach to take.

PROBLEM-SOLVING STEPS

There are five steps in the IDEAL problem-solving method (Bransford & Stein, 1984; Deno, 2013):

1. *I*dentify the problem.
2. *D*efine the problem.
3. *E*xplore alternate interventions.
4. *A*pply the selected intervention.
5. *L*ook at the effects.

Each step is uniquely important for effective problem solving and no step should be skipped. Each is described in detail.

Identify the Problem

The first step is to identify that there is a problem. This step corresponds with other research on what it takes for people to change. Prochaska and DiClemente (1992) suggest that there are five stages toward change and the first step is *precontemplation*. Precontemplation means that the individual does not (yet) acknowledge that a change is needed. But this is followed by the *contemplation* stage, at which point steps toward change are considered. Problem identification in the IDEAL model is like contemplation in the Prochaska and DiClemente change model. When the problem is identified—through contemplation—this does not mean it will automatically be solved, only that at least one person thinks there is a problem. Another analogy about problem identification is that it is the first moment when the problem appears on someone's "radar" (Brown-Chidsey & Steege, 2005). When a ship's captain sees something on the radar, it's not possible to know if the "blip" is small or large. Just like a blip on the radar, problem identification brings the problem to awareness, but additional steps are needed to do something about it.

Define the Problem

After a problem has been identified the next step is to define it. This is important because only once a problem has been defined can the importance of the problem be known. The best way to define a problem is to measure the distance between what is expected and what is occurring. This definition captures the nature of the problem for the stakeholders. In school settings the primary stakeholders are students and teachers. In general, school problems happen when there is a difference between what the teacher expects and what the student is doing or has done. When a student's performance is relatively close to the teacher's expectation, the situation is likely to be understood as a minor problem. Often, a teacher can provide reteaching or correction and the student can meet the stated goal. But when the difference between the teacher's expectations and the student's performance is large, the situation can seem very different. Then, a teacher might start to think that the student can never meet the goal, and the student might give up because the tasks are so hard. The larger the distance between the expectations and performance, the more likely it is that the problem is one that needs intervention.

In order to know the difference between what is expected and what is happening, a reliable and valid measurement of student performance is needed. Thankfully, there are many such measures available. For academic skills, curriculum-based measurement (CBM) works very well (and was actually designed for this purpose). For behaviors, information about how many discipline incidents have occurred, data from systematic classroom observations, and teachers' ratings of students' behaviors are all useful. In order to know if a student's current performance is different from other students, there needs to be some type of standard or basis of comparison. Such standards could be classroom specific, such as when a teacher expects all students to line up a certain way, or could be based on school, grade, district, or national norms. Once the student's performance and basis of comparison are known, then the team can decide if the difference between these is big enough to justify intervention.

If the difference is significant, then the team should consider different interventions and decide which one to try. Sometimes, the difference might not be big enough to justify intervention, but someone still thinks there is a problem. A classic example of this is when a parent thinks a child should be getting better grades, but the student's current performance meets or exceeds the school's standards. In such cases, it is important that a team member explain to the parent that the student's current performance is at or above the school's expectations. This is much better than not saying anything to the parent who might think the school did not pay attention to the concern or did not care. Certainly, many parents will want their children to do well in school and may benefit from understanding how the problem-solving method works. In some cases, it may be that the student should be referred for talented and gifted programming. Such programs are different from helping a student get higher grades, but could be an appropriate option for certain students. As schools implement the Common Core State Standards (CCSS), grade-level and schoolwide teams will want to learn how to compare student performance with those standards. See Box 20.1 for more information.

BOX 20.1. Understanding Student Performance and the CCSS

With the implementation of the CCSS (see Chapter 5), there is much greater consistency in what students will be expected to learn in each grade. As of 2015, 43 U.S. states and five territories had adopted and implemented the Standards. These standards are not a radical departure from prior learning goals, but do offer more consistency in what students will learn in each grade level across the United States. This is important because U.S. students are increasingly mobile during their school-age years. With common standards, students will be more likely to experience the same learning content even if they move among schools, districts, or states. Most education publishers have aligned their materials with the Standards but additional resources for teachers to understand the CCSS are available. The National Governors Association Center for Best Practices, Council of Chief State School Officers (2010)—which developed the standards—has a website with resources for teachers and parents:

www.corestandards.org/resources

In addition there is an "app" available for both Apple and Android devices that can be downloaded to smartphones and tablet computers for easy reference.

Apple version: *https://itunes.apple.com/us/app/common-core-standards/id439424555?mt=8*

Android version: *https://play.google.com/store/apps/details?id=com.masteryconnect.CommonCore&hl=en*

At first, the standards can seem overwhelming, so teachers may want to choose one area to learn at a time. State-level assessments matched to the standards were implemented by states starting in 2014–2015 and the data from these assessments will provide more information about how individual students are doing in relation to expected learning outcomes.

Explore Alternate Interventions

Once a team has determined that a student's school difficulty is sufficiently different from the expectations to warrant intervention, the next step is to consider possible interventions and select one. Over time, educators will become familiar with specific interventions for different behavioral and learning areas and this will help teams with the exploration process. There are many websites at which information about interventions can be found. Thanks to the Internet, there are reviews of different interventions that teams might want to consider. Table 20.1 includes a list of websites that include reviews of specific interventions. All of tthe sites listed in the table have conducted objective, thorough, and scientifically

TABLE 20.1. Websites with Reviews of Instruction and Intervention Materials

Name	Website
Best Evidence Encyclopedia	*www.bestevidence.org*
National Center on Intensive Intervention	*www.intensiveintervention.org*
Technical Assistance Center on Positive Behavioral Interventions and Supports	*www.pbis.org*
Center on Response to Intervention	*www.rti4success.org*
What Works Clearinghouse	*http://ies.ed.gov/ncee/wwc*

valid reviews of the interventions covered. None of the sites endorse any interventions, but instead provide information that educators can consider as they make instructional decisions. When a team is not certain about what intervention to use, it might be best to "test drive" two or three interventions in order to see what works best (Steege & Watson, 2009). When comparing interventions, it is important to use data collection and review procedures that allow accurate comparison of their effects. (See Chapter 22 for more information about how to compare interventions.)

Apply the Selected Intervention

Having decided on one intervention to use, the team needs to arrange for its implementation. Much of this work involves logistics of time, people, materials, and location. In addition, the team will need to select the progress measure to monitor the student's improvement over time. Keeping in mind that interventions are always in addition to core (Tier 1) instruction, the team should identify when in the school day the intervention will be provided (see Chapter 13). When there is a "skills" block or other time set aside each day for interventions, locating the time in the schedule is much easier. When there is no such time already set aside, the team will have to figure out what other time block in the student's day can be used for intervention. This process may lead the team to urge that the school add a skills block to the daily schedule! In addition to the time, there must be an interventionist provided to implement the intervention. Sometimes, a student may be joining an existing intervention group and so there is already a teacher, specialist, or paraprofessional offering such instruction. But if the right group for the student does not yet exist, the team needs to figure out who will provide the intervention. Importantly, the interventionist must be properly trained to use the selected intervention before the intervention begins. When a published intervention is used, there are often online or computer-based training materials available.

The specific materials for the intervention will be needed as well. It is helpful if there is one person in each building who coordinates the ordering and purchase of intervention materials. That person will be able to indicate when anything needs to be ordered. Knowing whether there are sufficient materials is important because it will affect the start date of the intervention. Where the intervention will take place is important as well. When a student will join an existing group, this is generally easy to determine, but when a new group is formed, space for the lessons will be needed. Second to time, space is a precious resource in schools so the team might need to review allv existing intervention space use and be sure that available locations are being used wisely. Over time, the team members will become familiar with locations in the school where interventions can happen. A final step in selecting and implementing the intervention is to choose a progress measure to be used. No intervention should be implemented without a corresponding progress measure. Unless there are data showing how the student is doing, educators will not know if it worked.

Progress Monitoring

As mentioned throughout this book, there are numerous existing progress measures that can be used to track student progress. Table 20.2 summarizes some of the most commonly used measures. This list is not exhaustive and certainly others can be used as well. The essential step for the team is to decide which measure will be used and how frequently. The National Center on Intensive Intervention (2014) recommends that students participating in Tier 2 interventions complete progress measures at least once a month, and that students participating in Tier 3 interventions complete progress measures at least once a week. Team members should keep in mind that the frequency of progress monitoring will affect how soon the data can be reviewed. There must be at least 3 data points before the effects of an intervention can be considered. If a student is monitored once a month, that will mean at least 3 months must pass before the data can be reviewed. In addition, the data need to be stable (see Chapter 21 for details). For

TABLE 20.2. Published Progress Monitoring Tools

Name	Website
AIMSweb	*www.aimsweb.com*
DIBELS	*http://dibels.org*
EasyCBM	*www.easycbm.com*
FastBridge Learning	*https://app.fastbridge.org/*
SWIS	*www.pbisapps.org/Applications/Pages/SWIS-Suite.aspx*

this reason, many school teams monitor Tier 2 students every 2 weeks, allowing the data to be reviewed after 6 weeks.

Look at the Effects

Once all of the above steps have been implemented, the team will have data indicating whether the intervention is working. Specific details about the technical review of data are provided in Chapter 22. Here, the focus is on the logistics of bringing the team together to look at data. Effective use of problem-solving methods requires that school teams create and use regular meetings to review data. As explained in Chapter 6, there is a process to creating effective teams, and for problem solving to be useful, teams need to spend time developing effective meeting procedures. Usually, it is not possible to review the data of all students participating in intervention on one day, in one meeting. But, given that students start and end intervention at different times, that is not necessary. Instead, effective school teams create schedules for reviewing student data at regular intervals. As explained above and in Chapter 21, the frequency of data collection drives the frequency of data review. There need to be at least 3 data points before data can be reviewed, but sometimes there will need to be more in order for the data to be stable.

With 3 or more data points plotted on a graph, the team can take a look at whether an intervention is having the desired effect. The easiest way for the whole team to see the data at once is to use a computer projector to display it on a wall of the meeting room. Be sure to close any curtains or doors to the room when displaying student data so that Family Educational Rights and Privacy Act (FERPA) rules are followed. With the data on the wall, the team can quickly see and discuss whether the intervention is having the desired effects for the student. The good news is that much of the time, when a research-based intervention has been implemented with integrity, it will be working and the team will quickly decide to maintain the intervention. In such cases, the data review takes about 2 minutes. This is important because it frees up time for discussion of students whose data indicate that the desired progress is not happening.

When reviewing data, school teams do need to consider whether the intervention was implemented with integrity. As explained in Chapter 17, without treatment integrity it is impossible to know exactly what led to the student's specific outcomes. Because schools are very busy places, when a student's data show adequate progress based on the goals, treatment integrity is assumed. While making this assumption has limitations, if the student's performance is improving, why mess with success? But when a student's data show limited or no progress, the team's first question should be "Was the intervention implemented with integrity?" This is important because it might be that the intervention could be effective if it were put into place exactly as intended. There are a number of reasons why an intervention might not get implemented correctly. If the student or interventionist is often absent, implementation can suffer. It may also be the case that the interventionist did not get adequate initial training for the specific intervention. When the student's data indicate a lack of progress, it is the school team's responsibility to investigate treatment integrity. If there is evidence that the intervention was not implemented with integrity, the next step is to start it over with integrity. To be certain that such integrity is reached, the steps outlined in Chapter 17 should be followed.

After investigating integrity and determining that it was adequate, the team needs to review the data again. When it shows good progress, the intervention can be continued. If it shows too little or no progress, the team needs to choose another plan. Often, there might be other possible interventions worth trying and the team will decide to implement another intervention and continue progress monitoring. If a student does not show progress over a period of time, then the team needs to discuss whether a referral for special education is justified. Each state, and some school districts, have spvecific policies about the process for referring students to special education after MTSS methods have been tried. Team members will need to learn and use the local and state guidelines about such referrals. Once a formal referral for special education is made, the rules and regulations concerning special education will need to be followed.

WHEN IS PROBLEM SOLVING NEEDED?

The steps included in the IDEAL problem-solving method are very thorough and certainly take a significant amount of time to implement correctly. For this reason it is important to consider whether every student with difficulties will require such detailed problem solving. Fuchs and Fuchs (2007) suggest that students and schools can benefit from using a combination of a "standard-protocol" and a problem-solving approach to an MTSS (see Chapter 18). A standard protocol refers to having a predetermined small number of research-based interventions available and ready to use as soon as students demonstrate difficulties. Often, schools use such standard protocols for Tier 2 interventions. The benefit of having such programs already set up and ready to go is that the process and time needed to start an intervention for a student is reduced. Research suggests that such standard protocols can be very effective for most students who require intervention. This alleviates the need for detailed problem solving for every student who presents with difficulties. But for those students who do not respond to a Tier 2 standard-protocol intervention, the problem-solving process is the best next step. Many schools employ the problem-solving method at Tier 3. Remember, only 5% of a school's total enrollment will need Tier 3 support if Tiers 1 and 2 are effective, so the total number of students who would be carefully reviewed using the problem-solving steps is quite small. This is important because it means that the team will have the time needed to review each student's situation carefully and to discuss possible solutions.

PROBLEM SOLVING IN ACTION

The following example illustrates the IDEAL problem-solving steps as applied for a student named Dean. As you will see, Dean displayed both academic and behavioral difficulties, both of which were addressed through the problem-solving process.

Background

Dean is a second-grade student at a small rural elementary school. Dean has attended the school since kindergarten, which consisted of a half-day program. Dean did not attend preschool prior to enrolling in kindergarten, but met all of the district's kindergarten-screening benchmarks. Both Dean's kindergarten and first-grade teachers reported that he was very quiet and shy, but he was well behaved and met all of the learning targets. In October of his second-grade year, Dean's teacher, Mrs. Doiron, shared concerns for him at the second-grade teachers' weekly grade-level team meeting. Mrs. Doiron was concerned about Dean because he was avoiding or refusing to do math assignments, and recently had "bolted" from the classroom on three occasions. She indicated that Dean was doing fine in reading and language arts, but not in math.

Tier 1

Dean's core instruction for math was the Everyday Mathematics program (McGraw-Hill Education, 2013). This program incorporates a "spiral" curriculum in which students are exposed to each topic or skill multiple times in each grade level, and then again at successive grade levels. Mrs. Doiron reported that she was teaching the program with integrity, but that she also added additional lessons during the core math instruction time because of her concern that Everyday Mathematics did not prepare the students well enough in computation fact fluency. The additional instruction included two parts: direct instruction of addition and subtraction math facts, and the peer-tutoring program called Peer Assisted Learning Strategies (PALS). For the initial fact teaching, Mrs. Doiron stood at the front of the room and used a computer projector to model the facts. The students had individual whiteboards on which they wrote answers to fact problems that Mrs. Doiron presented. These lessons were conducted for 15 minutes each, three times a week.

The PALS lessons consisted of the program-provided command card and student materials (Vanderbilt Kennedy Center, 2014). PALS lessons involve matching all students in pairs based on their current skills and then having them complete scripted coaching activities with each other. Prior to having the students coach each other, Mrs. Doiron provided four lessons in how to use PALS correctly. Once the students learned how to do the PALS sessions, they were incorporated into the class math instruction time two times per week for 15 minutes each. Mrs. Doiron reported that it was the PALS lessons that Dean appeared to avoid. During the second and third training sessions, Dean requested permission to go to the bathroom and was out of the classroom for most of the sessions. During the fourth training session when the students were supposed to practice the PALS coaching activities with their partners, Dean refused to speak to his partner and put his head on this desk. When Mrs. Doiron began the first formal PALS session the following week, Dean ran out of the classroom and hid in a hallway closet until the school psychologist, Mr. Gerard, convinced him to come to his office. This behavior was repeated two more times at the start of subsequent PALS sessions.

Tier 2

Based on the Tier 1 information that Mrs. Doiron shared, the grade-level team members asked Mrs. Doiron about Dean's general math performance and what other ideas she was considering. She reported that Dean scored between 70 and 80% correct on most math quizzes and tests. His fall math benchmark screening score was 1 point below the goal, so she has not yet put him into an intervention group. She has considered adding him to a group that meets during the school's daily skills block and that is run by the Title I math teacher. This group works on addition and subtraction fact fluency. Based on these details, the other teachers agreed that it made sense to have Dean attend the intervention block daily, starting right away. This was done and Dean's progress scores are shown in Figure 20.1. As shown in the graph, Dean made little progress toward the midyear second-grade math goal score of 14 after 4 weeks of the Tier 2 fact fluency lessons.

In early October, Mrs. Doiron again brought Dean's case to the second-grade team meeting to discuss his progress. In addition to sharing the graph, she also reported that Dean was continuing to run out of the room during all PALS sessions. Dean would go to the school office and sit near the secretary until Mrs. Doiron or Mr. Gerard could come and take him back to the classroom. Although Mrs. Doiron and Mr. Gerard had worked out a system for getting him back into the room, preventing his departure was the goal. This behavior was very disruptive and kept Dean away from a part of his math instruction. The team discussed whether Dean might dislike his assigned PALS partner or if the PALS activities were too hard for him. Mrs. Doiron reported that she did not think so, based on observing him in class and reviewing his other math work. Based on this information, the grade-level team recommended that Mrs. Doiron ask to meet with the building-level student assistance team (SAT) and discuss Dean's situation.

RSU #6
Year: 2014-2015

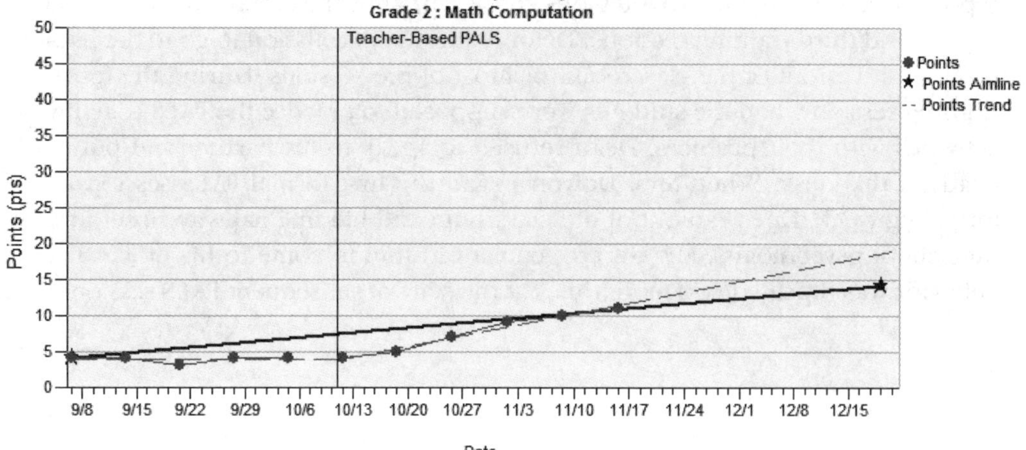

FIGURE 20.1. Dean's Tier 2 progress data.

Tier 3

In Dean's school district, when a student is referred to the SAT, it is considered Tier 3. But in this district, such a meeting does not automatically mean that the student will be referred for special education. Rather, the SAT often helps the teacher develop other interventions to be tried. Sometimes, the SAT also arranges for additional data about the student to be collected. After Mrs. Doiron shared Dean's data with the SAT, the members used the IDEAL steps to address the situation. First, the team affirmed that Mrs. Doiron and the other second-grade teachers viewed Dean's math performance as a problem (identify the problem). Next, Dean's current (e.g., October) math progress score was compared with the goal for second graders. The data showed that he was significantly below the goal and not on track to meet it by the middle of the school year. These data were similar to Dean's recent classroom math assessments, which showed that he got 50–60% of items correct. Based on these data, the SAT affirmed that Dean's math difficulties met the definition of a problem (define the problem).

Next, the team asked additional questions concerning Dean's classroom behaviors. For example, they wanted to know if he ever ran out of the classroom at any times other than during PALS, and how well he got along with the other students. Mrs. Doiron reported that Dean was very quiet, but polite with other students. He rarely initiated conversations with classmates, but he responded appropriately when classmates spoke to him, and he never ran away at other times. She indicated that Dean had a good sense of humor and he often smiled at other students' jokes, and he clearly followed along with instruction and class activities. The team members wanted to know if Dean showed any other math avoidance behaviors. Mrs. Doiron reported that he clearly did not favor math and had to be reminded to get out his math materials more often than other subjects. When given the choice to work on math or other tasks, he always picked another task. His independent math work was neat and accurate, but he often did not fully complete assignments despite using all the time available. Mrs. Doiron reported that Dean was fully engaged during her math fact lessons three times a week as well as during the daily Everyday Math lessons and activities.

The team members agreed that Dean's math difficulties appeared to be related to difficulties with fact fluency, but were not sure why he was engaged and compliant with the whole-class lessons and not the PALS lessons. After discussing whether to try a different fluency intervention, the team decided it wanted more information about Dean's behavior. It was decided that Mr. Gerard, a member of the SAT, would conduct a functional behavioral assessment (FBA) of Dean's behaviors during whole-class and small-group (Tier 2) math lessons. This meant that Dean would continue to participate in the small-group Tier 2 lessons while the FBA was conducted.

The FBA consisted of interviews with Mrs. Doiron, the Title I math teacher, and Dean's parents. Results indicated that Dean did not engage in running-away behaviors in any other settings. Observations conducted during the Tier 2 lessons showed that Dean was compliant with the teacher's directions, but he did not interact at all with the other students in the group. The group consisted of five students (three girls and two boys) from three different second-grade classrooms. The observations revealed that the three girls did most of the talking during the lessons and that the teacher directed much of her attention during the 30-minute lessons to keeping the three girls engaged in the math lesson. Mr. Gerard conducted three observations of Dean during his classroom math instruction. The first was on a Monday when Mrs. Doiron conducted a 15-minute math fact lesson after the Everyday Mathematics activities. During this lesson, Dean was quiet but engaged and wrote answers on his whiteboard as directed by Mrs. Doiron. Mr. Gerard noted that Dean's answers were not always correct and that Dean appeared to look at his neighbor's answers to see if he was right; when incorrect, Dean erased and quickly replaced his answer with the correct one. Dean did not ever volunteer to share his answers with the class, but did state them when called on by Mrs. Doiron.

A second observation was conducted on Tuesday of the same week when there was a PALS lesson scheduled. As the Everyday Math activities ended, Dean was observed to get up and ask Mrs. Doiron if he could go to the bathroom. She told him that he could go after all of his assigned math work was done. Dean walked slowly back to his desk and slumped down. When Mrs. Doiron told the students to get their PALS packets and sit with their partners, Dean got up as if to go and get his packet but then ran out the open classroom door. Having anticipated this, Mr. Gerard followed Dean out of the room and found him near the closet where he often ran. They went to Mr. Gerard's office to discuss the situation. On the past occasions when Dean had gone to Mr. Gerard's office after leaving the classroom, Dean had told Mr. Gerard that the reason he ran away was that doing PALS was "stupid" and a waste of his time. This time, Mr. Gerard asked Dean if maybe the reason he wanted to run away during PALS was that it was hard for him. Dean said that some of the problems were hard and that he hated having to talk to his partner. When asked if he did not like his partner, Dean started crying. After some waiting time, Dean told Mr. Gerard that talking with others has always been hard and he wished school did not require using words.

Mr. Gerard walked Dean back to the classroom and then conducted one additional observation on Thursday of the same week, the next day when PALS was planned. Unlike Tuesday, when Dean asked Mrs. Doiron if he could go to the bathroom before PALS, on Thursday he joined his partner for PALS, very briefly. Dean walked to the desk and started to sit down, then looked up at Mr. Gerard before running out of the room. Again, Mr. Gerard followed Dean out of the room and they went to Mr. Gerard's office to talk. By the time they got to Mr. Gerard's office, Dean was crying. After some time to calm down, Dean was able to tell Mr. Gerard that he just "can't" do PALS because he could not do math and talk at the same time. When asked if this had been a problem before in school, Dean said "no," because all other math had been "in my head." Mr. Gerard asked Dean why he was able to answer Mrs. Doiron's questions about math, and Dean said, "That's different. She's a teacher." Mr. Gerard then asked Dean if he would be willing to try doing PALS with a teacher to see if he could learn the steps. If that worked out, maybe he could try PALS with a student of his choosing. Dean said he would try PALS with a teacher if he and the teacher were the only people in the room. Mr. Gerard agreed that would be a good next step and walked Dean back to his classroom.

Mr. Gerard reported the results of the FBA to the SAT the next week. His conclusion was that Dean's "bolting" behavior functioned to help him avoid PALS, a task he found aversive. The SAT agreed with Mr. Gerard that Dean's behavior seemed to be specific to this situation and that a specialized intervention was needed to help Dean. But the team also agreed that it was worth trying out this intervention first, rather than refer Dean to special education. If Dean's fear of PALS could be addressed without special education, that would benefit everyone. Mr. Gerard outlined a possible intervention for Dean that involved having him work with one teacher alone to practice PALS during the skills block time when he had been attending the fact fluency group (explore alternate interventions). Mr. Ouellette, a fifth-grade teacher with a love of math who was on the SAT, volunteered to be the teacher to work with Dean for this intervention. The team worked out a 4-week schedule in which Dean would work with Mr. Ouellette each day to learn and become comfortable with the PALS procedures (apply the selected intervention). During this time, Dean's math skills would continue to be monitored weekly as before with AIMSweb M-COMP.

Dean's scores on weekly progress measures are shown in Figure 20.2. These data show that he made stable and significant progress toward the year-end math goal. Dean's progress in using PALS with a teacher was important because it suggested that PALS was an effective program for Dean, if Dean completed the steps. The next step for Dean was to have him use PALS with a classmate. To make this happen, and with Mr. Gerard's guidance, Mr. Ouellette asked Dean which one of his classmates he would be willing to have as his PALS partner. Dean indicated that Lisa, a quiet girl who was also a very good math student, would be his choice. With Dean's permission, Mr. Ouellette met with Lisa to explain the situation and ask her to attend PALS sessions with Dean during skills block. Lisa agreed and Mr. Ouellette had Lisa be part of the session with him for 2 weeks before he faded himself, 1 day at a time, over the next 5 weeks. Then, Mr. Ouellette talked with Dean about how Lisa had been his partner for a while and that maybe he was ready to do PALS in the class, with Lisa as his partner. This was arranged, and Dean was able to complete the PALS lessons with Lisa for 3 weeks in a row. Then, Mrs. Doiron met with Dean and suggested that maybe he was

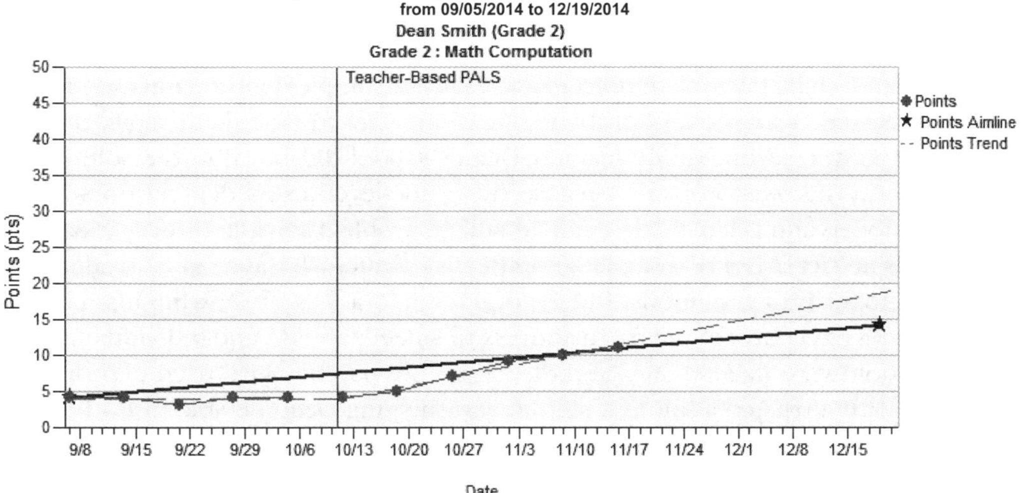

FIGURE 20.2. Dean's progress after a change to a teacher-based PALS intervention.

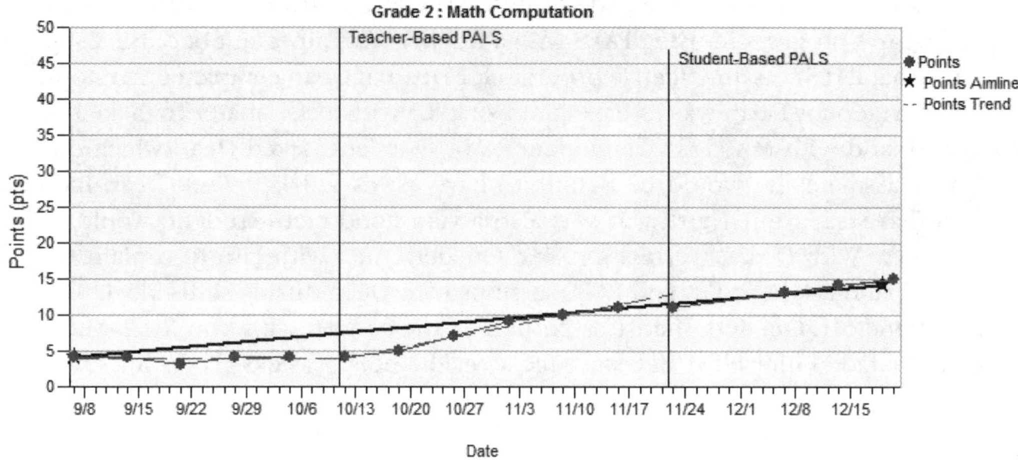

FIGURE 20.3. Dean's progress in PALS with a classroom-based peer. Copyright 2014 by NCS Pearson, Inc. Reprinted by permission. All rights reserved.

ready for a partner change (a typical event in PALS). Dean said he could try it and Mrs. Doiron assigned him to Brooke. Figure 20.3 shows Dean's progress from the beginning of the year to late December. The good news is that Dean met the midyear math goal and overcame his fear of doing PALS in the classroom.

By using the five steps of the IDEAL problem-solving method, Dean's teacher and colleagues were able to develop and implement an intervention that addressed Dean's school problem. It is important to note that despite their best efforts, the second-grade team at Dean's school did not find the solution he needed. This was probably because the grade-level teams depend on standard protocols and Dean needed individualized problem solving. Using standard protocols at Tier 2 is a reasonable and effective strategy because most students respond to such interventions. But Dean exhibited a fear of showing his math weaknesses to classroom peers. To address this need, an FBA and individualized intervention were needed. Mr. Gerard, the school psychologist, used exposure to PALS with a trusted adult as a step toward helping Dean be able to do PALS with a classmate. Such gradual exposure therapy is one of many tools that can be used with students who exhibit such fears. With these supports, Dean was able to overcome his fear of working with a classroom peer on math and he ended the year having met the second-grade math standards.

SUMMARY

Problem solving is an important tool that school teams can use to address the difficulties that students have. The IDEAL problem-solving method is one that has been validated in research studies as effective in school settings. The steps of the IDEAL method help the school team to identify and define school problems, evaluate possible interventions, apply the interventions, and look at the outcomes. If school teams use the IDEAL problem-solving method, they will recognize the importance of how each student's school difficulties are defined and understand that using functional solutions will lead to more student success and less stress for teachers. Importantly, problem solving with the IDEAL model should not be used with every student who experiences school difficulty. It is best reserved for Tier 3 because it is generally unnecessary at Tier 2 and it requires more time and resources. Yet, when needed, it is a very effective means of helping students with more unique school difficulties.

CHAPTER 21

Progress Monitoring

Progress monitoring is the backbone of tiered supports (Busch & Reschly, 2007; Fuchs, Fuchs, Compton, & Bryant, 2007; Griffiths, VanDerHeyden, Skokut, & Lilles, 2009). This chapter describes the features of progress monitoring for academics and behavior as well as how to keep student data organized for easy review. It emphasizes how progress monitoring is not optional and must be an integral part of the culture and practices of tiered supports.

WHAT IS PROGRESS MONITORING?

Progress monitoring refers to the regular and systematic collection of data about student progress. It is regular in that the data are collected at equally spaced intervals over time. By having regularly collected data, the school team can consider the student's rate of progress toward a specific learning goal. Progress data also need to be systematic so that the data from one point in time can be compared with those from another point in time. To be systematic, the data need to be based on equivalent forms that measure the same thing. For example, in collecting data on a student's oral reading, a teacher could assess progress over time by using reading passages with different stories as long as those passages are all at the same reading level. In addition, the passages would need to be administered in the same way each time. This combination of equivalent forms and consistent administration results in standardized forms of measurement. Thankfully, there are ready-made sets of progress measures (e.g., AIMSweb, DIBELS, Direct Behavior Rating—Single Item Scales, EasyCBM, FastBridge, SWIS) for many skills that teachers need to measure (Dynamic Measurement Group, 2014; Educational and Community Supports, 2015; FAST Research and Development,

2014; Houghton Mifflin Harcourt, 2014; NCS Pearson, 2014; National Center on Intensive Intervention, 2014).

The research on progress monitoring goes back over 30 years. Studies conducted by Stan Deno and Phyllis Mirken (Shinn, 1989) at the University of Minnesota in the 1970s showed that progress measures of equivalent difficulty could be used to monitor student progress (Shinn, 1989; Jenkins, Graff, & Miglioretti, 2009). In follow-up studies, the benefits of progress monitoring were made clear (Stecker, Lembke, & Foegen, 2008). The reliability of progress measures has been shown for both reading (Fuchs & Fuchs, 1992) and math (Foegen, Jiban, & Deno, 2007). Notably, measures have been shown to be reliable for students from preschool (VanDerHeyden, Broussard, & Cooley, 2006) through high school (Espin, Wallace, Lembke, Campbell, & Long, 2010; Ticha, Espin, & Wayman, 2009) and for students who are English language learners (ELLs) (McMaster, Wayman, & Cao, 2006). Research concerning progress monitoring continues, and recent studies have examined how best to control the equivalence of items (Cummings, Park, & Schaper, 2013), the number of data points needed to have a secure trend (Christ, Zopluoglu, Long, & Monaghen, 2012), and the cut points to use in decision making about student risk (Christ, Zopluoglu, Monaghen, & Van Norman, 2013).

SELECTING PROGRESS MEASURES

The key to selecting progress measures is to match the measure to the skill being taught. When considering measures it is important to think about both reliability and validity. Reliability is a measure of how accurate a test is when used over time. Validity is a measure of how well the test measures what it is supposed to measure. A test of reading should measure reading but not math, and so on. In order to select the best measure for a specific student, it is important to be clear on what skill(s) the student is learning and to know the details of the student's intervention. To do this it is often necessary to know the content area and specific subskill that the student needs to learn. For example, a student might be learning the social skill of waiting for a break in conversation to say something. Or, a student might be working on multidigit multiplication. Once the specific skill has been identified, the teacher or team can review existing available progress measures. The National Center on Response to Intervention (NCRTI) completed reviews of available measures in math and reading. The National Center on Intensive Intervention (2014) continued this work and has added reviews of behavior measures as well. These reviews cover reliability, validity, sensitivity, and rates of improvement.

Progress measures are brief assessments that show a student's growth in the target skill over time. Some progress measures are embedded in a specific intervention such as those within the interventions Accelerated Math and Accelerated

Reader 360 (Renaissance Learning, 2015). Such measures are typically mastery measures (MMs), which indicate whether a student has mastered specific skills taught by the program. Other progress measures are designed to measure student progress in any curriculum. These are known as general outcome measures (GOMs) because they indicate how a student is doing in relation to using general skills in new material. Most of the time GOMs are the best type of progress measure to use because they indicate the extent to which the student has generalized learning (see Chapter 14). When a student does not show progress with GOMs, using MMs help identify which skills the student has mastered and which still need to be learned. Other features of progress measures to consider are format, length, frequency, personnel needed, and cost.

Format

Many progress measures are now computerized or have a computer-based data recording option. Computerized monitoring has the benefit of not requiring as much teacher time and attention as well as having the data automatically recorded. Often, the student can see his or her graph immediately with computerized measures. Nonetheless, computerized assessments may result in teachers not being as aware of how each student is doing and whether the student attempted all items with care. Many progress monitoring tools remain available in paper and pencil formats and these allow the teacher to observe the student's behaviors during assessment. A downside to using paper and pencil is that the teacher must then score and enter the data after testing. A unique solution is available from some progress monitoring publishers (e.g., AIMSweb, DIBELS, FastBridge), which have browser-based scoring. This system involves having the student complete the task on paper but the teacher immediately enters the data on a tablet or laptop computer. With this method, the data are entered while the student completes each assessment, alleviating the time required to score each progress measure.

Length

While all progress measures are designed to be brief assessments collected frequently, they do vary in the amount of time required. The shortest academic measures are 1-minute oral reading, early literacy, and early numeracy measures. These are very easily administered at the beginning or end of an intervention session. However, most such 1-minute measures must be individually administered because of the nature of the tasks that the students complete. There are browser-based administration options for all early literacy, early math, and oral reading measures, and this method makes the process easier and faster. Still, the teacher must consider the number of students that can be monitored at one time in order to know how much total time it will take.

The shortest measures for behavior are Direct Behavior Rating—Single Item Scales, which allow teachers to very quickly rate a student's progress on a target skill (Direct Behavior Ratings, 2014). Other measures take longer, but can be administered to students in groups. For example, the reading maze task takes 3 minutes, but several students can complete it at one time. A longer measure is M-COMP from AIMSweb. This assessment requires 8 minutes regardless of student age or grade. Like the maze, it can be group administered but must be individually scored like the maze. Other measures include schoolwide data such as the number of ODRs a student has received. It is important to think about how much total testing time will be needed for progress monitoring at each tier. Assessment time takes away from instruction, so finding the progress measure that accurately shows a student's growth while taking as little student and teacher time as necessary is important.

Frequency

To be effective, progress measures need to be administered often enough to show student progress during intervention. The Center on Response to Intervention (American Institutes for Research, 2015) recommends that students participating in Tier 2 interventions be monitored at least once a month and students in Tier 3 be monitored at least once per week. These suggestions are minimum frequencies and many schools opt to monitor more often. You will recall that there must be at least 3 data points before progress data can be reviewed and interpreted. If monitoring is monthly, that means a student will need to participate in the intervention for at least 3 months before progress can be reviewed. More frequent progress monitoring allows for faster review of intervention effects. Some schools have opted to monitor Tier 2 students every 2 weeks, shortening the minimum intervention time to 6 weeks. Others monitor all students once a week because it is an easy schedule to remember and allows for one data review schedule for all students. When a student is significantly behind, and when the nature of the concern warrants it, monitoring daily or several times a week can be done. This is more common for behavioral interventions such as check-in/check-out, which provides a daily number—percentage of points earned—as an indicator of a student's behavior throughout each day.

Personnel

While there is no rule about who can or should administer progress measures, it is important that the personnel be assigned and trained. Anyone who has mastered the skill being measured can administer the assessment, once trained. The training is very important because it helps ensure that the obtained data will be accurate and useful. As described in Chapter 19 on universal screening, a range of people could be trained to conduct progress monitoring. Classroom teachers, specialists, paraprofessionals, administrators, other staff, and volunteers are all possible monitors. An important consideration in deciding who will conduct the assessments is practicality. For this reason, many schools have the person who provides the intervention be the one who collects the progress data. This system works well because the interventionist knows the student's schedule, sees him or her regularly, and can keep track of the data in preparation for team meetings. Importantly, the interventionist is likely to know and keep track of any missed progress monitoring sessions. This is important because it is necessary to have enough data before review can occur. If someone other than the interventionist will conduct progress monitoring, it is essential that a schedule be worked out and that assessment integrity be checked.

Cost

Teams are likely to consider how much each type of progress measure will cost the school. The format of the measures influences the amount and nature of the cost to a high degree. Those that can be downloaded and printed for a low cost or for free (e.g., DIBELS, Direct Behavior Ratings) will need to be photocopied, involving paper and printing costs. Measures that are entirely computerized generally have one of two cost structures: per student or as a site license. In either case, the school must decide how many students will need to have access to the computer program at one time. Some software is designed for use at the school level (e.g., SWIS) and a per-student cost does not apply. When planning which progress monitoring tools to purchase, school teams need to keep in mind that progress monitoring is essential for an MTSS to work at all. The money invested in progress monitoring tools will make it possible for more students to be successful later.

KEEPING DATA ORGANIZED

Progress data will be useful only when they are accessed and understood by all team members. In order to make sure that the progress data will be accessible, there needs to be a plan for where the data will be stored and who will be in charge of data management. Each school needs a recognized data manager who will keep track of progress data for that building. In addition, when an entire district has progress monitoring at multiple buildings, there is a need for a district-level data manager as well. Often, the personnel that manage progress data will be the same ones who keep track of the screening data and other sources of information about student progress. These staff are responsible for assigning data access user names and passwords on computerized systems, gathering and filing paper records, and sometimes compiling reports about student progress over time. Progress data managers do not necessarily need to have a background in computer science or assessment. As long as they know how to use and train others to use the selected progress monitoring systems, educators with diverse backgrounds can serve in a data manager position.

In addition to training others how to use the progress monitoring measures, data managers also need to be able to facilitate and check on data collection schedules and integrity. This means checking to confirm that data have been collected at the specified times and that the measures were given correctly. Checking the integrity of progress monitoring can be done by setting up a schedule to observe all those who use progress measures once or twice a year. Given how brief progress measures are, it does not take a long time to conduct integrity observations. Most of the publishers of progress monitoring tools have assessment integrity checklists that can be used to conduct such observations. If an observation reveals that an assessment is being given incorrectly, the data manager should provide immediate retraining so that the measure will be used correctly as soon as possible. Keep in mind that the criterion for accuracy is for the assessment to be completed with 90% or better accuracy. It is also important that the data themselves be entered into the data management system with integrity. Some online systems, such as SWIS, provide data integrity monitoring that can alert data managers to data that are likely erroneous. It is recommended that data managers spot-check data that have been entered to ensure that they have been entered accurately.

DATA-DRIVEN TEACHING

The benefit of taking the time to set up a progress monitoring system is that teachers will be able to know quickly whether efforts to help students are working. This fosters a way of thinking about student achievement that might be different from what has been common in the school before. Data-driven teaching involves using student data to make decisions about the type of instruction a student needs and how long that instruction should continue. Often, teachers find that having student progress data changes their whole way of lesson planning and implementation. For example, in the past a teacher might have planned out lessons for the quarter based on the content the district expected him or her to teach. She would plan to "cover" the information and test students, but not necessarily change instruction based on student test scores. In data-driven instruction, the teacher adjusts instruction daily (sometimes hourly) based on how the students are doing. This means that teaching is more fluid, and yet more precise at the same time.

In the case of students who are participating in interventions, data-driven instruction includes teaching key knowledge and skills that they have not yet learned, but that are expected for the grade level. This can be challenging when a student starts out significantly behind. In such cases, the student needs to learn at an accelerated pace in order to catch up to classmates. In the book *Annual Growth for All Students, Catch-Up Growth for Those Who Are Behind*, Fielding, Kerr, and Rosier (2007) explain how students who start out behind must make progress at a faster pace than other students in order to have a chance to meet their current grade-level learning goals. This is because new learning goals are set every year that a student attends school. So, if a third grader enters in the fall reading at a middle first-grade level, then that student is 1.5 years behind in reading. But by the end of third grade, the school expects all students to have gained a school year's worth of progress (i.e., 9 months). For a third grader who starts out reading like a midyear first grader, the progress needed is really 2.5 years because his or her classmates will be moving ahead, too (we hope).

This is exactly why frequent progress monitoring is essential for tiered supports to be effective. As noted in Chapter 3, any student who starts out behind will stay behind unless he or she can gain at a rate faster than peers. And, in order to be sure that the student stays on track to catch up, there must be data showing progress. Many of the major published progress measures (e.g., AIMSweb, DIBELS, EasyCBM, FastBridge) have a metric known as the rate of improvement (ROI) for typically achieving students. The ROI tells how much gain on the specific measure should be expected for typically achieving students. For example, in the AIMSweb system, third graders at the 50th percentile are expected to gain 1.11 words per week on reading curriculum-based measurement (R-CBM). If a student who is enrolled in third grade starts the year reading at a mid-first-grade level, and gains only 1 year's growth during third grade, he or she would finish somewhere in the middle of second grade by the end of the year. In contrast, his or her classmates would end third grade ready for fourth-grade reading. In order to figure out the rate of progress that a student needs to have in order to meet a specific learning goal, teachers can set an aimline and then monitor the student's progress with a trendline (see also Chapter 22).

Aimline

An aimline is a line on a graph showing the goal for the student's performance at a future point in time. Aimlines can be determined based on the end-of-year grade-level goal or by the team's consensus of what type of performance the student needs to attain. The aimline is important in progress monitoring because it provides a clear visible reminder of the student's goal.

Trendline

A trendline is another line on a progress graph. The trendline shows the student's actual progress once the intervention begins. The graphed progress from one data point to another data point shows how the student is doing; often this line is up and down, showing some variability. This is normal because of expected variations in how the student does from one day to another. Adding a trendline to a graph helps to make sense of a student's up-and-down data. The trendline is a straight line through the obtained intervention data and it shows the general direction—or trend—of the data. The trendline can be helpful because it can show whether the student's data are on track to meet the aimline. This will indicate whether the student will meet the goal.

Figure 21.1 shows a sample graph of data for a student whose target skill is increasing the number of polite statements made during a class. The first 3 data points are the baseline and show that the student ranged from one to two polite statements per class. Prior to the intervention, the team set a goal for the student to make eight polite statements per class period. The horizontal line near the top of the graph shows the aimline and the goal of having the student increase polite statements to eight within 10 class periods. A dashed line separates baseline from the intervention. Once the intervention began, the student made more polite statements. The obtained data show that the student's number of polite statements went in an upward direction, but the increase was not linear. A trendline is shown through the intervention data and shows that after eight classes, the general direction of the data is improving and the student is on track to meet the goal by the tenth class. Adding trendlines to graphs is a helpful way for teams to be able to see a student's projected progress over time.

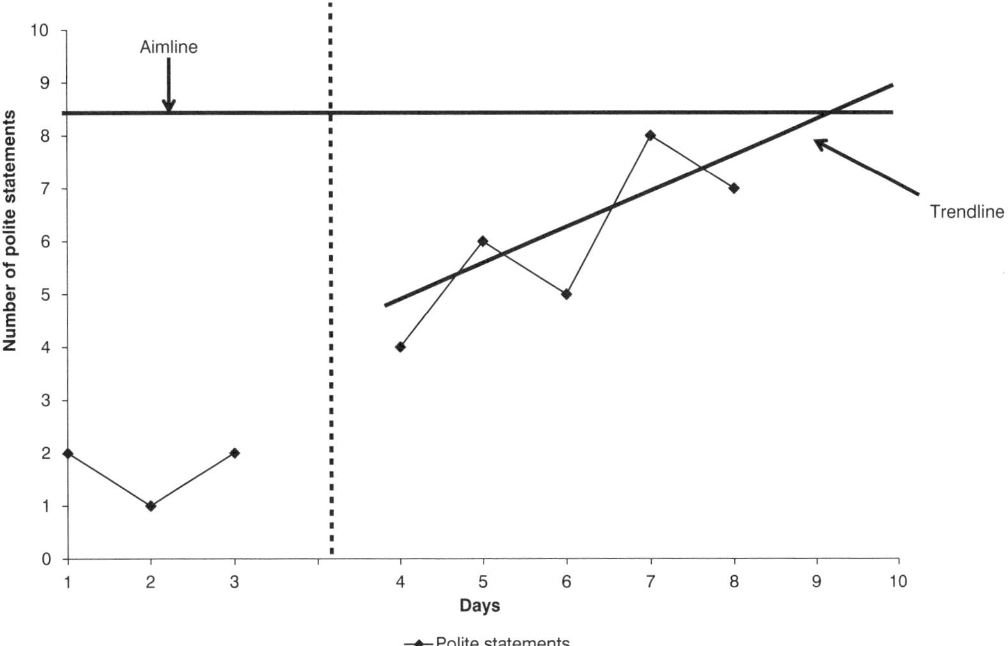

FIGURE 21.1. Sample graph showing an aimline and a trendline.

SUMMARY

Progress monitoring is an essential part of an MTSS. It provides evidence of whether a student is making progress toward specific learning goals. The use of progress monitoring as an effective way to accurately track student improvement has been validated in many studies. There are a number of published progress monitoring assessments available. School teams should consider the format, length, frequency, personnel, and cost of progress measures as they plan interventions. When progress monitoring is in place and used with integrity, it makes it possible for teachers to engage in data-driven instruction. By knowing a student's starting point and goals, teachers can identify how much growth a student needs in order to catch up.

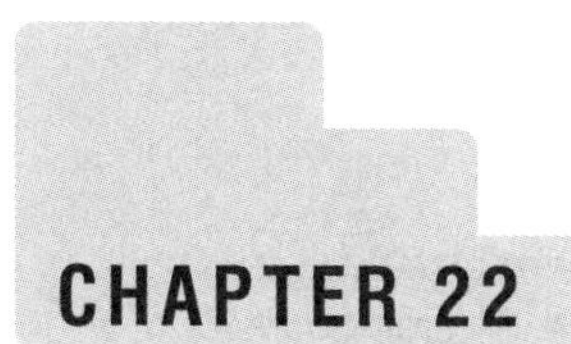

CHAPTER 22

Understanding Student Data

In order for progress data to be meaningful and useful, they must be reviewed at regular intervals. This chapter explains how to review such data and use them to make instructional decisions. One of the best methods for tracking student progress is called single-case design (SCD). This method can be used with one student at a time and lends itself to easily graphing the data for easy interpretation. The chapter explains how to set up such graphs in paper and computer formats, as well as the rules for how to plot the scores and show whether there has been a change in intervention conditions. Examples of student data for a variety of learning goals—both academic and behavioral—are included throughout the chapter (see Box 22.1). The examples show cases when the student met the goal, as well as when the student's improvement was positive but limited, resulting in the need for more intensive intervention.

SINGLE-CASE DESIGN

SCD is a method of data collection that was developed by psychologists who wanted to be able to test specific interventions with a small number of test subjects (Kazdin, 2010). Although the method has the name "single case," it can also be used with small groups of students. There are several subtypes of SCD and the ones most helpful for evaluating an individual student's progress are described here. For a more thorough explanation of SCD, the book *Evaluating Educational Interventions: Single-Case Design for Measuring Response to Intervention* by Chris Riley-Tillman and Matthew Burns (2009) is an excellent resource. The three SCD methods described here are (1) case study, (2) removal, and (3) multiple interventions. First, some basic features of SCD are explained.

BOX 22.1. Why Data Are Plural

Throughout this chapter (and others) you will notice that we use the word *data* in the plural form. This is because the word *data*—in Latin—is plural. The singular form of the word is *datum* and it is rarely used. Having one *datum* is not very helpful because we don't know if there is a trend (as described in this chapter). We use the plural for *data* to conform to the grammatical rules for both English and Latin and because it emphasizes how it is essential to have 3 or more *data* points before one can know if the data *are* important and useful. So, when thinking about *data*, think plural!

Notation

Single-case methods use a letter-notation system to indicate each phase of an experiment or intervention. SCD applications typically start with an A phase; this phase is also called "baseline." Baseline includes a period of time before the intervention is applied when specific data about the student's behavior are collected. The first (or only) treatment phase comes after baseline. This phase is labeled B and the most basic type of SCD is one that uses an AB design. In such a design, there are only two phases, A and B, in which A is baseline and B is the intervention. When there are more phases of intervention, additional letters are used to indicate those phases. The next most common type of SCD is one in which there is baseline, then intervention, then removal of intervention. The notation for this type of design is ABA because when the intervention is removed it can amount to a return to baseline. A third type of SCD is to add additional different phases such that the notation would be ABC, or if there is a return to baseline in between interventions, ABAC, and so on (see Kazdin, 2010, for more details).

Phase

As is shown below, all SCD data are displayed on a graph, which makes them easy to understand. Every time there is a change in the condition experienced by the student, there is a new phase. Each phase corresponds to a letter notation as described above, such that there is an A phase, a B phase, and so on. Whenever there is a phase change, a vertical line is made on the graph between the data for each phase. This shows that the conditions experienced by the student changed from one point in time to another. A more complete description of phases can be found in Cooper, Heron, and Heward (2007).

X-Axis

The *X*-axis is the horizontal direction on the graph. In SCD, the *X*-axis is always used to display units of time. Most often, this means that the days when data were collected are shown in order. Sometimes the days are consecutive, but not always. For academic measures like CBM, the data are usually collected either weekly or monthly. For behavior measures, the data are often collected daily, but sometimes more than once a day. Usually, the actual dates when data were collected are printed along the bottom of the *X*-axis.

Y-Axis

The *Y*-axis is the vertical direction on the graph. The *Y*-axis displays whatever measure was used to collect data about the student. For example, the *Y*-axis could show how many words were read correctly, the percentage of on-task intervals, or how many times a student raised his or her hand during discussion. The *Y*-axis is labeled with numbers that reflect the measure being used. If a percentage is depicted, then the numbers usually range from 1 to 100 in units of tens (e.g., 10, 20, 30). The range of numbers for the *Y*-axis should always reflect the possible scores or units a student's data would include.

Baseline

As mentioned above, an important feature of all SCD methods is the use of a baseline phase. This is a period of time when data about the student's preintervention behaviors are collected; it is also known as the A phase. In order to collect baseline data, the school team needs to identify the outcome variable that will be measured. There are some measures that are already available that can be used, such as CBM or behavior observations. In other cases, the team will need to develop and define the measure. For example, a team might use a daily behavior report card (DBRC) as a data collection tool, but the actual behavior(s) tracked on the report card will have to be defined by the team. It is best if the behavior is something positive that the student can strengthen such as more words read or more frequent positive social interactions with peers. Sometimes, though, if a student is engaging in very disruptive problem behaviors, it might make more sense to measure the frequency of those behaviors with the goal of reducing and eliminating them as quickly as possible. Baseline data are typically collected until a stable trend is observed. In order to know this, there must be a minimum of 3 data points during baseline, but sometimes baseline will last longer than 3 data points to be certain that the data are stable.

Stability

Stability refers to whether data points in a given phase are close together or highly variable. When a student's behavior is consistent across days or settings, the data points should be stable. Having stable baseline data is important because it shows the general level of the skill or behavior being measured. If a student was asked to complete three of the same type of reading assessment and scored very differently on each one, it would suggest that unknown variables are influencing the student's reading. Instead, if the student's reading score is about the same on each one, then the scores would show a reliable estimate of the student's current reading skill. Stability is important because it documents the student's consistency of performance. If data are not stable, it is difficult or impossible to know whether the changes observed in a student's academic skills or behavior were related to the intervention, or another variable. For this reason, unless there is an emergency, intervention does not begin until the student's baseline data are stable. Having stable baseline (e.g., preintervention) data will make it much easier to detect changes in student performance during the intervention. When the data are consistently different (but stable) after the intervention is implemented, it is easy to see that the intervention contributed to the changes in the student's performance. If a student's data are unstable during baseline (i.e., scores are widely variable), then more data need to be collected until they are stable.

Trend

In SCD, trend refers to the general direction of the data. There are three main types of data trends: increasing, stable, and decreasing. In order to identify the trend, there need to be multiple data points. With 2 data points, it is impossible to determine a trend because there is a 50% chance that the next data point will go up or down from the first two. For this reason, at least 3 data points are needed to consider a trend. Sometimes, the first 3 data points in a phase will be unstable and not interpretable. When the data are highly variable, it is important to collect more data until the data are stable enough to show a trend. A trend in the data provides information about whether an intervention is working. Once a trend is present, then the school team can interpret the data.

INTERPRETING STUDENT DATA

When the team follows the basic rules of SCD as described above, there will be data about an individual student's learning progress. As described in the section about trend, there are really only three possible interpretations of such data. In many (and hopefully most) cases, a student's data will show progress in the direction desired. When the goal is to strengthen a behavior, this means there will be an increase in the target skill or behavior. For example, the student will raise his or her hand more often before speaking in class. When the goal is to weaken a behavior, we would like to see a decrease in number on the graph. An example is a student's goal to get out of his or her seat less without permission. Both of these examples would suggest that the intervention is working. When a student's data trend shows that the intervention is working well enough that the student will meet the goal set for the end of the school year, then the intervention should be continued.

Sometimes, an intervention will be working, but not strongly enough. In such cases, the student is making progress but the trend is weak and the student is not likely to meet the year-end goal. In such cases, the intervention should be strengthened. This means that more of the intervention needs to be provided, much like a medical doctor might increase the dosage of a medication. For example, if a student was making progress with an intervention like CICO, in which he or she "checked" in with a specific teacher at certain times each day, but his or her progress was not strong enough to meet a year-end goal, then it would make sense for the team to increase the frequency of check-ins so that the student would see the teacher more often (Crone, Hawken, & Horner, 2010). This could mean that if the student was checking in with the teacher five times per day, the team could arrange for the student to check in with the teacher more frequently throughout the day. The team would continue to collect data about the student's progress with the same outcome measure and would check it at regular intervals. Since the intervention strength increased from five check-ins per day to more frequent check-ins, a phase-change line would be added to the student's progress graph.

In other cases, a student might not respond to the intervention at all, or show data with a trend in the opposite direction from the goal. In such cases, the intervention should be changed right away. When there are 3 or more stable data points indicating that a student has not responded to an intervention, the school team has an ethical obligation to change the intervention and keep collecting data about student progress. For example, if a student was provided with a reading fluency intervention four times a week and had stable weekly progress data showing no increase in reading fluency after 4 weeks, the team should identify and implement another reading fluency intervention. Sometimes, subtle differences between interventions for the same academic skill or behavior can make a big difference in student response. The student would be monitored using the same type of outcome measure and a phase-change line would be added to the graph.

When a student is making effective progress in an intervention, careful attention to the progress data may not seem important because the student is getting better at the skill. But if the student is not doing well, his or her skills or behavior are not improving or might be getting worse. For this reason, it is essential that school teams review student data on a regular basis. For students at Tier 2 or 3, this means taking a look at the scores at least every 3–4 weeks. As noted above, there must be at least 3 data points before a set of data can be reviewed. In some schools or districts, the policy is that data are reviewed every 4 weeks because it gives an extra data point and puts data review on a monthly schedule. Regardless of whether a school uses a 3- or 4-week schedule, the most important thing is that the data are looked at by the school team on a regular basis to see if the student is making progress (or not). When a student is making effective progress, the data review process is easy and fun. The team members look at the graph and celebrate the success. But when a student is not making adequate progress, the data review process is *critical*. This is because without careful review of the data, the team will not know that the intervention is not working. This might leave the student in an ineffective intervention for a long time. This is neither fair nor ethical for the student.

EXAMPLES

Three examples of student graphs and data are presented and shared. With each one, the pros and cons of each SCD type are explained as well. There is no perfect data collection method for the varied things that are measured in an MTSS, and school teams need to consider which methods might be used and which one will be the most effective for a given student.

Case Study

The case study SCD is referred to as the AB design. This means that there is a baseline (A) phase and one intervention (B) phase. The AB design has the benefit of quickly showing whether a specific intervention is working. First, a minimum of 3 baseline data points are collected. If these data are stable, then the intervention begins. After at least 3 intervention data points, the team can review the data to decide if the intervention is working. Figure 22.1 shows a graph for Maria, a third-grade student. Maria is an engaged student and she loves school. From the first day in Mr. Sanchez's classroom, Maria has participated in every activity and eagerly helped other students. Although Maria has been eager to help other students, she does not always raise her hand to be called upon by Mr. Sanchez. In the first 3 weeks of class, Maria raised her hand once. Despite raising her hand only once, Maria talked often and even gave answers for other students. Mr. Sanchez was pretty sure that other students wanted to speak, but that they did not have time to speak before Maria did.

Mr. Sanchez decided to see what would happen if he provided praise to those students who raised their hands before speaking in class. Before starting the praise intervention, Mr. Sanchez asked the school psychologist, Mrs. Starling, to observe his class for 10 minutes on 3 separate days in order to collect baseline data. After these baseline data were collected, Mr. Sanchez started praising each student when he or she raised a hand and waited to be called upon before speaking in class. Specifically, when a student raised a hand before speaking, Mr. Sanchez said "Thank you for raising your hand." Mr. Sanchez provided such praise every day for several weeks. To see if the intervention worked, Mrs. Starling came to the class once a week while the intervention was in place and observed how often Maria spoke with and without raising her hand. As shown in Figure 22.1, Mr. Sanchez's intervention worked very well to change Maria's behavior in class. The baseline data showed a stable trend of Maria not raising her hand before speaking. After the intervention was put into place, Maria did not talk without raising her hand as often as before. The trend during the intervention was a strong increase in Maria's hand raising. These data suggest that Mr. Sanchez's praise intervention was effective.

Removal

A second type of SCD that can be useful in MTSS is a removal design. The notation for the removal technique is ABA. This method includes collecting baseline data, implementing the intervention, and then removing it to see whether it was truly the intervention that led to any changes in behavior. Figure 22.2 shows what this could look like if Mr. Sanchez removed his praise intervention for Maria after 4 weeks. Again, Mrs. Starling observed the class once per week to see if Maria's behavior changed. As shown in the graph, once Mr. Sanchez stopped praising the students for raising their hands, Maria did not raise her hand very often. Like the trend during the intervention, the data were trending strongly in a specific direction, except this time there was a decrease in Maria's hand raising. These data suggest that the praise intervention worked and that Mr. Sanchez should probably start using it again, perhaps gradually fading it over time, if he wants Maria to raise her hand before speaking in class.

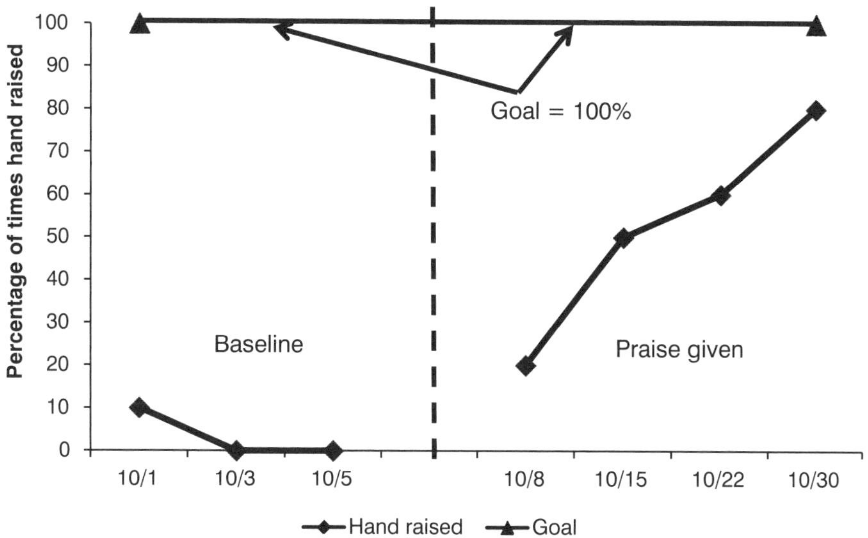

FIGURE 22.1. Maria's response to a praise intervention for hand raising.

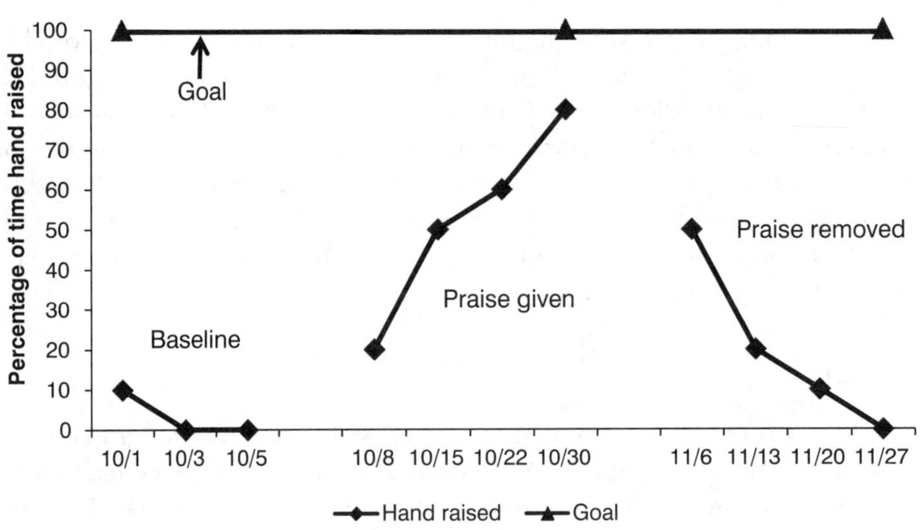

FIGURE 22.2. Maria's response when the praise intervention for hand raising was removed.

Removal can be an effective SCD method to use when the behavior of concern is not dangerous and the teacher wants to know for certain whether the specific intervention was really linked to the behavior change. The benefit of a removal condition is that it can confirm whether it was the intervention and not something else that led to a change in behavior. This can be important to know before using the same intervention with other students or in another classroom. But removal will not work for all behaviors or skills because some behaviors and skills do not revert to baseline levels once an intervention is removed. For example, once a student learns how to read, it is unlikely that the student will stop being able to read when an intervention is removed. For this reason, removal is used mostly with behavioral interventions for mild behaviors that do not pose a danger. When a student's behavior is severe or could cause harm, an intervention that appears to be working should not be removed.

Multiple Interventions

A third type of SCD method that can be used with all types of skills and behaviors is the implementation of multiple interventions. This method normally is used only if the first intervention tried either did not work or was not effective enough. An example of multiple interventions is shown in Figure 22.3. This graph shows reading data for Sean, a third grader. In the fall, Sean completed an oral reading screening using the third-grade DIBELS Next oral reading fluency (DORF) passages. His score on the screening was 33 words read correctly, while the third-grade fall benchmark goal on the DORF is 70. Sean's teacher, Mr. Peterson, was worried about his low score, so he followed up with two additional DORF assessments later that week. Sean's scores on these probes were similar to his fall benchmark, so Mr. Peterson worked with his grade-level team to implement a Tier 2 reading intervention for Sean. The team decided to implement a repeated reading (RR) intervention because RR has been shown to be effective for improving reading fluency. This intervention began the following week and was implemented 5 days a week, 30 minutes per day for 4 weeks.

Sean completed weekly third-grade DORF progress monitoring passages. After 4 weeks, the team reviewed Sean's data. Sean's scores during the intervention ranged from 36 to 41. These data suggested that Sean's reading fluency was improving, but not very quickly. Although these data were stable, the trend was weak and indicated that Sean would not meet the next benchmark screening goal of 86. The trendline for Sean's data from the RR intervention is shown in Figure 22.3 and indicates that if the RR intervention were continued, Sean would not meet the next DORF benchmark. Knowing that students who are not reading on grade level by the end of third grade are at high risk for additional school difficulty, the third-grade team agreed that Sean should participate in a more intensive reading intervention.

Based on this recommendation, Sean began participating in a new reading intervention called Corrective Reading (CR). CR is an intensive direct-instruction reading intervention designed for students like Sean who are significantly below grade level in reading. Sean attended daily 45-minute CR lessons for 4 weeks. At the end of that time, the team again reviewed Sean's data. This time, the rate of Sean's progress was higher and the trend of the data stronger. The trendline for the second intervention is shown in Figure 22.3 and indicates that Sean was likely to be just below the winter DORF benchmark. These data suggested that CR was a much better intervention for Sean and one more likely to help him

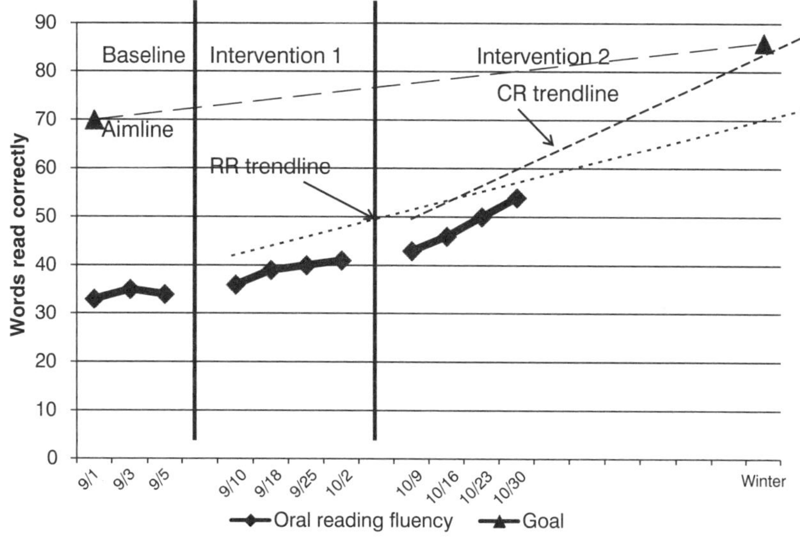

FIGURE 22.3. Multiple interventions for reading.

meet the grade-level reading goals. Still, the data indicated that Sean was likely to barely meet the winter goal, and the team would probably want to discuss whether any other additional interventions might be tried. Sean's case shows how using more than one intervention can be very important for a student. The SCD data collected during each phase made it possible for Sean's teacher and the team to know which intervention was best for Sean.

GRAPHS

As shown throughout this chapter, graphs are essential for tracking student progress. All of the graphs shown in this chapter were created using Microsoft Excel software. Several authors have provided detailed guidance about how to use Excel to create such graphs and readers are encouraged to consult a chapter by Cummings and Martinez (2013) that gives step-by-step instructions for such graphs. In addition, Google Drive has a spreadsheet program, Google Sheets, that can be used to track student progress. Many of the progress monitoring data management software programs (e.g., FastBridge, 2015; SWIS, Educational and Community Supports, 2015) have automatic graphing built in so that it is not necessary to create a separate graph for each student. When such graphs are provided by the software, they can be projected, printed, or shared electronically with team members for data review with just a few clicks.

As mentioned in Chapter 21, there are two additional lines often used on SCD graphs that can be very helpful for interpreting the data: aimlines and trendlines, respectively, show the desired and actual direction of the data over time. Together, aimlines and trendlines provide a means of comparing a student's actual scores with his or her target scores at any given point in time during an intervention. Figure 22.3 displays both an aimline and two trendlines.

Aimline

An aimline is drawn on the graph to show the goal, or target, score(s). The goal score for academic skills is usually the end-of-year benchmark score for the student's grade level. For behavioral skills, the goal can be set at the desired level of behavior. The benefit of having an aimline on a graph is that it shows the rate of progress that the student needs to make in order to reach the goal. Having an aimline on the graph can help both the student and teacher see the student's learning goal for the rest of the school year.

Trendline

A second type of line used on SCD graphs is the trendline. A trendline shows the direction of the student's actual scores over time. Trendlines are important because they show whether the student is making adequate progress toward the goal. When both an aimline and a trendline are on the graph, it is easy to see if the student is likely to reach the end-of-year goal as a result of the current intervention.

In situations where computerized graphing is not feasible, a handwritten graph can be used. Figure 22.4 includes a reproducible graph that can be used for any sort of student data. Teachers may discover that they want to have students complete a handwritten graph in addition to a computer-based one, as there are additional benefits to having students graph their own scores. Fuchs and Fuchs (1986), and DiGangi, Maag, and Rutherford (1991) found that when students graphed their own data, they demonstrated improvements above and beyond the intervention itself. An excellent summary of the benefits of having students graph their own intervention data can be found in Gunter, Miller, Venn, Thomas, and House (2002).

Allowing students to graph their own data improves outcomes because it gives them an additional feedback loop on their performance. After completing an intervention lesson and/or progress assessment, the student might have some idea of how he or she is doing, but this impression is not necessarily in relation to prior data. When the student writes the new score on the graph and connects a line showing the trend of the data, he or she can see whether he or she is making progress. When the intervention is working, the feedback from seeing the improvement provides reinforcement as well as additional motivation and encouragement to the student over time. If the intervention is not working, the student would be justified in wanting a different intervention. Either way, the feedback is useful and important for planning next steps.

SUMMARY

SCD is the best system for recording and understanding student intervention data. This method works well for school-based interventions because it can be used for one student at a time in relation to a specific intervention. It also has the capacity to show whether one or more interventions were effective for the student. Three types of SCD most useful for an MTSS are the case study (AB), removal (ABA), and multiple intervention (ABC) methods. The key to making SCD easy and useful is to graph the student data at regular intervals. Once graphed, student data can be interpreted in relation to whether the intervention is working well enough for the student to meet the learning goal, or if a change is needed. By understanding the phases, stability, and trend of a student's data, the school team can make decisions to improve overall learning outcomes.

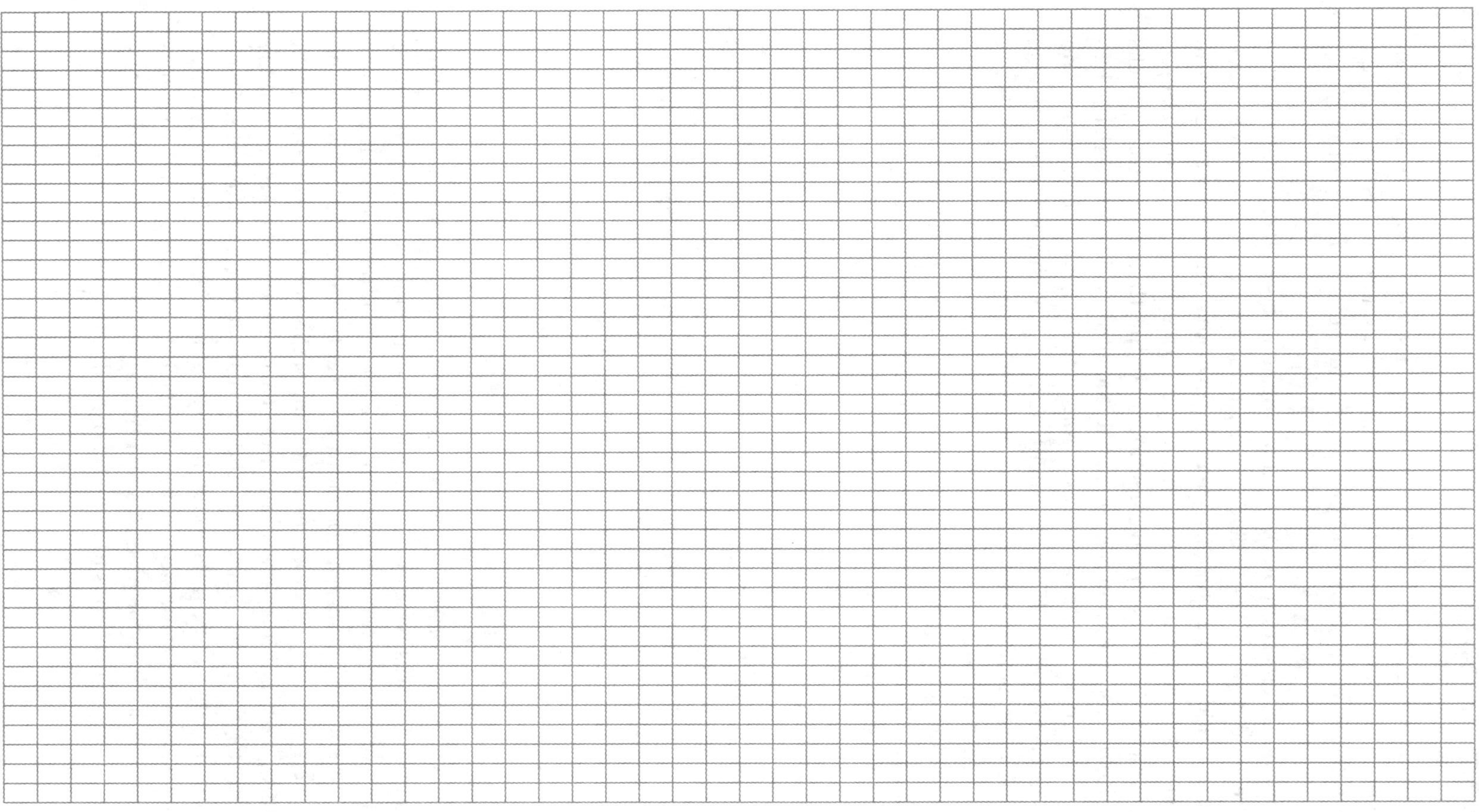

FIGURE 22.4. Basic graph.

PART VI

Connecting an MTSS with Other Supports

An MTSS is a general education method for supporting all students. Nonetheless, it has connections to programs for school-age students with disabilities, including Section 504 of the Rehabilitation Act of 1973, the Individuals with Disabilities Education Act (IDEA), and the Americans with Disabilities Act. All three of these laws have corresponding state rules requiring public schools to provide specialized supports for students with disabilities. The chapters in this section include the history of special education identification procedures, the consideration of whether it is necessary to use categories of special education services, and the possible eligibility for special education services for those students who do not respond to intervention. The first chapter in this section (Chapter 23) examines the type of supports provided at Tier 3 and how this tier provides a unique and necessary level of intensive intervention. Chapter 24 returns to the themes covered at the beginning of the book and reviews how an MTSS integrates supports that all students to access and benefit from their education. Finally, Chapter 25 describes how as MTSS fits well with the requirements for Section 504 plans and eligibility decisions for a specific learning disability, including detailed steps for how to use MTSS data for such decisions.

CHAPTER 23

What Is Tier 3?

This section of the book is designed to explain what intensive intervention looks like. The first chapter in this section answers the question "What is Tier 3?" The answer technically varies across the United States because each state has its own guidance for MTSS practices. Features such as very small groups, one-on-one instruction, daily sessions of 30 minutes or more, function-based behavior support plans, and alternative core programs are explained. In addition, the need for more frequent progress monitoring and data review is covered. The goal of this chapter is to help readers understand that Tier 3 is designed to ensure that there are highly intensive supports available for students who do not respond to Tier 1 + Tier 2 interventions. Guidance on how to decide the exact features of a student's Tier 3 program is provided.

THE FUNCTION OF TIER 3

The purpose of Tier 3 is to provide intensive intervention for students who have not yet been successful with Tier 1 + Tier 2. This is an important function because there will always be students whose needs require such intensive supports. Some of these students might have a disability and eventually be supported with special education. Others have life circumstances that have made school success difficult. For example, a student's parent(s) might be deployed by the military, lose a job, have a death in the family, or face other unexpected challenges that can impede school success. Conversely, a student might have a long-standing pattern of interfering behavior that has limited his or her access to instruction for some time, resulting in pronounced social and academic deficits. In some cases, the challenges will be temporary, but in others a student might need longer-term intensive supports. For all of these situations, Tier 3 is a means of continuing to support a student while determining the source(s) of difficulty and the best long-term solution.

There have been varied definitions and descriptions of Tier 3 services in relation to multi-tiered models. For example, Fuchs and Fuchs (2008) recommended that Tier 3 be part of special education services. By contrast, others see special education as different from the three tiers. The state of Georgia implemented a four-tiered model with Tier 4 being specialized services (Georgia Department of Education, 2011). Others have suggested that Tier 3 is a transition point during which more specialized data about a student are collected for the purpose of determining the best future plans (Brown-Chidsey & Steege, 2010).

The exact nature of Tier 3 interventions and progress monitoring can vary quite a bit. How the team proceeds at Tier 3 depends on the nature of the data from Tier 2. Most of the time, Tier 3 will involve a more intensive intervention than what has been tried before. In other cases, when a student's Tier 2 data indicate that there is a serious problem that most likely cannot be solved with Tier 3 intervention, the team might decide to initiate a special education referral. In such cases, all due process protections and procedures must be followed. This means that once a student is officially referred for a comprehensive evaluation, no individualized diagnostic testing can be conducted until written parent consent for evaluation is obtained. But, if a special education referral is made, the current intervention should still continue, as well as weekly progress monitoring, both of which do not require parent consent.

If a school team refers a student for Tier 3 supports, by definition, there are unresolved problems or needs. In such situations, it is likely that the team needs additional information in order to find the right supports for the student. For these reasons, we recommend that Tier 3 be utilized as a transition point during which more detailed data are collected. Such data could eventually be part of a referral for special education, but in other cases might indicate that the student's needs can be met with more intensive general education supports. An important consideration at Tier 3 is the type of intervention that is provided while additional assessment is conducted. Intervention should continue during Tier 3 and it is the progress data from the intensive instruction that generally constitutes the additional information that the team will consider.

TYPES OF INTERVENTIONS

Tier 3 interventions are the most intensive, meaning that they are likely to require more time to implement. In relation to Caplan's model (see Chapter 2), Tier 3 interventions are called "tertiary." This means that they occur after primary (Tier 1) and secondary (Tier 2) supports have been provided and are used only with students who have the most significant needs. In schools, Tier 3 interventions often involve a very small student to teacher ratio and are usually provided every school day. The amount of time necessary for Tier 3 interventions will always be in addition to the Tier 1 and 2 interventions already in place. For example, if a classroom teacher spends 15 minutes of each day on Tier 1 PBIS instruction and review, and a few students in the class also participate in another 15 minutes of a Tier 2 intervention like CICO, then those students are already receiving 30 minutes each day of behavioral instruction and intervention. However, if the Tier 2 intervention is showing zero benefit for the student, then that intervention could be replaced with another one that is implemented with the Tier 3 intervention, or the time allocated for Tier 2 could be pooled with additional time to allow an intensive intervention requiring 60 minutes per day beyond core instruction. Such an intervention could be to assess the function of the student's interfering behavior and implement a function-based behavior support plan for that student. It is essential that Tier 3 interventions not take away from existing supports because students who are struggling need more, not less, instruction.

There is no question that finding time for Tier 3 interventions is the most challenging aspect of an MTSS. There are a finite number of minutes in each school day, and a host of activities competing for that limited time. As described in Chapter 13, when a Tier 2 "intervention" or "skills" block is built into the daily school schedule, it means that every student in the school is given adequate time for Tier 1 and Tier 2; not all students will need Tier 2 and those who don't can use that time for enrichment activities. Those students who need Tier 2 will be able to access it on a regular basis. This means that there will be a very small number of students for whom finding time for Tier 3 is needed. In some cases, it may be necessary for the student's schedule to be adjusted so that the Tier 3 intervention will be in place of another activity or class for a defined period of time. While we do not want to take away any student's access to instruction without careful consideration, if a student's other needs are significant, a short-term Tier 3 intervention to test the hypothesis that the student's skills will improve can be justified. It is essential that such a schedule change be approved by the parent(s) in advance, that there be a definite time frame and end date for the intervention, and that an appropriate progress measure be identified and used regularly while the intervention is in place.

As noted, the number of students who participate in Tier 3 interventions is very small compared with the other tiers. It would be typical for only one student in each classroom to require Tier 3 intervention at a given time. For this reason, such interventions are more likely to be implemented by interventionists such as behavior or reading specialists, special educators, school psychologists, or social workers. One notable and common exception is that a function-based behavior support plan, while designed and supported by a behavior analyst, must be implemented by the teacher(s) and support staff working directly with the student throughout the day. Sometimes Tier 3 interventions will be individualized such that the student works with the interventionist individually each day. In other cases, several students from different classes will be in the intervention group. This is very likely to be the case if the intervention includes opportunities for the student to practice key skills in an analogue setting. For example, if an intervention focuses on helping students develop specific social skills such as initiating interactive play, and those students would benefit from practicing those skills in a controlled setting before practicing them in the natural setting, having several students in the group is necessary. The specific skills to be taught and practiced should guide decisions about how many students to include in a Tier 3 intervention group. Sometimes, a group might begin a little bigger (e.g., four students), and based on student progress (or lack thereof) be reduced in size.

The final key feature of Tier 3 interventions is that they happen at least every school day. This is because the student needs to acquire and work on developing fluency with one or more skills. As the team develops the intervention, it needs to consider exactly how the intervention will fit into the student's and interventionist's daily schedules. Tier 3 interventions are implemented with high frequency so that the student gets many practice opportunities for the target skill(s). If the intervention is less than daily, the skills will develop too slowly to be useful or will not develop at all. In some cases, Tier 3 interventions might be implemented more than once a day. This would be done in cases where more frequent student learning and practice are needed. For example, a student struggling with frustration tolerance during academic instruction might benefit from the opportunity to take scheduled or requested breaks at key times throughout the day.

Tables 23.1 and 23.2 include lists of interventions that have been identified as good choices at Tier 3 for academics and behavior, respectively. We include these examples because we want readers to know that there are prepared intensive interventions that work well at Tier 3 that teams do not have to develop themselves. But it is also important to remember that there will always be new interventions, and readers are cautioned that the examples we have included here are not necessarily endorsements for a given intervention for a particular student. Instead, these are examples of some of the many programs with strong research evidence. Note that each entry in Tables 23.1 and 23.2 has a research citation with it. These citations are a reminder that teams must locate and review the research evidence for any and all suggested interventions before deciding which ones to use. Future research will validate other programs and that is what is most important. As with the interventions used at Tiers 1 and 2, there must be a research base for any programs used as Tier 3 interventions.

Intensive Academic Interventions

The best Tier 3 academic interventions are those that include direct instruction (DI) methods. As described in Chapter 14, DI has been validated in numerous

TABLE 23.1. Examples of Tier 3 Academic Interventions

Mathematics	Reading	Writing
Academy of Math	Reading Mastery	Self-Regulated Strategy Development (SRSD)
Torlaković, E. (2011). Academy of MATH® Efficacy Report—Westwood Elementary School. Retrieved from *www.intensiveintervention.org/chart/instructional-intervention-tools/12923*	Carlson, C. D., & Francis, D. (2002). Increasing the reading achievement of at-risk children through direct instruction: Evaluation of the Rodeo Institute for Teacher Excellence (RITE). *Journal of Education for Students Placed at Risk*, *7*, 141–166.	Harris, K., Graham, S., & Mason, L. (2006). Improving the writing, knowledge, and motivation of struggling young writers: Effects of self-regulated strategy development with and without peer support. *American Educational Research Journal*, *43*, 295–340.
Corrective Math	Corrective Reading	Spelling Mastery
Crawford, D. B., & Snider, V. E. (2000). Effective mathematics instruction: The importance of curriculum. *Education and Treatment of Children*, *23*, 122–142.	Lingo, A. S., Slaton, D. B., & Jolivette, K. (2006). Effects of corrective reading on the reading abilities and classroom behaviors of middle school students with reading deficits and challenging behavior. *Behavioral Disorders*, *31*, 265–283.	Darch, C., Eaves, R. C., Crowe, D. A., Simmons, K., & Conniff, A. (2006). Teaching spelling to students with learning disabilities: A comparison of rule-based strategies versus traditional instruction. *Journal of Direct Instruction*, *6*, 1–16.

TABLE 23.2. Examples of Tier 3 Behavioral Interventions

Coping Cat

Beidas, R. S., Benjamin, C. L., Puleo, C. M., Edmunds, J. M., & Kendall, P. C. (2010). Flexible applications of the Coping Cat program for anxious youth, cognitive and behavioral practice. *Cognitive and Behavioral Practice, 17,* 14–153.

The Incredible Years

Webster-Stratton, C., & Reid, M. J. (2003). Treating conduct problems and strengthening social and emotional competence in young children: The dina dinosaur treatment program. *Journal of Emotional and Behavioral Disorders, 11*(3), 130–143.

Choice as an Antecedent Intervention

Kern, L., & Clemens, N. (2007). Antecedent strategies to promote appropriate classroom behavior. *Psychology in the Schools, 44,* 65–75.

Response Independent Reinforcement (also referred to at Noncontingent Reinforcement)

van Camp, C. M., Lerman, D. C., Kelley, M. E., Contrucci, S. A., & Vorndran, C. M. (2000). Variable-time reinforcement schedules in the treatment of socially maintained problem behavior. *Journal of Applied Behavior Analysis, 33*(4), 545–557.

Opportunities to Respond

Sprick, R., Knight, J., Reinke, W., McKale Skyles, T., & Barnes, L. (2010). *Coaching classroom management: Strategies and tools for administrators and coaches* (2nd ed.). Eugene, OR: Pacific Northwest Publishing.

Token Economy

Boerke, K. W., & Reitman, D. (2011). Token economies. In W. W. Fisher, C. C. Piazza, & H. S. Roane (Eds.), *Handbook of applied behavior analysis* (pp. 370–382). New York: Guilford Press.

research studies as the single most effective teaching method for students with academic difficulties. Table 23.1 includes four examples of DIinterventions that would be appropriate at Tier 3. These interventions all have at least one peer-reviewed research study documenting the effectiveness of the method and one of the studies for each intervention is listed in Table 23.1. All of these interventions can be used with individual students or with small groups, and they can be used with students in all grades.

Math Interventions

The first math intervention is Academy of Math. It is a relatively new computerized intervention that helps students learn and use foundational math skills quickly. Students work individually at Internet-connected computers to learn and practice specific skills identified and monitored by a teacher. A second math intervention is Corrective Math, which has been around for many years. It is a DI method and includes daily lessons for students who are 2 or more years behind grade level in math skills (Crawford & Snider, 2000).

Reading Interventions

The first intervention for reading is Reading Mastery. This program has been published for several decades and there are many older studies of its effectiveness, but a more recent study of over 20,000 students in Texas showed that students provided with Reading Mastery lessons outperformed comparison students (Carlson & Francis, 2002). A second intervention that can be used with students 2 or more years behind in reading, including secondary students, is corrective reading (CR). CR is a DI program designed for students who are significantly behind in reading skills (Lingo, Slaton, & Jolivette, 2006).

Writing Interventions

There are two intervention examples provided for writing. The first is the Self-Regulated Strategy Development method. This method includes a large number of specific writing strategies that are explicitly taught to students (Harris, Graham, & Mason, 2006). The second writing example, Spelling Mastery, uses DI to teach students how to spell increasingly longer and more difficult words using a combination of phonemic, morphemic, and whole word methods (Darch, Eaves, Crowe, Simmons, & Conniff, 2006).

Intensive Behavioral Interventions

Intensive behavioral interventions are typically function-based individual behavioral interventions, which require the expertise of a school psychologist or behavior analyst to develop. Nevertheless, there are some intensive interventions available for purchase. Several examples of function-based behavioral interventions and two examples of packaged Tier 3 behavioral interventions are presented in Table 23.2. The first packaged intervention is called Coping Cat (Beidas, Benjamin, Puleo, Edmunds, & Kendall, 2010). This intervention, along with the companion version for adolescents known as the C.A.T. Project, was developed from research about the effectiveness of cognitive-behavioral therapy for children with anxiety. It includes a student workbook, parent guide, and therapist manual and can be used with individuals or small groups. The second packaged intervention is The Incredible Years, an evidence-based intensive intervention for behavior problems that includes training for parents, teachers, and students (Webster-Stratton & Reid, 2003).

The remaining examples of Tier 3 behavior interventions are evidence-based strategies that have been developed for use with struggling students within the field of applied behavior analysis. The first of these interventions is called antecedent strategies, a term that refers to changes made to the environment that increase the likelihood that a student will be successful (Kern & Clemens, 2007). The second strategy is noncontingent reinforcement, which involves providing reinforcement according to a schedule rather than according to a student's behavior (van Camp, Lerman, Kelley, Contrucci, & Vorndran, 2000). The third strategy, opportunities to respond, is an intervention that increases student engagement by increasing the number of statements, questions, and gestures intended to elicit an academic response from students (Sprick, Knight, Reinke, McKale Skyles & Barnes, 2010). Finally, a token economy is a system in which students are provided with small rewards, such as poker chips or tickets, contingent upon desired behaviors (Boerke & Reitman, 2011). While the small rewards are not themselves valuable, they become valuable when they can be exchanged for items or privileges that the student values. Each of these interventions has a strong research base and can be used to address individual students' behavior challenges. While these Tier 3 strategies do not come prepackaged, they can become reliable and relied-upon interventions given the training and support of someone with behavioral expertise. Such methods are an important tool at Tier 3 where individualized intervention is needed.

PROGRESS MONITORING

Careful progress monitoring is essential for effective Tier 3 interventions. Tier 3 progress monitoring needs to be done more often than at other tiers because the students served at this level are at higher risk. For this reason, the NCRTI recommends that Tier 3 progress monitoring be done at least weekly. However, it depends on the behavior(s) being monitored whether weekly is sufficient or if more frequent monitoring is needed. A key to understanding progress monitoring is measurement sensitivity (see Chapter 21 for more information). A measure's sensitivity reflects how accurately it can detect changes in a specific indicator or behavior. For example, a bathroom scale is designed to be sensitive to changes in pounds or kilograms of body weight. A bathroom scale would not be sensitive to weight changes in grams or micrograms because it is not designed for that level of measurement.

Just like a bathroom scale, any assessment tool will be sensitive to different types and amounts of change over time. When selecting a progress monitoring tool for a Tier 3 intervention, educators need to select one that will reflect the expected changes in the student's behavior. For academic skills such as math, reading, and writing, curriculum-based measures (CBM) work well for weekly progress monitoring. This is because such skills have been observed to grow at predictable rates when effective instruction is provided. For example, the typical growth rate for reading fluency is less than one word per week in the middle elementary school years. When matched to the student's instructional level (i.e., level at which intervention is provided), CBM will show whether the student's skills improve from week to week.

For behavior skills like meeting classroom behavior expectations, an inverse measure can be effective. Specifically, teachers can track how often the student is disruptive in the classroom. This is the opposite of the skill we want the student to master, but is an effective metric to see whether a student's classroom behavior is improving. A common way of measuring interfering behavior is through office discipline referrals (ODRs). For students receiving Tier 3 behavioral intervention, we can assess the effectiveness of an intervention aimed at improving behavior by monitoring the extent to which students engage in interfering behavior less often (or have fewer ODRs).

Unlike acquisition of math, reading, and writing skills, social skills develop at more student-specific rates. Some students with problem behaviors may act out a few times per week and so weekly monitoring could be appropriate. Other students might be acting out multiple times each day; in such cases daily progress monitoring is needed. The types of progress monitoring tools that can be used to keep track of behavior improvement include tools like the daily behavior report card (DBRC). The DBRC, which is used in the CICO intervention described above, is a progress monitoring tool that can be used to track the extent to which students are meeting behavioral expectations each day (Vannest, Davis, Davis, Mason, & Burke, 2010). The DBRC is an effective tool to track student behavior progress because it allows tracking of student-specific behaviors with high frequency. As Vannest et al. showed, the DBRC is most effective when used to track behaviors throughout the school day.

When the DBRC is used throughout the school day, students receive timely feedback across activities, subjects, and settings. The data from DBRCs are most often tracked as an overall percentage based on the number of points earned divided by the number of points possible. Alternatively, teams can track the percentage of points earned for each criterion for each day. Joshua Rosenthal has developed a free electronic system for implementing a paper-free DBRC system that educators using this intervention might find useful (Rosenthal, 2015). School teams should recognize that monitoring improvements in student prosocial behaviors at Tier 3 requires daily progress monitoring to be effective. If this frequency seems daunting, it is essential to keep in mind that in any school, no more than 5% of students (e.g., one student per classroom) should need such monitoring. Moreover, the investment in time will likely be recovered in time not spent responding to challenging behavior.

DECISION MAKING

The data collected during Tier 3 eventually need to be reviewed and interpreted by the school team. As explained in the chapters about school teams (Chapters 6–8), it is usually a schoolwide team that will review data related to Tier 3 interventions. It is important that those educators who participate in Tier 3 data review understand the implications of the decisions they will make. At Tier 3, a student's school difficulties have persisted for a long time and have not been resolved with "easier" approaches like Tier 2 intervention. There are two main choices that a team can make at Tier 3: (1) refer the student to special education, or (2) maintain the intensive Tier 3 intervention. A third option, gradually reducing and then removing the Tier 3 intervention, is used in cases when a student's data show that desired improvements have occurred and the intervention should be faded. Referring the student means that a comprehensive evaluation will be conducted according to the federal IDEA and state special education rules. Details about this process will be discussed below. In order to decide whether the current Tier 3 intervention will be continued, there must be data indicating that it is working.

As described in the chapter on understanding data (Chapter 22), students are understood to be making improvement when they show progress data points different from the baseline data. The determination that a student is making *effective* progress is based on whether the trendline of the data shows that the student will meet the end-of-year goal for the specific target behavior or skill. For example, a third grader who is participating in Tier 3 intervention for math skills could have a progress graph that shows that he or she went from a fall screening score of 7 to a current progress score of 28. If the third-grade end-of-year goal for this student is 43, then this student is likely to meet that goal. Figure 23.1 depicts data for a student, Steve Seal. Steve's data indicate that he is responding well and will surpass the end-of-year goal. In this case, we would gradually fade the Tier 3 intervention back to Tier 1 + Tier 2 intervention. But what if Steve's data looked

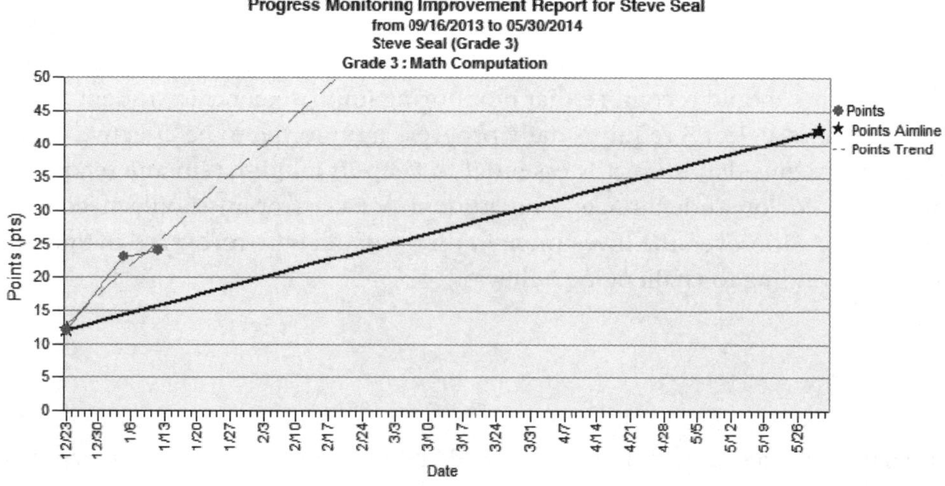

FIGURE 23.1. Steve Seal's math skills progress monitoring graph (a).

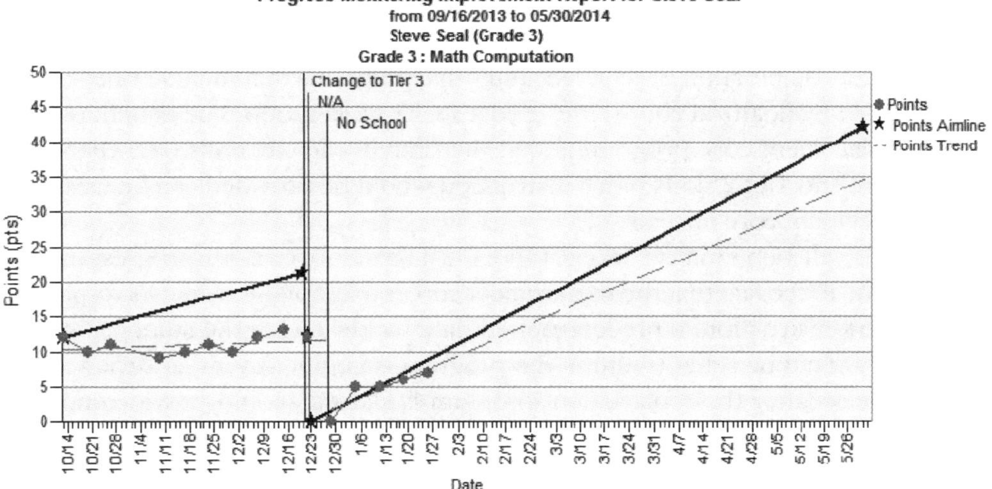

FIGURE 23.2. Steve Seal's math skills progress monitoring graph (b). Copyright 2014 by NCS Pearson, Inc. Reprinted by permission. All rights reserved.

like Figure 23.2? In this case, Steve made no progress since the fall and when he returned after the winter break he was still very behind. As a result of Steve's January screening score and Tier 2 progress monitoring, the team remained very concerned about Steve's progress. After the winter break, Steve's score was even lower. As a result, the team initiated Tier 3 intervention. Steve's initial progress at Tier 3 was very slow and indicated that he was not likely to catch up in time to meet the third-grade spring benchmark goal. In this case, we would verify that interventions were provided with integrity and refer Steve to special education for a comprehensive evaluation.

Replacing a Core Program

In a small number of cases, a team might decide that it is worth providing a different core instruction program, with added intervention, for a student who is significantly behind. The decision to replace core instruction with other materials and methods must be done very carefully and with parent approval. Making such a replacement should rarely be done because doing so means that the student will no longer be provided with the instruction otherwise guaranteed to all students. Still, if a student has not responded to a combination of supports that include Tier 1 core instruction, Tier 2 supplemental instruction, and Tier 3 intensive supplemental instruction, it might be worth using a replacement core program. When a replacement program is used, it tests the hypothesis that the student's lack of progress is due to the nature of the instructional materials. Replacement academic core programs are highly intensive in nature and usually require 120–150 minutes per subject each day. There are no stand-alone replacement core behavior programs, but a student with behavior difficulties could participate in a combination of "layered" intensive programs that include Check and Connect, individualized counseling, and a social skills group. The benefit of trying a replacement core program is that the time in the student's day when the Tier 1 core and Tier 2 skills block instruction would be provided can be used for the replacement core instead.

As with all Tier 3 interventions, there must be daily to weekly progress monitoring. Due to the fact that the replacement core is a test of the student's response to different instruction, a predetermined date for reviewing the student's progress data should be set at the time the program is begun. An initial review date of 3–6 weeks after the replacement program is started should provide enough time to see if the new program is helping. If the student responds to the new program and makes effective progress, the team will need to decide whether to maintain the new program for the rest of the school year as a Tier 3 intervention, or to refer the student for a comprehensive evaluation. The major factor in deciding which option to pursue is whether the student is likely to catch up to his or her peers within a reasonable time frame, or if the student will continue to lag behind the grade-level expectations. Students who are likely to catch up probably do not have a disability. Students who continue to lag behind might have a disability that should be addressed through special education.

COMPREHENSIVE EVALUATION

When a student does not respond to multiple tiers of intervention, it is appropriate to refer the student for a formal special education evaluation. Being nonresponsive to intervention is one of the ways that a student can be identified as a student with a disability. But a student might be exhibiting symptoms of another condition that needs to be addressed. When a student's Tier 3 data are similar to those in Figure 23.2, a nonresponse to intervention is suggested; such a student could have a specific learning disability (SLD), but such a student might have another condition such as a medical condition that impairs cognitive skills. When a student's Tier 3 data indicate that the year-end academic or behavior goals will not be met, a referral to special education is appropriate. Such a referral will initiate an individualized evaluation to determine if the student has a disability that requires special education.

The individualized evaluation requirements of IDEA were put in place to ensure that the needs of each student who presents with significant school difficulties would be considered. Students with disabilities have unique and specific instructional needs that can be met through special education. An individualized comprehensive evaluation incorporates academic, behavioral, cognitive, psychological, physical, occupational, and/or speech and language assessments of a student's current learning needs. The information collected during the individualized comprehensive evaluation is organized into one or more reports presented to the individualized education program (IEP) team. The IEP team is charged with determining whether a student has a qualifying disability and is eligible for special education. In order for a student to be eligible for special education, there must be evidence that the student (1) has a recognized disability that affects his or her education, (2) is not meeting age- and/or grade-level learning expectations, and (3) requires special education services in order to make effective school progress. If a student has data to indicate that all three of these conditions are met, then an IEP team is justified in determining that the student is eligible for special education services. Keep in mind that there are students who will need Tier 3 services who do not have a disability. As noted, life's circumstances could affect a student's school experience in a way that requires the extra help of tiered supports. Therefore, some students will need help for a defined period of time and then be fine. Other students who struggle, even with Tier 3 support, have a disability and will need the additional supports that IDEA provides.

SUMMARY

Some students will continue to struggle in school despite support at Tiers 1 and 2. Tier 3 support, which is usually individualized and intensive, should be provided to such students. Students who make effective progress with Tier 3 supports are generally understood not to have a disability and so do not need special education. Instead, such students have temporary challenges to school success and continuing Tier 3 services is recommended. Those students whose progress data during Tier 3 indicate a lack of response to intervention might have a disability that is affecting school progress. In fact, a key step in determining if a student is eligible for special education services is to provide Tier 3 intervention and progress monitoring. Students who do not make adequate progress when provided with effective Tier 3 support should be referred for a comprehensive individualized evaluation of educational and psychological needs. When such an evaluation indicates that a disability is present, then the IEP team must consider whether special education is necessary.

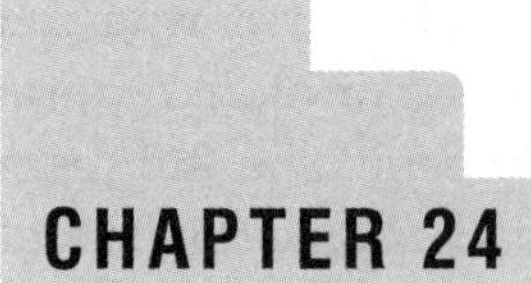

Education for All

As noted throughout this book, an MTSS is often thought to be about special education eligibility, but in truth it is *not*. As we have explained, an MTSS is a general education initiative designed to provide supports for all students. It is a mindset with corresponding practices that permeates every part of planning, teaching, assessing, and helping students. Nonetheless, guidance and regulation at both the federal and state levels formally includes MTSS procedures for one, and only one, special education eligibility category: specific learning disability (SLD). This chapter explains the history behind U.S. special education policies, how language about MTSS came to be included in federal and state laws, and lingering questions about whether applying labels to students' learning needs makes sense at all. In many ways this chapter circles back to the basic premise of the book to connect education policy with the social context of children's lives. For those eager to learn the details about how an MTSS might fit with special education decision making, Chapter 25 explains the details of using data from an MTSS for SLD eligibility decisions.

A HISTORY OF LEARNING DISABILITIES

There have always been some students who found school difficult. Until school attendance became mandatory in the United States starting in the 1890s, little attention was paid to students who struggled because they could generally leave school and be successful in their local communities. As the U.S. economic system went from a focus on local agriculture to the mass production of goods during the industrial revolution, the importance of school-based formal education increased. At about the same time as this economic shift, educators and psychologists began to conduct research into the source of student learning problems (Winzer, 1993). From the beginning, much of the research on what later became known as learning disability (LD) focused on reading problems. From the 1890s through the 1920s, researchers in Europe and the United States considered various possible causes for LDs. Research during this period built on interest in brain–behavior relationships that had begun in the early 1800s (Hallahan & Mercer, 2013; LD Online, 2013; Stanberry, 2013).

Several European physicians are credited with advancing the understanding of LD in the period before World War I. A German researcher, Adolph Kussmaul, coined the term *word blindness* to describe adults who had reading problems despite average intelligence and education. The British physicians James Hinshelwood and Pringle Morgan conducted autopsies of adults and children with specific reading problems. Their results suggested that there was a physical origin to the reading problems (Hallahan & Mercer, 2013). In the 1920s, Dr. Samuel Orton began work examining reading problems in U.S. children, leading him to conclude that children with average intelligence and reading difficulties could benefit from alternate reading instruction. Orton and his colleagues developed one of the first methods for teaching reading with systematic phonics instruction. Later termed the Orton–Gillingham method for the contributions of Anna Gillingham, this method was one of the first treatments for reading disability.

While much of the early research concerning students with school difficulties focused on reading, there was an awareness that some students struggled in other areas, too. Grace Fernald and Marion Monroe experimented with treatments in both clinic and school settings during the 1940s and 1950s. This early research created an awareness that not only were there children who were predicted to do well in school but did not, but also that there were instructional methods that could benefit these students. The term *learning disability* was developed by Samuel Kirk, who had been a student of Monroe's. Kirk used the term in his 1962 text *Educating Exceptional Children* and then again at a public lecture in 1963 (Hallahan & Mercer, 2013). The term has been used ever since to describe children who have learning difficulties despite no other clear medical or psychological impairments.

In the late 1960s, the U.S. Department of Education began to consider how to offer supports for students with LD. Two task forces were commissioned to consider the needs of such students and how to define LD. These groups initially referred to LD symptoms as "minimal brain dysfunction" (Hallahan & Mercer, 2013). In 1969, advocates for children with LD succeeded in having the Children with Specific Learning Disabilities Act passed. This act provided small amounts of funding to support instruction for students with LD. It also included the first federal definition of LD, which was very similar to the definition in use today. When passing this act, many advocates and members of Congress thought that the percentage of students with LD was no more than 1–3% of all students.

The 1960s and 1970s were a period of major social change in the United States. In addition to advances in rights for African Americans, Hispanic Americans, indigenous peoples, and women, there were major gains on behalf of individuals with disabilities in the 1970s. Because of a history of not being allowed to attend public schools, many of the efforts to support students with disabilities during the 1960s and 1970s focused on making a case for these students' rights under federal and state laws, as had been done for African American students (Winzer, 1993). The basic premise behind advocacy for students with disabilities is that all U.S. states are required to provide education for all students. Notably, some states initiated special education programs before a federal law was passed in 1975. For example, Massachusetts and Pennsylvania created laws requiring state special education programming before the landmark federal law Public Law 94-142 was passed by the U.S. Congress. The rationale for enacting such legislation was that the education clauses of each state's constitution do not limit which students are allowed to attend school. Instead, the broad language found in most states' constitutions refers to a requirement to provide education for all students.

Leading up to the passage of Public Law 94-142, two landmark legal cases established the legal rights of children with disabilities to access education. A 1971 lawsuit brought by the Pennsylvania Association for Retarded Citizens (PARC) succeeded in establishing the precedent that a state must provide access to education for all students, regardless of disability (Public Interest Law Center of Philadelphia, 2013). In another case in 1972, *Mills v. Board of Education of the District of Columbia*, the court made a similar ruling (Kids Together, Inc., 2013). These cases led the U.S. Congress to investigate the extent to which children with disabilities were being excluded from public schools. Findings showed that other states also prevented students with certain disabilities from attending school. Congress then took action to create a federal law requiring that all public schools provide instruction for all students, including those with disabilities. The focus of these legal cases was on the students' right to be in school. None of these cases, nor the subsequent law, stipulated what type of instruction each student should receive. Instead, the impetus of the court cases that led to special education focused on the legal right of all students to attend school.

The first U.S. federal special education law was the Education for All Handicapped Children Act (EHCA), passed in 1975. Also known as Public Law 94-142, this law reiterated that all children have a right to a free and appropriate public education (FAPE) in the least restrictive environment (LRE). The court decisions that contributed to the passage of Public Law 94-142 related to students with *mental retardation* (the term used at the time) or other severe disabilities. Nonetheless, advocates for students with LD participated in the efforts to create a national special education requirement and specific learning disability (SLD) was included as one of the disabilities for which special education could be provided. The EHCA has been revised several times and is now called the Individuals with Disabilities Education Act (IDEA), which was most recently reauthorized in 2004.

The definition of SLD incorporated into Public Law 94-142 was largely the same as had been used in the 1969 act. Most advocates and LD organizations agreed with the definition, but there was a lack of clarity in how to measure SLD. With the passage of Public Law 94-142, the federal government funded five SLD research centers during the late 1970s and early 1980s. These centers were housed at different universities and sought to develop measurement tools that could be used to assess whether a student has an SLD and if the student responds to instruction over time. Notably, the centers came up with discordant findings that created additional confusion about how to identify and monitor students with an SLD (Hallahan & Mercer, 2013). Two trends related to SLD during the late 1980s and 1990s are worth recounting: the Regular Education Initiative (REI) and inclusion.

In the decade following the passage of the EHCA, there were renewed efforts to define SLD, this time by different organizations. These efforts reflected a lack of national consensus about exactly what an SLD looks like. At the same time, the number of students with an SLD grew rapidly and faster than any other special education category. Looking back, Hallahan and Mercer (2013) noted that from 1976 through 1999 the number of students identified as having an SLD doubled. This rapid growth in a category that had once been considered a mild disability was concerning to teachers, administrators, and policymakers. In an effort to address the higher than expected number of students with an SLD, the Reagan administration developed the Regular Education Initiative (REI; Ackerman, 1987; Hallahan, Keller, McKinney, Lloyd, & Bryan, 1988). This was an administrative letter to the state directors of special education that indicated that they should be sure that students with disabilities were educated in the "regular" (now called general) education classroom as much as possible. The REI was not very effective in reducing the number of students with an SLD who were receiving services. Critics noted that the REI ignored the need for teacher training (Coates, 1989; Semmel & Abernathy, 1991) and that it likely violated student rights to a free and appropriate public education (FAPE; Bryan, Bay, & Donahue, 1988; Chisholm, 1988).

The REI tried to help teachers understand the idea of FAPE, but it did not succeed in reducing the number of students with an SLD. During the 1990s, a new effort to focus on students with disabilities emerged. Known as ***inclusion***, this initiative was led by advocates for students with more severe disabilities (Fuchs & Fuchs, 1994; Kubicek, 1994). Similar to the REI, inclusion focused on having all students with disabilities included in the general education classroom and curriculum as much as possible. In schools where full inclusion was adopted, all IEP services were supposed to be delivered in the general education classroom instead of in a specialized setting. While inclusion was aimed at giving students more access to the "normal" general education classroom, this was not always the outcome. The unintended consequence of the inclusion movement is that many students with disabilities stopped getting the very specialized services they needed.

RIGHTS AND INSTRUCTION

Broadly, special education has two primary missions: guaranteeing the rights of students with disabilities in schools *and* providing effective instruction for these students. At times, the special education community has seemed to focus more on one of these goals than the other. The initial efforts of Public Law 94-142 focused primarily on effective instruction for students with disabilities. This was a huge step forward for children who had previously not always been allowed to attend school at all. As the number of students with disabilities grew in the 1980s, there was a shift in policy focus to maintaining the rights of all students to access the general curriculum. By focusing more narrowly on the right to inclusion in the general education classroom, schools may have neglected the importance of effective instruction for all students. As the new century began, education policy began to focus much more on effective education for all students.

No Child Left Behind

In 2001, newly elected U.S. president George W. Bush signed a law passed by Congress known as the No Child Left Behind Act (NCLB; West, 2003). This law was based on research and preparation done primarily during the Clinton administration that focused heavily on achieving effective learning outcomes for all students. The catalyst of the NCLB was growing awareness that U.S. students were falling behind those from other industrialized nations in key measures of student achievement (see also Chapter 5). To address this concern, NCLB included key provisions designed to hold teachers and schools accountable for student outcomes. For example, under NCLB, at least 95% of all students were required to participate in the state's annual assessment. Unlike the past, students with mild disabilities like an SLD would not be exempted from this requirement. In addition, each school would be required to submit data to the state indicating whether or not it met key schoolwide learning objectives toward all students' adequate yearly progress (AYP). States were required to publish each school district's record of progress, indicating whether each school met its own stated goals toward AYP. The goal of NCLB was to increase the learning outcomes of all students, but its broad reach acknowledged that schools are responsible for the learning of all students, including those with disabilities.

THE PRESIDENT'S COMMISSION ON SPECIAL EDUCATION

Since the 1975 passage of the U.S. federal special education law, studies have shown that educational outcomes for students with disabilities have not improved as much as hoped. Kavale and Forness (2000) found that students with disabilities often made much less progress than general education students when an inclusion model was used. In response to evidence that students with disabilities were lagging behind other students, President George W. Bush appointed the President's Commission on Excellence in Special Education (PCESE; Federal Register, 2001). The charge to commission members was to identify what changes were needed in special education to make it more effective. In this regard, the PCESE focused more on effective practices than ensuring access to general education programs. The PCESE was important in the history of special education because it identified how the needs of students with disabilities were sometimes overlooked as a result of efforts to ensure their inclusion in general education. The recommendations of the PCESE were then incorporated, alongside provisions from NCLB, into the revision of the Individuals with Disabilities Education Improvement Act (IDEA), which was passed by the U.S. Congress in 2004.

INDIVIDUALS WITH DISABILITIES EDUCATION IMPROVEMENT ACT OF 2004

This new version of the law included several notable changes regarding eligibility for special education services. Part D, Subpart 3(C)5F of the statute noted that the intent of the law included:

> providing incentives for whole-school approaches, scientifically-based early reading programs, positive behavioral interventions and supports, and early intervening services to reduce the need to label children as disabled in order to address the learning and behavioral needs of such children . . .

This language is notable for emphasizing both scientifically based instruction as well as a focus on whole-school programs to reduce the number of students needing special education. Compared with earlier versions of the IDEA, the 2004 law recognized that prevention and early intervention would be important in efforts to support children with disabilities. The implementing regulations (2006) took the essence of both science and prevention even further and included important changes in prereferral requirements as well as in how school teams could determine if a student has an SLD (see Chapter 25).

The IDEA 2004 regulations incorporated the definition of scientifically based research from NCLB and also allowed schools to use up to 15% of their portion of IDEA funds to pay for professional development and delivery of prevention services (§300.225). Although the definition of an SLD was not changed from prior versions of the law in relation to the SLD category, additional guidance was provided that clarified the identification process. As noted in the general history above, there have long been questions about exactly how to identify an LD. For many years the standard method was to administer an IQ test and an academic achievement test, and see if the student's achievement was significantly below what was expected given the student's IQ score. This method was developed based on the general definition of LD originally created by Kirk (1962), but it has not been confirmed to be an accurate way to identify an SLD. The use of IQ–achievement discrepancy scores has long been debated in the research literature and has generally been found to be inaccurate in showing whether a student has an SLD (Floyd & Kranzler, 2013; Francis et al., 2005). IDEA 2004 remedied the reliance on such a discrepancy for identifying an SLD in §300.307:

> (a) *General.* A State must adopt, consistent with §300.309, criteria for determining whether a child has a specific learning disability as defined in §300.8(c)(10). In addition, the criteria adopted by the State—
>
> (1) Must not require the use of a severe discrepancy between intellectual ability and achievement for determining whether a child has a specific learning disability, as defined in §300.8(c)(10);
> (2) Must permit the use of a process based on the child's response to scientific, research-based intervention; and
> (3) May permit the use of other alternative research-based procedures for determining whether a child has a specific learning disability, as defined in §300.8(c)(10).

This language was a significant departure from earlier regulations because, for the first time, it barred states from requiring evidence of an IQ–achievement score discrepancy. Critics of the discrepancy method urged the changes seen in the IDEA 2004. It is important to note that the regulations did not bar all uses of IQ–achievement discrepancies, but rather barred states from requiring them. This means that local school districts could still chose to use them.

In addition, for the first time the regulations included a provision that required states to allow school teams to use data from a tiered-supports model such as an MTSS. In 2006, the most commonly used term for such supports was RTI and this term was used in the rule. The rule also allowed for the use of other methods that might not have been defined at the time that the rule was passed. This new language provided more options for how to identify an SLD than ever before in federal rules. Nonetheless, much of the real work needed to provide school personnel with working definitions and procedures about SLD was left to the states, primarily due to the nature of U.S. governance and the right of states to determine educational practices in their jurisdiction. Hauerwas et al. (2013) conducted a comprehensive review of all 50 states' regulations and guidance concerning SLD identification practices. This study revealed that the majority of states left decisions about SLD identification procedures up to the local school districts. Similar to findings from Zirkel and Thomas (2010), Hauerwas et al. showed that only 11 states required the use of RTI data as the primary source of data in the identification of an SLD. Thus, although federal law has allowed such data for SLD identification since 2006, few states have opted to mandate it and the majority of the process is guided by local school district policies and procedures.

Concurrent with the development of alternate procedures to identify an SLD, important research was ongoing into behavioral and social supports for all students. Based on work started at the University of Oregon, a comprehensive model of tiered supports for students' school behaviors became known as PBIS. Although not expressly written into the law or regulations concerning special education identification, PBIS has a very strong record of providing support to prevent significant behavioral and social difficulties (Sugai & Horner, 2010). While there is no mandate to do so, school teams can certainly use data from tiered PBIS as part of the process to consider a student's educational needs. For SLD and all other eligibility categories, using as many sources of data as possible in the process of determining a student's needs is simply best practice.

From the beginning in 1975, special education rules have required that teams use more than one source of data, and a general standard is to use at least three sources of data. The information gathered from tiered supports is one of the best possible sources of data concerning a student's current school performance. For this reason, school teams are urged to set up systems that collect such data and to use them regularly when a student is referred for special education services. Kovaleski, VanDerHeyden, and Shapiro (2013) offer excellent guidance about the exact data and steps needed to determine whether a student meets the criteria for SLD and special education services; these steps are reviewed in Chapter 25.

While MTSS data offer important information about recent student performance, it is essential that all educators understand that using tiered supports cannot interfere with a parent's right to request an evaluation. As with all prior versions of the law, the IDEA 2004 retained a parent's right to request an evaluation at any time. Once a referral for an evaluation has been initiated, the procedures fall under the due process protections of the law, including the requirement that any evaluations be completed in a timely manner. The protection of a parent's right to request an evaluation was reiterated in an administrative memo from the U.S. Office of Special Education Programs (OSEP) in November 2007 (Musgrove, 2007). As articulated in the 2007 memo, no school team can delay a comprehensive evaluation on the basis of ongoing intervention. Thus, once a formal request has been made, the required deadlines for completion of the comprehensive evaluation must be followed. Even when a parent has initiated a request, the evaluation can include data from tiered supports as long as the collection of the data does not delay the evaluation process. For example, if a student is having math difficulties and the school had already begun providing daily Tier 2 math intervention with weekly progress monitoring, the progress data could be included in the evaluation as another source of information. But it would not be appropriate to delay any part of the evaluation for the purpose of collecting more data or trying another intervention.

The revisions present in IDEA 2004 were the culmination of many years of efforts to make identification of an SLD easier and more accurate. Despite the many years of effort to understand and identify students' learning needs, some researchers and advocates have suggested that requiring the use of a "label" or category such as those employed for SLD identification has hampered true breakthroughs in supporting effective school outcomes for all students. The final section of this chapter considers how noncategorical approaches to supporting students might be a better alternative.

DO LABELS MATTER?

Since the beginning of special education, there have been discussions and debates about whether the students served needed to be identified by their diagnosis or category. During the period of time leading up to passage of Public Law 94-142, there were debates surrounding the effects of such "labels." Massachusetts, which passed one of the first state special education laws in 1973 (i.e., Chapter 766), intentionally created a state system of special education that was noncategorical (Brown-Chidsey, Seppala, & Segura, 2000). Testimony in hearings on the Massachusetts law included references to studies of how "labeling" students according to specific disabilities would hurt them in terms of self-esteem and school performance. In passing the federal special education law, the U.S. Congress decided to include categories and this requirement has continued through the 2004 revisions. Indeed, the OSEP requires that states submit counts of how many students are being served under each eligibility category each year. As of 2014, Iowa was the only remaining U.S. state to use a noncategorical system for identifying and supporting students with disabilities.

When U.S. special education policy was taking shape in the 1970s, there was a vigorous debate about whether a categorical system was in the best interests of students. Ultimately, Congress decided to include labels for the categories of disabilities (then called handicaps) that children might have. As early as 1977, there were calls for revising the categories being used in special education eligibility. Hallahan and Kauffman (1977) wrote a persuasive argument for doing away with categorical assignments for the so-called mild disabilities of "learning disabled, emotionally disturbed, and educable mentally retarded" (p. 139; these terms were those used at the time). Their justifications for collapsing these categories into one and using behavioral data to evaluate educational needs were that the definitions for these categories were imprecise and that many of the defining features overlap among the three. In supporting efforts to implement noncategorical tiered supports, Hallahan and Kauffman suggested that:

> children should be considered candidates for special education on the basis of specific social or academic performance deficits, and not judged solely on standardized

> test scores or clinical impressions. Children should be grouped for instruction according to their performance on remedial tasks. Such grouping would demand continuous assessment of the child's performance and flexibility in grouping children differently at different times, depending on the nature of the task and the child's progress. Chronological age, sex, and characteristic social behavior must be considered in grouping children for games and other social experiences, but specific academic skill level must be the criterion for grouping for remedial academic instruction. (p. 146)

These suggestions include many of the practices essential for an MTSS. In order to group children, screening would be conducted, and students receiving extra help would be monitored through "continuous assessment" such as progress monitoring. Hallahan and Kauffman recognized that for some students with disabilities, truly diagnostic or categorical methods were appropriate. For example, for students with hearing and vision impairments, the category of service directly indicated the instruction needed. Their argument was that for students with highly similar and overlapping mild "disabilities," a dynamic and flexible needs-based system would be better. Such programming would rely on the students' specific and current learning needs instead of an arbitrary and difficult to measure label such as learning disability or emotional disturbance. Thirty years after Hallahan and Kauffman's article, Sabornie, Evans, and Cullinan (2006) conducted a review of data showing learning outcomes among the three groups of students with mild disabilities (e.g., LD, emotional disturbance [ED], mild intellectual disability). The results indicated that indeed a continuous grouping of students with mild disabilities might be just as effective as the categorical method still in place as of IDEA 2004. It is important to note that Hallahan and Kauffman had made this suggestion well before the number of students with mild disabilities had skyrocketed.

As several chapters have noted, a continuing concern about special education has been the growing number of students who are served. In fact, MTSS practices were developed in part because so many students are being served in special education and some question whether all of them have a true disability. Ironically, in the early days of special education, there were concerns that too few students were being supported. Edgar and Hayden (1984) described how some special education teachers and administrators worried that their efforts to identify children with disabilities (known as Child Find) were not sufficient because fewer students than expected were identified for services. Interestingly, Edgar and Hayden also noted that "definitions of handicapping conditions, whether they are included in legislation or whether they are derived from other sources, must be reviewed periodically. We must continue to impose upon ourselves a system of checks and balances—a system that does not allow a compounding of errors" (p. 525). This statement from 1984 resonates with many of the issues that have surrounded the implementation of tiered supports in recent years. If all children might need support at one time or another, what is the correct role of special education and what role should categorical labels have in support systems?

In the years 1981–1994, the number of students in special education did rise. In 1981, about 8% of the total school population received special education services and by 1994 that number was about 10% (Edgar & Hayden, 1984; Reschly, 1996). More noticeable was the jump in the percentage of students who received special education in the category of SLD. In 1981, 3% of students were identified with an SLD; this percentage matched the estimated population prevalence of school-age children with an SLD (Edgar & Hayden, 1984). By 1994, the percentage of students receiving special education who qualified under the SLD category was 51%, fully half of all students receiving special education services (Reschly, 1996). This jump began in the 1980s and is what spurred the U.S. Department of Education to advocate for the REI. In reviewing the large increase in the number of students with an SLD, Reschly (1996) noted that there were problems both in the process of such an identification as well as in programming for them.

A related issue in SLD research includes long-standing concerns with the reliability of the assessments commonly used to identify an SLD. As Reschly and others have pointed out, it's not really possible to distinguish between students with an SLD and those who are "slow learners" (Reschly, 1996). Once a student has been identified with an SLD, few of the older, traditional measures used for identification can assist with instruction planning, although more recently this challenge has been addressed through the use of curriculum-based measurement (CBM). In addition to these technical problems, there are important social and psychological ones as well. As the number of students with an SLD increased, the percentage of identified students who were racial, linguistic, or cultural minorities was disproportionate to the total number of those students in schools (Reschly, 1996). Additionally, some students identified as having an SLD experienced a negative stigma and perceived themselves to be less capable than other students.

Given the drawbacks to using categorical systems of support, other methods have been suggested. Deno's (1985) problem-solving model was articulated as one possible alternative approach. Reschly (2005) reviewed the ongoing concerns with categorical service delivery and offered an updated description of how problem-solving-based methods could eliminate the problems with categorical services while improving outcomes for more students. Previously, Reschly (1996) provided guidance on how funding a noncategorical system need not be more expensive than categorical approaches. Recently, Gage, Lierheimer, and Goran (2012) updated and expanded the review conducted by Sabornie et al. in 2006. The Gage et al. study reviewed outcomes from students with mild disabilities as well as students with mild autism, attention deficit hyperactivity disorder (ADHD), and speech or language impairments. All of the latter categories have shown an increasing number of students in recent years. Gage et al. found that, except for students under the emotional disturbance category who had significant acting-out behaviors, all of the students showed similar outcomes and probably could have been grouped together by learning needs instead of by special education category.

Despite years of discussion and research, many supports for students are still organized in relation to specific categories of disability. It appears unlikely that special education is going to change this practice in the near future, but using an MTSS does offer a more flexible and noncategorical option for students who present with mild difficulties. Instead of placing students in mutually exclusive groups that never interact, an MTSS begins with all students together for initial instruction. For those students who need extra help, Tier 2 provides additional instruction but does not remove students from their Tier 1 core activities. For the small number of students who require intensive support, Tier 3 adds even more instructional time. Again, the students remain with classmates for most of the day, but get specific extra help when needed. Importantly, the tiers are fluid in that students can move back and forth between support at different tiers if they need more or less help, creating a dynamic approach to supporting all students.

The noncategorical and inclusive approach to supporting students used in an MTSS will stay that way only if educators can prevent themselves from adopting categorical language and behavior that they might have used in relation to special education. There is a danger that we might think of students in terms of "Tier 2 kids" rather than as Omar, Lilly, or Karen. While some form of organizational structure for any system is essential, this structure can become a barrier when it takes over the system and hides the reason—the function—of the instruction. When we stop thinking of students as individuals with unique learning needs, we have moved to a reliance on the system, instead of ourselves as educators, as agents of change. An MTSS works when all of the educators in a building agree on core principles and carry them out daily in their work with children. The "system" cannot do this work by itself. The system is people who care that every student has access to an effective education.

SUMMARY

The intersection of tiered supports with special education happens when a student does not make effective progress toward learning goals. One category of special education services, SLD, has an interesting history of diagnostic challenges. Ongoing research and discussions from the 1960s through the 1990s contributed to a shift in federal policy concerning SLD identification. As revised in 2004, the IDEA allows the use of data collected during specific interventions as part of one particular method for identification of SLD. Progress data collected during interventions can be used as part of a comprehensive evaluation for the other eligibility categories as well, but it must be accompanied by additional required criteria. A parent's right to initiate an evaluation for special education at any time was retained in the IDEA 2004 and the OSEP confirmed this protection in 2007.

Improving student outcomes does not depend on what we call the learning problem(s). Rather, it depends on using effective instruction at increasing levels of intensity and monitoring student outcomes. The use of categorical labels as part of systems to support students who are struggling has existed for over 40 years in U.S. education. Despite these labels, the number of students needing help has grown larger over time. Using an MTSS offers a noncategorical method of supporting students based on their educational need so that they can achieve specific learning goals. By focusing on the student's current learning need, tiered supports can be brief and dynamic so that all students can access them if needed. For those students with moderate to severe disabilities, special education is a very important resource. Nonetheless, research suggests that students with diverse learning difficulties, that may or may not be mild disabilities, can achieve improved learning outcomes without labels.

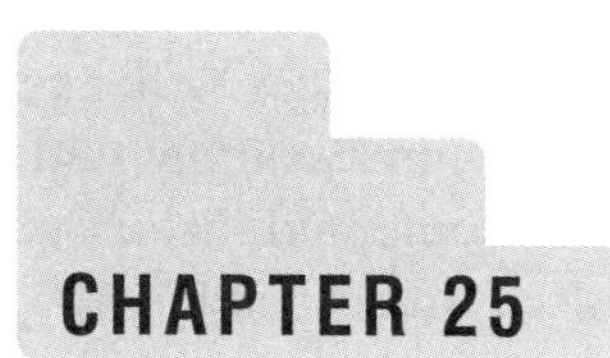

CHAPTER 25

Recognition and Support for Disabilities

SECTION 504 PLANS AND SPECIAL EDUCATION

Throughout this book we have emphasized how an MTSS is a general education initiative and is designed to support all students. While this is true, there are important ways that an MTSS connects with services for students who have identified disabilities. In the United States, there are two major laws related to school-age students who have disabilities: Section 504 of the Rehabilitation Act of 1973 and the Individuals with Disabilities Education Act (IDEA). Although these are federal laws, they have requirements that must be implemented by the states. This chapter provides information about how tiered supports have connections to U.S. laws and regulations for school-age students with disabilities. In addition, it explains how MTSS data have a unique role in the rules pertaining to the identification of students with a specific learning disability (SLD).

SECTION 504 PLANS

U.S. federal legislation passed in 1973 provides supports and protections for individuals of any age with disabilities. Known as Section 504 of the Rehabilitation Act, this law was primarily designed to prevent employment discrimination against people with disabilities. Nonetheless, the law applies to all organizations that receive federal funding, including public schools. Key provisions of the law prohibit denying (1) "qualified individuals the opportunity to participate in or benefit from federally funded programs, services, or other benefits"; and (2) "access to programs, services, benefits or opportunities to participate as a result of physical barriers" (U.S. Department of Health and Human Services Office of Civil Rights, 2015). All schools that receive federal funding must comply with Section 504. In the United States, any student who has a documented history of a recognized disability might be eligible for accommodations under Section 504.

History

The Rehabilitation Act was passed in 1973 as U.S. soldiers, some disabled, were returning from service in Vietnam. Because of the general unpopularity of the Vietnam War, some veterans experienced difficulty reentering the workforce. The early 1970s also saw the culmination of efforts to expand civil rights for many groups, including African Americans, indigenous peoples (i.e., Native Americans), women, and people with disabilities. It was in this historical and social context that the Rehabilitation Act was passed. The Rehabilitation Act provided protections for all persons with disabilities so that they could find employment. Section 504 of the act is where specific language that affects schools is found. Section 504 requires that any organization that receives funding from the U.S. government (i.e., federal sources) must provide services for those with identified disabilities. The original version of Section 504 only applied to a small percentage of students, though, as it focused primarily on assistance for individuals with physical disabilities.

In 1990, the U.S. Congress passed the Americans with Disabilities Act (ADA). This act was designed to provide more comprehensive protections for anyone with a disability, but used the same definition of disability as that in Section 504 (Zirkel, 2009). ADA emphasized that a disability affects a person's major life activities such as learning and working. In addition to barring employment discrimination, it also prohibits discrimination against individuals with disabilities in state and local government services, public accommodations, commercial facilities, and transportation (U.S. Department of Justice). Unlike Section 504, ADA did not include any contingencies in relation to federal funding (Zirkel, 2009). In other words, ADA is the "law of the land" regardless of an organization's funding source(s). Therefore, all U.S. schools must comply with the ADA and provide necessary supports for all students and staff who have recognized disabilities.

The ADA was revised in 2008 and the revisions included changes to Section 504 as well (Cortiella & Kaloi, 2010). Interestingly, these amendments put a special emphasis on ensuring that veterans of the wars in Iraq and Afghanistan did not face discrimination due to disability. These changes have implications for schools as well, whether they receive federal funding or not. The most significant changes relate to the list of major life activities protected under ADA and 504. In addition to basic physical activities, the covered activities now include *eating, sleeping, walking, standing, lifting, bending, reading, concentrating, thinking,* and *communicating.* Except for sleeping, the newly added activities are all things likely to happen in schools on a daily basis. Zirkel (2009) noted that the expanded disability definition in the revision is open-ended rather than restricted like the eligibility categories in IDEA.

Cortiella and Kaloi (2010) suggested that students in schools who might not have been eligible for Section 504 supports previously might be now as a result of the 2008 amendments. In addition to expanding the list of covered activities, the revisions also explicitly made clear that if a person's condition is in remission or treated through medication, services under Section 504 and ADA cannot be denied. In other words, evidence of the condition must be documented when symptoms are present and/or nonmedicated, but effective treatment is not a reason to deny services. As a result of these changes, students with conditions like asthma, diabetes, or attention deficit hyperactivity disorder (ADHD) whose disabilities are ameliorated by medications might be eligible for support services.

For many years after the passage of Section 504, and the original special education law—the Education of All Handicapped Children Act (EHCA) of 1975—many educators thought that Section 504 did not apply to schools because such protections were covered under EHCA and its successor, the IDEA. In 1991, the Office of Civil Rights (OCR) issued a policy memorandum that reminded schools that they actually are responsible for enforcing Section 504 as well as the IDEA (Shaw & Madaus, 2008).

The OCR memo clarified that when a student was found to have a disability but was not eligible for special education, he or she might be eligible for a Section 504 plan. As Madaus and Shaw note, Section 504 is separate and distinct from special education and is, therefore, a general education policy. Although Section 504 is a general education requirement in all U.S. states, research by Madaus and Shaw showed that many general educators had never received any training on the subject.

Section 504 Implementation

Section 504 has now been around for over 40 years, yet very little research has been conducted about its implementation. One reason for limited research is that it does not require as much procedural paperwork as the IDEA. Still, general patterns in Section 504 implementation are present. As noted, Section 504 requires that a person have a disability that ***significantly interferes with a major life activity***. For school-age students, any condition that affects being able to engage in daily school activities might qualify. As noted, the 2008 ADA amendments include a more inclusive definition of disability than either Section 504 or the original ADA. In order for a student to be eligible for Section 504 supports, there must be evidence of a disability. Zirkel (2009) suggested that any student who has compelling evidence of a disability might qualify for supports under Section 504. In some cases, the student might have been referred for a comprehensive evaluation for special education and the team decided that he or she was not eligible. If the team concludes that a disability is present but the student does not need special education, then a Section 504 plan could be created. In any situation when a school-age student has evidence of a recognized disability, application of Section 504 rules should be considered.

Another situation in which a student might be found eligible for a Section 504 plan is when the family has documentation of a disability but has already decided that special education is not needed. For example, a student who has orthopedic impairments and uses a wheelchair but does not need any specialized instruction could have a Section 504 plan to ensure access to all parts of the school building. Such a plan might include being allowed to use the school's elevator even though other students are not allowed to use it. In other cases, students who previously had special education services might benefit from Section 504 plans. Students who are deaf or hard of hearing but who do well in school when using hearing aids with a directional microphone might have had special education in the primary grades but no longer need such services as long as preferential seating and use of the assistive technology is available. School-based Section 504 plans are a way for educators to make sure that all students, regardless of disability, are able to have physical access to the school building and the curriculum.

Section 504 plans are different from special education because they should be fully implemented by general education teachers. The types of supports included in Section 504 plans vary from ensuring a student's access to a classroom with a wheelchair ramp to instructional accommodations. While definitions of accommodations vary from school to school, they typically include adjustments to the learning environment to make it accessible for a specific student. Examples include having students with hearing and vision impairments sit near the front of the room as well as repeating directions for a student with ADHD. The expanded definition of disability under the revised ADA makes available a broader array of services that a student might need.

One way to think about the difference between Section 504 plans and special education is to make a distinction between accommodation and modification. *Accommodate* means to "make room for." In relation to education, accommodations are steps taken to make sure that students with disabilities can access the general education curriculum. Section 504 plans should rely entirely on accommodations that allow students to access their education. This is different from educational modifications, which entail changing the instructional materials and/or expectations of students. *Modifications* are used in special education because the student's disability requires altering the instruction itself in order for the student to be successful in school.

Section 504 and an MTSS

Section 504 is perfectly aligned with an MTSS because they share the same goal: giving students access to learning. The main difference between Section 504 plans and an MTSS is the scope. Section 504 plans are individualized for each student who needs one. Generally, it is up to the student to demonstrate a need for a Section 504 plan and provide documentation of the disability. An MTSS is a universal system for supporting all students and seeks to discover which students need extra help and provide it to them. In this regard, an MTSS is a policy extension of the thinking behind Section 504. When Section 504 was passed, the mindset was that all persons (in the case of schools, students) have a right to certain opportunities (e.g., education). By creating a law to this effect, Congress sought to make employment and education options more equitable for those with disabilities. This was not a bad idea, but it was a reactive effort rather than a preventive effort. In other words, the right to access was given, but individuals with disabilities would have to advocate for themselves and document eligibility. As noted in many chapters of this book, an MTSS is prevention based, so it does not wait for a student to fail, but identifies what every student needs and provides it.

Another way of thinking about how Section 504 and an MTSS are two different ways to reach the same goal is to compare standard protocol and problem-solving efforts to support students (see also Chapter 20). Standard protocol methods involve using the current best science as the starting point for all individuals. Such methods are often used in fields other than education. For example, in medicine, the standard protocol for treating a fever in children is to use acetaminophen (e.g., Tylenol). It is used because it has been shown to be very effective and safe in the vast majority of children who have fevers. But if a child has muscle aches and no fever, acetaminophen is not recommended. Instead, ibuprofen (e.g., Advil), which is a medication that reduces pain from inflammation, is a better choice because of its anti-inflammatory properties. The same idea can be used in education. Research shows that all children benefit from direct instruction of decoding skills as a step toward learning how to read. Given that this is generally useful for all children, schools can adopt a standard protocol that includes teaching decoding as part of reading instruction. The benefit of standard protocols is that they create an efficient way to provide effective programming for a large number of people. The downside to a standard protocol is that it will not work for 100% of students. For this reason, problem-solving methods are also important.

A problem-solving approach involves looking carefully at the needs of each individual and coming up with a unique solution for each person. This can be very effective, but it is not efficient, or perhaps even possible, for each student. When there is a large number of students who have needs, stopping to create a unique solution for each one is probably going to take a long time, delay care for some, be difficult to sustain, and perhaps not be successful. For this reason, problem solving is best used as a second or third stage of support. Health care does this all the time. When a child's fever does not respond to Tylenol, the physician will then consider other treatments. The same is often true when a course of antibiotics is prescribed. If the first one does not work, then a second, or sometimes a third, is needed. Again, the same principles apply in education. When a student does not find success with the standard protocol(s), then problem solving is the right course of action.

MTSS Standard Protocols

Tiered supports typically include standard teaching protocols at Tier 1. This is most evident at Tier 1 where the programming is referred to as "core" instruction. As explained in Chapters 5 and 15, schools should select one core instructional program for each area of the curriculum. By having such core programs, there is one standard set of materials and methods provided for all students. In addition to making access to instruction equitable, using a core program is the best way to help the majority of students meet the stated learning goals. As noted many times in this book, not all students will be successful with Tier 1 alone. For the up to 20% of students who are still struggling despite an otherwise effective Tier 1 standard protocol of instruction, Tier 2 provides additional instruction in the specific area(s) of the students' need. In this regard, Tier 2 can have elements of both a standard protocol and problem solving.

Tier 2 involves providing students with additional instruction in one or more specific areas of need. It is always in addition to Tier 1 because students who are struggling need more time to learn and practice. Typically, Tier 2 sessions are provided three to five times per week for about 30 minutes each with small groups of students. The small-group format makes Tier 2 a standard protocol because all students in the group receive the same instruction. This is helpful because it means that more students can benefit from support at the same time. The choice of what instruction to use with each Tier 2 group is based on analysis of the students' prior performance in the classroom and on screening assessments (e.g., AIMSweb, DIBELS, FastBridge, SWIS). For the support to be effective it needs to be matched to the students' current learning needs. In order to make that match, some amount of problem solving is needed. Brown-Chidsey and Steege (2005, 2010) referred to the use of both a standard protocol and problem solving as a hybrid approach to supporting students. The use of both types of support at Tier 2 is what makes such intervention both effective and practical.

Many—even most—students who participate in Tier 2 will make the needed gains and not need more intensive support. Nonetheless, a small number of students will not find success and will need the more intensive methods used at Tier 3. By definition, Tier 3 supports are based on problem-solving activities. This is because by the time that Tier 3 becomes a consideration, several standard protocols have been tried and not worked. It would be foolish to keep trying such group-based methods when a student needs a more individualized solution. Tier 3 interventions are typically provided individually and include either additional minutes of intervention or a replacement core program. All such materials are selected based on the student's data from Tiers 1 and 2 and should be carefully matched to a specific learning need. Tier 3 problem solving requires more resources than the other tiers, but it is required by the 5% or fewer students who have not been successful with Tier 1 + Tier 2.

The original vision of Section 504 plans included the intensive and individualized problem solving that is found in Tier 3. The problem with this approach is that the intensity of the process limits how many students can be effectively supported. An MTSS, however, is geared toward helping as many students as possible with the fewest resources needed. This does not mean that an MTSS is less effective, just that it uses a public health prevention mindset that prioritizes how resources are distributed based on evidence of need. As mentioned earlier in this book, the term *triage* is widely used to describe the process of determining who needs what treatment. It is often used in emergency settings where physicians and nurses need to know quickly which patients to see first. Using an MTSS with a combination of standard protocol and problem-solving steps is a form of triage in education. It helps teachers identify which students need help the most and soonest.

Using an MTSS complements the requirements of Section 504 by providing a structured system for identifying which students need help in order to be successful in school. When implemented correctly, an MTSS goes beyond the basic requirements of Section 504 because it includes universal screening, as well as supports, for students regardless of disability. Still, an MTSS is a very good approach to addressing the new requirements of the 2008 ADA/Section 504 amendments. The 1973 language in Section 504 focused on severe and profound impairments, which are now typically identified well before a child reaches school age. Students with significant disabilities likely will have an individualized education program (IEP) before, or soon after, entering school. The students whose difficulties have not yet been detected and who might have a mild disability are those with some of the conditions recently added to the law, particularly reading, concentrating, thinking, and communicating. These are activities necessary for many aspects of school success and which can be supported very well using an MTSS.

Specifically, students with mild disabilities that affect their reading, concentrating, thinking, and communicating are likely to respond well and benefit from tiered supports. This is because when a condition is mild, it may not be noticed in nonschool settings. So, a student who did fine in home-based or preschool play settings could find the more challenging demands of school difficult. Tier 2 interventions are designed to provide such students with a brief but consistent "nudge" toward meeting learning goals. Some students will benefit quickly from these supports and not need them for a long period. Others may require sustained intervention because the expectations for students become more demanding each year. Either way, the supports provide exactly the kind of general education triage that the updated provisions of Section 504 require.

As noted throughout this book, a small number of students will not show progress despite participating in tiered supports. Such students might have either a persistent form of a mild disability or a more moderate undiagnosed condition. The good news is that the MTSS data can be used as part of the process of determining if a student has a disability that requires either more intensive Section 504 supports or special education. Importantly, at any point in time the parents of a child with school difficulties can request a comprehensive evaluation, and schools must not use tiered supports as a way to avoid providing special education services. In terms of meeting the requirements of Section 504, an MTSS offers schools a perfect system to identify and help all students. For those students with mild disabilities who don't need an IEP, tiered supports can be used within Section 504 plans to meet their needs. For those students who might have more persistent difficulties or a disability that requires special education, the MTSS process offers a way to document and identify the nature of the student's needs. And if a student is eventually diagnosed with a disability, he or she can be provided with either a Section 504 plan that uses the tiered supports or an IEP.

IDEA 2004

The IDEA of 2004 included important changes designed to improve outcomes for students with disabilities. Using findings from the President's Commission on Excellence in Special Education (PCESE; see Chapter 24; Federal Register, 2001), IDEA 2004 included an emphasis on effective instruction for students with disabilities.

Purposes of Special Education

There are two primary goals for special education: ensuring that student rights are protected and providing effective instruction. In order for special education to be effective, it is important that both students' rights and effective instruction are considered. As noted in the findings of the PCESE (Federal Register, 2001), the history of U.S. special education programming has not fulfilled the promise of effective instruction. Too many students with disabilities do not achieve each state's learning outcomes. Sadly, many students with disabilities end up dropping out of school (Goss & Andren, 2014).

The mechanism by which students are found eligible for special education is the team meeting. Congress included a requirement that a team made up of the student's parent(s), teacher(s), and other professionals be responsible for determining whether a student is eligible for special education. The team method was included because of prior school practices in which school personnel only, sometimes a single person, made decisions about whether a student could attend school or not. Importantly, the team must include at least one of the student's parents or a legal guardian. Again, this was because parents had rarely been included in decisions about their child's access to instruction in the past. The goal of having a team-based decision process was to ensure that all of the right stakeholders would be involved in determining a student's educational program.

Starting with the 1975 federal law, there have been specific categories of disability supported through special education. The current categories are shown in Table 25.1 (National Dissemination Center for Children with Disabilities, 2013). There are a total of 14 categories, but one of these, developmental delay, can be used with children ages 3–9 only. It is important to understand that these *categories* are not *diagnoses*. Instead they are general descriptors of the most common behaviors and symptoms that a school-age child with a disability is likely to demonstrate. In order for a student to qualify for special education, several conditions must be met. First, there needs to be evidence of a disability. Such evidence often consists of a diagnosis made by a licensed physician, psychologist, or other health care provider. Such a diagnosis will be based on the student's presenting symptoms as well as the classification system used by that professional to identify various conditions. Two frequently used classification systems are the *Diagnostic and Statistical Manual of Mental Disorders* (DSM) published by the American Psychiatric Association (2013) and the *International Classification of Diseases* (ICD) published by the World Health Organization (2010). A diagnosis based on either DSM or ICD criteria does not, by itself, mean that a student will be eligible for special education.

In addition to a diagnosis, there must be evidence that the student's disability has an adverse effect on the student's education such that specially designed

TABLE 25.1. Categories for Special Education Services According to the Individuals with Disabilities Improvement Act (IDEA) of 2004

1. Autism
2. Deaf-blindness
3. Deafness
4. Emotional disturbance
5. Hearing impairment
6. Intellectual disability
7. Multiple disabilities
8. Orthopedic impairment
9. Other health impairment
10. Specific learning disability
11. Speech or language impairment
12. Traumatic brain injury
13. Visual impairment (including blindness)
14. Developmental delay: If a state or local education agency chooses, this term can be used for children ages 3–9 only

instruction is necessary. While states can develop their own definitions of adverse effect, some indicators of student learning outcomes that are often used to show whether a student's education is adversely effected by his or her disability include outcomes on statewide, district-level, and classroom assessments, as well as disciplinary evidence and evidence of functional impairment. There are more specific criteria in the IDEA 2004 regulations for specific learning disability. For all disability categories, there should be evidence across multiple sources of data that the student's ability to access his or her education is adversely effected by his or her disability before he or she is considered for special education. The purpose of this criterion is based on the reality that some students with diagnosed disabilities may make very effective progress in school and not need a special education. For example, a student with cerebral palsy that affects his or her legs may need crutches, a walker, or a wheelchair, but not necessarily specialized instruction. The school would be required to meet the physical access provisions of the ADA and provide ramps and elevators, but these must be provided no matter what and are not specific to special education.

The final criterion for special education eligibility is evidence that the student will benefit from specialized instruction that addresses the needs presented by his or her disability. This is the other side of the requirement that a student's education is adversely effected by his or her disability. When a student who has a disability is not making effective progress, it is generally assumed that he or she would benefit from specialized instruction. In this situation, a team is likely to decide that the student qualifies for special education. Then, the team's next job is to develop an IEP that addresses the student's specific learning needs. As with eligibility, IEP development must be team based so that no single person is making decisions about the student's future and that the parent(s) or guardian(s) are involved in the process. Once completed and approved by the parent(s), the IEP is a legally binding document that the school is required to implement with integrity.

Many Bumps on the Road of Life

The special education procedures outlined above are designed to ensure that students who have diagnosed disabilities and who are not making effective progress in school are able to access education just like children who do not have disabilities. The problem with limiting access to additional supports like special education is that having a diagnosed disability is not the only reason that a student might experience school difficulties. There are many reasons that a student could have non-disability-related problems in school. School difficulties can arise from many events that occur outside of school such as frequent family moves, parent unemployment, military deployment, and unexpected illness or death of a family member. All of these circumstances are likely to affect a student's school progress in some way. When a student experiences any of these difficult life events over a prolonged time, or encounters multiple such events, he or she is even more likely to struggle in school (see Chapter 4 about risk factors).

A challenge that special educators have faced in the years since Public Law 94-142 was passed is that special education is often seen as the only way that a student can get extra help in school. When additional help in school was limited to special education alone, many nondisabled students either "slipped through the cracks" because there was no system of supports available, or were found eligible for special education despite not having a true disability. An MTSS is designed to provide additional supports for all students so that none can slip through the cracks. Unfortunately, there is no way to guarantee that school will go easily for every student every day, week, or year. But educators can ensure that there are supports available for all students over both short- and long-term circumstances. Tier 1 is a long-term support designed to help every student have a good start with school progress. Most students will succeed with Tier 1 by itself, but some will need Tier 2 + Tier 3. These tiers are generally short-term supports to help students get through brief periods of school difficulty. If a student demonstrates persistent difficulty despite tiered supports, then the school team must consider whether the student has a disability that is influencing school progress. Special education is another long-term support that is designed to ensure that students with disabilities receive access to effective instruction in relation to the disability.

SPECIAL EDUCATION ELIGIBILITY

IDEA 2004 included language that allows school-based teams to use data from an MTSS as part of the process of determining whether a student has an SLD. Although MTSS data can be used as part of a comprehensive evaluation, it is important that all teachers understand that the MTSS process cannot be used to delay special education referral or services. Melody Musgrove, then director of the Office of Special Education Programs at the U.S. Department of Education, sent a memo to all of the U.S. state directors of special education in November 2007 reminding them that MTSS (then called RTI) procedures could not be used to delay access to special education services (Musgrove, 2007). Specifically, Dr. Musgrove reminded state directors that "States and LEAs [local educational agencies] have an obligation to ensure that evaluations of children suspected of having a disability are not delayed or denied because of implementation of an RTI strategy" (Musgrove, 2007, p. 1). This reminder is very important for those who seek to implement an MTSS because it reiterates that parents of students with suspected disabilities have the right to obtain a comprehensive evaluation paid for by the school district. This evaluation is then used by the team to decide whether a child qualifies for special education services. While MTSS procedures have the potential to provide additional data about how a student is doing in school, they must never be used to delay the process of referring a student for special education.

IDEA Language

The section of IDEA that includes reference to MTSS data is §300.307. This section is specific to the identification of an SLD only. It includes three options for how to identify an SLD (see Chapter 24 for details):

1. Unless prohibited by state law, a number based on the difference between the student's IQ and the score on a test of achievement in the area of concern (i.e., reading, math, or writing);
2. Data showing the child's response to scientific, research-based intervention; or
3. Another research-based procedure.

It is important to note that §300.307 gave states the option to bar the use of an IQ–achievement difference, but states cannot require this method.

State Rules

Since education in the United States is governed by the states, each state must create its own special education rules and regulations. A state's rules must meet the minimum federal standards (i.e., IDEA), but have the option to go beyond the federal standard. As of 2014, 16 states had adopted special education rules that require the collection and use of RTI data as part of the process of determining whether a student has an SLD (Zumeta, Zirkel, & Danielson, 2014). Of these 16 states, four have additional language requiring supplemental testing. Georgia, Idaho, and Maine require cognitive testing to document the student's cognitive processing, and Louisiana requires additional testing to document the student's strengths and weaknesses. The remaining 34 states allow school teams to utilize any one of the three methods included in the IDEA.

The presence of different methods for identifying an SLD has created confusion among educators. Although this section of IDEA 2004 was designed to reduce the overall number of students with an SLD, it has led to more diverse practices for SLD identification. Some states have developed detailed guidance about how to use MTSS data for SLD decisions, while others have not (Boynton Hauerwas, Brown, & Scott, 2013). Despite the availability of such guidance in many states, there does not appear to be any relationship between a state's MTSS guidance and the percentages of students with an SLD in that state. Since 2005, the national number of students identified as having an SLD has gone down, but there have been significant increases in certain other categories such as autism and other health impairment (Cortiella & Horowitz, 2014). The lack of alignment between states' MTSS policies and the number of students with an SLD is a good reminder that an MTSS is not about screening students for special education. Instead, it is about helping all students be successful in school. Nonetheless, if a student does not respond to carefully selected and implemented interventions, then it might be appropriate to consider whether the student has an SLD. In such cases, student data collected during MTSS activities is the best starting point for such an evaluation.

Specific Procedures

In states where specific procedures for using MTSS data as part of an evaluation for an SLD are required, those should be followed consistently and carefully. In those states without such procedures, there are two excellent resources that can be used by team members. These resources are also likely to be helpful for those working in states that require use of the MTSS data method. The first resource is a book by Kovaleski et al. (2013) titled *The RTI Approach to Evaluating Learning Disabilities*. The second is an online toolkit from the National Center for Learning Disabilities (NCLD; 2014).

Kovaleski et al. (2013) developed a model for identifying an SLD that includes four criteria. Two of these are criteria that must be "ruled in." The other two are factors that must be "ruled out." The four criteria are

Rule in

1. Failure to meet one or more specific learning standards.
2. A pattern of strengths and weaknesses—or—lack of progress in response to scientifically based instruction.

Rule out

3. Other type of impairment, cultural factor, environmental issue, or limited English proficiency.
4. Lack of effective instruction by qualified personnel as shown through repeated assessments.

In addition to the four criteria, there must be an observation of the student in the learning environment.

Ruling In

The first step of the Kovaleski et al. (2013) criteria comes from §300.308 of IDEA 2004 and involves examining the student's academic achievement data and determining whether he or she has failed to meet age- or grade-level standards in one or more of the following areas:

1. Oral expression
2. Listening comprehension
3. Written expression
4. Basic reading skills
5. Reading fluency
6. Reading comprehension
7. Mathematics calculation
8. Mathematics problem solving

If there is evidence that the student has not met one or more identified standards in any of the above areas, then the team can proceed with the evaluation. It is important to note that if the student is meeting all standards in the above areas, consideration of an SLD is not appropriate. Only by "ruling in" low performance in one of the eight areas listed in IDEA 2004 can a team move forward with an evaluation for an SLD.

The second criterion comes from IDEA 2004 section §300.309 and includes two options. The team can use data that show that either (paraphrased from IDEA 2004):

1. The student did not make sufficient progress to meet age- or state-approved grade-level standards in one or more of the areas identified in criterion 1 after using a process based on the student's response to scientific, research-based intervention; or
2. The child exhibits a pattern of strengths and weaknesses in performance, achievement, or both, relative to age, state-approved grade-level standards, or intellectual development.

Notably, option 2 is not as specific as option 1 and there remains uncertainty about exactly what scores should be used for this option. Kovaleski et al. (2013) recommend that teams use option 1 and gather the data from progress assessments used during an MTSS process. When using option 1, the team would consider whether the student's data indicate a lack of improvement as a result of one or more interventions. More details about how to interpret student progress data can be found in Chapters 21 and 22. If the student's data confirm that the student did not make sufficient progress to reach the grade-level standard, then the team moves on to consider whether there is another reason for the student's lack of progress.

Ruling Out

Criterion 3 of the Kovaleski et al. (2013) method involves considering whether the student's lack of progress is due to the presence of another type of disability, cultural factors, environmental deprivation, or limited English proficiency. Specifically, the team must consider whether any of the following factors are a better explanation for the student's academic difficulties:

1. Visual impairment
2. Hearing impairment
3. Orthopedic impairment
4. Intellectual disability
5. Emotional disturbance
6. Cultural factors
7. Environmental disadvantage
8. Limited English proficiency

If the team concludes that any of the above offers a better explanation for the student's school difficulties, then an SLD is not identified. But if the team rules out all of the above factors, it can consider the other rule-out criterion.

The fourth and final criterion in the Kovaleski et al. (2013) method is to consider whether the student received appropriate and adequate instruction by qualified personnel. There are two primary indicators of appropriate instruction. First, the credentials of the teacher can be verified. All states have requirements for teachers and, therefore, it should be the case that the teacher(s) of any student referred for an SLD evaluation was certified or licensed by the state's department of education. The second indicator of effective instruction is information about the learning outcomes of other students in the same classroom. As noted by Kovaleski et al., the easiest way to determine whether most of the students in a classroom are making effective progress is to review triannual screening data. Triannual screenings are a cornerstone of an MTSS and show the relative progress of all students in each classroom. They are important because they indicate whether the selected Tier 1 core programs are working for the majority of students in a specific population.

As described in Chapter 18, it is important that at least 80% of students in every classroom, grade, school, and district meet specific goals for mastery of basic academic skills. As with many aspects of prevention and public health, it is understood that some students will not meet these learning goals. Over time, it has been shown that if 80% or more of students meet the goals as a result of Tier 1 core instruction, then the teachers are doing their job well and the curriculum is a good match for the students. Therefore, the second step in determining if appropriate and adequate instruction was provided for a student referred for an SLD is to examine the triannual screening data for the student's classroom and grade. Such data will show whether 80% or more of students met the grade-level goal in the fall, winter, and spring of each academic year. If the data show that 80% or more of students have met the goal, and the student in question has had good attendance, then the adequacy of instruction is confirmed. But if less than 80% of students in the referred student's classroom or grade (depending on grade level) have met the goal, or the student has had poor attendance, then the adequacy of instruction cannot be confirmed.

What If the Adequacy of Instruction Cannot Be Confirmed?

This is a difficult question, but a very important one. If data show that less than 80% of the students in a classroom did not meet the benchmark goals for the grade, additional data review is needed. First, the team should check to see if 80% or more of the students in last year's classroom met the benchmark. If so, then the referred student will have experienced at least 2 years of ineffective instruction and really needs help as soon as possible. If the referred student is 2 or more years behind the benchmark goal for his or her grade, then additional support is justified, regardless of inadequate instruction. Technically, Title I programs were designed to address the needs of such students. But if the student is behind fewer than two grade levels, the focus of support needs to be at the Tier 1 classroom level.

In addition to reviewing the classwide data for the referred student, the team will need to look at the Tier 2 and Tier 3 data to consider whether these interventions were provided accurately and with integrity. If the team concludes that all of the interventions were provided with adequate integrity, then the referred student's ongoing difficulties can be interpreted as a manifestation of an SLD. But if there were problems with the implementation of the intervention(s), the team should suspend the evaluation and request that more data be collected under conditions in which the intervention is implemented correctly.

In jurisdictions where the RTI method has been adopted as the only pathway to determining the presence of an SLD, if the team concludes that the instruction or intervention provided to a student—at any level—was incomplete or inadequate, then it must suspend the evaluation process and seek to gather more data. This is very important because data resulting from inadequate instruction are not reliable. The team will need to consult with the student's parents about such situations and explain why more data are needed. If a parent insists that the evaluation be completed according to the initial deadline, then the team might need to use diagnostic teaching procedures in order to gather enough data in a timely manner. Diagnostic teaching refers to instruction designed to show whether a student has learned specific knowledge or skills. Diagnostic teaching is a method of working with one student individually in a way that shows whether the student learns from each lesson. It is an effective method for identifying learning problems because it shows whether the student made progress during each brief lesson.

Observation

IDEA 2004 requires that there be an observation of the student in the student's current learning environment. SLD is the only IDEA category that requires such an observation. The observation can be conducted by any member of the IEP team except the current classroom teacher. The purpose of the observation is to see how the student behaves and responds to classroom instruction. A variety of observation methods can be used, but systematic recording procedures are recommended. Systematic recordings include collection of data about a student's classroom behaviors at specified time intervals. There are a number of published systematic recording methods including the behavior observation of students in schools (BOSS; Pearson Education, Inc., 2014). There are both paper and online versions of the BOSS and it is very easy to use.

The NCLD Toolkit

The National Center for Learning Disabilities (NCLD) published a toolkit for school teams seeking to complete an MTSS data-based evaluation of an SLD. The toolkit is organized around six criteria that must be met to verify the presence of an SLD:

1. Failure to meet age- or grade-level state standards in one of eight areas when provided with appropriate instruction.
2. Lack of sufficient progress in response to scientific, research-based intervention in the area(s) identified in criterion 1.
3. Findings are not primarily the result of a visual, hearing, or motor disability; an intellectual disability, emotional disturbance, cultural factors, environmental or economic disadvantage, or limited English proficiency.
4. Underachievement is not due to lack of appropriate instruction in reading or math.
5. Observation(s) of student in the learning environment documents academic performance and behavior in areas of difficulty.
6. Specific documentation for eligibility determination includes required components.

Criteria 1–5 of the toolkit are the same as those found in Kovaleski et al. (2013). The additional requirement is that there be specific documentation of all five criteria. The NCLD website includes many resources for the toolkit, including descriptions and examples of each criterion and a form that teams can use to assist them with compiling the required documentation (NCLD, 2014).

If a student's data show that he or she failed to meet grade-level standards—both initially and after scientifically based instruction—and that he or she was provided with appropriate and effective instruction, as confirmed by observations and repeated assessments, then the student can be identified as a student with an SLD. The biggest challenge that school teams face in using MTSS data for SLD identification is having the necessary data. In order for the team to have such data, the school will need to have established and implemented MTSS policies and procedures several years before. Once such systems are put into place, the data needed for SLD identification will be available. Until such systems are in place, schools should focus on creating teams, making sure they work effectively, gathering screening and progress data, and verifying the integrity of all levels of instruction. With such components in place, use of MTSS data for SLD identification is possible.

SUMMARY

Using an MTSS is well aligned with the requirements of both Section 504 of the Rehabilitation Act and IDEA 2004. The MTSS method fits with Section 504 because it includes both standard protocol and problem-solving components that address students' learning needs. Tiered supports ensure that students, regardless of disability, have access to help when school is difficult. Although broader in scope than Section 504, an MTSS includes universal supports that help to distribute school resources in relation to all students' needs. Importantly, when tiered supports are in place, schools will have the additional instruction and data needed to document accommodations for students with disabilities.

An MTSS has important connections with special education as well. While U.S. special education provides procedures so that students with disabilities who are struggling in school can access IEPs, many students have difficulties in school that are not related to a disability. Circumstances such as frequent family moves, parent unemployment, military deployment, and unexpected illness or death of a family member can mean that a student falls behind in school and fails to meet grade-level goals. An MTSS offers a way to support all students, regardless of disability, and ensure that any short-term difficulties that students face do not have to become long-term handicaps. Nonetheless, it is essential that all educators understand that the use of an MTSS cannot result in delaying a student's referral for a comprehensive evaluation for special education services. There are specific steps that teams must follow in order to use MTSS data for special education decision making. By following these steps, teams will ensure students' rights and have important data for effective decision making.

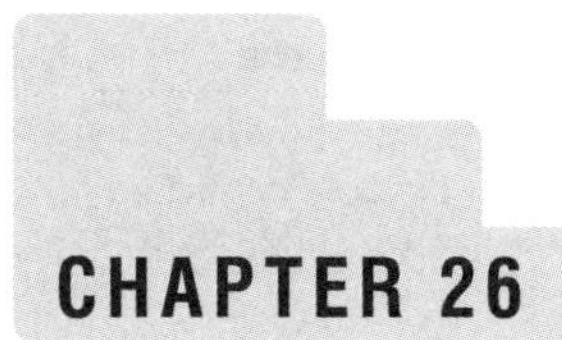

CHAPTER 26

Case Example

BUILDING TIERED SUPPORTS

This final chapter includes an example of the process used in one school district to plan, develop, implement, and evaluate a comprehensive MTSS. In order to maintain confidentiality, the details of the example are taken from a number of different schools and districts in which we have worked; all names and locations have been changed. But each and every step and process described is one that we have used in at least one setting to establish an effective MTSS. The exact process will be different for each school, but this example is designed to show the level of detail required to make an MTSS successful.

APPLEWOOD SCHOOL DISTRICT

Applewood is a medium-size school district with a total student enrollment of 9,575 students. The district includes a small urban center as well as several suburban neighborhoods. There are three high schools, four middle schools, and six elementary schools in the district. In the district as a whole, about 25% of students qualify for free and/or reduced lunch, but the percentages are quite different across the buildings. Table 26.1 provides a summary of student demographics for each school. The community of Applewood has experienced significant changes in its economy in recent years. In decades past it served as a manufacturing hub, but many of the companies moved their operations outside of the United States and there are very few manufacturing jobs left. Most of the remaining jobs include retail and entertainment-related positions in restaurants

TABLE 26.1. Applewood School District Student Demographic Data

School	Total enrollment	Percent receiving free and/or reduced-price meals	Percent proficient on state exam
Lincoln Elementary	350	57%	32%
Taft Elementary	300	7%	89%
Carter Elementary	425	23%	44%
Adams Elementary	400	14%	56%
Jefferson Elementary	325	4%	92%
Wilson Elementary	450	42%	54%
Jackson Middle School	925	32%	69%
Roosevelt Middle School	950	55%	48%
Harrison Middle School	900	22%	77%
Kennedy Middle School	850	5%	84%
Reagan High School	1100	5%	88%
Truman High School	1200	11%	76%
Madison High School	1400	44%	68%

and small businesses. Some community members work in a larger nearby urban center and commute to and from the greater Applewood area, typically living in the newer and more affluent neighborhoods.

DISTRICT SCORES ON STATE TESTS

Students in Applewood complete a mandated state assessment each spring. As shown in Table 26.1, student performance varies. The final column of the table shows the percentage of students in each school who earned a proficient score on the test. Overall student achievement is much higher in some schools than others. The members of the Applewood School Board are very concerned about the low achievement in certain schools. If such achievement persists, the state will take over and run the low-performing schools, something board members do not want to see happen. The lower-performing schools have received additional funding from the state to implement steps to improve student outcomes but, so far, little change has been observed. The board has let the superintendent know that if scores do not improve significantly at the lower-performing schools in the next 2 years, she will be dismissed.

Creating a District-Level Team

Knowing that her job is on the line, the superintendent, Dr. Lisa Crawford, reviewed the many improvement efforts that the district implemented in recent years. These efforts included additional paraprofessionals in low-performing buildings, release time for teachers to review student data, and a stricter discipline policy for the middle and high schools. Despite these steps, the schools did not make progress. Dr. Crawford decided to review available research literature about effective school improvement systems. She examined the resources at federally funded online technical assistance centers, read a number of articles, and talked with fellow superintendents. As a result of these steps, Dr. Crawford concluded that effective and lasting student improvement can happen only if (1) all educators understand and make a commitment to different practices; and (2) school-level teams develop, implement, and evaluate practices that support improved student outcomes. Such practices fit within an MTSS model and Dr. Crawford decided to develop such a model for Applewood. As a next step, Dr. Crawford decided to convene a meeting of all the principals and assistant principals in the district. At this meeting she explained the scope of change she envisioned. She presented information about creating an MTSS and gave the leaders two articles to read. She explained her plan to appoint a districtwide MTSS planning team that would work over the course of a full academic year to develop a 3- to 5-year plan to implement the MTSS in each school. She explained that the following year, school-level teams would be appointed to develop building-level plans and procedures. Dr. Crawford concluded the meeting by asking all principals to nominate two staff from their buildings to serve on the district team. The meeting ended with a date set for another meeting at which the district team members would be announced.

Before the next meeting with the principals, Dr. Crawford contacted and talked with each one of the staff members nominated for the district team. She explained the scope of the work to be done, the time required, and the length of the commitment: 3 years. Based on these discussions, Dr. Crawford identified which staff were best suited to serve on the district team. In addition, Dr. Crawford wrote a description of the planned districtwide team and sent it to all staff and board members, as well as to the local newspaper. At the next principals' meeting, Dr. Crawford announced the members of the district team, noting that she would be a member but not the chair. She then asked each principal and assistant principal to share his or her ideas and concerns about the MTSS project. All ideas were recorded in the meeting minutes so that they could be given to the district team members for later review. The first district team meeting was held on a scheduled professional development day. Dr. Crawford explained the MTSS project to the team members and they spent the entire day discussing the benefits and drawbacks to this project. All ideas were categorized as either barriers or enhancers and recorded in the meeting minutes. By the end of the first meeting, the team had selected a chair, set up its schedule for the school year, and assigned each member to collect specific information that the team would need to do its work. For example, team members were assigned to bring to the next meeting the lists of currently adopted core curricula, what each school was doing to support prosocial behavior, and interventions that were used in each building, along with other related information.

Dr. Crawford arranged for the district team to be trained in the Team-Initiated Problem-Solving (TIPS) process. The team used TIPS, as well as the data that they had, to document and guide their work and to guide their decision-making process. During the rest of the school year, the district team met regularly to discuss and plan specific steps toward creating an MTSS for Applewood. This work was driven by a master schedule that was brought to each meeting and on which specific steps were written as they were determined. Many of the team's activities included identifying strengths and weaknesses in current instruction as well as a time frame and process to select new materials and methods. Similarly, the team reviewed all current assessments being used and identified which ones provided useful information and which ones did not. The team identified areas for teacher professional development that would contribute to building an effective MTSS.

The team then worked to identify and arrange professional development for the schools in their district about what an MTSS is and how to implement it with integrity. The team utilized resources for selecting professional development, such as the blueprint for professional development available at the National Technical Assistance Center on Positive Behavioral Interventions and Supports (Lewis et al., 2010). They also identified people in their state with expertise and experience in building and sustaining an MTSS across buildings, and vetted those people based on what they learned about best practices in professional development from the resources they consulted. Once professionals with expertise and experience were selected, plans were made to develop trainings that would support the work of the teams and the educators in each building who would be charged with implementing the MTSS.

In May, the team shared its work and plans at an all-district professional development day. At this event, the team described how each building would go about appointing an MTSS planning team for the next year and the activities that those teams would lead. The primary goal of the May event was to generate interest and questions among all staff. At the conclusion of the meeting, all staff were asked to complete a brief survey indicating whether they supported the planned MTSS and if they thought it would work. The responses to this survey were then reviewed by the district team to learn how much support was initially present across the district. The survey results showed that 82% of staff supported the idea, but only 65% thought it would work. These data indicated that the district had enough buy-in to begin—the goal is 80% support—but that the team needed to focus on showing staff how tiered supports would result in student improvement. Before the school year ended, the district team decided to revise its planned fall activities and in addition to appointing building-level teams, it gathered data from existing interventions and organized the data to show team members how students made improvements over time. The district team's 5-year MTSS plan is shown in Table 26.2.

School-Level Teams

During the second year of implementation, two school-level activities were added to what the district team had already begun. First, two school-level teams were set up for each school: a behaviorally focused team and an academically focused team. The building representatives on the district team served as the convening chairs of the school teams. They met with their principals to identify possible team members and then the principal personally contacted each nominee. Such personal contact was used to convey to nominees the importance of the team's role in the school's work. The principal or assistant principal of each building served as a member of each team, but not as the chair. Once each team's membership was confirmed, first meetings were held at which the chair explained the work of the district team as well as the school teams' tasks for the school year. The school teams were trained in TIPS and were then ready to begin their work.

There were two main tasks that each academic school team took on: identifying all current interventions and corresponding assessments, and supporting the professional development provided to all building staff about an MTSS. Importantly, the academic teams focused on inventorying only current interventions that were being used above and beyond the Tier 1 core curricula that the district team identified. The purpose of having each school share its academic interventions was to create an honest summary of what was actually being used. When assessments were being used to monitor student progress, these were noted as well. The process of learning what interventions and assessments were used was broken down by grade level and content area. Team members were assigned to interview teachers, specialists, and other staff to identify the practices that were in place. Once gathered, this information was put into a table that summarized the information for the building. The district team representative then took the summary back to the district team to compile a master list.

In contrast, the behavior teams were tasked with taking the school year to develop a universal system for supporting prosocial behavior among students. To accomplish this, the teams employed the representative model described in Chapter 7 in which they developed plans and then sought and incorporated the feedback of their colleagues. Through that process, each team identified three to five positively stated expectations that could be applied schoolwide and that reflected the values of the school community. Once identified, the teams developed plans for teaching those expectations to students. Teaching plans included developing matrices for schoolwide settings and events, which depicted what it would look like to meet each of the expectations in each of those contexts. Based on those matrices, the teams developed lesson plans for teaching the expectations in each context for teachers to employ with their students. Each building behavior team went on to develop a schoolwide acknowledgment system that would allow educators to encourage and maintain expected behaviors.

TABLE 26.2. Five-Year District MTSS Implementation Plan

Group	Year 1	Year 2	Year 3	Year 4	Year 5
District team	1. Inventory existing practices and prioritize needs. 2. Develop materials and methods to prepare others at the school level, including long-term PD needs. 3. Identify, vet, and retain people with expertise and experience to provide PD. 4. Develop 5-year district MTSS plan.	1. Using the developed plan, review current curricula, and select new materials as needed. 2. Develop a comprehensive list of approved interventions for each tier. 3. Conduct districtwide PD to support the MTSS. 4. Review 5-year plan and set annual goals.	1. Review current curricula and select new materials at needed. 2. Provide monthly PD for all newly adopted curricula. 3. Provide initial and refresher assessment and intervention training for all staff. 4. Review 5-year plan and set annual goals.	1. Review current curricula and select new materials as needed. 2. Gather data about implementation integrity at each school. 3. Address implementation problems as needed. 4. Provide initial and refresher assessment and intervention training for all staff. 5. Review 5-year plan and set annual goals.	1. Review current curricula and select new materials as needed. 2. Gather data about implementation integrity at each school. 3. Address implementation problems as needed. 4. Provide initial and refresher assessment and interventions training for all staff. 5. Create new 5-year plan and set annual goals.
School academic teams	NA	1. Develop a written action plan for the year. 2. Implement TIPS. 3. Review existing intervention and assessment practices and share findings with district team.	1. Develop a written action plan for the year. 2. Conduct universal screening for academics and review data to identify trends by grade levels and content areas.	1. Develop a written action plan for the year. 2. Conduct universal screening for academics and review data to identify trends by grade levels and content areas.	1. Develop a written action plan for the year. 2. Conduct universal screening for academics and review data to identify trends by grade levels and content areas.

		4. Support PD provided to all building staff about the MTSS and their role in it. 5. Develop 5-year MTSS school plan.	3. Develop and implement meeting protocols for grade-level teams. 4. Review 5-year plan and set annual goals.	3. Develop ongoing supports for teachers such as coaching. 4. Review and implement meeting protocols for grade-level teams. 5. Review 5-year plan and set annual goals.	3. Review and refine ongoing supports for teachers. 4. Review and support meeting protocols for grade-level teams. 5. Create new 5-year plan and set annual goals.
School behavior teams		1. Develop a written action plan for the year. 2. Implement TIPS. 3. Develop a universal system of behavior support (see Table 26.3).	1. Develop a written action plan for the year. 2. Implement the universal system developed in Year 2. 3. Prepare for Tier 2 (see Table 26.3).	1. Develop a written action plan for the year. 2. Adapt Tier 1 as needed. 3. Conduct universal screening for behavior and review data to identify trends by areas of need. 4. Implement the Tier 2 system developed in Year 3. 5. Plan for Tier 3 (see Table 26.3).	1. Develop a written action plan for the year. 2. Adapt Tiers 1 and 2 as needed. 3. Conduct universal screening for behavior and review data to identify trends by areas of need. 4. Implement the Tier 3 system developed in Year 4 (see Table 26.3).
Grade-level teams	N/A	N/A	1. Review academic and behavior data to identify students at risk. 2. Implement approved interventions and monitor progress.	1. Review academic and behavior data to identify students at risk. 2. Implement approved interventions and monitor progress.	1. Review academic and behavior data to identify students at risk. 2. Implement approved interventions and monitor progress.

With plans developed for teaching and acknowledging expected behaviors, the teams turned their attention to developing systems for responding to problem behavior. Those systems included differentiating between minor behaviors, which would be managed by staff, and major behaviors, which would be managed by school administration. Operational definitions were developed for each identified behavior, and an office discipline referral (ODR) form was developed for each school. Each team developed a flowchart to depict the process by which staff would respond to problem behavior when it occurred. Finally, the teams adopted a data management system by which they could track and analyze their ODR data and assess the effectiveness of their behavior support efforts.

The final task for the school teams to complete during Year 1 was to develop a building-level 5-year school MTSS plan. These plans were modeled on the district plan and incorporated activities for the school team, grade-level teams, and individual teachers. The purpose of building-level plans is to help teachers and other staff take ownership for the changes in daily practice needed in order to implement an MTSS with integrity. Table 26.3 shows a sample school-level plan from Lincoln Elementary School. Since the school teams began work a year after the district team, this plan does not have activities in Year 1. Starting in Year 2, the school teams will have specific duties. In addition, the planned steps for the grade-level teams are more specific and reflect each building's needs. In the case of Lincoln Elementary, it is the lowest-performing school in the district, thus the school team established a goal of setting schoolwide learning priorities for students each year. In addition, individual professional development for teachers was included as a means of improving the instruction and support for all students.

Individual Teacher Plans

Included in the sample school plan are steps for individual teachers and other staff. This level of detailed planning is important because it documents how each staff person plays a role in making an MTSS successful. Teachers will have various backgrounds and experiences with tiered supports. In order for it to work over the long term, all staff have to understand and implement the components. The planning steps for teachers and other staff include annual development of personal goals. When a school is working to develop and implement an MTSS, it is helpful if each staff person's personal work goals incorporate the learning needed to implement the MTSS. All staff have a role to play in making the tiered supports succeed. Classroom teachers have the most visible role, but specialists and support staff have essential roles as well. How a cafeteria worker responds when a student acts out in line, or how a special education teacher reacts in response to a student who does a great job on a difficult task, can influence the success of the MTSS.

KEY DETAILS

A part of the district plan is the use of universal screening assessments starting in Year 3. This was a step developed and adopted by the district team and not by individual schools. Certain aspects of an MTSS will be most effective when developed and implemented at the district level instead of the school level. The reason for this is that every school district is recognized at the state and federal levels as the local educational agency (LEA). An LEA has the legal responsibility to provide effective education for all students in its jurisdiction. States grant this authority to LEAs along with funding to implement practices. Therefore, the LEA is the smallest unit of curriculum decision making in the U.S. public education system. Given the importance of using EBI for academics and behaviors, the LEA has the responsibility to identify, select, and evaluate instructional practices in all its member schools.

Similarly, LEAs have the responsibility to select, administer, and report the results from assessments of student achievement. In order for such assessment data to be useful, the assessments must be carefully matched to the curriculum of instruction. Having districtwide assessments matched to districtwide instruction ensures that the information collected about all students is reliable and valid. Both the screening assessments and progress measures need to be matched to the instruction that students receive. For these reasons, it is best for the district-level team to select the universal (Tier 1) screening assessments, but for school and grade-level teams to select progress measures. As noted in Chapter 21, the specific progress measure must reflect and be sensitive to the specific skill that the student is learning. This level of assessment precision cannot be determined by a district-level team, but can be understood by either school- or grade-level teams.

An additional detail included in both the district- and school-level MTSS plans is professional development (PD). Since an MTSS includes practices that may be new to veteran teachers, it is essential that both the district and school provide PD for teachers and other staff to learn and use new practices. Steps such as universal benchmark screening, using CBM for progress monitoring, and certain interventions might be totally new to some teachers. In other cases, a teacher might have learned about the practice in college, but might not have used it in many years. In order for any teaching practice to be effective, the teacher must use it accurately and with integrity. For these reasons, initial and ongoing PD to support an MTSS is necessary.

Action Plans

The academic and behavior teams at each school will need to have specific steps and goals for each year of their work. Often, teams refer to such plans as "action" plans because they guide the work during the course of each academic year.

TABLE 26.3. Five-Year MTSS Implementation Plan for Lincoln Elementary School Beginning in Year 2 of the District Initiative

Group	Year 2	Year 3	Year 4	Year 5	Year 6
School academic team	1. Review existing intervention and assessment practices and share findings with district team. 2. Educate all building staff about the MTSS and their role in it. 3. Develop 5-year MTSS school plan that boosts student outcomes by 5% each year.	1. Use universal screening data to identify target learning areas by grade levels and subject areas. 2. Develop and implement meeting protocols for grade-level teams. 3. Set annual goals for 5% or more improvement.	1. Use universal screening data to identify target areas by grade levels and subject areas. 2. Develop ongoing supports for teachers such as coaching. 3. Review and improve meeting protocols for grade-level teams. 4. Set annual goals for 5% or more improvement.	1. Use universal screening data to identify target areas by grade levels and subject areas. 2. Review and refine ongoing supports for teachers. 3. Review and improve meeting protocols for grade-level teams. 4. Set annual goals for 5% or more improvement.	1. Develop next 5-year plan 2. Use universal screening data to identify target areas by grade levels and subject areas. 3. Review and refine ongoing supports for teachers. 4. Review and improve meeting protocols for grade-level teams. 5. Set annual goals for 5% or more improvement.
School behavior team	1. Develop a written action plan for the year. 2. Implement TIPS. 3. Develop a universal system of behavior support, including schoolwide expectations, plans for teaching expectations, plans for rewarding expectations, a system for responding to problem behavior, and plans for sustainability.	1. Develop a written action plan for the year. 2. Implement the universal system developed in Year 2. 3. Prepare for Tier 2 by identifying areas of need for at-risk students, identifying and acquiring interventions that would address those needs, and providing corresponding PD.	1. Develop a written action plan for the year. 2. Adapt Tier 1 as needed. 3. Conduct universal screening for behavior and review data to identify trends by areas of need. 4. Implement the Tier 2 system developed in Year 3. 5. Plan for Tier 3 by identifying areas of need for students who need intensive	1. Develop a written action plan for the year. 2. Adapt Tiers 1 and 2 as needed. 3. Conduct universal screening for behavior and review data to identify trends by areas of need. 4. Implement the Tier 3 system developed in Year 4.	1. Develop a written action plan for the year. 2. Adapt Tiers 1, 2, and 3 as needed. 3. Conduct universal screening for behavior and review data to identify trends by areas of need.

			intervention, identifying staff with behavioral expertise to design and implement that intervention, and providing corresponding PD.		
Grade-level teams	N/A	1. Conduct universal screening of all students and review data to identify students at risk. 2. Implement approved interventions and monitor progress.	1. Conduct universal screening of all students and review data to identify students at risk. 2. Review progress data from students participating in intervention and determine efficacy.	1. Conduct universal screening of all students and review data to identify students at risk. 2. Implement approved interventions and monitor progress. 3. Identify needed intervention changes.	1. Conduct universal screening of all students and review data to identify students at risk. 2. Implement approved interventions and monitor progress. 3. Identify needed intervention changes.
Individual teachers and other staff	N/A	N/A	1. Develop individual PD goals aligned with the MTSS. 2. Select and attend PD activities based on personal goals. 3. Implement new or improved instructional practices based on PD. 4. Review and evaluate professional growth that supports the MTSS with supervisor.	1. Develop individual PD goals aligned with the MTSS. 2. Select and attend PD activities based on personal goals. 3. Implement improved instructional practices based on PD. 4. Review and evaluate professional growth that supports the MTSS with supervisor.	1. Develop individual PD goals aligned with the MTSS. 2. Select and attend PD activities based on personal goals. 3. Implement improved instructional practices based on PD. 4. Review and evaluate professional growth that supports the MTSS with supervisor.

There are no formal rules for how to develop and implement such action plans, but having them is an important component of making the MTSS planning and implementation move forward. Tables 26.4 and 26.5 show action plans based on the PBIS model (Colvin, 2007). Table 26.4 includes the steps that a school's behavior team might want to take during the first year (gear-up) for PBIS implementation. Table 26.5 shows the action plan for a behavior team using a PBIS model during Year 2 (implementation).

EVALUATION

The success of the MTSS will be determined by students' academic and behavior data. Student progress toward identified goals shows whether the steps implemented are having the desired result. Academic progress is usually measured through student performance on the state-mandated annual assessment. In coming years, this assessment will include those developed to evaluate student learning of the CCSS (e.g., Partnership for Readiness of College and Careers, 2014; Smarter-Balanced Assessment Consortium, 2014). In addition, school districts might opt to use additional assessments such as the Measures of Academic Progress (MAP; Northwest Evaluation Association, 2014).

Each school and district will need to review the data from such assessments to decide whether its specific goals were met. In addition, schools and districts should set annual improvement goals, a practice initiated with NCLB. The effectiveness of the system for supporting student behavior can be assessed through the School-Wide Information System (SWIS). SWIS provides a platform through which schools can enter, manage, and analyze their ODRs. In addition to being able to monitor how student behavior responds to the efforts put in place as part of the school-wide positive behavior support system (SWPBS), schools can compare their ODR data trends with those of schools across the country that have agreed to share their data in aggregate form in order to provide national norms for student behavior.

SUMMARY

With each successive year of MTSS implementation, schools and districts will become more skilled at selecting and using effective instruction and assessment practices that work for the students they serve. Effective MTSS implementation requires careful long-term planning and effective communication among all parties. The case example in this chapter documents how starting with a district-level plan that leads to school-level plans will help make development, implementation, and evaluation of an MTSS effective for teachers and students.

TABLE 26.4. Phase 1 PBIS Timeline: Preparing for Gear-Up

Action step	Personnel involved	Time frame	Major activities	Outcome indicator
Conduct the School-wide Evaluation Tool (SET) and Self-Assessment Survey (SAS), and collect baseline discipline data.	Administrators and PBIS facilitator	April 2015–July 2015	• Facilitator interviews administrator, staff, and students. • Administrator provides facilitator with discipline data, handbook, and other permanent products.	• School evaluation report • Baseline discipline data
Hold a faculty meeting at which the PBIS facilitator presents an overview of SWPBS along with the school's data.	Administrators, faculty, and PBIS facilitator	April 2015–July 2015	• Provide information about SWPBS. • Demonstrate a need for SWPBS based on school's data. • Generate interest and support of faculty and staff.	• Increased awareness of, interest in, and support for SWPBS.
Attain 80% faculty buy-in.	Administrators and faculty	April 2015–July 2015	• Discuss the costs and benefits of adopting SWPBS and of maintaining status quo. • Vote, or in some other way, reach a decision about adopting SWPBS.	• School Readiness Checklist and commitment
Form a representative team.	Administrators, faculty, and PBIS facilitator	July 2015–September 2015	• Nominate or in some way identify potential representatives. • Secure commitments. • Ensure that the team is representative of all school constituencies (faculty, paraprofessionals, support staff, administrators, parents, students, etc.). • Define the roles and responsibilities of team members.	• Universal team
Establish ongoing facilitation.	Administrators and PBIS facilitator	July 2015–September 2015	• Secure funding for support of SWPBS activities, including facilitation and PD. • Negotiate the amount of time needed.	• Facilitation contract
Plan a biweekly to monthly meeting schedule that will include facilitation and Monthly Team Checklist.	Universal team and facilitator	July 2015 – September 2015	• Consider the academic schedule, the facilitator's schedule, the schedules of the team members • Address the need to accommodate (work around, compensate, etc.) hourly employees	• Meeting schedule
Schedule ongoing training and PD.	Universal team, administrators, and PBIS facilitator	July 2015–September 2015	• Determine the training needs of the faculty and staff. • Identify training opportunities in the academic calendar.	• Training and PD schedule

TABLE 26.5. Phase 2 PBIS Timeline: Gear-Up for Schoolwide PBIS by Creating, Teaching, and Acknowledging Schoolwide Behavior Expectations

Action step	Personnel	Time frame	Major activities	Outcome indicator
Develop a purpose statement.	Universal team, in conjunction with full staff and facilitator	September 2015	• Identify the essential features that the faculty would like to include in the approach to schoolwide discipline. • Generate a brief statement that encapsulates those features.	First draft of a PBIS handbook, including: • SET report • An action plan • A purpose statement • Three to five expectations • Plans for teaching expectations • Plans for acknowledging student behavior • Guidelines for active supervision • A list of office-managed behaviors with operational definitions • A list of staff-managed behaviors with operational definitions • A functional ODR • Written procedures for when and how to refer students for additional support • TICs
Establish three to five positively stated schoolwide behavior expectations.	Universal team, in conjunction with full staff and facilitator	September 2015–October 2015	• Define desirable behaviors of students that enable efficient teaching and learning. • Identify three to five broad, positive, distinct concepts that capture the desirable behaviors.	
Generate plans for teaching the schoolwide expectations.	Universal team, in conjunction with full staff and facilitator	November 2015–January 2016	Create: • Matrices for school settings and school events. • Lesson plans for each matrix juncture. • A schedule for presenting each lesson plan. • A procedure for prompting, precorrecting, and encouraging appropriate displays of expectations. • A system for determining the extent to which students have acquired and are displaying the expectations.	
Develop a system for maintaining the behavior expectations by acknowledging student behavior.	Universal team, in conjunction with full staff and facilitator	February 2016–March 2016	• Develop an acknowledgment system. • Train full staff in modeling, teaching, and acknowledging expectations. • Train full staff in active supervision.	
Develop plans for correcting problem behavior.	Universal team, in conjunction with full staff and facilitator	April 2016–June 2016	• Determine office-managed versus staff-managed behaviors. • Operationally define office-managed behaviors. • Create a functional office discipline referral (ODR) form. • Develop procedures for making an office referral. • Assess and ensure administration's ability to respond to referred behavior problems. • Develop procedures for staff to follow for staff-managed behaviors, including when and how to refer problems to a behavior support team or to the administration. • Train staff in procedures for responding to problem behavior.	
Complete monthly/quarterly Team Implementation Checklist (TIC).	Universal team, in conjunction with facilitator	September 2015–June 2016	• Complete an implementation checklist each month and each quarter to monitor progress. • Discuss the results and identify areas of priority.	

Glossary of Important MTSS Terms

Academic specialist: School staff person whose job is to develop and implement academic interventions, teach students with academic difficulties, and to consult with teachers who work with these students.

Adoption: The formal decision by a school board or district to purchase and use a specific instructional program or curriculum product.

Aimline: A line on a student progress graph that shows the goal level that a student is working to meet.

AIMSweb: An Internet-based set of CBM in the areas of early reading, early numeracy, math, reading, spelling, and writing for students in grades K–8.

Barriers: People, events, or systems that interfere or block the implementation of an MTSS.

Behavior specialist: School staff person whose job is to develop and implement behavior interventions, teach students with behavior difficulties, and to consult with teachers who work with these students.

Benchmark: A specific measureable student performance goal that is based on nationally normed data indicating the likelihood of a student meeting a later standard on a local or national assessment.

BICS: Basic interpersonal communication skills. These are the first new language skills to develop when a student is learning a new language, including English. BICS typically developed within 2 years of immersion in a new language.

Buy-in: The extent to which the staff members of a school or district agree that developing an MTSS is a good idea and are willing to help make it happen.

CALP: Cognitive academic language proficiency. These are advanced language skills needed to learn and be fully proficient in a new language. CALP typically require 5–7 years of focused instruction to develop.

CBM: Curriculum-based measurement. Brief timed assessments of math, reading, spelling, and writing that show a student's relative progress toward specific learning goals.

CCSS: Common Core State Standards. The instructional goals developed by the National Governors Association for use in and by public schools in U.S. states and territories, pending adoption by each state or territory.

Coach: A school staff person whose job is to work with classroom teachers for the purpose of improving instruction and student learning outcomes.

Consultant: A school staff person or contracted professional who works with teachers, administrators, and other school staff to implement and/or improve specific instructional practices.

Content-area team: All of the teachers in a building who teach the same curriculum content (e.g., English, math, science, social studies).

Core instruction: The materials and methods in one or more learning areas adopted by a school or district to be used in all Tier 1 general education classrooms.

Curriculum: An adopted set of courses or learning activities leading to a specific goal.

DIBELS: Dynamic Indicators of Basic Early Literacy Skills. A type of CBM that includes measures of early literacy as well as oral and silent reading. Companion DIBELS for Math measures include assessments of early numeracy, computation, and problem solving.

Differentiation: Practice of adjusting classroom instruction to meet the needs of individual students and small groups of students.

Diffusion of responsibility: The tendency of group members to assume that others in the group are taking care of important tasks and they do not need to do anything. This often results in key tasks not being done because every group member thinks another person did it, but actually no one took responsibility and completed the task.

EasyCBM: An Internet-based set of CBMs in the areas of early reading, early numeracy, math, and reading, for students in grades K–8.

Effect size: A research statistic that shows how much better or worse the experimental group's performance was compared with the control group. The effect size number is given in standard deviation (SD) units and shows how many more (or less) *SD* units the experimental group's performance was compared with the control group.

Evidence based: A term meaning that a standardized instructional program has been found to work effectively with students from diverse backgrounds in two or more experimental research studies.

Exploration: The first stage of the change model proposed by Fixsen, Naoom, Blase, Friedman, and Wallace (2005). This stage includes activities that allow staff members to consider whether changes in current practices are needed.

Externalizing behaviors: Behaviors such as acting out, physical and verbal aggression, and excessive physical activity that are symptoms of student distress. In some cases, specific externalizing behaviors are linked with certain diagnostic criteria for a mental disorder.

Facilitator: (1) A school staff person or hired contractor whose job is to help the staff develop, implement, and evaluate school and/or districtwide instructional programs. (2) People, events, or systems that promote and support the implementation of an MTSS.

FAST and FastBridge: Also called the Formative Assessment System for Teachers. An Internet-based assessment system that includes both adaptive measures and CBMs for reading and math, as well as measures of behavior. There are adaptive measures of math and reading for grades 1–12 and CBM in the areas of early reading, early numeracy, math, and reading for grades K–6. The behavior measures cover all grades.

Food insecurity: A person or family's lack of access to enough food to be healthy. In severe forms, food insecurity can lead to malnutrition.

Formative assessment: Assessment that is conducted at multiple points in time (e.g., weekly to monthly) during instruction. Formative assessments are generally tied to the instruction and show whether a student learning what is being taught.

Free and reduced-cost lunch: A U.S. Department of Education program that provides daily breakfast and/or lunch meals for students whose parents meet low-income criteria.

GOM: General outcome measure. An assessment that measures a student's relative progress and proficiency on a specific learning standard. Examples include nationally normed CBMs.

Grade-level team: All of the teachers in a building who teach the same grade(s) students. Grade-level teams can include teachers who teach multiple grades.

Implementation: The process of putting an MTSS system into place, including consideration of schedules, areas covered, meetings, communication, and progress review.

Implementation driver: A step that an organization takes so that any given innovation is effective.

Implementation science: The study of how people working in a given setting (e.g., schools) develop, implement, and evaluate changes in their daily routines and practices.

Innovation: A change that improves on existing materials and practices.

Inoculation: Intentionally exposing an individual to a very small dosage of a pathogen or treatment for the purpose of strengthening the individual's response to a large dosage.

Installation: Behind the scenes steps to prepare for implementation of an MTSS.

Internalizing behaviors: Behaviors such as being excessively quiet and withdrawn, overly anxious, and having limited social interaction that are symptoms of student distress. In some cases, specific internalizing behaviors are linked with certain diagnostic criteria for a mental disorder.

Mastery measure: An assessment that measures a student's relative expertise (e.g., mastery) of a specific skill. Such measures are narrow in focus and help teachers know when a student is ready to move on to new instruction.

Metacognition: The skill of reflecting on one's own learning.

Minutes taker: A school team member whose role during meetings is to keep track of time allotted for each agenda item and remind others when it is time to move on to a new item.

MTSS: Multi-tiered system of support. A school and/or districtwide set of procedures that provides increasingly more intensive instruction based on each student's individual needs.

NCLB: No Child Left Behind Act of 2001. This was the additional name given to the 2001 reauthorization of the Elementary and Secondary Education Act. It added many more requirements for state education agencies to implement in order to be eligible for federal education funding.

ODR: Office discipline referral. ODR refers to each and every time a student is sent from a classroom to the principal's office because he or she was displaying inappropriate behavior in the classroom.

PALS: Peer Assisted Learning Strategies. This is a peer-teaching curriculum developed by Doug and Lynn Fuchs, researchers at Vanderbilt University. There are versions of PALS in both math and reading for grades K–6.

PBIS: Positive behavioral interventions and supports. A school and/or districtwide method of preteaching desired social behaviors and praising students for engaging in those behaviors. As needed, PBIS also includes targeted (Tier 2) and intensive (Tier 3) interventions for students who need them.

PLC: Professional learning community. A specific model for school-based teams that focuses on developing teachers' knowledge and skills for the purpose of improving student outcomes.

Poverty: Having less than a usual or socially acceptable amount of money or material possessions. Students in poverty often face additional challenges because they lack the time or money needed to invest in education.

Prevention model: A three-stage progression of activities that seek to prevent behavior, health, and learning problems as early as possible.

Primary prevention: Stage 1 of the prevention model. This stage includes steps taken to educate and treat all persons in a population before a problem develops.

Problem-solving intervention: A type of school intervention that is individualized for a specific student based on his or her response to prior instruction.

Problem-solving team: A schoolwide team of teachers, specialists, and administrators that reviews individual and group student data to develop, implement, and evaluate improvements in student outcomes.

Program: Published materials developed for the purpose of teaching students specific knowledge and/or skills.

Progress monitoring: Regular administration, scoring, and graphing of specific student assessments for the purpose of showing whether an intervention is working.

Public health: A field of study that gathers, evaluates, and reacts to population data about human welfare, including education, health, safety, and sanitation.

Reciprocal teaching: A specific type of peer tutoring for reading comprehension skills that involves having students work in pairs to practice and improve reading skills.

Replacement core: An instructional program used at the Tier 3 level that replaces the general education Tier 1 core program.

Risk factors: Specific events or situations that are associated with negative behavior, education, and health outcomes.

RTI: Response to intervention. RTI refers to the changes in a student's academic skills in response to a specific intervention.

Scientifically based: Materials and methods *based on* practices found to be effective in prior research but which have themselves not been validated in two or more experimental studies.

Screening: A system for collecting uniform school outcome data about every student in a grade, school, or district. Screening data are used alongside other sources of information to identify students who need additional tiers of support.

SD: Standard deviation. The average amount of variation in a given set of scores.

Standard protocol: A type of instruction or intervention that is provided to all students with the same type of need.

Secondary prevention: Prevention efforts initiated at the first sign of a problem so that the problem is eliminated altogether.

Special education: Instruction provided for a student who has been identified as having difficulty in school, having a disability, and requiring specialized instruction. In the United States, such services are provided according to the Individuals with Disabilities Education Improvement Act (IDEA) 2004 and related state laws and regulations.

Stakeholder: Everyone who has something to gain or has some level of involvement in an MTSS. Stakeholders include students, parents, teachers, administrators, and other school staff.

Standards: Officially adopted learning goals for all students in a given school, district, or state.

Summative assessment: An assessment of learning administered at the end of a specified period of instruction (e.g., learning unit or grade level).

Sustainability: The extent to which an implemented initiative such as an MTSS can be continued into the future with success.

SWIS: School-Wide Information System. An Internet-based system for recording and tracking data related to positive behavioral interventions and supports (PBIS).

Tertiary prevention: Prevention efforts applied well after the onset of problems or symptoms for the purpose to reducing the effects of the condition or problem over the lifespan.

Tier 1: The first level of instruction in an MTSS. Also known as the universal level, Tier 1 includes all of the academic and behavioral instruction provided to all students in a school. Sometimes, Tier 1 is known as the general education curriculum. It is expected that 80% or more of students will be successful with Tier 1 alone.

Tier 2: The second level of instruction or intervention in an MTSS. Tier 2 includes instruction or intervention activities that are implemented in addition to Tier 1 with the goal of having all participating students meet the academic and behavior learning goals. It is expected that 15% of students will be successful with Tier 2 in addition to Tier 1 (i.e., for a total of 95% student success).

Tier 3: The third level of instruction or intervention in an MTSS. Tier 3 includes very intensive and highly specialized instruction or intervention activities that are implemented in addition to Tiers 1 and 2. In some cases, Tier 3 interventions are provided as replacement core programs.

Timekeeper: The member of a school team who keeps track of and reminds others of the time allotted and passed for each item on the team's meeting agenda.

TIPS: Team Initiated Problem Solving. This is a model for how to run problem-solving meetings that involves using a specific agenda format and information-gathering process.

Treatment fidelity: The extent to which any given instruction or intervention is implemented faithfully, according to the program's research-based directions. *Treatment integrity* is the preferred term.

Treatment integrity: The extent to which any given instruction or intervention is implemented completely and accurately, according to the program's research-based directions.

Trend: The general direction of data points collected and graphed to show student performance during Tier 2 and Tier 2 interventions. In order to calculate a trend there must be at least 3 data points, but usually more are required to have a reliable trend.

Trendline: A line drawn through data points on a graph to show the general direction of performance. There are formulas for calculating trendlines (e.g., split-half) and computer programs can calculate them automatically.

Triage: A method for prioritizing treatment in relation to the level of individual need. This term is often used in medical settings but can be used in schools to determine which students need support at Tiers 1, 2, and 3.

Universal screening: A process of gathering academic and behavior data about all the students in a class, grade, school, or district in order to identify which students need additional assistance to meet learning goals.

Universal team: A school-based representative group that includes teachers, specialists, administrators, and sometimes parents that meets on a regular basis to develop, implement, and evaluate an MTSS, and to review schoolwide student data to improve practices and outcomes.

References

Ackerman, B. P., Brown, E. D., & Izard, C. E. (2004). The relations between persistent poverty and contextual risk and children's behavior in elementary school. *Developmental Psychology, 40*, 367–377.

Ackerman, R. D. (1987). Regular education initiative [Letter to the editor]. *Journal of Learning Disabilities, 20*, 514–515.

Alessi, G. (1987). Generative strategies and teaching for generalization. *Analysis of Verbal Behavior, 5*, 15–27.

Algozzine, B., Wang, C., & Violette, A. S. (2011). Reexamining the relationship between academic achievement and social behavior. *Journal of Positive Behavior Interventions, 13*(1), 3–16.

All Things PLC. (2013). About PLCs. Retrieved from *www.allthingsplc.info/about/about-PLC.php*.

Aloe, A. M., Amo, L. C., & Shanahan, M. E. (2014). Classroom management self-efficacy and burnout: A multivariate meta-analysis. *Educational Psychology Review, 26*, 101–126.

American Diabetes Association. (2013). Who is at greater risk for type 2 diabetes? Retrieved from *www.diabetes.org/diabetes-basics/prevention/risk-factors*.

American Institutes for Research. (2015). Center on response to intervention. Retrieved from *www.rti4success.org*.

American Psychiatric Association. (2013). *Diagnostic and statistical manual of mental disorders* (5th ed.). Arlington, VA: Author.

American Public Health Association. (2015). APHA history and timeline. Retrieved from-*www.apha.org/news-and-media/newsroom/online-press-kit/apha-history-and-timeline*.

Barrera, M. (2006). Roles of definitional and assessment models in the identification of new or second language learners of English for special education. *Journal of Learning Disabilities, 39*, 142–156.

Barrera, M., & Liu, K. (2010). Challenges of general outcomes measurement in the RTI progress monitoring of linguistically diverse exceptional learners. *Theory Into Practice, 49*, 273–280.

Batsche, G. (2013). Developing a plan. Retrieved from *www.rtinetwork.org/getstarted/develop/developingplan*.

Beidas, R. S., Benjamin, C. L., Puleo, C. M., Edmunds, J. M., & Kendall, P. C. (2010). Flexible applications of the Coping Cat program for anxious youth. *Cognitive and Behavioral Practice, 17*, 142–153.

Bickford, R. S. (2012). *Promoting students' social and academic success through teacher praise* (doctoral dissertation). Gorham: University of Southern Maine.

Bidwell, A. (2014, March). The politics of common core. *U.S. News and World Report*. Retrieved from *www.usnews.com/news/special-reports/a-guide-to-common-core/articles/2014/03/06/the-politics-of-common-core*.

Blanchett, W. J., Klingner, J. K., & Harry, B. (2009). The intersection of race, culture, language, and disability: Implications for urban education. *Urban Education, 44*, 389–409.

Blase, K., Kiser, L., & Van Dyke, M. (2013). *The hexagon tool: Exploring context*. Chapel Hill: National Implementation Research Network, FPG Child Development Institute, University of North Carolina at Chapel Hill.

Boerke, K. W., & Reitman, D. (2011). Token economies. In W. W. Fisher, C. C. Piazza, & H. S. Roane (Eds.), *Handbook of applied behavior analysis* (pp. 370–382). New York: Guilford Press.

Boynton Hauerwas, L., Brown, R., & Scott, A. (2013). Specific learning disability and response to intervention: State-level guidance. *Exceptional Children, 80*, 101–120.

Bradshaw, C. P., Pas, E. T., Goldweber, A., Rosenberg, M. S., & Leaf, P. J. (2012). Integrating school-wide positive behavioral interventions and supports with tier 2 coaching to student support teams: The PBISplus model. *Advances in School Mental Health Promotion, 5*, 177–193.

Bransford, J. D., & Stein, B. S. (1984). *The IDEAL problem solver: A guide for improving thinking, learning, and creativity*. New York: Freeman.

Brown-Chidsey, R., Bronaugh, L., & McGraw, K. (2009). *RTI in the classroom: Recipes and guidelines for success*. New York: Guilford Press.

Brown-Chidsey, R., & Gritter, A. (2012, February). *Comparing administration personnel: Curriculum-based measures of reading and math*. Paper presented at the annual meeting of the National Association of School Psychologists, Philadelphia, PA.

Brown-Chidsey, R., Seppala, M., & Segura, M. L. (2000). Chapter 766: Massachusetts special education law. In *American Education Annual*. New York: Gale.

Brown-Chidsey, R., & Steege, M. W. (2005). *Response to intervention: Principles and strategies for success*. New York: Guilford Press.

Brown-Chidsey, R., & Steege, M. W. (2010). *Response to intervention: Principles and strategies for success* (2nd ed.). New York: Guilford Press.

Bryan, T., Bay, M., & Donahue, M. (1988). Implications of the learning disabilities definition for the regular education initiative. *Journal of Learning Disabilities, 21*, 23–28.

Bryant, D., Bryant, B., Gersten, R., Scammacca, N., & Chavez, M. (2008). Mathematics intervention for first- and second-grade students with mathematics difficulties: The effects of tier 2 intervention delivered as booster lessons. *Remedial and Special Education, 29*, 20–32.

Burke, N. J., Hellman, J. L., Scott, B. G., Weems, C. F., & Carrion, V. G. (2011). The impact of adverse childhood experiences on an urban pediatric population. *Child Abuse and Neglect, 35*, 408–413.

Burns, M. K. (2007). Reading at the instructional level with children identified as learning disabled: Potential implications for response-to-intervention. *School Psychology Quarterly, 22*, 297–313.

Burns, M. K., VanDerHeyden, A. M., & Jiban, C. L. (2006). Assessing the instructional level for mathematics: A comparison of methods. *School Psychology Review, 35*, 401–418.

Busch, T., & Reschly, A. R. (2007). Progress monitoring in reading: Using curriculum-based measurement in a response-to-intervention model. *Assessment for Effective Intervention, 32*, 223–230.

Cantrell, S. C., & Hughes, H. K. (2008). Teacher efficacy and content literacy implementation: An exploration of the effects of extended professional development with coaching. *Journal of Literacy Research, 40*, 95–127.

Caplan, G. (1964). *Principles of preventive psychiatry*. New York: Basic Books.

Carlson, C. D., & Francis, D. (2002). Increasing the reading achievement of at-risk children through direct instruction: Evaluation of the Rodeo Institute for Teacher Excellence (RITE). *Journal of Education for Students Placed at Risk, 7*, 141–166.

Cartledge, G., & Kourea, L. (2008). Culturally responsive classrooms for culturally diverse students with and at risk for disabilities. *Exceptional Children, 74*, 351–371.

Casey, T., & Maldonado, L. (2012). *Worst off: Single-parent families in the United States*. New York: Legal Momentum: The Women's Legal Defense and Education Fund.

Castle, S., Deniz, C. B., & Tortora, M. (2005). Flexible grouping and student learning in a high-needs school. *Education and Urban Society, 37*, 139–150.

Castro, M. J. (2013). The future of Spanish in the United States. Retrieved from *www.languagepolicy.net/archives/Castro1.htm*.

Centers for Disease Control and Prevention. (2013a). State vaccination requirements. Retrieved from *www.cdc.gov/vaccines/vac-gen/laws/state-reqs.htm*.

Centers for Disease Control and Prevention. (2013b). Ten great public health achievements—United States, 1900–1999. Retrieved from *www.cdc.gov/mmwr/preview/mmwrhtml/00056796.htm*.

Chard, D. J. (2013). Systems impact: Issues and trends in improving school outcomes for all learners through multitier instructional models. *Intervention in School and Clinic, 48*, 198–202.

Chisholm, D. P. (1988). Concerns respecting the regular education initiative. *Journal of Learning Disabilities, 21*, 487–501.

Christ, T. J., Zopluoglu, C., Long, J. D., & Monaghen, B. D. (2012). Curriculum-based measurement of oral reading: Quality of progress monitoring outcomes. *Exceptional Children, 78*, 356–373.

Christ, T. J., Zopluoglu, C., Monaghen, B. D., & Van Norman, E. R. (2013). Curriculum-based measurement of oral reading: Multi-study evaluation of schedule, duration, and dataset quality on progress monitoring outcomes. *Journal of School Psychology, 51*, 19–57.

Cirino, P. T., Vaughn, S., Linan-Thompson, S., Cardenas-Hagan, E., Fletcher, J. M., & Francis, D. J. (2009). One-year follow-up outcomes of Spanish and English interventions for English language learners at risk for reading problems. *American Educational Research Journal, 46*, 744–781.

Coates, R. D. (1989). The regular education initiative and opinions of regular classroom teachers. *Journal of Learning Disabilities, 22*, 532–536.

Collier, V. (2011). *Seven steps to separating difference from disability*. Thousand Oaks, CA: Corwin Press.

Colvin, G. (2007). *Seven steps for developing a proactive schoolwide discipline plan: A guide for principals and leadership teams*. Thousand Oaks, CA: Corwin Press.

Common Core State Standards Initiative. (2015). Standards in your state. Retrieved from *www.corestandards.org/standards-in-your-state.*

Condly, S. J. (2006). Resilience in children: A review of literature with implications for education. *Urban Education, 41*, 211–236.

Cook, C. R., Rasetshwane, K. B., Truelson, E., Grant, S., Dart, E. H., Collins, T. A., et al. (2011). Development and validation of the Student Internalizing Behavior Screener: Examination of reliability, validity, and classification accuracy. *Assessment for Effective Intervention, 36*, 71–79.

Cook, C. R., Volpe, R. J., & Livanis, A. (2010). Constructing a roadmap for future universal screening research beyond academics. *Assessment for Effective Intervention, 35*, 197–205.

Cooper, H. (1989). Synthesis of research on homework. *Educational Leadership, 47*(3), 85–91.

Cooper, H., Lindsay, J. J., Nye, B., & Greathouse, S. (1998). Relationships among attitudes about homework, amount of homework assigned and completed, and student achievement. *Journal of Educational Psychology, 90*, 70–83.

Cooper, H., Robinson, J. C., & Patall, E. A. (2006). Does homework improve academic achievement?: A synthesis of research, 1987–2003. *Review of Educational Research, 76*, 1–62.

Cooper, J. O., Heron, T. E., & Heward, W. L. (2007). *Applied behavior analysis* (2nd ed.). Upper Saddle River, NJ: Pearson.

Cortiella, C., & Horowitz, S. (2014). *The state of learning disabilities: Facts, trends and emerging issues.* New York: National Center for Learning Disabilities.

Cortiella, C., & Kaloi, L. (2010, February). Meet the new and improved section 504. *EP Magazine*, pp. 14–15.

Coyne, M. D., Kame'enui, E. J., & Simmons, D. C. (2004). Improving beginning reading instruction and intervention for students with LD: Reconciling "all" with "each." *Journal of Learning Disabilities*, 37, 231–239.

Crawford, D. B., & Snider, V. E. (2000). Effective mathematics instruction: The importance of curriculum. *Education and Treatment of Children, 23*, 122–142.

Crone, D. A., Hawken, L. S., & Horner, R. H. (2010). *Responding to problem behavior in schools: The behavior education program* (2nd ed.). New York: Guilford Press.

Cummings, J. A., & Martinez, R. S. (2013). Visual representation of progress monitoring and academic achievement data. In R. Brown-Chidsey & K. J. Andren (Eds.), *Assessment for intervention: A problem-solving approach* (2nd ed., pp. 321–343). New York: Guilford Press.

Cummings, K. D., Park, Y., & Schaper, H. A. B. (2013). Form effects on DIBELS Next oral reading fluency progress-monitoring passages. *Assessment for Effective Intervention, 38*, 91–104.

Cummins, J. (1981). Empirical and theoretical underpinnings of bilingual education. *Journal of Education, 163*, 16–29.

Danielson Group. (2013). The 2013 framework for teaching evaluation instrument. Retrieved from *http://danielsongroup.org/books-materials.*

Danielson, L., Doolittle, J., & Bradley, R. (2007). Professional development, capacity building, and research needs: Critical issues for response to intervention implementation. *School Psychology Review, 36*, 632–637.

Darch, C., Eaves, R. C., Crowe, D. A., Simmons, K., & Conniff, A. (2006). Teaching spelling to students with learning disabilities: A comparison of rule-based strategies versus traditional instruction. *Journal of Direct Instruction, 6*, 1–16.

David, J. L. (2007). Classroom walk-throughs. *Educational Leadership, 65*(4), 81–82.

Deno, S. L. (1985). Curriculum-based measurement: The emerging alternative. *Exceptional Children, 37*, 229–237.

Deno, S. L. (2002). Problem solving as "best practice." In A. Thomas & J. Grimes (Eds.), *Best practices in school psychology IV* (Vol. 1, pp. 37–55). Washington, DC: National Association of School Psychologists.

Deno, S. L. (2005). Problem-solving assessment. In R. Brown-Chidsey (Ed.), *Assessment for intervention: A problem-solving approach.* (pp. 10–40). New York: Guilford Press.

Deno, S. L. (2013). Problem-solving assessment. In R. Brown-Chidsey & K. Andren (Eds.), *Assessment for intervention: A problem-solving approach* (2nd ed., pp. 10–38). New York: Guilford Press.

Denton, C. A., Fletcher, J., Anthony, J., & Frances, D. (2006). An evaluation of intensive intervention for students with persistent reading difficulties. *Journal of Learning Disabilities, 39*, 447–466.

Denton, C. A., & Hasbrouck, J. (2009). A description of instructional coaching and its relationship to consultation. *Journal of Educational and Psychological Consultation, 19*, 150–175.

DiGangi, S. A., Maag, J. W., & Rutherford, R. B. (1991). Self-graphing of on-task behavior: Enhancing the reactive effects of self-monitoring of on-task behavior and academic performance. *Learning Disabilities Quarterly, 14*, 221–230.

Direct Behavior Ratings. (2014). Retrieved from *www.directbehaviorratings.org/cms.*

Dixon, L. Q., Zhao, J., & Shin, J. (2012). What we know about second language acquisition: A synthesis from four perspectives. *Review of Educational Research, 82*, 5–60.

Doll, B., Pfohl, W., & Yoon, J. (2010). *Handbook of youth prevention science.* New York: Routledge.

Driscoll, M. J. (2008). *Embracing coaching as professional development.* Reston, VA: National Association of Secondary School Principals.

Drummond, T. (1994). *The Student Risk Screening Scale* (SRSS). Grants Pass, OR: Josephine County Mental Health Program.

Dufour, R. (2004). What is a professional learning community? *Educational Leadership, 61*(8), 6–11.

Durlak, J. A., & DuPre, E. P. (2008). Implementation matters: A review of research on the influence of implementation on program outcomes and the factors affecting implementation. *American Journal of Community Psychology, 41*, 327–350.

Dynamic Measurement Group. (2011). DIBELS Next assessment manual. Retrieved from *www.dibels.org.*

Dynamic Measurement Group. (2014). Dynamic Indicators of Basic Early Literacy Skills [DIBELS] Next. Retrieved from *https://dibels.org/dibelsnext.html.*

Edgar, E., & Hayden, A. H. (1984). Who are the children special education should serve?: And how many children are there? *Journal of Special Education, 18*, 523–539.

Education Week. (2004, August 4). Student mobility. Retrieved from *www.edweek.org/ew/issues/student-mobility.*

Educational and Community Supports. (2015). SWIS Suite. Retrieved from *www.pbisapps.org/Applications/Pages/SWIS.-Suite.aspx.*

Edwards, O. W., Mumford, V. E., & Serra-Roldan, R. (2007). A positive youth development model for students considered at-risk. *School Psychology International, 28*, 29–45.

Erchul, W. P. (2011). School consultation and response to intervention: A tale of two literatures. *Journal of Educational and Psychological Consultation, 21*, 191–208.

Espin, C., Wallace, T., Lembke, E., Campbell, H., & Long, J. D. (2010). Creating a progress-monitoring system in reading for middle-school students: Tracking progress toward meeting high-stakes standards. *Learning Disabilities Research and Practice, 25*, 60–75.

Esposito, D. (1973). Homogeneous and heterogeneous ability grouping: Principal findings and implications for evaluating and designing more effective educational environments. *Review of Educational Research, 43*, 163–179.

Evans, G. W., & Kim, P. (2013). Childhood poverty, chronic stress, self-regulation, and coping. *Child Development Perspectives, 7*, 43–48.

Fairbanks, S., Sugai, G., Guardino, D., & Lathrop, M. (2007). Response to intervention: Examining classroom behavior support in second grade. *Exceptional Children, 73*, 288–310.

FastBridge Learning. (2015). Retrieved from *www.fastbridge.org*.

Federal Register. (2001). President's Commission on Excellence in Special Education. Retrieved from *www.gpo.gov/fdsys/pkg/FR-2001-10-05/pdf/01-25344.pdf.*

Federal Register. (2008, October 17). Title III of the elementary and secondary education act of 1965 (ESEA), as amended by the No Child Left Behind Act of 2001 (NCLB), Vol, 73, No. 202. Retrieved from *www2.ed.gov/legislation/FedRegister/other/2008-4/101708a.html.*

Ferguson. R. F. (2006). Five challenges to effective teacher professional development. *Journal of Staff Development, 27*(4), 48–52.

Fielding, L., Kerr, N., & Rosier, P. (1998). *The 90% reading goal: 90% of our students will read at or above grade level by the end of third grade*. Kennewick, WA: New Foundation Press.

Fielding, L., Kerr, N., & Rosier, P. (2007). *Annual growth for all students: Catch-up growth for those who are behind*. Kennewick, WA: New Foundation Press.

Figueroa, R. A., & Newsome, P. (2006). The diagnosis of LD in English learners: Is it nondiscriminatory? *Journal of Learning Disabilities, 39*, 206–214.

Filter, K. J., McKenna, M. K., Benedict, E. A., Horner, R. H., Todd, A. W., & Watson, J. (2007). Check in/check out: A post-hoc evaluation of an efficient, secondary-level targeted intervention for reducing problem behaviors in schools. *Education and Treatment of Children, 30*, 69–84.

Fixsen, D. L., Blase, K. A., Duda, M. A., Naoom, S. F., & Van Dyke, M. (2010). Implementation of evidence-based treatments for children and adolescents: Research findings and their implications for the future. In A. E. Kazdin & J. R. Weisz (Eds.), *Evidence-based psychotherapies for children and adolescents* (pp. 3–9). New York: Guilford Press.

Fixsen, D. L., Naoom, S. F., Blase, K. A., Friedman, R. M., & Wallace, F. (2005). *Implementation research: A synthesis of the literature*. Tampa: University of South Florida, Louis de la Parte Florida Mental Health Institute, The National Implementation Research Network (FMHI Publication No. 231).

Fletcher, J. M., & Vaughn, S. (2009). Response to intervention models as alternatives to traditional views of learning disabilities: Response to the commentaries. *Child Development Perspectives, 3*, 48–50.

Florida Center for Reading Research. (2013). Frequently asked questions about reading instruction: Why is it important to have a 90 minute reading block? Retrieved from *www.fcrr.org/curriculum/curriculumInstructionFaq1.shtm#3.*

Florida Department of Education. (2014). Florida's MTSS: A multi-tier system of supports. Retrieved from *www.floridarti.org/educatorResources/MTSS_Book_ImplComp_012612.pdf.*

Floyd, R. G., & Kranzler, J. H. (2013). The role of intelligence testing in understanding students' academic problems. In R. Brown-Chidsey & K. Andren (Eds.), *Assessment for intervention: A problem-solving approach* (2nd ed., pp. 229–249). New York: Guilford Press.

Foegen, A., Jiban, C., & Deno, S. (2007). Progress monitoring measures in mathematics: A review of the literature. *Journal of Special Education, 41*, 121–139.

Forman, S. G., Shapiro, E. S., Codding, R. S., Gonzales, J. E., Reddy, L. A., Rosenfield, S. A., et al. (2013). Implementation science and school psychology. *School Psychology Quarterly, 28*, 77–100.

Francis, D. J., Fletcher, J. M., Stuebing, K. K., Lyon, R. L., Shaywitz, B. A., & Shaywitz, S. E. (2005). Psychometric approaches to the identification of LD: IQ and achievement scores are not sufficient. *Journal of Learning Disabilities, 38*, 98–108.

Fryling, M. J., Wallace, M. D., & Yassine, J. N. (2012). Impact of treatment integrity on intervention effectiveness. *Journal of Applied Behavior Analysis, 45*, 449–453.

Fuchs, D., & Fuchs, L. S. (1994). Inclusive schools movement and the radicalization of special education reform. *Exceptional Children, 60*, 294–300.

Fuchs, D., & Fuchs, L. S. (2008). Implementing RTI. *District Administration, 10*, 73–76.

Fuchs, D., Mock, D., Morgan, D. L., & Young, C. L. (2003). Responsiveness-to-intervention: Definitions, evidence, and implications for the learning disabilities construct. *Learning Disabilities Research and Practice, 18*, 157–171.

Fuchs, L. S., & Fuchs, D. (1986). Effects of systematic formative evaluation: A meta analysis. *Exceptional Children*, 53, 199–208.

Fuchs, L. S., & Fuchs, D. (1992). Identifying a measure for monitoring student reading progress. *School Psychology Review, 21*, 45–58.

Fuchs, L. S., & Fuchs, D. (2007). A model for implementing responsiveness to intervention. *Teaching Exceptional Children, 39*(5), 14–20.

Fuchs, L. S., Fuchs, D., Compton, D. L., & Bryant, J. D. (2007). Mathematics screening and progress monitoring at first grade: Implications for responsiveness to intervention. *Exceptional Children, 73*, 311.

Gage, N. A., Lierheimer, K. S., & Goran, L. G. (2012). Characteristics of students with high-incidence disabilities broadly defined. *Journal of Disability Policy Studies, 23*, 168–178.

Gamse, B. C., Jacob, R. T., Horst, M., Boulay, B., & Unlu, F. (2008). *Reading First Impact Study Final Report Executive Summary* (NCEE 2009-4039). Washington, DC: National Center for Education Evaluation and Regional Assistance, Institute of Education Sciences, U.S. Department of Education.

Garcia, S. G., Jones, D., Holland, G., & Mundy, M. (2013). Instructional coaching at selected middle schools in south Texas and effects on student achievement. *Journal of Instructional Pedagogies, 11*, 1–16.

Genesee, F., Lindholm-Leary, K., Saunders, W., & Christian, D. (2005). English language learners in U.S. schools: An overview of research findings. *Journal of Education for Students Placed at Risk, 10*(4), 363–385.

Georgia Department of Education. (2011). Response to intervention. Retrieved from *www.gadoe.org/Curriculum-Instruction-and-Assessment/Curriculum-and-Instruction/Pages/Response-to-Intervention.aspx*.

Gilbertson, D., Maxfield, J., & Hughes, J. (2007). Evaluating responsiveness to intervention for English-language learners: A comparison of response modes on letter naming rates. *Journal of Behavioral Education, 16*, 259–279.

Gladwell, G. (2011). *Outliers: The story of success*. Boston: Back Bay Books.

Glasgow, N. A., & Farrell, T. S. C. (2007). *What successful literacy teachers do: 70 research-based strategies for teachers, reading coaches, and instructional planners*. Thousand Oaks, CA: Corwin Press.

Goss, C. L., & Andren, K. J. (2014). *Dropout prevention*. New York: Guilford Press.

Gravois, T. A., & Rosenfield, S. A. (2006). Impact of instructional consultation teams on the disproportionate referral and placement of minority students in special education. *Remedial and Special Education, 27*, 42–52.

Griffiths, A., VanDerHeyden, A. M., Skokut, M., & Lilles, E. (2009). Progress monitoring in oral reading fluency within the context of RTI. *School Psychology Quarterly, 24*, 13–23.

Gumm, R., & Turner, S. (2013). 90 minutes plus [Florida Center for Reading Research]. Retrieved from *www.fcrr.org/staffpresentations/Ruth/90MRBfinal2.pdf.*

Gunter, P. L., Miller, K. A., Venn, M. L., Thomas, K., & House, S. (2002). Self-graphing to success. *Teaching Exceptional Children, 35*(2), 30–34.

Haager, D. (2007). Promises and cautions regarding using response to intervention with English language learners. *Learning Disability Quarterly, 30*(3), 213–218.

Hacker, D. J., & Tenent, A. (2002). Implementing reciprocal teaching in the classroom: Overcoming obstacles and making modifications. *Journal of Educational Psychology, 94*, 699–718.

Hallahan, D. P., & Kauffman, J. M. (1977). Labels, categories, behaviors: ED, LD, and EMR reconsidered. *Journal of Special Education, 11*, 139–149.

Hallahan, D. P., Keller, C. E., McKinney, J. D., Lloyd, J. W., & Bryan, T. (1988). Examining the research base of the regular education initiative: Efficacy studies and the adaptive learning environments model. *Journal of Learning Disabilities, 21*, 29–35, 55.

Hallahan, D. P., & Mercer, C. D. (2013). Learning disabilities: Historical perspectives [National Resource Center for Learning Disabilities]. Retrieved from *www.nrcld.org/resources/ldsummit/hallahan.pdf.*

Haring, N. C., Lovitt, T. C., Eaton, M. D., & Hansen, C. L. (1978). *The fourth R: Research in the classroom*. Columbus, OH: Merrill.

Harris, K., Graham, S., & Mason, L. (2006). Improving the writing, knowledge, and motivation of struggling young writers: Effects of self-regulated strategy development with and without peer support. *American Educational Research Journal, 43*, 295–340.

Hart, B., & Risley, T. R. (1995). *Meaningful differences in the everyday experience of young American children*. Baltimore, MD: Brookes.

Harvard School of Public Health. (2013). The benefits of physical activity. Retrieved from *www.hsph.harvard.edu/nutritionsource/staying-active-full-story.*

Hattie, J. (2009). *Visible learning: A synthesis of over 800 meta-analyses relating to achievement*. New York: Routledge.

Hattie, J. (2011). *Visible learning for teachers: Maximizing impact on learning*. New York: Routledge.

Hattie, J., & Yates, G. C. R. (2013). *Visible learning and the science of how we learn*. New York: Routledge.

Hauerwas, L. B., Brown, R., & Scott, A. (2013). Specific learning disability and response to intervention: State-level guidance. *Exceptional Children, 80*, 101–120.

Hawley, W. D., & Valli, L. (1999). The essentials of effective professional development: A new consensus. In L. Darling-Hammond & G. Sykes (Eds.), *Teaching as the learning profession: Handbook of policy and practice* (pp. 127–150). San Francisco: Jossey-Bass.

Herbers, J. E., Cutuli, J. J., Supkoff, L. M., Heistad, D., Chan, C.-K., Hinz, E., et al. (2012). Early reading skills and academic achievement trajectories of students facing poverty, homelessness, and high residential mobility. *Educational Researcher, 41*, 366–374.

Hernandez, D. J. (2012). *Double jeopardy: How third grade reading skills and poverty influence high school graduation*. Baltimore, MD: Annie E. Casey Foundation.

Hill, H. C. (2009). Fixing teacher professional development. *Phi Delta Kappan, 90*, 470–476.

Hochberg, E. D., & Desimone, L. M. (2010). Professional development in the accountability context: Building capacity to achieve standards. *Educational Psychologist, 45*, 89–106.

Hoover, J. J. (2011). Making informed instructional adjustments in RTI models: Essentials for practitioners. *Intervention in School and Clinic, 47*(2), 82–90.

Houghton Mifflin Harcourt. (2014). EasyCBM. Retrieved from *www.riversidepublishing.com/products/easycbm/overview.html*.

Huebner, T. (2010). Differentiated instruction. *Educational Leadership, 67*(5), 79–81.

Institute of Education Sciences. (2013a). Reading First Impact Study: Final report. Retrieved from *http://ies.ed.gov/ncee/pubs/20094038*.

Institute of Education Sciences. (2013b). What Works Clearinghouse. Retrieved from *http://curry.virginia.edu/research/centers/castl*.

Jenkins, J. R., Graff, J. J., & Miglioretti, D. L. (2009). Estimating reading growth using intermittent CBM progress monitoring. *Exceptional Children, 75*, 151–163.

Jorissen, K. T., Salazar, P., Morrison, H., & Foster, L. (2008). Instructional coaches: Lessons from the field. *Principal Leadership, 9*(2), 16.

Joyce, B., & Showers, B. (2002). *Student achievement through staff development* (3rd ed.). Alexandria, VA: Association for Supervision and Curriculum Development.

Kalberg, J. R., Lane, K. L., & Menzies, H. M. (2010). Using systematic screening procedures to identify students who are nonresponsive to primary prevention efforts: Integrating academic and behavioral measures. *Education and Treatment of Children, 33*, 561–584.

Kansas State Department of Education. (2014). Kansas multi-tier system of supports. Retrieved from *www.kansasmtss.org*.

Kavale, K. A., & Forness, S. R. (2000). History, rhetoric, and reality. *Remedial and Special Education, 21*, 279–297.

Kazdin, A. E. (2010). *Single case research designs: Methods for clinical and applied settings*. (2nd ed.). Oxford, UK: Oxford University Press.

Kellam, S. G., Ling, X., Merisca, R., Brown, C. H., & Ialongo, N. (1998). The effect of the level of aggression in the first grade classroom on the course and malleability of aggressive behavior into middle school. *Development and Psychopathology, 10*, 165–185.

Keller-Margulis, M. A. (2012). Fidelity of implementation framework: A critical need for response to intervention models. *Psychology in the Schools, 49*, 342–352.

Kern, L., & Clemens, N. (2007). Antecedent strategies to promote appropriate classroom behavior. *Psychology in the Schools, 44*, 65–75.

Kids Together, Inc. (2013). Mills v. Board of Education of the District of Columbia. Retrieved from *www.kidstogether.org/right-ed_files/mills.htm*.

Kirk, S. A. (1962). *Educating exceptional children*. Boston: Houghton Mifflin.

Klingner, J., Artiles, A., Kozleski, E., Harry, B., Zion, S., Tate, W., et al. (2005). Addressing the disproportionate representation of culturally and linguistically diverse students in special education through culturally responsive educational systems. *Education Policy Analysis Archives, 13*, 38.

Klingner, J. K., Ahwee, S., Pilonieta, P., & Menendez, R. (2003). Barriers and facilitators in scaling up research-based practices. *Exceptional Children, 69*, 411–429.

Klingner, J. K., & Edwards, P. A. (2006). Cultural considerations with response to intervention models. *Reading Research Quarterly, 41*(1), 108–117.

Knight, J. (2005). *A primer on instructional coaches.* Reston, VA: National Association of Secondary School Principals.

Konold, K. E., Miller, S. P., & Konold, K. B. (2004). Using teacher feedback to enhance student learning. *Teaching Exceptional Children, 36*(6), 64–69.

Koutsoftas, A., Harmon, M., & Gray, S. (2009). The effect of tier 2 intervention for phonemic awareness in a response-to-intervention model in low-income preschool classrooms. *Language, Speech, and Hearing Services in Schools, 40,* 116–130.

Kovaleski, J. F., Van Der Heyden, A. M., & Shapiro, E. S. (2013). *The RTI approach to evaluating learning disabilities.* New York: Guilford Press.

Kubicek, F. C. (1994). Special education reform in light of select state and federal court decisions. *Journal of Special Education, 28,* 27–43.

Kulik, J. A., & Kulik, C.-L. C. (1988). Timing of feedback and verbal learning. *Review of Educational Research, 58,* 79–97.

Kung, S. H. (2009). *Predicting the success of state standards test for culturally and linguistically diverse students using curriculum-based oral reading measures.* Unpublished doctoral dissertation, University of Minnesota.

Lane, K. L., Menzies, H. M., Oakes, W. P., & Kalberg, J. R. (2012). *Systematic screenings of behavior to support instruction: From preschool to high school.* New York: Guilford Press.

Lane, K. L., Oakes, W. P., Carter, E. W., Lambert, W. E., & Jenkins, A. B. (2013). Initial evidence for the reliability and validity of the Student Risk Screening Scale for Internalizing and Externalizing Behaviors at the middle school level. *Assessment for Effective Intervention, 39,* 24–38.

LD Online. (2013). Timeline of learning disabilities. Retrieved from *www.ldonline.org/article/11244.*

Leafstedt, J. M., Richards, C. R., & Gerber, M. M. (2004). Effectiveness of explicit phonological-awareness instruction for at-risk English learners. *Learning Disabilities Research and Practice, 19,* 252–261.

Lembke, E. S., McMaster, K. L., & Stecker, P. M. (2010). The prevention science of reading research within a response-to-intervention model. *Psychology in the Schools, 47,* 22–35.

Lesaux, N. K., Lipka, O., & Siegel, L. S. (2006). Investigating cognitive and linguistic abilities that influence the reading comprehension skills of children from diverse linguistic backgrounds. *Reading and Writing: An Interdisciplinary Journal, 19,* 99–131.

Lewis, T., Barrett, S., Sugai, G., & Horner, R. H. (2010). Blueprint for school-wide positive behavior support training and professional development. Retrieved from *www.pbis.org/common/cms/files/pbisresources/PBIS_PD_Blueprint_v3.pdf.*

Linan-Thompson, S., Cirino, P. T., & Vaughn, S. (2007). Determining English language learners' response to intervention: Questions and some answers. *Learning Disability Quarterly, 30,* 185–195.

Lingo, A. S., Slaton, D. B., & Jolivette, K. (2006). Effects of corrective reading on the reading abilities and classroom behaviors of middle school students with reading deficits and challenging behavior. *Behavioral Disorders, 31,* 265–283.

Mahdavi, J. N., & Beebe-Frankenberger, M. E. (2009). Pioneering RTI systems that work: Social validity, collaboration, and context. *TEACHING Exceptional Children, 42*(2), 64–72.

Major-League Obie Role-Based System. (2013). 2013 MORPS roto draft tool update. Retrieved from *http://morps.mlblogs.com/category/morps.*

Makibbin, S. S., & Sprague, M. M. (1997). The instructional coach: A new role in instructional improvement. *National Association of Secondary School Principals: NASSP Bulletin, 81*(586), 94.

Marsh, J. A., Sloan McCombs, J., & Martorell, F. (2010). How instructional coaches support data-driven decision making: Policy implementation and effects in Florida middle schools. *Educational Policy, 24*(6), 872–907.

Mayam, L. (2013). Kentucky Derby 2013 winner predictions: Twitter accounts to watch. Retrieved from *http://voices.yahoo.com/image/2608990/index.html?cat=2*.

McCollum, J. A., Hemmeter, M. L., & Hsieh, W. Y. (2013). Coaching teachers for emergent literacy instruction using performance-based feedback. *Topics in Early Childhood Special Education, 33*, 28–37.

McGraw-Hill Education. (2013). Everyday mathematics. Retrieved from *www.everydaymath.com*.

McIntosh, K., Frank, J. L., & Spaulding, S. A. (2010). Establishing research-based trajectories of office discipline referrals for individual students. *School Psychology Review, 39*, 380–394.

McLoyd, V. C. (1990). Minority children: Introduction to the special issue. *Child Development, 61*, 263–266.

McMaster, K. L., Wayman M. M., & Cao, M. (2006). Monitoring the reading progress of secondary-level English learners: Technical features of oral reading and maze tasks. *Assessment for Effective Intervention, 31*(4), 17–31.

Mendez, L. R., Ogg, J., Loker, T., & Fefer, S. (2013). Including parents in the continuum of school-based mental health services: A review of intervention program research from 1995 to 2010. *Journal of Applied School Psychology, 29*, 1–36.

Merton, R. K. (1968). The Matthew effect in science: The reward and communication systems of science are considered. *Science, 159*(3810), 56–63.

Methe, S. M., & Hintze, J. M. (2003). Evaluating teacher modeling as a strategy to increase student reading behavior. *School Psychology Review, 32*, 617–623.

Michigan Department of Education. (2014). Multi-tiered system of supports. Retrieved from *http://michigan.gov/mde/0,4615,7-140-28753_65803-322534—,00.html*.

Michigan's Integrated Behavior and Learning Support Initiative. (2015). Student risk screening scale. Retrieved from *http://miblsi.cenmi.org/MiBLSiModel/Evaluation/Measures/StudentRiskScreeningScale.aspx*.

Moore, J., & Whitfield, V. (2009). Building schoolwide capacity for preventing reading failure. *The Reading Teacher, 62*, 622–624.

Mueller, M. M., Palkovic, C. M., & Maynard, C. S. (2007). Errorless learning: Review and practical application for teaching children with pervasive developmental disorders. *Psychology in the Schools, 44*, 691–700.

Musgrove, M. (2007, November). Memorandum: A response to intervention (RTI) process cannot be used to delay–deny an evaluation for eligibility under the Individuals with Disabilities Education Act (IDEA). Retrieved from *www2.ed.gov/policy/speced/guid/idea/memosdcltrs/osep11-07rtimemo.doc*.

Najman, J. M., Clavarino, A., McGee, T. R., Bor, W., Williams, G. M., & Hayatbakhsh, M. R. (2010). Timing and chronicity of family poverty and development of unhealthy behaviors in children: A longitudinal study. *Journal of Adolescent Health, 46*, 538–544.

National Center for Learning Disabilities. (2014). RTI-based SLD identification toolkit. Retrieved from *www.rtinetwork.org/getstarted/sld-identification-toolkit*.

National Center for Response to Intervention. (2012). Screening tools chart. Retrieved from: *www.rti4success.org/screeningTools*.

National Center on Intensive Intervention. (2014). Tools charts. Retrieved from *www.intensiveintervention.org/resources/tools-charts.*

National Council for Teacher Quality. (2013). Teacher prep review 2013 report. Retrieved from *www.nctq.org/dmsStage/Teacher_Prep_Review_2013_Report.*

National Council of Teachers of Mathematics. (2013). Agenda for action: More math study. Retrieved from *www.nctm.org/standards/content.aspx?id=17285.*

National Dissemination Center for Children with Disabilities. (2013). Categories of disability under IDEA. Retrieved from *http://nichcy.org/disability/categories.*

National Governors Association Center for Best Practices & Council of Chief State School Officers. (2010). *Common Core State Standards for English language arts and literacy in history/social studies, science, and technical subjects.* Washington, DC: Author.

National Implementation Research Network. (2015). Retrieved from *http://nirn.fpg.unc.edu.*

National Lightning Safety Institute. (2013). Lighting strike probabilities. Retrieved from *www.lightningsafety.com/nlsi_pls/probability.html.*

NCS Pearson, Inc. (2014). AIMSweb. Retrieved from *www.aimsweb.com.*

Neisser, U., Boodoo, G., Bouchard, T. J., Boykin, A. W., Brody, N., Ceci, S. J., et al. (1996). Intelligence: Knowns and unknowns. *American Psychologist, 51,* 77–101.

Nellis, L. M. (2012). Maximizing the effectiveness of building teams in response to intervention implementation. *Psychology in the Schools, 49,* 245–256.

Nelson, J. R., & Epstein, M. H. (2002). Report on evidence-based interventions: Recommended next steps. *School Psychology Quarterly, 17,* 493–499.

Newton, J. S., Horner, R. H., Algozzine, B., Todd, A. W., & Algozzine, K. (2012). A randomized wait-list controlled analysis of the implementation integrity of team-initiated problem solving processes. *Journal of School Psychology, 50,* 421–441.

Newton, J. S., Horner, R. H., Algozzine, R. F., Todd, A. W., & Algozzine, K. M. (2009). Using a problem-solving model to enhance data-based decision making in schools. In W. Sailor, G. Dunlop, G. Sugai, & R. Horner (Eds.), *Handbook of positive behavior support* (pp. 551–580). New York: Springer.

Newton, J. S., Horner, R. H., Todd, A. W., Algozzine, R. F., & Algozzine, K. M. (2012). A pilot study of a problem-solving model for team decision making. *Education and Treatment of Children, 35*(1), 25–49.

Newton, J. S., Todd, A. W., Algozzine, K., Horner, R., & Algozzine, B. (2009). *The Team Initiated Problem Solving (TIPS) Training manual.* Eugene: Educational and Community Supports, University of Oregon.

Northwest Evaluation Association. (2014). Measures of academic progress. Retrieved from *www.nwea.org/assessments/map.*

O'Connor, E. P., & Freeman, E. W. (2012). District-level considerations in supporting and sustaining RtI implementation. *Psychology in the Schools, 49,* 297–310.

Onchwari, G., & Keengwe, J. (2008). The impact of a mentor-coaching model on teacher professional development. *Early Childhood Education Journal, 36,* 19–24.

Orosco, M. J., & Klingner, J. (2010). One school's implementation of RTI with English language learners: "Referring into RTI." *Journal of Learning Disabilities, 43,* 269–288.

Ortiz, A. A., & Artiles, A. J. (2010). Meeting the needs of ELLs with disabilities: A linguistically and culturally responsive model. In G. Li & P. A. Edwards (Eds.), *Best practices in ELL instruction* (pp. 247–272). New York: Guilford Press.

Ortiz, A. A., Wilkinson, C. Y., Robertson-Courtney, P., & Kushner, M. I. (2006). Considerations in implementing intervention assistance teams to support English language learners. *Remedial and Special Education, 27,* 53–63.

Ortiz, S. O., Flanagan, D. P., & Dynda, A. M. (2008). Best practices in working with culturally and linguistically diverse children and families. In A. Thomas & J. Grimes (Eds.), *Best practices in school psychology V* (pp. 1721–1738). Washington, DC: National Association of School Psychologists.

Pacheco, J. S., & Plutzer, E. (2008). Political participation and cumulative disadvantage: The impact of economic and social hardship on young citizens. *Journal of Social Issues, 64*, 571–593.

Parker, D. C., McMaster, K. L., & Burns, M. K. (2011). Determining an instructional level for early writing skills. *School Psychology Review, 40*, 158–167.

Parker, S., Greer, S., & Zuckerman, B. (1988). Double jeopardy: The impact of poverty on early child development. *Pediatric Clinics of North America, 35*, 1227–1232.

Partnership for Readiness of College and Careers. (2014). PARCC assessment. Retrieved from *www.parcconline.org/parcc-assessment*.

Pas, E. T., Bradshaw, C. P., & Mitchell, M. M. (2011). Examining the validity of office discipline referrals as an indicator of student behavior problems. *Psychology in the Schools, 48*, 541–555.

Patti, J., Holzer, A. A., Stern, R., & Brackett, M. A. (2012). Personal, professional coaching: Transforming professional development for teacher and administrative leaders. *Journal of Leadership Education, 11*, 263–274.

Pearson Education, Inc. (2013). Reading street common core. Retrieved from *http://pearsonschool.com/index.cfm?locator=PS1gC9*.

Pearson Education, Inc. (2014). Behavior observation of students in schools. Retrieved from *www.pearsonclinical.com/education/products/100000780/behavioral-observation-of-students-in-schools-boss.html#tab-details*.

Phillips, D., Voran, M., Kisker, E., Howes, C., & Whitebrook, M. (1994). Child care for children in poverty: Opportunity or inequity? *Child Development, 65*, 472–492.

Pollard-Durodola, S. D., Mathes, P. G., Vaughn, S., Cardenas-Hagan, E., & Linan-Thompson, S. (2006). The role of oracy in developing comprehension in Spanish-speaking English language learners. *Topics in Language Disorders, 26*, 365–384.

Positive Behavioral Intervention and Supports. (2014). Universal screening for behavior. Retrieved from *www.pbis.org/common/cms/files/Forum12/A4_Rose_Owens.pptx*.

Prochaska, J. Q., & DiClemente, C. C. (1992). Stages of change in the modification of problem behaviors. In M. Hersen, R. M. Eisler, & P. M. Miller (Eds.), *Progress in behavior modification* (pp. 184–214). Sycamore, IL: Sycamore Press.

Public Interest Law Center of Philadelphia. (2013). Pennsylvania Association for Retarded Citizens (PARC) v. Commonwealth of Pennsylvania. Retrieved from *www.pilcop.org/pennsylvania-association-for-retarded-citizens-parc-v-commonwealth-of-pennsylvania*.

Public Law 94-142. (1975). Education of All Handicapped Children Act. Retrieved from *www.gpo.gov/fdsys/pkg/STATUTE-89/pdf/STATUTE-89-Pg773.pdf*.

Ransdell, S. (2012). There's still no free lunch: Poverty as a composite of SES predicts school-level reading comprehension. *American Behavioral Scientist, 56*, 908–925.

Renaissance Learning. (2015). *Accelerated Reader, Accelerated Math*. Retrieved from *www.renaissance.com*.

Reschly, A. L., Busch, T. W., Betts, J., Deno, S. L., & Long, J. D. (2009). Curriculum-based measurement oral reading as an indicator of reading achievement: A meta-analysis of the correlational evidence. *Journal of School Psychology, 47*, 427–469.

Reschly, D. J. (1996). Identification and assessment of students with disabilities. *The Future of Children, 6*(1), 40–53.

Reschly, D. J. (2005). Learning disabilities identification: Primary intervention, secondary intervention, and then what? *Journal of Learning Disabilities, 38*, 510–515.

Reyes, M. R., Brackett, M. A., Rivers, S. E., White, M., & Salovey, P. (2012). Classroom emotional climate, student engagement, and academic achievement. *Journal of Educational Psychology, 104*, 700–712.

Riedel, S. (2005). Edward Jenner and the history of smallpox and vaccination. *Proceedings* [Baylor University Medical Center], *18*(1), 21–25.

Riley-Tillman, C., & Burns, M. K. (2009). *Evaluating educational interventions: Single-case design for measuring response to intervention*. New York: Guilford Press.

Rinaldi, C., Averill, O. H., & Stuart, S. (2010). Response to intervention: Educators' perceptions of a three-year RTI collaborative reform effort in an urban elementary school. *Journal of Education, 191*, 43–53.

Rinaldi, C., & Samson, J. (2008). English language learners and response to intervention: Referral considerations. *TEACHING Exceptional Children, 40*(5), 6–14.

Robinson, J. D., & Jon, F. N. (2004). Grounding research and medical education about religion in actual physician–patient interaction: Church attendance, social support, and older adults. *Health Communication, 16*, 63–85.

Rogers, E. M. (2003). *Diffusion of innovations* (5th ed.). New York: Free Press.

Rogers, E. M., & Mortimore, F. J. (1969). *Diffusion of innovations: Educational change in Thai government secondary schools*. East Lansing: Michigan State University.

Rosenthal, J. (2015). *Electronic Daily Report Card* (eDRC). Retrieved from *https://e-drc.com*.

Rothwell, J. (2014). Still searching: Job vacancies and STEM skills. Retrieved from *www.brookings.edu/research/interactives/2014/job-vacancies-and-stem-skills#/M10420.*

Rouse, H. L., & Fantuzzo, J. W. (2009). Multiple risks and educational well-being: A population-based investigation of threats to early school success. *Early Childhood Research Quarterly, 24*, 1–14.

Sabornie, E. J., Evans, C., & Cullinan, D. (2006). Comparing characteristics of high-incidence disability groups: A descriptive review. *Remedial and Special Education, 27*, 95–104.

Samson, J. F., & Lesaux, N. K. (2009). Language-minority learners in special education: Rates and predictors of identification for services. *Journal of Learning Disabilities, 42*, 148–162.

Samuels, C. (2010, November 19). Number of students classified as learning disabled continues to drop. Retrieved from *http://blogs.edweek.org/edweek/speced/2010/11/number_of_students_with_learni.html.*

Sanetti, L. M. H., Gritter, K. L., & Dobey, L. M. (2012). Treatment integrity of interventions with children in the Journal of Positive Behavior Interventions from 1999 to 2009. *Journal of Positive Behavior Interventions, 14*, 29–46.

Sanetti, L. M. H., & Kratochwill, T. R. (2005). Treatment integrity assessment within a problem-solving model. In R. Brown-Chidsey (Ed.), *Assessment for intervention: A problem-solving approach* (pp. 304–328). New York: Guilford Press.

Sanetti, L. M. H., & Kratochwill, T. R. (2013). Treatment integrity assessment within a problem-solving model. In R. Brown-Chidsey & K. Andren (Eds.), *Assessment for intervention: A problem-solving approach* (2nd ed., pp. 297–320). New York: Guilford Press.

Sanetti, L. M. H., & Reed, F. D. D. (2012). Barriers to implementing treatment integrity procedures in school psychology research: Survey of treatment outcome researchers. *Assessment for Effective Intervention, 37*, 195–202.

Sanger, D., Friedli, C., Brunken, C., Snow, P., & Ritzman, M. (2012). Educators' year long reactions to the implementation of a response to intervention (RTI) model. *Journal of Ethnographic and Qualitative Research, 7*, 98–107.

Schulte, A. C., Easton, J. E., & Parker, J. (2009). Advances in treatment integrity research: Multidisciplinary perspectives on the conceptualization, measurement, and enhancement of treatment integrity. *School Psychology Review, 38*, 460–475.

Scott, A., Boynton Hauerwas, L., & Brown, R. (2014). State policy and guidance for identifying learning disabilities in culturally and linguistically diverse students. *Learning Disability Quarterly, 37*, 172–185.

Seligman, M. E. P., Ernst, R. M., Gillham, J., Reivich, K., & Linkins, M. (2009). Positive education: Positive psychology and classroom interventions. *Oxford Review of Education, 35*(3), 293–311.

Seligman, M. E. P., Reivich, K., Jaycox, L., & Gillham, J. (1995). *The optimistic child*. New York: Houghton Mifflin.

Semmel, M. I., & Abernathy, T. V. (1991). Teacher perceptions of the regular education initiative. *Exceptional Children, 58*, 9–24.

Shaler, N. S. (1891). Individualism in education. *Atlantic Monthly, 67*, 82–91.

Shapiro, E. S., & Lentz, F. E. (1985). Assessing academic behavior: A behavioral approach. *School Psychology Review, 14*, 325–338.

Shaw, S. F., & Madaus, J. W. (2008). Preparing school personnel to implement section 504. *Intervention in School and Clinic, 43*, 226–230.

Shifrer, D., Muller, C., & Callahan, R. (2011). Disproportionality and learning disabilities: Parsing apart race, socioeconomic status, and language. *Journal of Learning Disabilities, 44*, 246–257.

Shinn, M. R. (1989). *Curriculum-based measurement: Assessing special children*. New York: Guilford Press.

Shinn, M. R. (Ed.). (1998). *Advanced applications of curriculum-based measurement*. New York: Guilford Press.

Simonsen, B., Fairbanks, S., Briesch, A., Myers, D., & Sugai, G. (2008). Evidence-based practices in classroom management: Considerations for research to practice. *Education and Treatment of Children, 31*, 351–380.

Skiba, R. J., Horner, R. H., Chung, C., Rausch, M. K., May, S. L., & Tobin, T. (2011). Race is not neutral: A national investigation of African American and Latino disproportionality in school discipline. *School Psychology Review, 40*(1), 85–107.

Slopen, N., Fitzmaurice, G., Williams, D. R., & Gilman, S. E. (2010). Poverty, food insecurity, and the behavior for childhood internalizing and externalizing disorders. *Journal of the American Academy of Child and Adolescent Psychiatry, 49*, 444–452.

Smarter-Balanced Assessment Consortium. (2014). Item writing and review. Retrieved from *www.smarterbalanced.org/smarter-balanced-assessments/item-writing-and-review*.

Snow, C., Burns., S., & Griffin, P. (1998). *Preventing reading difficulties in young children*. Washington, DC: National Academy Press.

Solomon, D., Battistich, V., & Hom, A. (1996). Teacher beliefs and practices in schools serving communities that differ by socioeconomic level. *Journal of Experimental Education, 64*, 327–347.

Sprick, R., Knight, J., Reinke, W., McKale Skyles, T., & Barnes, L. (2010). *Coaching classroom management: Strategies and tools for administrators and coaches* (2nd ed.). Eugene, OR: Pacific Northwest Publishing.

St. Croix River Education District. (2013). Outcomes. Retrieved from *www.scred.k12.mn.us/outcomes/research*.

Stanberry, K. (2013). The history of learning disabilities. Retrieved from *www.ncld.org/types-learning-disabilities/what-is-ld/history-special-education*.

Stanovich, K. E. (1986). Matthew effects in reading: Some consequences of individual differences in the acquisition of literacy. *Reading Research Quarterly, 21*, 360–407.

Steckel, R. H., & Rose, J. C. (Eds.). (2002). *The backbone of history: Health and nutrition in the western hemisphere*. Cambridge, UK: Cambridge University Press.

Stecker, P. M., Fuchs, D., & Fuchs, L. S. (2008). Progress monitoring as essential practice within response to intervention. *Rural Special Education Quarterly, 27*(4), 10–17.

Stecker, P. M., Lembke, E. S., & Foegen, A. (2008). Using progress-monitoring data to improve instructional decision making. *Preventing School Failure, 52*(2), 48–58.

Steege, M. W., & Watson, T. S. (2009). *Conducting school-based functional behavioral assessments: A practitioner's guide*. New York: Guilford Press.

Stokes, T. F., & Baer, D. M. (1977). An implicit technology of generalization. *Journal of Applied Behavior Analysis, 10*, 349–367.

Sugai, G., & Horner, R. H. (2005). School-wide positive behavior supports: Achieving and sustaining effective learning environments for all students. In W. L. Heward (Ed.), *Focus on behavior analysis in education: Achievements, challenges, and opportunities* (pp. 90–102). Upper Saddle River, NJ: Pearson Prentice-Hall.

Sugai, G., & Horner, R. [H.] (2010). Schoolwide positive behavior supports: Establishing a continuum of evidence-based practices. *Journal of Evidence-Based Practices for Schools, 11*, 62–83.

Sugai, G., Horner, R. H., Algozzine, R., Barrett, S., Lewis, T., Anderson, C., et al. (2010). *Implementation blueprint and self-assessment*. Eugene: University of Oregon. Available at *www.pbis.org/Common/Cms/files/pbisresources/SWPBS_Implementation-Blueprint_vSep_23_2010.pdf*.

Taylor, E. S., & Tyler, J. H. (2012). Can teacher evaluation improve teaching? *Education Next, 12*(4), 78–84.

Teemant, A. (2014). A mixed-methods investigation of instructional coaching for teachers of diverse learners. *Urban Education, 49*, 574–604.

Ticha, R., Espin, C. A., & Wayman, M. M. (2009). Reading progress monitoring for secondary-school students: Reliability, validity, and sensitivity to growth of reading-aloud and maze-selection measures. *Learning Disabilities Research and Practice, 24*, 132–142.

Tilly, D. W. (2009). Pinning the pendulum to the wall: Practical strategies to create lasting change in schools. Retrieved from *http://cech.uc.edu/content/dam/cech/centers/student_success/docs/summer-institute-2009/pendulum_hos_final.pdf*.

Todd, A. W., Newton, J. S., Algozzine, K., Horner, R. H., & Algozzine, B. (2014). *The team initiated problem solving (TIPS II) training manual*. Eugene: University of Oregon, Educational and Community Supports. Available at *www.uoecs.org*.

Toppino, T. C., & Cohen, M. S. (2010). Metacognitive control and spaced practice: Clarifying what people do and why. *Journal of Experimental Psychology: Learning, Memory, and Cognition, 36*, 1480–1491.

Torlaković, E. (2011). Academy of MATH® efficacy report—Westwood Elementary School. Retrieved from *www.rti4success.org/tools_charts/popups_instruction/programPopup.php?url=aca*.

Tuckman, B. W. (1965). Development sequence in small groups. *Psychological Bulletin, 63*, 348–399.

Tuckman, B. W., & Jensen, M. A. C. (1977). Stages in small group development revisited. *Group and Organizational Studies, 2*, 419–427.

University of Kansas Center for Research on Learning. (2013). Instructional coaching. Retrieved from *www.instructionalcoach.org*.

U.S. Department of Commerce, Bureau of the Census. (2013). Current population survey: Annual social and economic supplement. Retrieved from *www.census.gov/hhes/www/poverty/publications/pubs-cps.html*.

U.S. Department of Education, National Center for Education Statistics. (2009). Basic reading skills and the literacy of the America's least literate adults: Results from the 2003 national assessment of adult literacy (NAAL) supplemental studies. Retrieved from *https://nces.ed.gov/pubsearch/pubsinfo.asp?pubid=2009481*.

U.S. Department of Education, National Center for Education Statistics. (2010). *Status and Trends in the Education of Racial and Ethnic Minorities* (NCES 2010-015), Indicator 8.

U.S. Department of Education, National Center for Education Statistics. (2013a). Fast facts: Dropout rates. Retrieved from *http://nces.ed.gov/fastfacts/display.asp?id=16*.

U.S. Department of Education, National Center for Education Statistics. (2013b). Fast facts: English language. Retrieved from *http://nces.ed.gov/fastfacts/display.asp?id=96*.

U.S. Department of Education, National Center for Education Statistics. (2013c). Fast facts: Students with disabilities. Retrieved from *http://nces.ed.gov/fastfacts/display.asp?id=64*.

U.S. Department of Education, National Center for Education Statistics. (2015). Trends in international mathematics and science study. Retrieved from*https://nces.ed.gov/TIMSS/results11.asp*.

U.S. Department of Education Office of Elementary and Secondary Education. (2012). Report to congress on the Elementary and Secondary Education Act: State-reported data for school year 2009–10. Retrieved from *www2.ed.gov/about/reports/annual/nclbrpts.html*.

U.S. Department of Education Office of Special Education Programs. (2015). *National technical assistance center on positive behavioral interventions and supports*. Retrieved from *www.pbis.org/about_us/default.aspx*.

U.S. Department of Health and Human Services Office of Civil Rights. (2015). *Discrimination on the basis of a disability*. Retrieved from *www.hhs.gov/ocr/civilrights/understanding/disability/index.html*.

U.S. Food and Drug Administration. (2013). Nutrition facts label. Retrieved from *www.fda.gov/downloads/Food/IngredientsPackagingLabeling/UCM275412.pdf*.

U.S. National Commission on Excellence in Education. (1983). *A nation at risk: The imperative for educational reform: A report to the nation and the secretary of education, United States Department of Education*. Washington, DC: Author.

Utley, C. A., Obiakor, F. E., & Jeffrey P., B. (2011). Culturally responsive practices for culturally and linguistically diverse students with learning disabilities. *Learning Disabilities: A Contemporary Journal, 9*(1), 5–18.

van Camp, C. M., Lerman, D. C., Kelley, M. E., Contrucci, S. A., & Vorndran, C. M. (2000). Variable-time reinforcement schedules in the treatment of socially maintained problem behavior. *Journal of Applied Behavior Analysis, 33*(4), 545–557.

Vanderbilt Kennedy Center. (2014). Peer Assisted Learning Strategies [PALS]. Retrieved from *http://kc.vanderbilt.edu/pals*.

VanDerHeyden, A. M., Broussard, C., & Cooley, A. (2006). Further development of measures of early math performance for preschoolers. *Journal of School Psychology, 44*, 533–553.

VanDerHeyden, A. M., & Witt, J. C. (2008). Best practices in can't do/won't do assessment. In A. Thomas & J. Grimes (Eds.), *Best practices in school psychology V* (pp. 131–139). Bethesda, MD: National Association of School Psychologists.

Vannest, K. J., Davis, J. L., Davis, C. R., Mason, B. A., & Burke, M. D. (2010). Effective intervention for behavior with a daily behavior report card: A meta-analysis. *School Psychology Review, 39*, 654–672.

Vaughn, S., Linan-Thompson, S., Kouzekanani, K., Bryant, D. P., Dickson, S., & Blozis,

S. A. (2003). Reading instruction grouping for students with reading difficulties. *Remedial and Special Education, 24*, 301–315.

Vaughn, S., Mathes, P., Linan-Thompson, S., Cirino, P., Carlson, C., Pollard-Durodola, S., et al. (2006). Effectiveness of an English intervention for first-grade English language learners at risk for reading problems. *Elementary School Journal, 107*, 153–180.

Vaughn, S., Mathes, P. G., Linan-Thompson, S., & Francis, D. J. (2005). Teaching English language learners at risk for reading disabilities to read: Putting research into practice. *Learning Disabilities Research and Practice, 20*, 58–67.

Vaughn, S., Wanzek, J., Murray, C. S., Scammacca, N., Linan-Thompson, S., & Woodruff, A. L. (2009). Response to early reading intervention examining higher and lower responders. *Exceptional Children, 75*, 165–183.

Wadsworth, M. E., Raviv, T., Reinhard, C., Wolff, B., Santiago, C. D., & Einhorn, L. (2008). An indirect effects model of the association between poverty and child functioning: The role of children's poverty-related stress. *Journal of Loss and Trauma, 13*, 156–185.

Wagmiller, R. L., & Adelman, R. M. (2009). Childhood and intergenerational poverty: The long-term consequences of growing up poor. Retrieved from *www.nccp.org/publications/pdf/text_909.pdf*.

Wagner, R. K., Francis, D. K., & Morris, R. D. (2005). Identifying English language learners with learning disabilities: Key challenges and possible approaches. *Learning Disabilities Research and Practice, 20*, 6–15.

Walker, H. M., Horner, R. H., Sugai, G., Bullis, M., Sprague, J. R., Bricker, D., et al. (1996). Integrated approaches to preventing antisocial behavior patterns among school-age children and youth. *Journal of Emotional and Behavioral Disorders, 4*, 194–209.

Walker, H. M., Ramsey, E., & Gresham, F. M. (2003–2004, Winter). Heading off disruption: How early intervention can reduce defiant behavior and win back teaching time. *American Educator*, pp. 6–21.

Wasserman, G. A., Keenan, K., Tremblay, R. E., Coie, J. D., Herrenkohl, T. I., Loeber, R., et al. (2003, April). Risk and protective factors of child delinquency. *OJJDP Child Delinquency Bulletin* Series, 1–14. Retrieved from *www.ncjrs.gov/pdffiles1/ojjdp/193409.pdf*.

WebMD. (2013). Understanding cholesterol numbers. Retrieved from *www.webmd.com/cholesterol-management/guide/understanding-numbers*.

Webster-Stratton, C., & Reid, M. J. (2003). Treating conduct problems and strengthening social and emotional competence in young children: The dina dinosaur treatment program. *Journal of Emotional and Behavioral Disorders, 11*(3), 130–143.

Webster-Stratton, C., Reid, M. J., & Stoolmiller, M. (2008). Preventing conduct problems and improving school readiness: Evaluation of the Incredible Years Teacher and Child Training Programs in high-risk schools. *Child Psychology and Psychiatry, 49*, 471–488.

Webster-Stratton, C., Reinke, W. M., Herman, K. C., & Newcomer, L. L. (2011). The Incredible Years teacher classroom management training: The methods and principles that support fidelity of training delivery. *School Psychology Review, 40*, 509–529.

Welner, K. G., & Oakes, J. (1996). (Li)ability grouping: The new susceptibility of school tracking systems to legal challenges. *Harvard Educational Review, 66*, 451–470.

West. (2003). No Child Left Behind (NCLB) Act of 2001, 20 U.S.C.A. §6301 *et seq*.

Whyte, G. (1991). Diffusion of responsibility: Effects on the escalation tendency. *Journal of Applied Psychology, 76*, 408–415.

Wight, V. R., Chau, M., & Aratani, Y. (2011). Who are America's poor children?: The official story. Retrieved from *www.nccp.org/publications/pdf/text_1001.pdf*.

Wilcox, K. A., Murakami-Ramalho, E., & Urick, A. (2013). Just-in-time pedagogy: Teachers' perspectives on the response to intervention framework. *Journal of Research in Reading, 36*(1), 75–95.

Wilkinson, C. Y., Ortiz, A. A., Robertson, P. M., & Kushner, M. I. (2006). English language learners with reading-related LD: Linking data from multiple sources to make eligibility determinations. *Journal of Learning Disabilities, 39*(2), 129–141.

Wilson Language Training Corp. (2010). Wilson reading system. Retrieved from *www.wilsonlanguage.com/fs_program_wrs.htm*.

Winsor Learning, Inc. (2013). Sonday system 1. Retrieved from *http://winsorlearning.com/winsorshop/sonday-system-1.html*.

Winzer, M. A. (1993). *The history of special education: From isolation to integration*. Washington, DC: Gallaudet University Press.

World Health Organization. (2010). International classification of diseases (10th ed.). Geneva, Switzerland: Author. Retrieved from *http://apps.who.int/classifications/icd10/browse/2010/en*.

Zirkel, P. A. (2009). Legal eligibility of students with learning disabilities: Consider not only RTI but also 504. *Learning Disability Quarterly, 32*(2), 51–53.

Zirkel, P. A., & Thomas, L. B. (2010). State laws and guidelines for implementing RTI. *TEACHING Exceptional Children, 43*(1), 60–73.

Zumeta, R. O., Zirkel, P. A., & Danielson, L. (2014). Identifying specific learning disabilities: Legislation, regulation, and court decisions. *Topics in Language Disorders, 34*, 8–24.

Index

Note. f or *t* following a page number indicates a figure or a table.
Page numbers in bold refer to terms in the Glossary.

B

E

F

G

H

I

L

M

N

O

P

R

S

U

W